Theatre and Celebrity in Britain, 1660–2000

Theatre and Celebrity in Britain, 1660–2000

Edited by

Mary Luckhurst

and

Jane Moody

Introduction, editorial matter and selection
© Mary Luckhurst and Jane Moody 2005
All chapters © their respective authors 2005

All rights reserved. No reproduction, copy or transmission of this publication may be made without written permission.

No paragraph of this publication may be reproduced, copied or transmitted save with written permission or in accordance with the provisions of the Copyright, Designs and Patents Act 1988, or under the terms of any licence permitting limited copying issued by the Copyright Licensing Agency, 90 Tottenham Court Road, London W1T 4LP.

Any person who does any unauthorised act in relation to this publication may be liable to criminal prosecution and civil claims for damages.

The authors have asserted their rights to be identified as the authors of this work in accordance with the Copyright, Designs and Patents Act 1988.

First published in 2005 by
PALGRAVE MACMILLAN
Houndmills, Basingstoke, Hampshire RG21 6XS and
175 Fifth Avenue, New York, N.Y. 10010
Companies and representatives throughout the world.

PALGRAVE MACMILLAN is the global academic imprint of the Palgrave Macmillan division of St. Martin's Press, LLC and of Palgrave Macmillan Ltd. Macmillan® is a registered trademark in the United States, United Kingdom and other countries. Palgrave is a registered trademark in the European Union and other countries.

ISBN-13: 978–1–4039–4682–9 hardback
ISBN-10: 1–4039–4682–5 hardback

This book is printed on paper suitable for recycling and made from fully managed and sustained forest sources.

A catalogue record for this book is available from the British Library.

Library of Congress Cataloging-in-Publication Data

    Theatre and celebrity in Britain, 1660–2000 / edited by Mary Luckhurst and Jane Moody.
      p. cm.
    Includes bibliographical references and index.
    Contents: Introduction : the languages of theatrical celebrity / Mary Luckhurst and Jane Moody – Public intimacy : the prior history of "it" / Joseph Roach – Wilde : the remarkable rocket / Peter Raby – The many masks of Clemence Dane / Maggie B. Gale – Stolen identities : mimicry and the invention of Samuel Foote / Jane Moody – The celebrity of Edmund Kean : an institutional story / Jacky Bratton – Infamy and dying young : Sarah Kane, 1971–1999 / Mary Luckhurst – Celebrity and rivalry David [Garrick] and Goliath [Quin] / Peter Thomson – Actresses and the economics of celebrity, 1700-1800 / Felicity Nussbaum – Private lives and public spaces : reputation, celebrity, and the late Victorian actress / Sos Eltis – Siddons, celebrity, and regality : portraiture and the body of the aging actress / Shearer West – "Some of you might have seen him" : Laurence Olivier's celebrity / Peter Holland
      ISBN 1–4039–4682–5 (cloth)
      1. Actors – Great Britain – Biography. 2. Fame. I. Luckhurst, Mary. II. Moody, Jane, 1967–

PN2597.T44 2005
792.02′8′092241—dc22   2005049679

10 9 8 7 6 5 4 3 2 1
14 13 12 11 10 09 08 07 06 05

Printed and bound in Great Britain by
Antony Rowe Ltd, Chippenham and Eastbourne

Contents

List of Figures	vii
Acknowledgements	ix
Notes on the Contributors	x

1 Introduction: The Singularity of Theatrical Celebrity   1
   Mary Luckhurst and Jane Moody

Part I   Public Intimacy

2 Public Intimacy: The Prior History of 'It'   15
   Joseph Roach

3 Wilde: The Remarkable Rocket   31
   Peter Raby

4 The Many Masks of Clemence Dane   48
   Maggie B. Gale

Part II   Notoriety

5 Stolen Identities: Character, Mimicry and the Invention of Samuel Foote   65
   Jane Moody

6 The Celebrity of Edmund Kean: An Institutional Story   90
   Jacky Bratton

7 Infamy and Dying Young: Sarah Kane, 1971–1999   107
   Mary Luckhurst

Part III   Markets

8 Celebrity and Rivalry: David [Garrick] and Goliath [Quin]   127
   Peter Thomson

9 Actresses and the Economics of Celebrity, 1700–1800   148
   Felicity Nussbaum

10 Private Lives and Public Spaces: Reputation, Celebrity and the Late Victorian Actress   169
   Sos Eltis

Part IV Nation

11 Siddons, Celebrity and Regality: Portraiture and
    the Body of the Ageing Actress   191
    Shearer West

12 'Some of you may have seen him': Laurence
    Olivier's Celebrity   214
    Peter Holland

Select Bibliography   233

Index   238

List of Figures

3.1	Bernard Partridge, *The Decadent Guys, Punch*, 10 November 1894.	33
3.2	Bernard Partridge, *Fancy Portrait: Quite Too-Too Puffickly Precious!! Punch*, 5 March 1892.	35
4.1	Photograph of Clemence Dane. Courtesy of the Mander and Mitchenson Theatre Collection.	59
5.1	Samuel Foote by William Greatbach, after Joshua Reynolds. By kind permission of the Victoria Art Gallery, Bath and North East Somerset Council.	66
5.2	Mr. Foote as Mrs. Cole in *The Minor* (1777). Engraving published by T. Lowndes and Partners. Courtesy of the Victorian and Albert Picture Library.	79
8.1	William Hogarth, Portrait of Quin (*c.* 1739), Tate Gallery, London.	131
8.2	Joshua Reynolds, *Garrick between Tragedy and Comedy* (1761), courtesy of the Garrick Club, London.	143
9.1	China statue of Peg Woffington. By courtesy of the Trustees, Fitzwilliam Museum, Cambridge.	160
9.2	*The Rival Queens of Covent Garden and Drury Lane Theatres, at a Gymnastic Rehearsal* (BM 6126). By kind permission of the Trustees of the British Museum.	161
10.1	Lillie Langtry as *Rosalind* in Shakespeare's *As You Like It*. St. James's Theatre, London (1890), photographed by Lafayette Studios of Dublin. Photograph courtesy of the Victoria and Albert Picture Library.	174
10.2	Ellen Terry as Nance Oldfield in Cicely Hamilton's *A Pageant of Great Women*. Photograph by Lena Connell, published by the Suffrage Shop (1910), courtesy of the Victoria and Albert Picture Library.	185
11.1	Thomas Lawrence, *Mrs. Siddons* (1804). Copyright Tate London 2004.	198
11.2	Henry Perronet Briggs, *Sarah Siddons* and *Fanny Kemble* (1830), courtesy of the Boston Athenaeum.	201
11.3	Joshua Reynolds, *Mrs. Siddons as the Tragic Muse* (1784). Courtesy of the Henry E. Huntington Library, Art Collections, and Botanical Gardens, San Marino, California.	202

11.4 Thomas Lawrence, *Queen Charlotte* (1789) by
kind permission of the National Gallery, London. 203
11.5 L. Gahagan, *Engraving of Her Most Gracious
Majesty Queen Charlotte* (c. 1817), courtesy of the
National Portrait Gallery, London. 207

Acknowledgements

This book has its origins in a conference held at the University of York in 2002 supported by the Department of English and Related Literature and the Centre for Eighteenth Century Studies. We would like to thank everyone who participated in this very lively day for their enthusiasm and interest. Special thanks go to the speakers, to the students who helped us on the day (John Biggin, Liz Brace, James Disley, Sarah Lowes and Nancy Walker), to colleagues who chaired individual sessions (Kate Newey, Kerry Powell and Richard Rowland) and to David Mayer and Viv Gardner for mounting a wonderful exhibition of theatrical photographs. Our contributors have responded to queries and suggestions with great patience throughout the process of preparing this volume for publication: we are most grateful for their inspiration and good humour. For encouragement and help at various stages we should like to thank a number of colleagues and friends: Jessica Chaney, Michael Cordner, Tracy Davis, Joe Donohue, Peter Holland, Joel Kaplan, John Kerrigan and John Stokes. The Department of English and Related Literature has provided financial support for the completion of this project through the Leavis Fund, and we are delighted to record our gratitude for such invaluable assistance. At Palgrave Macmillan, Emily Rosser took an energetic interest in this project from the beginning and we appreciate her encouragement and support. Thanks are also due to Paula Kennedy and Helen Craine who have seen the volume through the press. In addition we would like to record our thanks to Palgrave Macmillan's readers for their advice. Finally, a special word of thanks to our editorial assistant, Vike Plock, who has collated the typescript and prepared the index with meticulous care and attention: it has been an enormous pleasure for us to work with her.

Notes on the Contributors

Jacky Bratton is Professor of Theatre and Cultural History at Royal Holloway, University of London. Her book *New Readings in Theatre History* was published by Cambridge University Press in 2003. Her recent publications include *King Lear Text and Archive*, a CD-Rom, and various essays (in *Theatre Survey* and in books edited by Catherine Burroughs, Tracy Davis and Ellen Donkin) about the writer/actor/manager Jane Scott. In 2002 she collaborated with Gilli Bush-Bailey on a practice as research project to revive Scott's melodramas in performance.

Sos Eltis is a Fellow and Tutor in English at Brasenose College, Oxford. She is the author of *Revising Wilde: Society and Subversion in the Plays of Oscar Wilde* (1996), and of various articles on Oscar Wilde, Bram Stoker's *Dracula* and nineteenth-century theatre. She is currently working on treatments of the fallen woman on stage from 1850 to the present day.

Maggie B. Gale is Professor of Drama at the University of Manchester. She has published widely on mid-twentieth-century British theatre and on gender, theatre and historiography. Her publications include *West End Women: Women and the London Stage 1918–1962* (1995); *British Theatre between the Wars 1918–1939* (2000) with Clive Barker; and *Women, Theatre and Performance: New Histories, New Historiographies* (2000) with Viv Gardner.

Peter Holland is the McMeel Family Professor in Shakespeare Studies in the Department of Film, Television, and Theatre at the University of Notre Dame. His publications include *The Ornament of Action: Text and Performance in Restoration Comedy* (1979); *English Shakespeares: Shakespeare on the English Stage in the 1990s* (1997); and *Theorizing Practice: Redefining Theatre History* (2003). He is the editor of *Shakespeare Survey* and general editor, with Stanley Wells, of *Oxford Shakespeare Topics*.

Mary Luckhurst is Senior Lecturer and co-director of the Drama initiative at the University of York. She is the author of *Dramaturgy: A Revolution in Theatre* (2005), and co-author of *The Drama Handbook* (2002). She is currently editing two companions for Blackwell: *The Companion to Modern British and Irish Drama* and the *Companion to Contemporary British and Irish Drama*. She is also a director and playwright and most recently directed Caryl Churchill's *Far Away* at the York Theatre Royal.

Jane Moody is Professor in the Department of English and Related Literature at the University of York She is the author of *Illegitimate Theatre in London, 1770–1840* (2000) and a number of essays in journals and edited collections on the history of British theatre. She is co-editing the *Cambridge Companion to British Theatre, 1730–1830* with Daniel O'Quinn and completing a monograph on literary and theatrical censorship in Britain.

Felicity Nussbaum is Professor in the Department of English at the University of California at Los Angeles. She is the author of numerous works including *The Autobiographical Subject: Gender and Ideology in Eighteenth-Century England* (1989); *Torrid Zones: Maternity, Sexuality and Empire in Eighteenth-Century English Narratives* (1995) and *The Limits of the Human: Fictions of Anomaly, Race and Gender in the Long Eighteenth Century* (2003).

Peter Raby is a Fellow of Homerton College, Cambridge. He is the author of *Fair Ophelia: A Life of Harriet Smithson Berlioz* (1982), as well as biographies of Samuel Butler (1990) and Alfred Russel Wallace (2001) and a study of Oscar Wilde (1988). He has edited the *Cambridge Companions* to Wilde and Pinter, and edited a collection of Wilde's plays for the *World's Classics* Series.

Joseph Roach is the Charles C. and Dorothea S. Dilley Professor of Theatre and English at Yale University. His books and articles include *Cities of the Dead: Circum-Atlantic Performance* (1996), which won the James Russell Lowell Prize from the Modern Language Association and the Calloway Prize from New York University; *The Player's Passion: Studies in the Science of Acting* (1993), which won the Barnard Hewitt Award in Theatre History, and essays in *Theatre Journal*; *Theatre Survey*; *The Drama Review*; *Theatre History Studies*; *Discourse*; *Theater*; *Text and Performance Quarterly* and others.

Peter Thomson is Emeritus Professor of Drama at the University of Exeter. He is the author of books on Shakespeare and Brecht, and a volume of essays entitled *On Actors and Acting* (2000). He is an elected Research Associate of the *New Dictionary of National Biography* and General Editor of the three-volume *Cambridge History of British Theatre* (2004).

Shearer West is Professor of Art History at the University of Birmingham. She is the author of *The Image of the Actor: Verbal and Visual Representation in the Age of Garrick and Kemble* (1991); *Fin de Siècle, The Visual Arts in Germany 1890–1940* (1993); and *Portraiture* (2003); as well as editor of *Italian Culture in Northern Europe in the Eighteenth Century* (1998); *The Victorians and Race* (1996); and, with Marsha Meskimmon, *Visions of the 'Neue Frau': Women and the Visual Arts in Weimar Germany* (1995). She is also the author of many articles and essays on the relationships between art and theatre in the eighteenth and nineteenth centuries.

1
Introduction: The Singularity of Theatrical Celebrity

Mary Luckhurst and Jane Moody

Celebrity, the condition of being much talked about, is hardly an invisible phenomenon in the history of British theatre. On the contrary, its discourses constitute a silent yet pervasive presence in the accounts of performing lives through which that history has been written. Theatrical celebrity leaves behind many forms of material evidence: plays, anecdotes, photographs, cartoons, programmes, reviews, portraits and costumes. But despite its ubiquity, the nature of celebrity on and off the stage has scarcely begun to be addressed.

Much of the scholarship done by theatre historians in this area has been concerned with fame (the nature of the exceptional life) rather than with celebrity (a concept which focuses attention on the interplay between individuals and institutions, markets and media). There is a well-established tradition of theatrical biography which plots the life of a famous individual. Typically, these books explore the stage reputation of a particular actor or writer but pay little attention to the markets and institutions through which their fame was produced. More recently, in a fascinating collection of essays entitled *Extraordinary Actors* (2004), critics have examined a range of celebrated performers from the early modern period to the present day in order to consider how and why certain performers produced such powerful responses in their audiences.[1] Comparative perspectives on an individual's fame are also valuable: a study such as *Three Tragic Actresses: Siddons, Rachel, Ristori* (1996) deserves mention here because it illuminates connections between the acting lives and tragic art of three female performers who enjoyed international fame.[2]

Several scholars have reflected from a theoretical perspective on the material traces of theatrical celebrity. In *Interpreting the Theatrical Past* (1989), Thomas Postlewait highlights the idea of the performer as someone whose trade in the creation of identities prompts further questions about the construction and dissemination of public selves.[3] An essay in the same volume by Leigh Woods analyses how Edmund Kean sought to construct his own legacy and to convert life and performance into legend. His argument exposes theatrical biography as a kind of performance which frequently extends forms of myth-making instigated by the actor. Wood thus draws attention to the challenges presented by interpreting the artefacts which celebrity leaves behind.[4] Another important contribution to this area has been made by Michael Quinn, whose semiotic analysis of stage celebrity presents the star actor as a figure who subverts economic, critical and artistic authority. What is radical about Quinn's approach is his insistence that celebrity is the discourse through which the dynamics of acting are revealed. It is only by investigating these transactions between individuals, audiences and institutions, he suggests, that performance can be fully understood.[5]

Since celebrity has received wide attention from cultural theorists and sociologists as well as film analysts, it is helpful to consider to what extent this criticism can be deployed in the analysis of the theatre. In his seminal book, *The Image: or What Happened to the American Dream?* (1961), Daniel Boorstin defines modern fame as the manufacture of secular human heroes. Boorstin argues that celebrity in twentieth-century America has become an alternative structure of authority and route to political power. Leo Braudy's monograph, *The Frenzy of Renown* (1986), is another significant piece of scholarship, offering a history of fame from Alexander the Great to the present day. Braudy's work is relevant to this volume because it deploys theatrical terminology to explore the relationship between the famous and their audiences and subjects. As Braudy demonstrates, monarchs have always found ways of performing power in order to secure their authority; in more recent periods, however, the performer has become 'the model of how to be and how to be seen'.[6] In the last decade, cultural critics have begun to pay particular attention to the pervasive presence of celebrity in contemporary society. According to Marjorie Garber, for instance, its ubiquity is a symptom of both desire and loss, encapsulating a longing for objective standards and nostalgia for hierarchy.[7]

A number of studies of this subject have been published in the last few years.[8] The most significant of these is *Celebrity* by Chris Rojek (2001). Rojek identifies three existing frameworks for the analysis of celebrity: subjectivism, structuralism and post-structuralism. Subjectivism is distinguished by a focus on the supposed qualities possessed by a celebrated individual, such as aura and charisma. Structuralism concentrates on economic factors, and its adherents assert that celebrity is an instrument through which capitalism has set out to subdue and exploit the masses. Post-structuralism, by contrast, entails a critique of subjectivism's emphasis on the individual. Scholars adopting this last approach focus on the intricate sets of negotiations through which the production, consumption and representation of celebrity take place. Each of these frameworks, Rojek suggests, has something useful to contribute to our understanding of this subject.

As Rojek observes, the origins of celebrity can be located in the history of the British stage. The theatre, he argues, has been 'an important laboratory in the evolution of the rhetorical, didactic, sexual and comedic repertory of the public face'.⁹ Several of the contributors to *Theatre and Celebrity in Britain, 1660–2000* have drawn on Rojek's theoretical vocabulary – notably the concepts of ascribed, achieved and attributed celebrity – in their discussions of fame on and off the stage. The essays in this volume also make clear that an investigation of theatrical celebrity demands the consideration of various disciplinary perspectives.

In film studies, it is often assumed that celebrity is simply a product of the twentieth century. On the contrary, as Christine Gledhill states, it was the theatre which provided the model of stardom subsequently appropriated by film.¹⁰ For a variety of reasons, cinematic approaches¹¹ to celebrity are problematic. The most significant distinction between theatre and film is that theatre is a live event: the power of theatrical performance has to do with the uniqueness of the occasion and the impossibility of its reproduction. Live performers are seen and experienced by audiences without the forms of mediation characteristic of film. Put simply, the celebrity of performers is about the experience of seeing an actor in the flesh. Moreover, live performance has always been feared in the history of the British theatre, because of its potential to disrupt the political status quo. The capacity of performers to circumvent theatre censorship and for audiences to respond to a play in unpredictable ways is exactly what has made the regulation and censorship of the theatre so difficult.

The history and organisation of theatrical institutions are also significant factors in shaping the discourses of fame on and off the stage. Until the twentieth century, the actor-manager was a major force in shaping the production of theatrical celebrity. Such figures played leading roles in many shows and also took responsibility for theatre finance and the selection of repertory. The prominence of and cultural value ascribed to the playwright's script by contrast with that of the screenwriter is another distinguishing feature of theatrical performance. In the last hundred years, too, the playwright has emerged as a personality in his or her own right.

This volume offers the first collection of essays about the nature and operation of theatrical celebrity from the eighteenth to the twentieth century. The eighteenth century is widely recognised as the historical moment when fame takes a recognisably modern form.¹² The rationale for this argument arises from the conviction that celebrity is above all a media production: only in the eighteenth century does an extensive apparatus for disseminating fame emerge. Although the essays in this book concentrate on actors and playwrights, theatrical celebrity in the twentieth century has proliferated to an unprecedented degree: it is now possible for directors, designers and producers to become stars as well.

The broad scope of the volume highlights common themes and agendas in the discourses of celebrity across the three centuries, although the essays also reveal ambiguities and discontinuities in its construction. One of the challenges involved in writing about this subject is its pervasive but intangible quality. The concepts around which we have chosen to organise the book seek to address this problem and thereby to challenge how we think about celebrity. These concepts perform a number of functions. First, they seek to determine a vocabulary for understanding the relationships between stars and their audiences. Second, they seek to explore the power of celebrity as an economic tool in the theatrical marketplace. Third, they demonstrate the ways in which stars appropriate nationhood for the production of their own fame. Fourth, they elucidate the changing lexicon of celebrity, confirming the necessity for a more historically nuanced terminology for thinking about the nature of theatrical fame. Above all, our categories set out to anchor an apparently mysterious phenomenon in a range of social, economic, moral, aesthetic and political negotiations.

Although this volume takes the eighteenth century as its starting point, the lexicon of theatrical fame pre-dates this period. Before the early modern era, the language of celebration was inseparable from the discourse of religion. By the end of the sixteenth century, however, celebration had started to lose its religious connotations and to become associated with the circulation of fame. The verb 'celebrate', meaning 'to make publicly known, proclaim, publish abroad', has a first citation of 1597; 'celebrity' appeared *circa* 1600; and 'celebrated' was in use by 1665.

Although the word 'fame' emerged as early as 1290, 'famous' only began to gain currency in Shakespeare's time. Indeed, the foundation of a professional theatre in Britain seems to have provided the institutional context for an expansion in the vocabulary of stage celebrity. Shakespeare's *Much Ado About Nothing* is cited in the *OED* as an early source for the word 'favourite' ('one who stands unduly high in the favour of a prince; one chosen as an intimate by a superior').[13] Another word which has a significant place in the embryonic terminology of celebrity is 'wonder', connoting the possession of miraculous gifts or powers. By 1615, Stow's *Annales* was referring to Richard Tarlton, Elizabeth I's favourite clown, as 'the wonder of his time'.

Public intimacy

Our first organising principle sets out to investigate the nature of those qualities associated with the charisma of a celebrated performer. Film critics have examined this subject extensively and the absence of substantial discussion in theatre history is most puzzling. The medium of film, and particularly the representation of the face in close-up, offers the most detailed image of physical proximity to a performer. As Richard Schickel states, 'We do not see our closest friends so intimately, or the people who share our homes, or our lives, except perhaps in the act of making love.'[14] In live performance the nature of proximity is experienced and mediated in different ways. In this part of the volume, we offer a theoretical lens for investigating this territory, followed by two case histories exploring playwrights' construction and presentation of personality.

Joseph Roach's pioneering criticism positions public intimacy as the illusion which mediates the relationship between stars and their audiences.[15] As Roach demonstrates, intimacy is a kind of public performance produced expressly for the purposes of stimulating theatrical consumption. This illusion makes possible the creation of desire, familiarity and identification. Roach's essay seeks to define a vocabulary for investigating a performer's charisma. He is interested in the nature of the actor's seductive arts: the multifaceted genius of the factor called 'It'. That genius is made up of elusive qualities related to sex appeal, glamour, beauty, acting technique and aspects of what we now call a performer's lifestyle. Roach's argument suggests that charisma is a product of both strength and weakness. He coins the term 'charismata' to describe a celebrity's positive features or 'marks of strength', and the word 'stigmata' to connote marks of vulnerability. The co-existence in a single body of charismata and stigmata is a particularly tantalising combination. Sometimes, one set of characteristics may outweigh the other; at other times, both overlap or contradict one another; on occasion, the stigmata may dominate to disastrous effect, producing a crisis. Sarah Siddons, for example, succeeded in making her charismata prevail despite the physical changes to her body. In the same way, James Quin's voice and acting style beguiled audiences time after time though his physique was far from perfect.

Several essays in this volume are concerned with the nature of public intimacy. In her essay on eighteenth-century actresses, Felicity Nussbaum actively draws on Roach's vocabulary. Her argument investigates the strategic elision of public and intimate knowledge and the deliberate exposure of supposedly private information for the purpose of cultivating an alluring image. Oscar Wilde's fame, too, was produced by public intimacy of a distinctive and transgressive kind. Peter Raby examines how Wilde created his own model of the playwright as personality. What is remarkable about Wilde is the flagrant way in which he staged his private life. In particular, he defined himself as the centre of a coterie characterised by forms of sartorial and sexual controversy.[16] At the moment immediately before his fame turned to notoriety, Raby argues, Wilde was presenting himself as a pyrotechnical display: flamboyant, unpredictable and socially dazzling. Ultimately, however, his marks of vulnerability were judged to have compromised in scandalous ways his marks of strength. The result was catastrophic ostracism.

The concept of public intimacy also offers a fascinating perspective on the curious invisibility of Clemence Dane in theatre historiography. Dane's early career was marked by notoriety. However, she went on successfully to reinvent herself as a conservative figure and a voice of the Establishment. Significantly, this transformation involved the erasure of her sexual identity. While Dane foregrounded aspects of celebrity in many of her plays, she remained notably silent about her private life. If Roach is right, and sexuality is a major component of the 'It' factor, then the playwright unwittingly abandoned the very identity which might have secured her enduring fame. Moreover, the fact that she wrote under a pseudonym throughout her life suggests another kind of self-erasure. Rather than simply condemning Dane for this suppression, we need to consider the kinds of agency which might be at work in such public performances of the private self.

Notoriety

Notoriety is an important concept in this volume because it has to do with the making and breaking of reputations.[17] Notoriety tends to be attributed to a person rather than to a text or event; it can be a positive or a negative attribute, accidentally won or self-consciously pursued. Above all, notoriety is inseparable from questions of confrontation, challenge and transgression.

Contributors to this volume explore the relationship of notoriety to terms such as controversy (a public dispute, whether moral, political or aesthetic, usually fuelled by cultural commentators or institutional authorities), scandal (usually involving a sexual transgression in the private life of an individual) and sensation (a term which now connotes artefacts or events designed to provoke shock). Scandals which have to do with the publication of private life can create or destroy a celebrity. Controversy, on the other hand, does not necessarily implicate the private domain.

Notoriety's position in the borderland territory between fame and disgrace is a crucial aspect of its fascination. Although a notorious reputation may be recuperated, it may also become difficult to escape. Infamy, however, connotes a scandalous or shameful reputation of an altogether more serious kind; in law, it can result in the loss of a citizen's rights. Moments of notoriety figure in the lives of many playwrights and actors under discussion in this volume. In the case of Samuel Foote, Edmund Kean and Sarah Kane, however, notoriety has become a distinguishing feature of how they are remembered. For a player or a playwright to acquire a notorious reputation before the twentieth century could be risky. For Samuel Foote, however, notoriety became a profitable identity. The actor's satirical imitations of powerful contemporary figures represented a sequence of high-wire acts. Jane Moody argues that Foote used his notoriety as a means of acquiring aristocratic patronage and as a device for making extraordinary cultural interventions. Precisely because he was the performer of his own material Foote could find ever more inventive ways of subverting the licensing laws; as an actor manager, Foote acquired far-reaching cultural authority, which he exploited for the comic production of public scandal.

The fame of Edmund Kean was inseparable from forms of aesthetic and political transgression. Kean's electric, often violent style of performance, particularly in Shakespearean roles, provided a stark contrast with the elegant classicism of John Philip Kemble; indeed, his acting came to be associated with the language of political radicalism. Jacky Bratton's essay focuses on a moment when the prosecution of Kean for illicit sexual relations threatened to bring about his disgrace. She demonstrates how Kean's transgression was construed as an offence against middle-class public mores. In this episode, Kean's notoriety was appropriated and manipulated as part of a campaign for moral reform in the theatre.

Notoriety is often associated with the limits of representation on stage, particularly in relation to sex and violence. From the outset, Sarah Kane's plays were associated with the production of sensation. Cultural institutions, however, also decided to cultivate Kane's notoriety as a profitable commodity. Mary Luckhurst's essay examines the complex interplay between Kane's own agency, her controversial reception, and her appropriation as a cultural brand in domestic and international theatrical markets. An interesting feature of Kane's career is the way it crossed the boundaries between notoriety and infamy: the obsession of the press with Kane's identity as a young woman, and with the circumstances of her death, are critical factors in these attributions.

Markets

Selling celebrity, in the theatre as in any other area of culture, is a business. With one notable exception, however, the economics of the theatre remains a seriously neglected area.[18] This part of the volume seeks to explore ways in which individual performers sell and market themselves. It also draws attention to the by-products of fame (biographies, autobiographies and various kinds of print ephemera) through which celebrities and their agents have shaped their public reputations and commercial value. Contributors are also interested in how theatrical institutions have promoted celebrity at particular moments. The creation and manipulation of rivalry between star performers, for example, has provided a significant means of creating a competitive market.

This part addresses the different devices employed by stars and institutions to maximise their fame. The word 'star' describes 'a person of brilliant reputation or talents'; 'an actor, singer, etc. of exceptional celebrity, or one whose name is publicly advertised as a special attraction to the public' (*OED*). The entry of this term into the lexicon of celebrity has to do with managers' recognition of certain performers as valuable commodities. The idea of the star emerged during the late Georgian period to describe the engagement of metropolitan performers at so-called 'minor' theatres in London and at the provincial Theatres Royal in cities such as Norwich, Bristol and York. The arrival of the star, then, is related to fundamental shifts in the economics and geography of British theatrical production. Celebrated performers in this era commanded huge salaries: at the height of their careers, Sarah Siddons and Edmund Kean were each being paid £50 a night. Yet the commercial success enjoyed by star performers created envy and unease as well as raising questions about the authenticity of a performer's fame.

As Peter Thomson argues, publicity delights in partisanship. His essay explores the 'media hype' which brought the actors James Quin and David Garrick together on the same stage. At different moments in history, reviewers have pitched Olivier against Gielgud, Kean against Kemble, Garrick against Quin. Moreover, by providing a commercial forum for a confrontation between acting styles, rivalry can become a significant site for the recognition of aesthetic innovation.

The position of women in theatrical markets is the subject of contributions by Felicity Nussbaum and Sos Eltis. In the past, theatre historians have tended to emphasise the problems and difficulties women encountered as players and playwrights in institutions dominated by male actor managers. In different ways, both these essays challenge this history. Nussbaum's essay demonstrates the commercial power and economic influence of eighteenth-century actresses. The construction of public intimacy was a significant weapon for women in the dramatic market: print by-products such as memoirs helped to engender this illusion by linking actresses with their stage characters and by circulating details of their private lives.

The box-office appeal of these star actresses was matched by their earnings. As Nussbaum attests, leading actresses made considerably more money than successful women novelists; their financial independence – combined with their sexual freedom – was unprecedented. At the end of the nineteenth century, actresses also commanded a high value: by the age of 36, Sos Eltis points out, Ellen Terry was earning the highest salary of any woman in Britain. Like Nussbaum, Eltis highlights the position of women as agents of their own celebrity and demonstrates that the performance of public selves on and off the stage involves a complex set of transactions. Sarah Bernhardt's outrageous forms of self-advertisement were an example of her shrewd business acumen. Indeed, her publicity stunts anticipated the marketing strategies adopted by many contemporary theatre companies.

Eltis explores how celebrated actresses sold their talents and their bodies whilst simultaneously negotiating still powerful expectations about female virtue. She identifies the demand for portrayals of fallen women on the nineteenth-century stage and investigates the relationship between these controversial roles and the reputations which actresses sought to construct through life writing. Even as she exploited the theatrical fashion for morally compromised heroines, for example, Lillie Langtry carefully manipulated information about her private life. Ellen Terry, by contrast, made a career out of performing virtue. From a variety of perspectives, then, these essays highlight performers' negotiation of the competing and sometimes contradictory demands of the market.

Nation

The nation is a significant lens for this book because it reveals the ways in which particular celebrities have emerged as symbols of Britain's culture and identity. Celebrities in a variety of periods have appropriated the trappings and rhetoric of monarchy in order to define, defend and perpetuate their own fame in national and international marketplaces. Garrick portrayed himself as a quintessential Englishman; Sarah Siddons cultivated the image of herself as a queen, and Laurence Olivier's portrayal of Henry V famously provided an image of heroic monarchy in wartime. The idea that modern celebrities occupy the space left by a decline in the power of monarchy is a familiar one in the sociology of celebrity. The historical character of this process, however, is not properly understood. This part of the volume seeks to confront this problem by offering two examples of the construction of theatrical celebrity as a form of alternative monarchy.

The distinctive quality of the monarchy imagined and produced by theatrical celebrity arises from the capacity of performers such as Siddons or Olivier to represent the body and person of monarchs both historical and contemporary. As Joseph Roach observes, celebrities, like kings, 'have two bodies, the body natural, which decays and dies, and the body politic, which does neither' (p. 24). What is noticeable about Siddons' performance of queenliness or Olivier's characterisation of kingship is the elision between the historical figure and the monarch of the day. The plays of Shakespeare have provided performers with an extraordinary opportunity for staging the dissolution of these two bodies. From this perspective, then, to explore the relationship between celebrity and nationhood is to discover the centrality of Shakespeare in performers' dynamic construction of their own fame.

The British theatre has always provided a crucial site for imagining monarchy. It is noticeable, however, that the particular kinds of monarchical celebrity explored here appeared during periods of war and political instability. As West and Holland emphasise, Siddons and Olivier actively sought to define and manipulate monarchical images and to provoke patriotic emotions in their audiences. The creation of an alternative monarchy, however, is inherently collaborative and involves extensive dialogue between performers, audiences and institutions. Moreover, this process takes place in various kinds of media: portraiture and biography in the case of Siddons; film in the case of Olivier. These representations at moments of national crisis appear to support recent arguments about celebrity's conservative function in society and its significant role in containing cultural anxieties.

The performing bodies of Siddons and Olivier, however, complicate such claims. Siddons projects both violent energy and regal control; Olivier's pleasure in camp is at odds with his representation of raw masculinity. Ambiguity, conflict and contradiction are essential to the creation of these performers' fame. The essays in this part explore the bodies of Siddons and Olivier as sites of national definition, but also draw attention to the relationship between the performance of monarchy and the construction of reputation. The allure of monarchy for Siddons and Olivier may be as much about the desire to create a myth of immortality as it is a sign of their own theatrical distinction.

* * *

This is the first book explicitly to address the subject of celebrity in the history of British theatre. These original essays reveal the collaborative production of fame by individuals, organisations and audiences. Our volume argues that the discourses of celebrity are central to our understanding of agency, institutional politics and the economic structures of theatrical cultures. We have undertaken this project for the purposes of illuminating a neglected set of questions about British theatre history. At the same time, our investigation opens up important perspectives on the nature of celebrity in contemporary society. Above all, this volume is intended to stimulate new conversations about celebrity across periods and disciplines.

Notes

1 *Extraordinary Actors: Essays on Popular Performers*, ed. Jane Milling and Martin Banham (Exeter: University of Exeter Press, 2004).
2 Michael Booth, John Stokes and Susan Bassnett, *Three Tragic Actresses: Siddons, Rachel, Ristori* (Cambridge: Cambridge University Press, 1996).
3 Thomas Postlewait, 'Autobiography and Theatre History', in *Interpreting the Theatrical Past: Essays in the Historiography of Performance*, ed. Thomas Postlewait and Bruce A. McConachie (Iowa City: University of Iowa Press, 1989), pp. 248–72.
4 Leigh Woods, 'Actors' Biography and Mythmaking: The Example of Edmund Kean', in Postlewait and McConachie (eds.), *Interpreting the Theatrical Past*, pp. 230–47.
5 Michael L. Quinn, 'Celebrity and the Semiotics of Acting', *New Theatre Quarterly* 22:6 (May 1990), 154–61.
6 Leo Braudy, *The Frenzy of Renown: Fame and its History* (1986; repr. New York: Vintage Books, 1997), Afterword, p. 614.
7 Marjorie Garber, 'Greatness', in *Symptoms of Culture* (New York: Routledge, 1998), p. 18.
8 See, for instance, David Giles, *Illusions of Immortality: A Psychology of Fame and Celebrity* (Basingstoke: Macmillan, 2000); and David Gritten, *Fame: Stripping Celebrity Bare* (London: Allen Lane, 2002).
9 Chris Rojek, *Celebrity* (London: Reaktion, 2001), p. 112.
10 *Stardom: Industry of Desire*, ed. Christine Gledhill (London: Routledge, 1991), p. xiii.
11 The work of Richard Dyer has been pivotal here. See *Stars* (London: British Film Institute, 1979; revised edition 1998); *Heavenly Bodies: Film Stars and Society* (London: British Film Institute, 1986); and 'A Star is Born and the Construction of Authenticity', in Gledhill, *Stardom*, pp. 132–40.

12 Cf. P. D. Marshall, *Celebrity and Power: Fame in Contemporary Culture* (Minneapolis, MN: University of Minnesota Press, 1997). For celebrity on the early modern stage, see further Alexandra Halasz, ' "So beloved that men use his picture for their signs": Richard Tarlton and the Uses of Sixteenth-Century Celebrity', *Shakespeare Studies* 23 (1995), 19–38, 19; Andrew Gurr, *The Shakespearean Stage 1574–1642* (3rd edition; Cambridge: Cambridge University Press, 1992), pp. 91–4; and Alexander Leggatt, 'Richard Burbage: A Dangerous Actor', in Milling and Banham, *Extraordinary Actors*, pp. 8–20.
13 *Much Ado About Nothing*, III.i.9, in *Shakespeare: The Complete Works*, general editors Stanley Wells and Gary Taylor (Oxford: Clarendon Press, 1986), p. 620.
14 Richard Schickel, *Intimate Strangers: The Culture of Celebrity* (New York: Doubleday, 1985), p. 35.
15 See Joseph Roach, 'It', *Theatre Journal* 56:4 (2004), 555–68.
16 For a compelling study, see Joel H. Kaplan and Sheila Stowell, *Theatre and Fashion: Oscar Wilde to the Suffragettes* (Cambridge: Cambridge University Press, 1994). Cf. Stephen Calloway, 'Wilde and the Dandyism of the Senses', in *The Cambridge Companion to Oscar Wilde* ed. Peter Raby (Cambridge: Cambridge University Press, 1997), pp. 34–54.
17 The term first came into usage at the end of the sixteenth century. Only with the coinage of 'notorious' (in use from 1603), however, did the word acquire derogatory connotations. Interestingly, the *OED* cites a usage of notoriety (1837) in which the word is linked specifically to actors and implies persons of dubious reputation and morality.
18 See Tracy C. Davis's groundbreaking book, *The Economics of the British Stage, 1800–1914* (Cambridge: Cambridge University Press, 2000).

Part I
Public Intimacy

'One man in his time plays many parts.' (And so does a *woman*!)
Ellen Terry, remembering Shakespeare's *As You Like It*

2
Public Intimacy: The Prior History of 'It'
Joseph Roach

> I belonged to the Public and to the world, not because I was talented or even beautiful but because I had never belonged to anything or anyone else.
>
> Marilyn Monroe

There is a certain quality, easy to perceive but hard to define, possessed by abnormally interesting people. Call it 'it'. For the sake of clarity, let 'it', as a pronoun aspiring to the condition of a noun, be capitalised hereafter, except where it appears in its ordinary pronominal role. Most of us immediately assume that 'It' has to do with sex, and we're right, but mainly because everything has to do with sex. Most of us also think that 'It' necessarily entails glamour, and so it does, but not for long. Most of us think that 'It' is rare, and it is quite, even to the point of seeming magical, but 'It' is also everywhere to be seen. In fact, however elusive this quality may be in the flesh, some version of it will, at any given moment, fall within our direct view or easy reach as a mass-circulation image; and if not, a worthy substitute will quickly come to mind, even to the minds of those who, commendably, want to resist generalisations like these, along with the pervasive imposition of the icons they describe.

Let's not be unduly prim, however. This is the way of the world right now, and it has been so, with increasingly invasive saturation and ingenious manipulation since popular celebrities began to circulate their images in the place of religious and regal icons. Today's sacred totems can pop up anywhere. Just at the limit of my reach, on the magazine table at the barbershop on the corner of Chapel and High Streets, but close enough to touch, Uma Thurman returns my gaze from the cover of *GQ*. It's uncanny. She might, with minor adjustments perhaps, just as easily be looking up from the cover of *Cosmopolitan* in the check-out line of Stop & Shop at the Amity Mall, but here she is, sitting right beside me at Tony's, miraculously outshining the lesser deities of *Maxim* and *Esquire*. As *GQ*'s cover girl, she is fragile of feature – eyelids drooping, lips parted, hair bad – and negligent of dress, or about to be, the silken filament of one strap sliding down almost to her right elbow, carrying part of the lace bodice with it, the rest apparently soon to follow, if the insinuated narrative of volition or gravity is to keep its eye-catching promise.

Then again, let's not be wholly prurient either. Her image fascinates, not merely because she looks to be nearly naked, but also because she looks to be completely alone. Even as her eyes meet mine as seductively as they need to in order to do their work, her countenance somehow keeps a modicum of privacy where none seems possible, a discreet veil of solitude in a world brought into illusory fullness of being by the general congregation of unaverted stares. That countenance, the effortless look of public intimacy well known in actresses and models, but also common among high-visibility professionals of other kinds, is but one part, albeit an important one, of the multifaceted genius of 'It'.

A formula as oxymoronic as public intimacy may seem to be a purely modern and secular idea, but it is in fact rooted in traditional religious doctrine and, more deeply and lastingly, in popular religious feeling. Saints and martyrs must make themselves tangibly accessible to ordinary mortals even as they communicate with the divine. Like cover girls, they must seem at once touchable and transcendent, and like them also, and for that reason, they very often appear in representation semi-nude. Their images circulate widely in the absence of their persons – a good working definition of celebrity – but the very tension between their widespread visibility and their actual remoteness creates an unfulfilled need in the hearts of the public. One aspect of this need manifests itself as a craving to communicate with the privately embodied source of the aura, as in the 'I and Thou' relationship imagined to exist between a praying supplicant and a god, in which the archaic 'du' form of intimate second-person address allows the speaker to imagine a conversation with an abstract deity personified as if it had a body, a face and a voice.[1] To be efficacious, the 'I and Thou' experience of 'It' requires a mental picture or idea, not reducible to any single one of the materially circulating images of the celebrity, but nevertheless generally available by association when summoned to memory from the enchanted imagination of the speaker. This availability-to-be-known reaches its apogee when auratic celebrities, like gods or kings, are familiarly called by a single name, as in 'Elvis' or 'Cher'.

As a concept, 'It' has accumulated plenty of history, but as yet rather little theory.[2] It is not celebrity. It is rather the *sine qua non* of celebrity, the infrequently remarked but underlying cause of celebrity's runaway effects. The popular usage of the word was coined in 1927 by a British expatriate, romance-author and Hollywood taste-maker Elinor Glyn (1864–1943), writing in the foreword to *It*, one of her pulpiest fictions, also done into a screenplay for Paramount:

> To have 'It', the fortunate possessor must have that strange magnetism which attracts both sexes. He or she must be entirely unselfconscious and

full of self-confidence, indifferent to the effect he or she is producing, and uninfluenced by others. There must be physical attraction, but beauty is unnecessary. Conceit or self-consciousness destroys 'It' immediately. In the animal world 'It' demonstrates [itself] in tigers and cats – both animals being fascinating and mysterious, and quite unbiddable.[3]

Glyn royally dubbed silent film star Clara Bow 'The "It" Girl', a transferable title once openly aspired to by successive generations of Hollywood starlets, now demurely coveted again under the reactionary aegis of stealth post-feminism.[4] But as Glyn's liberally polymorphous definition suggests, men can have 'It' too. At the Eureka moment when she found the word, just as the Talkies were coming in but before her career as an unofficial chargé d'affaires for British culture in Hollywood burned out, she rechristened what was then only the latest and most powerful version of an oft-observed human phenomenon known by many aliases in the extensive annals of celebrity performance.

How many? For Quintilian, Latin *rhetor* in the rule of Vespasian, 'It' was *ethos*, the compellingly singular character of the great orator. For Zeami, the Zen-inflected theorist of Noh acting, 'It' was the ninth and highest level of *hana*, 'The Flower of Peerless Charm'. For Castiglione, It was *sprezzatura*, the courtly possessor of which turned every head when he, and he alone, suavely entered a room. For many religious thinkers, from the biblical prophets and apostles to modern theologians, 'It' was expressed by the word *charisma*, a special gift vouchsafed by God, a grace or favour, which the sociologist Max Weber then condensed into a principle of powerfully inspirational leadership or authority.[5] For adherents of science, 'It' was captured by the metaphoric terms of *magnetism* and *radiance*, which, taken together, neatly express the opposite motions instigated by the contradictory forces of 'It': drawing towards the charismatic figure as *attraction*; radiating away from him or her as broadcast *aura*. Such metaphors describe well the effects of the phenomenon, but they still explain very little of its mystery. No closer today to a satisfactory theory of 'It', contemporary speakers of proper English employ various synonyms, such as *charm, charisma* and *presence*. Americans also have recourse to a well-stocked slang lexicon, including *stuff, spunk* and *moxie*. What we still lack on both sides of the Atlantic, Glyn's pioneering effort from the 1920s aside, is an analysis of precisely what qualities, then and now, make moxie the cat's meow.

The most promising place to begin such an inquiry is with the received traditions that Glyn represented to the nascent American dream-factory in its wide-open early years – those she brought with her as baggage from England and those she imagined she had. With the possible exception of Edmund Burke, no writer has described the nature of the cultural legacy or burden Glyn inherited more cogently than the Victorian journalist Walter Bagehot, author of *The English Constitution* (1867), who cynically anatomised the irrationality of the political structures of the world into which Glyn and her generation were born. Woven into the snobbery of his largely persuasive account of the government and society of Great Britain in the middle of Victoria's reign is the unspecified but ubiquitous principle of 'It':

> To state the matter shortly, royalty is a government in which the attention of the nation is concentrated on one person doing interesting actions. A Republic is a government in which that attention is divided between many, who are all doing uninteresting actions. Accordingly, so long as the human heart is strong and the human reason weak, royalty will be strong because it appeals to diffused feeling, and Republics weak because they appeal to the understanding.

Moreover, there is for Bagehot a long-standing religious sanction to this aggregation of interesting actions in the hands of the illustrious one at the expense of the jejune many. This sanction did not lose its efficacy after 1867, Matthew Arnold notwithstanding, nor has it entirely since then, if religion is to be counted as the communal aspiration to belong to something larger and more important than ourselves. 'The English Monarchy strengthens our Government with the strength of religion,' concludes *The English Constitution*, with a pointed tautology.[6] One effect of looking at religious faith in Bagehot's socio-political way is to imagine an historic move directly from theocratic to theatrocratic rule. It is also to set aside, at least provisionally, the prevailing tendency of the human sciences to see 'rationality' and 'rational choice' everywhere in the emergence of modern democratic societies. It is to propose instead a lively repertoire of crowd-pleasing romantic comedies and tear-jerking histrionics as an alternative explanation of what passes for popular sovereignty in the age of mass communication, magnetic personalities, and endemic mendacity.

In discussing the sentimental hold of monarchy on the imaginations of the English people, Bagehot's keyword is *visibility*. Royalty, the aristocracy and the established Church (along with anyone else with glamour who might be recruited for the parade) provide the 'visible form' of English government, to which loyal emotion is due and by which it is extracted, whereas nameless, faceless bureaucrats provide the 'efficient form' of boring – hence invisible – service and regulation, the good offices of which effectively rule but do not reign. Bagehot explicitly compares the visible branch of government to the theatre:

> A common man may as well try to rival the actors on the stage in *their* acting, as the aristocracy in *their* acting. The higher world, as it looks from without, is a stage on which the actors walk their parts much better than the spectators can. The play is played in every district, [and] the climax of the play is the Queen.[7]

Let it be emphasised that such theatricality does not render the visible branch otiose. On the contrary, one of the great achievements of the English constitution, the most famous document in history never to have been written, is that the visible branch succeeds not only in dramatising itself, but also in concealing the efficient branch from view, which allows it to complete its secret work as if by magic:

> The apparent rulers of the English nation are like the most imposing personages of a splendid procession: it is by them that the mob are influenced; it is they whom the spectators cheer. The real rulers are secreted in second-class carriages; no one cares for them or asks about them, but they are obeyed implicitly and unconsciously by reason of the splendour of those who eclipsed and preceded them.[8]

Some of the apparent rulers enjoy their splendour *ex officio*; their charisma is ascribed. Others have charisma that is attained, promoting them, as their merits deserve, to the ranks of the visible, the celebrated and the inefficient.

The narrative of Elinor Glyn's life, a Victorian Crusoe castaway among flappers, charts the impromptu extension of the English constitution to Hollywood, where the visible also works to conceal the efficient. Here, in the magical, rapacious place that has since become the playing fields of Eton for American presidents and governors, Glyn refracted the light of star power through the lens of her romantic understanding of history and culture. Not everyone took her seriously then, and few do today, but in order to make my argument about the urgent role of public intimacy in the creation of 'It', I must take her any way I can get her, for she understood early on that the most charismatic celebrities are the ones we can only imagine, even if we see them naked everywhere.

Glyn thought of herself as a proper Englishwoman; this meant, of course, that her life was a tangled skein of contradictory idiosyncrasies. Born in Jersey to a relatively well-connected but impecunious family of Franco-Irish Canadians, she believed that she was descended from a titled but attainted follower of the Old Pretender. In 1896, she was presented at Court to Alexandra, Princess of Wales, during the absence due to illness of Queen Victoria herself, in a gown made for the occasion by her elder sister, the exceptionally resourceful couturiere 'Lucile', later Lady Duff-Gordon. But no mere actual royals then living, certainly not Hanoverians, could surpass in glamour those who reigned in the nostalgic, pre-French Revolutionary realms that Glyn called the 'Fairy Kingdoms' of her imagination:

> The outlook and the beliefs impressed upon me by my grandparents, already nearly a century out of date from the contemporary point of view, sank into my mind, and have never been entirely eliminated. They can be seen peeping out of every book I write, even when I fancy that I am being

entirely modern. A varied life containing much disillusionment, and which has witnessed the passing of the last vestiges of the *ancien régime* that I was taught so greatly to admire, has not completely removed my childhood's faith in the value of the aristocratic tradition. Even my constant touch with, and ten years' residence in democratic, modern America has not undermined my subconscious belief, born of many fairy tales, that princes and princesses are the natural heroes and heroines of romantic adventures![9]

Romance for Glyn, while deeply spiritual in abstract feeling, also required, for better or worse, bodies: a precocious free spirit even in her teens, she married well none the less; but after fifteen exciting and widely travelled years, Clayton Glyn exhausted both his weak liver and his considerable inheritance (tragically for Elinor, not in that order). With two children and a slowly dying invalid of a husband to support, she turned her hand to writing romances and snaring extended invitations as a house-guest of the rich and famous. In the end, both proved to be good career moves: her works included *Three Weeks*, a *succès de scandal*, featuring a memorable scene of erotic encounter, teasingly autobiographical, on a tiger-skin, which led to local ostracism from English society but international fame; her hosts ranged from the Russian Grand Duchess Cyril to the American William Randolph Hearst of the newspaper empire. Celebrity fascinated her at a distance and at close range, and long before her fateful rendezvous with Clara Bow, her way of understanding 'It' percolated through a number of filters of historical precedent and her own experience.

As a self-fashioning entrepreneur who sincerely believed that almost everything worth having in life is inherited, Glyn found her historical imagination excited most vividly by the Stuart Restoration of 1660. Meditating on the extreme carelessness of some aspects of her otherwise exemplary upbringing, she savoured the memory of being turned loose at the age of ten in her stepfather's library, where she found her way to the unexpurgated edition of Samuel Pepys' *Diary*. Undetected, she read it through with great curiosity and, what is worse, growing comprehension. Among other stimulations, Glyn recounts, 'Pepys awakened my great interest in the Charles II period, and strengthened my Stuart proclivities. I wrote under his picture, in a child's illustrated History of England which we had, the words "Dear Good King" and "Nasty old Beast!" under the portrait of Cromwell.'[10] Like Richard Eyre's *Stage Beauty* (2004), set at the moment in theatrical history when women replaced female impersonators at the behest of the restored King, Glyn's concept of the modern genesis of romantic celebrity, in which no bodice remains unripped, leans heavily on Pepys' account of the English Restoration's improvisatory mix of theatre, politics, religion and sex.

Pepys, however, was not writing pulp fiction. The period he documents in flesh-and-blood detail saw the reinstatement of the theatre in the repertoire of popular pleasures, but now under the legal and symbolic aegis of the monarchy and with the added attractions of painted scenes and painted women. For both Pepys and his royal sovereign, and not for them alone, the pre-eminent ' "It" Girl' of the Restoration stage was Nell Gwyn, whose sexuality, in the words of a distinguished historian of the first actresses, 'became the central feature of her professional identity as a player'.[11] But not the only feature: she also had moxie, which is the ability to project self-possession even at moments of apparent self-abandonment. On 2 March 1667, Pepys saw Gwyn in a breeches role and recorded what seems to have been a general response to the intimacy of her public presence, even from the women, though the most important spectators at that particular performance the diarist specifically names:

> there is a comical part done by Nell, which is Florimell, that I never can hope to see the like done again by man or women. The King and Duke of York was at the play; but so great performance of a comical part was never, I believe, in the world before as Nell doth this, both as a mad girle and then, most and best of all, when she comes in like a young gallant; and hath the motions and carriage of a spark the most that ever I saw any man have.[12]

That's 'It'.

The iconic status of the double-bodied King, God's Vicar on Earth and now titular head of the playhouse into the bargain, became ever so much more intimate in the strange twilight of sacral monarchy. Like the best of his actors and paramours, the 'Dear Good King' had 'It', not only on account of his widely reputed personal qualities, but also by virtue of his job description, which still empowered him to cure 'the King's Evil' by the laying on of his anointed hands and to commit adultery with social impunity. A number of the most telling episodes of his performance of public intimacy cluster around the theatre: carrying on flirtations and even open rows with his mistresses in the auditorium; passing notes with actors and actresses backstage; loaning his coronation robes to the players for use as costumes. Wrapped in the theatre's cloak of a thousand colours, flaunting his affairs with actresses so notorious that they were popularly known, as he was, by their first names, Charles nevertheless properly signed official documents, including the theatrical patents that legally incorporated the stage into his regime, 'Defender of the Faith'.

No wonder Glyn, the coiner of *It*, was attracted to him across the intervening centuries. Later in life a passionate believer in reincarnation (and, for a time, spiritualism) and always a fierce foe of Puritanism of any denomination, Glyn developed her own quirky, quasi-Christian-charismatic, neo-pagan religion. In the royalist Gospel according to Elinor, social order and aesthetic beauty unite in the ascent to 'romance', which was her godhead:

> As I see it, the word 'romantic' represents the true opposite of the word 'sordid'; romance is a spiritual disguise, created by the imagination, with which to envelop material happenings and desires, and thus bring them into greater harmony with the soul.[13]

She found her special doctrine of 'spiritual disguise' revealed in the heroes and heroines she created in fiction or sought out in her journeys, which took on the aura of pilgrimages. Her spiritual quest was for the iconic royals of an imagined dynasty of true glamour and *noblesse oblige* which ran from her putative Stuart forebears to their modern successors in Tinsel Town. When she unpacked her bags in the autumn of 1920 with a contract in hand from 'Famous-Players-Lasky' (later Paramount), she found herself in the right place at the right time: Douglas Fairbanks and Mary Pickford, Glyn recalls, were 'the acknowledged King and Queen of the cinema world when I reached Hollywood'.[14]

Not that this was an especially new idea to her or to the actors. Of Charles Hart's impersonation of Alexander the Great, the old prompter John Downes remembered in *Roscius Anglicanus* (1706): 'he Acting [the role] with such Grandeur and Agreeable Majesty, That one of the Court was pleas'd to Honour him with this Commendation; that *Hart* might Teach any King on Earth how to Comport himself'.[15] Of the whole institution of the stage under the later Stuarts, Charles Gildon, in his *Life of Thomas Betterton* (1710), wrote that it was a 'Mimic State'.[16] The key element of monarchical government, as Bagehot attests, is the public visibility of its sacred head, and His Majesty's Servants made their sovereign intimately visible through their daily performances of all genres in his name, not merely on those rare and dangerous occasions when, as in the Exclusion Crisis, they edged too close to current events and seemed to mimic a reigning monarch or his deputies directly and critically. Every performance, except the silenced ones, proceeded with explicit royal authorisation, like daily religious services, except Sundays. For anyone shaped by an idea of theatre as necessarily subversive or adversarial, to think of the stage as an organ of state like the Established Church seems counterintuitive, but the royal warrants and patents issued by Charles enjoined his patentees to manage their houses so that they might 'serve as moral instructions in human life', censoring by prior restraint any and all plays, old or new 'containing any passages offensive to piety or good manners'.[17]

That was the theory. In practice, results varied, but Glyn's best guide and ours, Samuel Pepys, recorded something like a religious conversion experience at a theatrical performance in 1668, a divine apparition resonant of bells and redolent of smells. Supported in full baroque splendour with music and machines, the revival of Dekker and Massinger's *The Virgin Martyr* featured Rebecca Marshall as the saintly Dorathea and Nell Gwyn as her guardian angel:

> With my wife and Deb to the King's House, to see *The Virgin Martyr*, the first time it has been acted in a great while; and it is mighty pleasant; not that the play is worth much but it is finely Acted by Becke Marshall. But that which did please me beyond anything in the whole world was the wind-musique when the Angell comes down, which is so sweet that it ravished me; and endeed, in a word, did wrap up my soul so that it made me really sick, just as I have formerly been when in love with my wife; that neither then, nor all the evening going home and at home, I was able to think of anything but remained all night transported.[18]

Nothing exactly like this seems to have happened to Pepys in church, though the habits he indulged there demonstrate that he felt a certain rapport between his experiences in the two different venues.[19] Apparently driven by the contradictory urges of his para-Episcopal attraction, Pepys went backstage to the dressing rooms after another performance of *The Virgin Martyr*. Here, much to his disillusionment, he found that the painted faces and coarse language of the same actresses now repelled him: 'but Lord, their confidence, and how many men do hover about them as soon as they come off the stage, and how confident they [are] in their talk'.[20] No other detail confirms more decisively the historic emergence of public intimacy than the convention of allowing gentlemen backstage at the playhouse to meet the actresses as they undressed. But it does not diminish the religious force of the impulse Pepys felt at the first appearance of the angel, whose offstage identity he well knew, in a sublime flourish of oboes and the raiment of ecstatic belief. In his voluptuous faith, as in Glyn's, fantasies have the efficacy of prayers, and flesh-and-blood actors, no less than kings, appear in the 'spiritual disguise' of gods.

By the time Glyn beatifically defined 'It', the cultural connection between long-standing traditions of religious life and modern life had already been thoroughly explored, perhaps even exhausted, by her more discursive contemporary, sociologist of religion Emile Durkheim. Chris Rojek in *Celebrity* (2001) summarises the pertinent argument of *The Elementary Forms of Religious Life* (1912): 'There are many striking parallels between religious belief and practice and celebrity cultures', he writes, citing the fan reception of film idols and rock stars. These parallels, which include reliquaries, death rites, ceremonies of ascent and descent, shamanic interventions, eucharistic offerings, confessions, resurrections, and promises of everlasting redemption, tend to 'reinforce the hypothesis that considerable partial convergence between religion and celebrity has occurred'.[21] Durkheim slyly but resolutely interpreted the structures of his own society in the defamiliarising light of the animistic beliefs of indigenous peoples. In each case, these structures and beliefs are expressed through 'totems', the unifying symbols around which a culture or a people coheres. No matter how 'advanced' the members of society may think that their special way of doing things is, their social life is *la vie religieuse*, however secular it may seem and however deeply entrenched its adherents' self-flattering sense of their own 'rationality' may have become. 'If the totem is the symbol of both the god and the society,' Durkheim asks rhetorically, 'is it not because the god and the society are one and the same?'[22]

For purposes of appreciating the persistence of Durkheim's influence and the attraction of his analysis of the religious basis of modern popular culture, historians of celebrity should return as frequently as is necessary to Roland Barthes' *Mythologies* (1957). While divulging the secret paths of meaning that connect sacred totems like 'Steak and Chips', 'Plastic' and 'The New Citroën', Barthes writes an ethnography of public intimacy in 'The Face of Garbo': 'The name given to her, *the Divine*, probably aimed to convey less a superlative state of beauty than the essence of her corporeal person, descended from heaven where all things are formed and perfected in the clearest light.'[23] Greta Garbo famously wanted to be left alone, but that pathetic wish succeeded only in summoning millions more to genuflect at her shrine. Consummately 'unbiddable' and yet everywhere to be seen, she took her place in the foremost ranks of the miracle-workers who turned mere bread and wine into bread and circuses.

Celebrities, like kings, have two bodies – the body natural, which decays and dies, and the body politic, which does neither. But the immortal body of the 'image', even though it is preserved on celluloid, on digitalised files or in the memory of the theatre-going public, always bears the nagging reminder of the former ('She looks great. Isn't she dead by now?') As their sacred images circulate in the demotic swirl of the profane imagination, celebrities foreground a peculiar combination of strength and vulnerability, expressed through outward signs of the union of their imperishable and mortal bodies. Let those marks of strength be called *charismata*; the signs of vulnerability, *stigmata*. They work cooperatively, like muscles in opposable pairs, and their beguiling interplay, now widely heralded among acting teachers, has a long history as well as popular currency as the source of public intimacy.

With or without the Stuarts, the theatre of the long eighteenth century provided a conduit through which the double body-type of the monarch devolved upon the most famous of his or her subjects. In this expansion of celebrity to a wider aperture of visibility, the stage produced totemic signs, by which the intimate persons of its stars became as familiar to the public as the heraldic trappings of monarchy once were and continued to be. Anne Bracegirdle's white teeth, David Garrick's flashing eyes and Dorothy Jordan's curly hair, for example, are celebrated *charismata* in English theatrical history. At the same time, Elizabeth Barry's asymmetrical face, David Garrick's short stature and Sarah Siddons' *embonpoint* are equally well-known *stigmata*.

In the creation of public intimacy, psyche and soma intertwine, and the stigmatising marks, visible or invisible, leave their emotional trace in every expression, especially the strongest.

As Achilles was a more compelling hero because of his heel, not in spite of it, so Thomas Betterton became a more effective tragedian in part because his increasingly vulnerable body contrasted so poignantly with his growing moral strength. Except for those by Pepys, the eyewitness accounts of him come from later in his career, most pertinently Tony Aston's reverent but clear-eyed portrait:

> Mr. Betterton (although a superlative good Actor) labour'd under ill Figure, being clumsily made, having a great Head, a short thick Neck, stoop'd in the Shoulders, and had fat short Arms, which he rarely lifted higher than his Stomach. His Left Hand frequently lodg'd in his Breast, between his Coat and Waist-coat, while, with his Right, he prepar'd his Speech. His Actions were few, but just. He had little Eyes, and a Broad Face, a little Pock-fretten, a corpulent Body, and thick Legs, with large Feet. He was better to meet, than to follow; for his Aspect was serious, venerable, and majestic; in his latter Time a little paralytic. His Voice was low and grumbling; yet he could Time it by an artful Climax, which enforc'd universal Attention, even from the Fops and Orange-Girls.[24]

In many religious traditions worldwide, 'shamans, sorcerers, and medicine men' are singled out by extraordinary physical marks or eccentricities of behaviour.[25] In modernity, actors are identified in much the same way, even if their oddity is abnormal perfection. Whatever its source, their apartness is no less important than their availability. With Betterton's physical peculiarity came a more powerfully distinguished magic, and contemporaries felt 'It'. Richard Steele's eulogy on the occasion of the actor's burial in Westminster Abbey conveyed the preternaturally vivid presence of the characters he created over a long career, as if he had, before Steele's astonished eyes, actually done the many extraordinary deeds attributed to the heroes and kings he represented and had actually suffered their extraordinary travails. In some sense, he had. In death, Steele realised, Betterton, son of an undercook in the service of Charles I, had officially joined the appropriate assembly in the pantheon of English worthies, avatars of a 'Free-born People': 'the Sacred Heads which lie buried in the Neighbourhood of this little Portion of Earth in which my poor Friend is deposited, are returned to Dust as well as he'. Steele further concluded that all differences among living men are 'merely Scenical' and 'that there is no Difference in the Grave between the Imaginary and the Real Monarch'.[26] With growing audacity, performers, whose celebrity was achieved, did not wait for the grave before they claimed their place in the public eye beside aristocrats and royals, whose celebrity was ascribed. This does not mean that they thereby became altogether socially acceptable, but it does mean that they became increasingly necessary.

That would certainly apply to the 'The Siddons'. Like Betterton, whose authority increased with the passing decades, Sarah Siddons became a more formidable tragedienne with the stigmatising *avoirdupois* than without it, for after seven pregnancies, her signature emotions of distressed maternity gained greater conviction as well as gravity. William Hazlitt's famous prayer to Mrs Siddons as the long-reigning deity of the stage captures both the intensity and the fragility of her charismatic hold on her public. In another time and place, the adulation he reports would be called 'Momism':

> The homage she has received is greater than that which is paid to queens. The enthusiasm she excited had something idolatrous about it; she was regarded less with admiration than with wonder, as if a superior order had dropped from another sphere, to awe the world with the majesty of her appearance. She raised tragedy to the skies, or brought it down from thence. It was something above nature. We can conceive of nothing grander. She embodied to our imagination the fables of mythology, of the heroic and deified mortals of elder time. She was not less than a goddess, or than a prophetess inspired by the gods. Power was seated on her brow, passion emanated from her breast as from a shrine. She was Tragedy personified. She was the stateliest ornament of the public mind.[27]

Less often noted is what Hazlitt says he is praying for: he is imploring Siddons to reconsider her ill-advised return to the stage in 1816, long enough after her retirement that the perfect balance between *charismata* and *stigmata* she had once been able to strike was no longer possible. Slow of speech and largely immobile, she now exhibited vulnerabilities that so surpassed her strengths that by coming again upon the boards she risked the almost certain destruction of her hard-won image as an 'idol' in the public mind. When *stigmata* so far overrun *charismata*, the embarrassed celebrity becomes too available to the identification of the audience, and that special quality of apartness, which Glyn describes as 'unbiddable', disappears, taking 'It' down with it. 'Players should be immortal', Hazlitt explains, 'if their own wishes or ours could make them so; but they are not'.[28]

The wish to sanctify 'idols' as inviolate, a wish that public intimacy both inspires and betrays, prompted Edmund Burke to name Sarah Siddons along with her precursor David Garrick in connection with the sufferings of Marie Antoinette in *Reflections on the Revolution in France* (1790) and, more radically, to propose the replacement of religion by the stage, at least for the duration of the emergency: 'Indeed, the theatre is a better school of moral sentiments than churches, where the feelings of humanity are thus outraged.'[29] Burke proved prophetic, but what for him was an impassioned expedient became a settled practice according to Bagehot's cooler analysis in *The English Constitution* three-quarters of a century later:

> In fact, the mass of English people yield a deference rather to something else than to their rulers. They defer to what we may call the *theatrical show* of society. A certain state passes before them; a certain pomp of great men; a certain spectacle of beautiful women; a wonderful scene of wealth and enjoyment is displayed, and they are coerced by it. Their imagination is bowed down; they feel they are not equal to the life which is revealed to them. Courts and aristocracies have the great quality which rules the multitude, though philosophers can see nothing in it – visibility.[30]

It's magical: visibility increases as reality vanishes. What Bagehot could be describing with equal familiarity is the relationship between the public and the motion picture industry in the twentieth century, or between the public and the whole expansive network of mediated spectacles in the twenty-first. Taking Glyn's personal history as the touchstone for a more general account of the rise of public intimacy yet to be written, the concept of 'It' might be speculatively assessed as useful to the creation of an invisible British Empire, one that not only survived the Second World War, but actually continues to flourish and grow, as the unwritten English constitution spreads itself worldwide like an oil slick. Meanwhile, to conclude, the barest outline of that argument might be tentatively suggested here by a tale of two women: one, a former bun-slicer at Nathan's on Coney Island, who became suddenly and completely visible; the other, the supposed descendent of the Old Pretender's liegeman, who was born to be efficient.

'American film producers had learnt all that I had to teach them', wrote Elinor Glyn grandly about her departure from Hollywood in 1927, 'and I realised that my work was done'.[31] But even adjusted to accommodate her vanity, Glyn's work did have consequences. It was she who persuaded earnest set-dressers at Famous-Players-Lasky that Baronial Halls of old English castles ought not to be provided with rows of spittoons. It was she who explained to Rudolph Valentino how to kiss the fleshy inside of a woman's palm instead of the knuckle on the top. And it was she who conjured and honed the image of 'The "It" Girl'. Paramount wanted Clara Bow to be an American girl-next-door, as adorable as Mary Pickford, but also to be self-confidently sexual, as overtly so in her own 'aw-shucks' kind of way as the exotic vamp popularised a few years earlier by Theda Bara (a pseudonymous anagram for 'Arab death'). This was a tall order, requiring real finesse, like cloning Anne Bracegirdle from Elizabeth Barry, and Glyn set grimly to work.

The publicity department at Paramount arranged for Bow and Glyn to spend time together and to be seen in public doing so. To that end, striking redheads both, they sped around Los Angeles together in a large Packard, accompanied by the actress's great red chow dog and a redundant driver provided by the Studio. Bow, who at best regarded speed limits and traffic lights as advisory, insisted on taking the wheel, while Glyn kept her upper lip stiff in the passenger's seat and the terrorised chauffeur wept and prayed in the back. What inter-societal connection opened up between these two women in their work together cannot be rationally specified, but one did, and it must have had to do with 'It', which for both of them, in their different genres, meant the ability to stand as if naked in the middle of a crowded room as if alone. For her part, Bow, an abused drop-out with the patois of the Brooklyn tenements stencilled on her tongue, suffered icy condescension and impeccably phrased reproof from her mentor. At the same time, Glyn, world authority on gracious living and romance, endured non-stop gum-popping, macaroni and cheese, and the special moniker reserved for her by her tough-cookie tutee: 'Shithead'.[32]

Looking back, however, Glyn remembered above all else Bow's leonine courage: on location in the Pacific for the movie version of *It*, shooting a shipwreck scene on a cold day when the shark-infested seas were too high, she watched 'The "It" Girl', who had barely learned to swim, laugh off the stunt-double and plunge cheerfully over the side. Nor did Bow ever hesitate to seduce the men she wanted or apologise for her success in doing so. Glyn respected her for that too, rather like something she might have encountered in the pages of Pepys or, with more demure diction, in her own novels, where self-assured women politely but decisively take charge of their erotic fates. Like Steele at Betterton's funeral, Glyn recalled the actress as having done in life the very deeds she enacted in representation, and at the end of the day, both women made their own livings by their talents and their looks, and both earned enough to well afford the men they supported. Glyn also believed that Bow's true emotional range was never really tested by the sexy little comedies in which she was invariably cast. Behind Bow's freakishly big eyes and brittle laugh, the novelist saw a sorrow that spoke of the special kind of loneliness peculiar to the age of public intimacy, when an actress or even a princess might plausibly come to the conclusion that she can belong to the world but not to anything or anyone else in it. Of course that will sell a lot of popcorn too.

Glyn rehearsed similarly melancholy and yet elevated thoughts in remembering the state funeral of Queen Victoria in 1901. The three things that struck her most forcefully were first, the tremendous emotion expressed in silence by the bereaved, adoring crowds; second, the resolute fortitude of the men, some quite elderly, who followed the gun-carriage on foot for the entirety of its long journey; and finally, the diminutive size, measured against the vast panoply of nation and empire, of 'the little, little coffin'. At the memory of her sight of this object, Glyn's thoughts turned again to the irrational but irresistible paradox of the Queen's two bodies, the body natural and the body politic, and the visible role that the former plays in creating the invisible dream-works of the latter:

> This reminder of the smallness, the feminine frailty, of the greatest ruler in the world, brought home to me for the first time the glorious romance of the British Empire, and the greatness of the British race. A sublime spirit of chivalry must be innate in a people whose highest response of loyalty and valour is always made to its Queens.[33]

This is Bagehot's 'visible government' quaintly working its magic the old-fashioned way, but a century later the anonymous producers of mass spectacle on a global scale continue to take their cue from its elementary but effective prestidigitation: now you see 'It' – hocus-pocus – now you don't.

Notes

1. David Aberbach, *Charisma in Politics, Religion and the Media: Private Trauma, Public Ideals* (London: Macmillan, 1996), p. x.
2. For the more recent history of 'It', see Joseph Roach, 'It', *Theatre Journal*, 56:4 (2004), 555–68.
3. Elinor Glyn, *It* (New York: The Macaulay Company, 1927), pp. 5–6.
4. Eugenia Peretz, 'The "It" Parade', *Vanity Fair* (September 2000), pp. 313–82.
5. Max Weber, *On Charisma and Institution Building*, ed. S. N. Eisenstadt (Chicago, IL: University of Chicago Press, 1968).
6. Walter Bagehot, *The English Constitution*, ed. R. H. S. Crossman (1867; repr. Ithaca, NY: Cornell University Press, 1966), p. 86.
7. Bagehot, *The English Constitution*, p. 248.
8. Bagehot, *The English Constitution*, p. 249.
9. Elinor Glyn, *Romantic Adventure* (New York: E. P. Dutton and Co., 1937), p. 11. For additional details and perspective, see Anthony Glyn, *Elinor Glyn: A Biography* (London: Hutchinson, 1955), Meredith Etherington-Smith and Jeremy Pilcher, *The 'It' Girls: Lucy, Lady Duff Gordon, the Couturiere 'Lucile', and Elinor Glyn, Romantic Novelist* (London: Hamish Hamilton, 1986); and Joan Hardwick, *Addicted to Romance: The Life and Adventures of Elinor Glyn* (London: André Deutsch, 1994). In *The Cat's Meow* (Lions Gate, 2002), Joanna Lumley plays Elinor Glyn to Kirsten Dunst's Marion Davies.
10. Glyn, *Romantic Adventure*, p. 23.
11. Elizabeth Howe, *The First English Actresses: Women and Drama 1660–1700* (Cambridge: Cambridge University Press, 1992), p. 34.
12. *The Diary of Samuel Pepys*, ed. Robert Latham and William Matthews, 13 vols (Berkeley, CA: University of California Press, 1970–83), VIII, p. 91.
13. Glyn, *Romantic Adventure*, p. 2.
14. Glyn, *Romantic Adventure*, pp. 300–1.
15. John Downes, *Roscius Anglicanus*, ed. Judith Milhous and Robert D. Hume (1706; repr. London: Society for Theatre Research, 1987), p. 41.
16. Charles Gildon, *The Life of Mr. Thomas Betterton, the Late Eminent Tragedian* (London: Printed for Robert Gosling, 1710), p. 10.
17. *Theatre in Europe: A Documentary History; Restoration and Georgian England, 1660–1788*, ed. David Thomas and Arnold Hare (Cambridge: Cambridge University Press, 1989), pp. 12, 17.

18 *The Diary of Samuel Pepys*, IX, pp. 93–4.
19 See Joseph Roach, 'Celebrity Erotics: Pepys, Performance, and Painted Ladies', *Yale Journal of Criticism*, 16:1 (2003), 211–30.
20 *The Diary of Samuel Pepys*, IX, p. 189.
21 Chris Rojek, *Celebrity* (London: Reaktion Books, 2001), p. 58.
22 Emile Durkheim, *The Elementary Forms of Religious Life*, trans. Karen E. Fields (1912; repr. New York: The Free Press, 1995), p. 208. See also Jeffrey Alexander and Phil Smith, 'Introduction', *The Cambridge Companion to Durkheim* (Cambridge: Cambridge University Press, 2005).
23 Roland Barthes, *Mythologies*, trans. Annette Lavers (1957; repr. New York: Hill and Wang, 1972), pp. 56–7.
24 Anthony Aston, *A Brief Supplement to Colley Cibber*, in *An Apology for the Life of Mr. Colley Cibber* (1740), ed. Robert W. Lowe. 2 vols (London: John C. Nimmo, 1889), II, pp. 299–300.
25 Rojek, *Celebrity*, p. 55.
26 Richard Steele, *The Tatler*, ed. Donald F. Bond, 3 vols (Oxford: The Clarendon Press, 1987), II, p. 424.
27 *Hazlitt on Theatre*, ed. William Archer and Robert Lowe (1895; repr. New York: Hill and Wang, n.d.), p. 94.
28 *Hazlitt on Theatre*, p. 93.
29 Edmund Burke, *Reflections on the Revolution in France*, ed. Conor Cruise O'Brien (1790; repr. London: Penguin, 1968), p. 176.
30 Bagehot, *The English Constitution*, p. 248. Emphasis Bagehot's.
31 Elinor Glyn, *Romantic Adventure*, p. 326.
32 Hardwick, *Addicted to Romance*, p. 263.
33 Hardwick, *Romantic Adventure*, p. 97.

3
Wilde: The Remarkable Rocket
Peter Raby

Wilde was arguably the first English-speaking playwright who systematically cultivated an image for himself. He was soon to be followed by George Bernard Shaw, who, while relishing the Celtic heritage he shared with Wilde, fashioned a distinctively contrasting public personality. Shaw, rival as well as colleague, also found himself in the role of critic when he began to write theatre notices for the *Saturday Review* in January 1895, and had to respond successively to *An Ideal Husband* and *The Importance of Being Earnest*, which marked Wilde's re-entry to the public arena of West-End theatre in the first months of that year. For a brief period, Wilde and Shaw mounted a combined assault on the West-End London stage, an outpost of mediocrity defended by serried ranks of Philistines, puppets and time-serving journalists, where the actor-managers offered to a complaisant public wholly predictable and limited theatrical fare. Shaw performed his role combatively in the columns of the *Saturday Review*, and in his energetic attempts to market his unpleasant plays through actor-managers such as Charles Wyndham and George Alexander. Wilde, prolific in both playscripts and scenarios, and distinctly more bankable, was eventually successful in placing *An Ideal Husband*, and agreed to compress *The Importance of Being Earnest* to satisfy Alexander's criteria.

Theatrical celebrity in the 1880s and 1890s belonged to the actor-managers, the controlling powers of theatre – Irving, Beerbohm Tree, Alexander, Wyndham – and to goddesses such as the divine Sarah Bernhardt, Ellen Terry, Lillie Langtry or Mrs Patrick Campbell. The playwright was almost incidental. The estimable Arthur Wing Pinero hardly ranked as a celebrity, while as for Henry Arthur Jones – '[W]ho is Jones?' enquired Wilde mischievously of Alexander, who had mentioned him in a speech: 'Perhaps the name as reported in the London papers was a misprint for something else. I have never heard of Jones. Have you?'[1]

Wilde, already adept at creating a public persona, deliberately invaded the theatrical arena, aspiring to dominate it as effortlessly as his alter ego in *A Woman of No Importance*, Lord Illingworth, commands a London

31

dinner-table: 'A man who can dominate a London dinner-table can dominate the world.' This essay examines some aspects of Wilde as a celebrity in the period between July 1894 and March 1895, when he was uneasily poised between fame and notoriety, the fame of social glitter and theatrical success crystallised by the reception to *Lady Windermere's Fan* and *A Woman of No Importance*, and the notoriety which followed his failed libel suit against the Marquess of Queensberry and the subsequent trials. The London theatre formed a kind of annex to the London drawing-room, and Wilde's plays deliberately mirrored the luxury, power and morality of upper-class English society. Although his audiences were by no means restricted to the wealthy and fashionable, their success depended on a positive London reception; and the line between success and failure was finely drawn, as Henry James found to his cost when *Guy Domville* was withdrawn and *The Importance of Being Earnest* substituted in its place. Wilde's kind of comedy invokes the complicity of the audience. The public had to decide whether or not to continue to be amused. A certain unease, an ambivalence, can be detected, for example, within the long tradition of hostility towards Wilde displayed in the cartoons of George Du Maurier in *Punch*, or by those of Harry Furniss. More surprising are the traits, physical and literary, pointed up by those who actually admired Wilde as an artist, as identified in the cartoons of Max Beerbohm and the parodies of Ada Leverson.

This uneasiness is powerfully illustrated in a *Punch* piece of 10 November 1894, 'The Decadent Guys',[2] which picks up both *A Green Carnation*[3] and Wilde's story 'The Remarkable Rocket', in addition to a whole range of Wilde's writings and sayings (Figure 3.1). Douglas is lampooned as Lord Raggie Tattersall, sitting in the peculiar kind of portable chair he most affected, Wilde as Fustian Flitters 'in a luxurious sort of hand-barrow'. 'I am very beautiful,' declares Raggie. 'And you, Fustian, you are so energetically inert. Are you going to blow up tonight? You are so brilliant when you blow up.' 'I have not decided either way,' replies Fustian. 'I never do. It will depend upon how I feel in the bonfire. I let it come if it will. The true *impromptu* is invariably premeditated.' The dialogue continues, as beautiful rose-coloured children chant their Fifth of November catches, and then depart, to be replaced by 'one of those unconsciously absurd persons they call policemen'. 'But what is this crude blue copper going to do with you and me?' Raggie asks Fustian. 'Can we be going to become notorious – *really* notorious – at last?' 'I devoutly trust not. Notoriety is now merely a synonym for respectable obscurity. But he certainly expects to be engaged in what a serious humourist would call "running us in".' 'How pedantic of him! Then shan't we be allowed to explode at all this evening?' 'It seems not. They think we are dangerous. How can one tell? Perhaps we are ...' And with gentle resignation, 'as martyrs whose apotheosis is merely postponed', Lord Raggie and Fustian Flitters are moved on 'by the rude hand of an unsympathetic Peeler'.

Wilde: The Remarkable Rocket   33

"My dear Raggie, you are looking very well this afternoon."

Figure 3.1   Bernard Partridge, *The Decadent Guys, Punch,* 10 November 1894.

Wilde's story, 'The Remarkable Rocket', was published in May 1888.[4] It is, among other things, a satire on James Whistler: Whistler's painting *Nocturne in Black and Gold – The Falling Rocket* provides the unifying central theme, the same painting which prompted John Ruskin's comment about 'flinging a pot of paint in the public's face',[5] and of which Wilde had written, while still an undergraduate, 'it is worth looking at for about as long as one looks at a real rocket, that is, for somewhat less than a quarter of a minute'.[6] (This is the sort of comment that many of Wilde's contemporaries would make about his own work.) But if 'The Remarkable Rocket' reads as an elaborate Whistler-tease, it also seems to mock Wilde himself; Wilde seems to infuse the Rocket's speech with his own tone and manner: 'I like hearing myself talk. It is one of my greatest pleasures.'[7] Wilde, who at times seems bent on promoting himself as an elaborate and spectacular firework display, has nevertheless an ironic and heightened mistrust of such brilliant and public dazzle. He was always aware of the difference between a subtle appreciation of art and the pyrotechnics which surrounded the selling of art in the late Victorian marketplace.

Wilde deployed the firework motif on a number of occasions, including the summer of 1894. Fireworks feature significantly in an important letter he wrote to George Alexander in July, in which he tries to sell his first scenario of *The Importance of Being Earnest* to the actor-manager for £150 (he was also obviously hoping to sell 'this amusing thing with lots of fun and wit' simultaneously to Albert Palmer for the American market).[8] The scenario ends with a projected post-curtain scenario, a parodic version of previous public encounters in that dangerous moment before a first-night audience.

> Author called. Cigarette called. Manager called. Royalties for a year for author.
> Manager credited with writing the play. He consoles himself for the slander with bags of red gold.
> Fireworks.

Teasingly, Wilde absents himself from this imagined scene. When the first night duly arrived, on 14 February 1895, Wilde tactfully, and sensibly, remained out of sight. Hesketh Pearson quotes Franklin Dyall – the actor who played Merriman – as his authority for Wilde's comment: 'I don't think I shall take a call tonight. You see, I took one only last month at the Haymarket, and one feels so much like a *German band.*'[9] (Wilde was reportedly called for by the first night audience of *An Ideal Husband*, an audience that included the Prince of Wales, and the politicians Balfour and Chamberlain, only for the audience to be informed by Beerbohm Tree that he had left the theatre.)[10] At the opening of *A Woman of No Importance*, Wilde's variation was to announce, from his box, 'Ladies and Gentlemen, I regret to inform you that Mr Oscar Wilde is not in the house.' Max Beerbohm records the occasion rather differently, and with a mischievous slant:

> The first night was very brilliant in its audience. I could not see a single nonentity in the whole house ... Balfour and Chamberlain and all the politicians were there. When little Oscar came on to make his bow there was a slight mingling of hoots and hisses, though he looked very sweet in a new white waistcoat and a large bunch of little lilies in his coat.[11]

On these occasions, the pyrotechnics were confined to the play. There was to be no repetition of the famous, or notorious, moment when Wilde strolled onto the stage after the opening of *Lady Windermere's Fan*, cigarette in hand, a 'modern' and casual gesture interpreted as a calculated insult to the audience, and which prompted a *Punch* cartoon, 'Fancy Portrait', with the sub-title 'Quite Too-Too Puffickly Precious!!', to accompany a caustic pseudo-scene, 'A Wilde "Tag" to a Tame Play' (Figure 3.2).[12]

Figure 3.2 Bernard Partridge, *Fancy Portrait: Quite Too-Too Puffickly Precious!!* Punch, 5 March 1892.

The stage at curtain call, and the box, represented conspicuously public territories for a fashionable playwright, the exposure of the stage being infinitely more dangerous than the box. Wilde wrote to Douglas in November 1894, after a visit to the theatre: 'The bows and salutations of the lower orders who thronged the stalls were so cold that I felt it my duty to sit in the Royal Box with the Ribblesdales, the Harry Whites and the Home Secretary.' (Lord Ribblesdale was Master of Buckhounds, White First Secretary at the US legation; the Home Secretary was Lord Asquith, to whose wife Margot Tennant Wilde had dedicated 'The Star Child') 'This exasperated the wretches. How strange to live in a land where the worship of beauty and the passion of love are considered infamous. I hate England ...'[13] This perceived public coldness was a new sensation for Wilde, who seems to turn here to seek protection from the upper classes, in his role as artist/jester to a court of his own construction. At a distance, he looked like a member of the upper classes: more carefully dressed perhaps, and with a more distinctive button-hole, but not, to the untutored eye, different in kind. In contrast, there could be no mistaking George Bernard Shaw for an English aristocrat, as he leaped about the stage in his reddish-brown Jaeger suit, responding to hisses or cheers with equal aplomb.[14] But if there was still a marked distance between the elegant Wilde and his anti-type, the guy Fustian Flitters, with a small magenta cauliflower in his button-hole, the transformation of Wilde's public image into something approaching the grotesque was gathering speed. The caricature by Beerbohm for *Pick-me-up* in September 1894 bears testimony to both Wilde's physical vulnerability and his power.[15] What seemed wittily to define him, or celebrate him, could also condemn him. This ambivalence is highlighted in 'The Remarkable Rocket', when the Rocket is lying in a ditch and is used by some boys as fuel for their fire. 'OLD STICK!' said the Rocket, 'impossible! GOLD STICK, that is what he said. Gold stick is very complimentary. In fact, he mistakes me for one of the Court dignitaries.'[16] Wilde's 'Gold Stick', wish-fulfilment versions of himself, can be discerned in his stage creations of Lord Illingworth and, even more exactly in terms of outward appearance, Lord Goring, complete with button-hole, silk hat, Inverness cape and Louis Seize cane. It must have been somewhat galling to see the actor Charles Hawtrey inhabit the latter role so effortlessly.

In contrast to Wilde's and Shaw's choice of fanciful dress, that other *enfant terrible* of late Victorian England, Samuel Butler, presented himself to the world as an entirely respectable Victorian bachelor. Utterly conventional in his daily public life, dressed in a black suit and accompanied by a black travelling bag that might well have doubled for Miss Prism's, he talked politely to the elderly ladies and family groups whom he met on holiday in Switzerland and Italy, and benignly concealed from them his radical views on Christianity, marriage and sex. Encountering him in a hotel in 1898, Charles Ricketts and Charles Shannon described him as 'an old buggins who looked like a sea-captain', before discovering his true identity.[17]

Butler's novels slipped surreptitiously into the world. They were published anonymously, or posthumously, their fuses sputtering unnoticed before they blew the edifice of Victorian values to pieces. Wilde, however, associated himself very publicly with his creations, like the jester/presenter in Aubrey Beardsley's picturings of *Salome*.

Wilde, in the summer of 1894, was juggling his various lives in an increasingly precarious manner. In order to write *The Importance of Being Earnest*, he chose to go, not to a country retreat on the Thames or the privacy of rooms in London, but to a rented house in the small seaside resort of Worthing, a 'genteel, quiet alternative' a few miles from the more fashionable Brighton, out of easy striking range of the Marquess of Queensberry.[18] The Wildes presumably went to Worthing because it was cheaper than many alternatives: it was certainly cheaper than normal that summer because the previous year there had been a serious typhoid epidemic, with 188 deaths. The Wildes paid 10 guineas a week. But even in Worthing, provincial to the core, Wilde decided to play the part of an extremely public figure. This was a man who was practically bankrupt, and who claimed to Alexander that he did not have the money for the railway fare to London. He had a family to support, school fees to pay and a play to write; and yet he had time to stroll about patronising the local entertainments, sometimes with his son Cyril, sometimes with Douglas on his fleeting visits; or he went sailing down the coast to Littlehampton with Alphonse Conway, the newspaper boy he met on the beach. Worthing was not Algiers, the destination of his January holiday with Douglas. One wonders what he was thinking about and, more pertinently, what Worthing was thinking about him. The citizens of highly respectable, not very fashionable Worthing seemed to have decided that he was an asset and welcomed him as a free advertisement. The Wilde of the 1880s had been exploited to sell soap, sewing-machines, cigars and comic opera: why not a seaside resort?

While the first draft of *The Importance of Being Earnest* lay scattered 'in Sibylline leaves'[19] about his room at 5, The Esplanade, Wilde was content to play the role of a famous writer. 'Last night,' he informed Douglas, 'you, and I, and the Mayor figured as patrons of the entertainment given by the vagabond singers of the sands. They told me that our names, which have been placarded all over the town, excited great enthusiasm … I was greeted with loud applause, as I entered with Cyril.' (He added, jokingly but uncomfortably, 'Cyril was considered to be you'.)[20]

It was not necessary, of course, to be a celebrity to have your name in the provincial newspapers. Lists of well-to-do or well-connected visitors at the smarter hotels were published regularly, an echo of the London society columns. Wilde's occasional visits to the Grand and Albion Hotels, Brighton, that summer can be partly traced in this way, and the records throw up intriguingly named fellow guests such as Mrs Bunbury. Wilde's stay, and public performance, at Worthing were enough to prompt a few paragraphs in the Brighton newspapers. Their first mention was in conjunction with notices about Sydney Grundy's latest play, *The New Woman*, which came to Brighton for a week in September with Rose LeClercq, who would be Lady Bracknell, appearing as the dragonish Lady Wargrave. In the foyer of the Theatre Royal, apparently, Oscar Wilde's latest *mots* were discussed. 'By the way, mentioning Mr Oscar Wilde reminds us that that clever gentleman has for some time been staying at Worthing, where he has of course been made a very public character.'[21] The 'clever', and perhaps the 'very public', convey a slight rebuke. The *Brighton Society* paragraph went on to report a speech that Wilde made in Worthing, on Saturday, 15 September. This was the day Wilde finished his first draft of *The Importance of Being Earnest*, and sent it to London to be typed.

The occasion for the speech was the Worthing Venetian Water Carnival, a grand climax to the holiday season. The pier was illuminated with Japanese lanterns and bracket lamps, and decorated with a device, in coloured lights, 'Go it Worthing'. Mr Wright's band performed on a moored steam launch, the pier band played in the Pavilion. Coloured fire burned, a procession of illuminated boats passed by and the evening ended with fireworks. Wilde presided, distributing the prizes and delivering the closing speech, in which he proposed a vote of thanks to the committee (chairman, Captain Fraser).

Wilde began by congratulating Worthing on 'the extremely beautiful scene that evening':

> He thought, however, there was one thing that marred the Regatta. There was a sailing boat, not belonging to Worthing, but coming from some wicked, tasteless spot, bearing a huge advertisement of a patent pill. He hoped that boat would never be allowed to enter Worthing again. (Much laughter) He could not help feeling the change that had taken place this year in the town, and expressing the great pleasure it gave visitors to return. He considered that such a charming town would become one of the first watering places on the South Coast. It had beautiful surroundings and lovely long walks, which he recommended to other people but did not take himself. (Much laughter)

('No gentleman ever takes exercise' – *The Importance of Being Earnest*, four-act version). Alluding to the EXCELLENT WATER SUPPLY, he said he was told that the total abstainers who visited Worthing were so struck with the purity and excellence of its water that they wished everybody to drink nothing else.

Then, in a finale, which seems to fit effortlessly with the tone of the play he had just completed, he concluded:

> Above all things, he was delighted to observe in Worthing one of the most important things, having regard to the fashion of the age – the faculty of

offering pleasure. To his mind few things were so important as a capacity for being amused, feeling pleasure, and giving it to others. He held that whenever a person was happy he was good, although, perhaps, when he was good he was not always happy. (Laughter) There was no excuse for anyone not being happy in such surroundings. This was his first visit, but it would certainly not be his last. (Applause)[22]

Captain Fraser then proposed a vote of thanks to Wilde for his kindness in presenting the prizes. Extracting more mileage from the event, 'Local Notes' in the *Worthing Gazette* picked up the comments of one of the nationals, the *Globe*:

> Oscar's very latest role is that of a patron of aquatic enterprises ... he made the highly original observation that anything as pretty he had never seen before. It was not brilliant, but then no one expects the great wit to say brilliant things in the provinces ...

'Captious criticism, this', commented 'Local Notes'. 'The writer should rather have given Mr Wilde praise for his good nature ...'[23] The *Brighton Society*, taking up a position somewhere between the *Worthing Gazette* and the *Globe*, commented that 'there was a good deal more in the same vein of semi-cynical banter with which the author of "The Decay of the Art of Lying" [sic] has made us rather agreeably familiar'.[24] Interestingly, the *Worthing Gazette* also observed, by way of introduction, 'Time was when Mr Oscar Wilde and his movements occupied no inconsiderable space in the public journals; but less attention has of late been given to him and his utterances.'[25] This view, if it had any validity, would soon change. The carefree Bunburying by the provincial seaside was coming to an end after a transitional period of farce played out by Wilde and Douglas in the Grand Hotel and Wilde's Brighton lodgings.[26]

September 15, coincidentally but significantly, also saw the publication of Robert Hichens' smart parody *The Green Carnation*, a malicious squib tied to Wilde's coat-tails, which captures Wilde's conversation as relayed to Hichens via Douglas.[27] Esme Amarinth, the Wilde persona, addresses Lord Reginald Hastings:

> Here we are at the railway station ... Railway stations always remind me of Mr Terriss, the actor. They are so noisy. The Surrey week is over. Soon we shall see once more the tender grey of the Piccadilly pavement, and the subtle music of Old Bond Street will fall fortuitously upon our ears.

(First scenario of *Earnest*: 'The country is demoralising: it makes you respectable.' 'The simple fare at the Savoy: the quiet life in Piccadilly: the solitude of Mayfair is what you need.'[28]) 'Put your feet up on the opposite cushion, dear boy, while I lean out of the railway carriage window and smile the people away. When people try to get into my compartment I always smile at them, and they always go away.' The cruel dimension embedded in this parody was echoed in Beerbohm's caricature for *Pick-me-up*, one week later.

Had Ada Leverson been the author, as Wilde and others first surmised, *The Green Carnation* might have been acceptable. Wilde was soon claiming to be delighted that his Sphinx was not a minx, but it would have been less insidious coming from her incisive but unpoisoned pen than this palpable hit from a very clever journalist. A fortnight later, Wilde wrote to the *Pall Mall Gazette* to deny the rumour that he was himself the author of *The Green Carnation* – he had invented that magnificent flower, but had 'nothing whatsoever to do with the middle-class and mediocre book that usurps its strangely beautiful name'.[29]

The Sphinx/minx joke refers to Ada Leverson's *Punch* piece of 21 July, a comic interview between the Sphinx and the Poet.[30] Leverson, who would later write sharply elegant novels, was beginning to experiment with and expand her writing, and Francis Burnand, editor of *Punch*, was in frequent correspondence with her about suitable subjects. Initially, he seems to have been lukewarm about Wildean topics and angles, warning her in November 1893: 'I don't want to *revive* any "cult" of *him* – it seems for the general public the "craze" which this illustrates is a bit out of date.'[31] The 'craze' or cult of Wilde to which Burnand refers was, presumably, the aesthetic, greenery-yallery Wilde of the 1880s, defined by sunflowers, lilies and six-mark teapots. In September 1894, there seems to have been a shift in Wilde's status. The accuracy of Beerbohm's and Hichens' darts, the knowledge of two impending plays, perhaps, too, the general – if entirely inaccurate – association of Wilde with the *Yellow Book*, propelled him back into the public arena. Wilde was a prisoner of his own public character. He might attempt to outwit commentary by such devices as his collaboration with Robert Ross, 'Mr Oscar Wilde on Mr Oscar Wilde; An Interview'[32] (*St James's Gazette*, 18 January 1895), but there was no escape. *Punch*, in spite of Burnand's earlier caution, printed four pieces specifically centred on Wilde between 12 January and 2 March 1895, plus a mildly dismissive comment on *An Ideal Husband* and a rather laboured joke linking him with Oscar Browning. (In the same period, Shaw received one mention.) It is noteworthy how centred *Punch* is on drama and dramatic form at this period, in spite of pervasive comments in newspapers and journals on the dearth and death of British drama. Actors, or aspects of drama, feature repeatedly as the subjects of cartoons; and the longer pieces frequently take the form of dramatic dialogue, in addition to extended Ibsen spoofs such as 'Little Mopseman, the very newest Dramatic Allegory from Norway.' Drama, and theatre, were no less central to the Victorians than politics and social life; and the codes of the audience quite as closely scrutinised as those of the stage. As Ada Leverson recorded in her *Punch* piece '1894':

> we may learn from the Caricatures of the day what the *Decadents* were in outward semblance; from the Lampoons what was their mode of life. Nightly they gathered at any of the Theatres where the plays of Mr Wilde were being given. Nightly, the stalls were fulfilled by Row upon Row of neatly-curled Fringes surmounting Button-holes of monstrous size.[33]

The theatre auditorium, like the rooms of the Royal Academy, provided a forum where taste and reputation could be judged. The decadent, the dandy or a particular celebrity was on public display. Wilde explored similar defining moments within his own plays, most notably in the arrival of Mrs Erlynne at Lady Windermere's ball: Lady Windermere, who has threatened to insult her when her name is announced by striking her across the face with her fan, merely bows coldly, while Mrs Erlynne glides triumphantly into society in a stunningly elegant dress.

Ada Leverson begins and ends the *Punch* sequence of commentary on Wilde. Her first, on 12 January, is charming: an 'Overheard Fragment of a Dialogue', in which Lord Goring talks to Lord Illingworth. 'It is perfectly comic, the number of young men going about the world nowadays who adopt perfect profiles as a useful profession.'[34] Wilde loved this – 'No other voice but yours is musical enough to echo my music.'[35] The following week, Wilde was under attack: the lampoon, in dramatic form, was entitled 'A Penny Plain – But Oscar Coloured' (An Entertainment Antagonistic to Amusement). 'Scene – Anywhere. Characters distributed about the Stage in more or less admired confusion.' The *dramatis personae* include Anybody; Charles his Friend; Somebody; Someone Else; A Casual Visitor; A Caller; A Lady; A Person; Another Person; A New Comer; The Audience; the Author:

> *A blasé Man of the World.* And yet, in spite of all this, I have had a pleasant evening.
> *Charles his Friend.* So has an author when he is laughing in his sleeve and confuses black with white.
> *Someone.* But does the author never know the difference?
> *Charles his Friend.* What does it matter? If he thinks himself right, everybody will know that he is wrong!
> *The Audience.* All this is very clever because it is unintelligible.
> *The Author.* So I believe. Only I stand upon my irresponsibility.[36]

Even in this exchange, one can detect the sound of a knife being sharpened, suggesting that the court wit may have outstayed his welcome. The earlier dialogue contains a more cryptic reference:

A Person. And a wife, if she found her husband in trouble, would surely cleave to him?
Charles his Friend. So she would, if she only knew where to find him.

By the time this lampoon was published, Wilde was in Algiers with Douglas. *Punch* continued the theme of Wilde as masquerading dramatist on 23 February, with 'The O.W. Vade Mecum' – post-*Earnest*; and post two interviews, Gilbert Burgess's in the *Sketch* (9 January 1895), and the dialogue with Robert Ross. The *Punch* piece begins:

Q. Is it easy to become a dramatist?
A. As easy as anything else.
Q. What are the requisites?
A. A West-end theatre, a first rate troupe of artists, a trained audience, and a personality.
...
Q. And what do you mean by a personality?
A. More or less – an *insouciant* manner, and a rather startling button-hole.
Q. Does the personality require a speech or a cigarette?
Q. Neither now, as both have ceased to be the fashion.

From the process emerges 'the product' – a trivial comedy for serious people.

Q. Why give a play such a title?
A. Why not?[37]

There is something distinctly modern about this transformation of an author into a personality, and the distillation of that personality into a manner, and a button-hole. It is almost as though Wilde has begun to float free from his literary creations, a process that he might argue was entirely apposite, even if it was anathema to his critics. More radically, and perhaps alarmingly, it conceals an intuition about the alliance between theatre, actors and audience, an unwitting conspiracy, with Wilde as the almost invisible magician, or catalyst. The power of a Wilde play to entertain and captivate an audience was a reality, however much the art that constructed the play might be called to account.

Ada Leverson's second Wildean parody, on 2 March, was 'The Advisability of Not Being Brought Up in a Handbag: A Trivial Tragedy for Wonderful People',[38] a title that would become uncomfortably ironic in the space of a few weeks. ('Title for *Punch* quite charming,' Wilde cabled. 'Rely on you to misrepresent me.'[39]) The cast of Ada Leverson's fragment was an amalgamation from different sources: Aunt Augusta – an Aunt; Cousin

Cicely – a ward; Algy – a flutter-pate; The Duke of Berwick – and Dorian – a button-hole. Not even in retrospect, some of the dialogue is remarkably pointed. Dorian is described as having 'brown Algerians who beat monotonously upon copper drums'. Cicely asks: 'Shall you like dining at Willis's with Mr Dorian tonight, cousin Algy?' To which Algy replies *'evasively'*: 'It's much nicer being here with you, Cousin Cicely.' The dialogue concludes:

> *Dorian.* To be really modern, one should have no soul. To be really mediaeval, one should have no cigarettes. To be really Greek – (*The* Duke of Berwick *rises in a marked manner, and leaves the garden*)
> Cicely (*writes in her diary, and then reads aloud dreamily*). The Duke of Berwick rises in a marked manner, and leaves the garden. The weather continues charming.

Ada Leverson both admired and liked Wilde, but her demarcation of his style and his life-style drew attention to those very aspects that antagonised conventional society. When the aristocracy rise and leave the garden, it may be in order to summon the police. By the time the article was published, the Marquess of Queensberry, after depositing his grotesque bouquet of vegetables at the stage door of the St James's Theatre, had delivered his fatal, written insult at the Albemarle Club.[40] These melodramatic interventions wrenched Wilde from his position as purveyor of verbal fireworks to the upper classes and put him in the stocks; but the subtler critique of the Sphinx, and of Max Beerbohm, helped to define that shift.

In tracing Wilde's erratic interaction with celebrity and with his various public images in the last nine months of his pre-trial life, one can detect both the precarious nature of his fame and a certain personal weariness with the whole business. 'If McClure wishes me to be interviewed he must pay me,' he wrote to Robert Sherard, suggesting the 'classical sum' of £20. 'Of course he won't do this: why on earth should he? But I certainly won't give him a column of conversation to amuse his readers for nothing. Besides, I am sick of my name in the papers.'[41] Wilde was drinking and smoking too much; his health was precarious; he was becoming isolated, with fewer reliable friends. He had embraced a very public life as a society dramatist, a role much harder to sustain than the mask of a genial summer visitor to a seaside resort. The conflicting demands of public and domestic life were a theme he chose to explore in *An Ideal Husband*, through the contrasting trajectories of Sir Robert Chiltern, the Under Secretary of State with a seat in the Cabinet, and Lord Goring, the first well-dressed philosopher in the history of thought who intends to live a wholly private existence. *An Ideal Husband* is set in London, the centre of government and social power. But even in Brighton and Worthing the upper classes were on display. One could not stay at the Grand Hotel or the Metropole without the fact being reported in the newspapers: miss a train, as Lady Bracknell commented, and you were exposed to comment on the platform; present the prizes at the Worthing

Water Carnival, and you risked mockery in the London papers for uttering a platitude.

It is remarkable that out of this inauspicious set of circumstances emerged Wilde's holiday play, *The Importance of Being Earnest*. At Worthing, however, more so than in the little parish of St James's, Wilde was surrounded by the full range of robust Victorian theatrical fare: the D'Oyly Carte production of *Utopia, Limited*, by Gilbert and Sullivan, Brandon Thomas's *Charley's Aunt*, Sanger's Circus presenting a Grand Military Spectacle, 'The War in Matabeleland', or Cissie Loftus, darling of the music-hall and Max Beerbohm's obsession, at the Pavilion; while in Brighton, Sydney Grundy's *The New Woman* was followed by that quintessential seaside farce, *The Foundling*, which Kerry Powell argued Wilde might have seen before perfecting his own plot.[42] Out of this popular context, he constructed his deliberately trivial, highly polished masterpiece, a collaboration with Victorian theatre and with the audience. He possessed supremely the faculty of offering pleasure, on this occasion with a display of fireworks both spectacular and deliberately fleeting.

Ada Leverson has left an evocative description of Wilde on the first night of *The Importance of Being Earnest*:

> He was dressed with elaborate dandyism and a sort of florid sobriety. His coat had a black velvet collar. He held white gloves in his small pointed hands. On one finger he wore a large scarab ring. A green carnation, echo in colour of the ring, bloomed in his buttonhole, and a large bunch of seals on a black moiré ribbon watch-chain hung from his white waistcoat. This costume, which on another man might have appeared perilously like fancy dress, and on his imitators was nothing less, seemed to suit him perfectly; he seemed at ease and to have the look of the last gentleman of Europe.[43]

She also recorded the scene outside the St James's Theatre:

> The street outside was crowded, not only with the conveyances and the usual crowd of waiting people, but with other Wilde fanatics who appeared to regard the arrivals as part of the performance. Many of these shouted and cheered the best-known people, and the loudest cheers were for the author, as he got out of his carriage with his pretty wife ...[44]

The whole evening was performative. According to Wilde, twenty policemen from Scotland Yard were guarding the theatre, while the Scarlet Marquis prowled about, chattering like a monstrous ape: he had even made a plot to usurp Wilde's role and address the audience. On this last first night, Wilde paid only a fleeting visit to the box where Ada Leverson sat with Aubrey and Mabel Beardsley; and there was no speech. The balance was poised precariously between celebrity and notoriety. Max Beerbohm's September cartoon, in which a corpulent Wilde, all chins and wavy hair, is designated by his trademark buttonhole, tiepin, ring and cane is the counterpoint to the Sphinx's generous portrait. Beerbohm, a little disingenuously, commented: 'One or two of those drawings have been thought rather cruel, I believe. I can't understand how anyone can resent a mere exaggeration of feature.'[45] As Joseph Bristow compellingly argues, the caricature shows how 'the pretensions of the human body, even when subjected to such close observation, maintain a compelling power over the viewer'.[46] The cruder cartoon of Fustian Flitters, wearing white cotton gloves, broken boots and a small magenta cauliflower in his button-hole, waits in the shadows.

The links between Wilde – his name, the public persona he constructed, and the counter-constructions of his contemporaries – and his works are complex. It is tempting to invoke the closing sequence of 'The Remarkable Rocket':

> The Rocket was very damp, so he took a long time to burn. At last, however, the fire caught him.
> 'Now I am going off!' he cried, and he made himself very stiff and straight. 'I know I shall go much higher than the stars, much higher than the moon, much higher than the sun. In fact, I shall go so high that – '
> Fizz! Fizz! Fizz! And he went straight up into the air.
> 'Delightful!' he cried, 'I shall go on like this for ever. What a success I am!'
> But nobody saw him.[47]

Wilde was, with a few striking exceptions, vilified by the press and the public in the months of the trials; the 'last gentleman of Europe' disappeared abruptly from the society pages; and his name was removed from the playbills of *The Importance of Being Earnest* at the St James's Theatre before the play itself was taken off. Against that general shunning is Wyndham's insistence on retaining Wilde's name when *An Ideal Husband* was briefly transferred. More surprising and significant, perhaps, is the fact that *An Ideal Husband* toured successfully in the provinces, including Brighton, when Wilde was still in prison; while as early as 1902, *The Importance of Being Earnest* was reintroduced to the West End. In *De Profundis*, Wilde critiqued aspects of his own duality, and a century of critical comment has since probed his reputation. In defiance of *Punch* and all that *Punch* represented, his celebrity has proved to be remarkably enduring: it is very difficult not to see Wilde, even if the dazzle makes it difficult to be certain about what one is seeing. As Wilde predicted in his letter to George Alexander, his unserious play has continued to illuminate the stage, and the supply of rockets seems inexhaustible.

Notes

1. *The Complete Letters of Oscar Wilde*, ed. Merlin Holland and Rupert Hart-Davis (London: Fourth Estate, 2000) p. 620.
2. *Punch*, 10 November 1894, p. 225. The cartoon is by Bernard Partridge (who as Bernard Gould played Sergius in George Bernard Shaw's *Arms and the Man*).
3. *The Green Carnation* (London: William Heinemann, 1894).
4. Oscar Wilde, *The Happy Prince and Other Tales* (London: David Nutt, 1888).
5. John Ruskin, *Fors Clavigera*, in *The Library Edition of the Works of John Ruskin*, 39 vols, ed. E. T. Cook and Alexander Wedderburn (London: George Allen, 1903–12), XXIX, p. 160.
6. Oscar Wilde, 'The Grosvenor Gallery', *Dublin University Magazine*, 90, July 1877.
7. This self-referential aspect is explored in the introduction to *The Fireworks of Oscar Wilde*, ed. Owen Dudley Edwards (London: Barrie and Jenkins, 1989).
8. *The Complete Letters of Oscar Wilde*, pp. 595–7.
9. Hesketh Pearson, *The Life of Oscar Wilde* (London: Methuen, 1946), p. 57.
10. Richard Ellmann, *Oscar Wilde* (London: Penguin, 1988), p. 404.
11. Hesketh Pearson, *Beerbohm Tree: His Life and Laughter* (London: Methuen, 1956), p. 71; Max Beerbohm's letter to Reggie Turner is quoted from David Cecil, *Max* (New York: Atheneum, 1985), p. 68. It is difficult to establish the accuracy of some of these recollections; however, Wilde's appearance, reception and the taking or avoiding of a curtain-call were all clearly part of the occasion.
12. *Punch*, 5 March 1892, p. 113.
13. *The Complete Letters of Oscar Wilde*, p. 622.
14. Michael Holroyd, *George Bernard Shaw: The Search for Love* (London: Chatto and Windus, 1988), p. 160.
15. See the discussion in *Wilde Writings: Contextual Conditions*, ed. Joseph Bristow (Toronto: University of Toronto Press, 2003), pp. 18–20.
16. *The Complete Works of Oscar Wilde* (London: HarperCollins, 1994), p. 301.
17. *Letters and Journals of Charles Ricketts*, ed. Cecil Lewis (London: P. Davies, 1939), pp. 26–7.
18. For commentary on Worthing, see D. Robert Elleray, *Worthing: Aspects of Change* (Chichester: Phillimore, 1985).
19. *The Complete Letters of Oscar Wilde*, p. 600.
20. *The Complete Letters of Oscar Wilde*, pp. 607–8.
21. 'Mr Oscar Wilde Dilates on Worthing's Charms', *Brighton Society*, 15 September 1894, p. 5.
22. 'Mr Oscar Wilde Dilates on Worthing's Charms', p. 5.
23. *Worthing Gazette*, 19 September 1894, p. 3.
24. 'Mr Oscar Wilde Dilates on Worthing's Charms', p. 5.
25. *Worthing Gazette*, 19 September 1894, p. 3.
26. See Wilde's letter to Douglas, 'De Profundis', in *The Complete Letters of Oscar Wilde*, pp. 696–9.
27. Robert Hichens' name appeared on the title-page of the fourth printing, 1895.
28. *The Complete Letters of Oscar Wilde*, p. 596.
29. *The Complete Letters of Oscar Wilde*, p. 617.
30. *Punch*, 21 July 1894, p. 33.
31. Julie Speedie, *Wonderful Sphinx: The Biography of Ada Leverson* (London: Virago, 1993), p. 63.
32. *St James's Gazette*, 18 January 1895.

33 Quoted in Speedie, *Wonderful Sphinx*, p. 69.
34 *Punch*, 12 January 1895, p. 24.
35 *The Complete Letters of Oscar Wilde*, p. 627.
36 *Punch*, 19 January 1895, p. 36.
37 *Punch*, 23 February 1895, p. 85.
38 *Punch*, 2 March 1895, p. 107.
39 *The Complete Letters of Oscar Wilde*, p. 632.
40 *The Complete Letters of Oscar Wilde*, p. 632.
41 *The Complete Letters of Oscar Wilde*, p. 624.
42 See Kerry Powell, *Oscar Wilde and the Theatre of the 1890s* (Cambridge: Cambridge University Press, 1990), pp. 108–10. *The Foundling* was written by William Lestocq Wooldridge and E. M. Robson.
43 Ada Leverson, 'The Importance of Being Oscar', in Violet Wyndham, *The Sphinx and Her Circle: A Biographical Sketch of Ada Levenson 1862–1933* (London: André Deutsch, 1963), p. 114.
44 Leverson, 'The Importance of Being Oscar', p. 110.
45 This comment forms part of 'A Few Words with Mr Max Beerbohm', an interview by Ada Leverson published in *The Sketch*, 2 January 1895. Beerbohm added: 'And I do not think that the men themselves whom I have drawn have ever been offended.' Leverson added, 'Perhaps their wives have been?'
46 *Wilde Writings*, p. 20.
47 *The Complete Works of Oscar Wilde*, p. 301.

4
The Many Masks of Clemence Dane

Maggie B. Gale

Theatre and politics: *A Bill of Divorcement*

Clemence Dane (1888–1965), born Winifred Ashton, was one of the most prolific British women playwrights, screenwriters and novelists of her generation.[1] Frequently mentioned in the recent centenary celebrations of Noël Coward's life and work, she was one of his inner circle of friends, but her own celebrity has been persistently downplayed. Dane never worked under her real name, but achieved extraordinary success in both theatre and film, and demonstrated a remarkable talent to reinvent her public image at various points in her career. She was awarded the CBE in 1953, moved among the leading theatrical and film stars of the day and showed a rare versatility as a writer and public speaker; it is therefore very odd that she figures so little in twentieth-century theatre history.

Dane was one of the few modern playwrights whose work was consistently produced from the 1920s to the 1960s. Her introduction to the stage as a playwright (she had been an actress working under the name Diana Cortis before the First World War) came through the ReandeaN (Basil Dean) production of *A Bill of Divorcement* at the St Martin's Theatre in 1921.[2] The play bypassed the usual try-out and went straight into commercial production, becoming a smash hit, running for over 400 performances. It was made into a silent film in 1922 starring Fay Compton, and subsequently provided the lead role for Katherine Hepburn in Selznick's 1932 film of the same name. (David O. Selznick made the film again in 1940 with a new cast, which included Maureen O'Hara and Dame May Whitty.) During the interwar years both professional and amateur productions of *A Bill of Divorcement* were frequently staged in London and in the regions. J. C. Trewin's comment that the play was 'extremely contentious in its time', but could also 'scorch a theatre years after the reform it called for', pays tribute to the way in which Dane's first play not only caught contemporary audiences' imaginations but also tapped into social and cultural anxieties which reverberated throughout the first half of the twentieth century.[3]

A Bill of Divorcement focuses on the moral and social dynamics of divorce. Set in a projected future of 1933, when the English divorce laws have been liberalised, Dane takes a contentious issue and dramatises it in terms of the specific effect of divorce on the different female generations of an English middle-class family and, more generally, on the welfare of the nation. The plot revolves around a new law which allows women whose husbands have been incarcerated because of mental illness to divorce and remarry. When Sydney Fairfield's father escapes from a psychiatric hospital, she decides that she is morally obliged to care for him despite these legal changes and breaks off her engagement. Her belief that his illness is hereditary as well as her espousal of eugenics make marriage unthinkable to her, yet she encourages her mother, Margaret Fairfield, to find happiness and elope with her lover to start a new 'healthy' family. Audiences found the play's audacious approach to divorce utterly arresting, and it quickly became a very contentious event. Critics hailed Dane as 'our leading woman dramatist' and claimed that *A Bill of Divorcement* was a play 'that pointed the way to the salvation of the London stage', containing 'straight-from-the shoulder drama, healthy sentiment, optimistic philosophy and … cleanliness through and through'.[4] The production provoked discussion in the media about the relevance of the divorce laws and the sanctity of marriage at a time when the aftermath of the First World War had created a discernible shift in women's domestic, social and economic roles: women, especially those from the growing middle classes, expected more from life. When asked for her opinion on the divorce question, Dane pointed out that she had clearly presented both sides of the argument in her play and suggested that the divorce laws needed revision: 'Can anyone believe that deception and repression can continue for a long period without making husband and wife mentally, morally, and physically worse characters?'[5] Dane was fully versed in the progress of the divorce law reforms just as she was in the basic tenets of the eugenics movement.[6] She was also aware that a great deal of the cultural anxiety about divorce derived from the belief that women were somehow 'fickle' and would take unfair advantage of any revised laws. But, as she would continue to do throughout her career, Dane argued the 'woman's side': 'Married women, even those who have been self-supporting before marriage, do not "yearn for freedom" as a rule, but only for release from an intolerable position … I believe they may be trusted to take no advantage of amended divorce laws.'[7]

Dane's arrival as a playwright certainly located her as politically radical, but she had in fact already acquired an infamous reputation. Trained at the Slade School of Art, Dane was an experienced teacher and published novelist and was considered by the media to be one of the most notorious feminists of her generation. The impact of her best-selling novel *Regiment of Women* (1917), a 'lesbian vamp'/'forbidden love' narrative which explored the relationships between single women teaching in a private school,[8] had caused a sensation; like Wilde and Coward, Dane was able to turn the reactions of outrage and intrigue to her advantage.

The critical reception of *A Bill of Divorcement* placed Dane firmly within the main celebrity circles of the time and, in popular usage of the term during the 1920s, within a *feminist* group. The notoriety of *Regiment of Women*, in addition to Dane's friendships with sexually controversial individuals such as Violet Trefussis and Vita Sackville-West, not surprisingly influenced the play's reception.[9] One reviewer called Dane 'the most discussed of all women writers' and saw *A Bill of Divorcement* as a battle between the 'womanly woman' and the 'emancipated "regiment of women"'.[10] Another perceived Dane as a dangerously inflammatory playwright, who might convert uneducated classes of women to a new radical politics:

> The unprecedented success of Miss Clemence Dane's first dramatic offering has set all the highbrow dovecots in a flutter. The 'regiment of women' who are her most ardent admirers do not quite know whether to be pleased at her conquest of the unintellectual masses or annoyed that the masses are really showing signs of unexpected intelligence.
>
> However, the be-jumpered and bobbed young women are flocking to the St Martin's, and I also noticed Lady Rhondda in the stalls the other night. Her car, by the way, was 'manned' by an extremely pretty girl chauffeur.[11]

This notice is typical of the class and gender prejudice that *A Bill of Divorcement* attracted. The phrase 'unintellectual masses' exposes this particular critic's anxiety about the 'new theatre audiences' (allegedly lower middle-class females) who were perceived as going to the theatre in larger numbers than before. The 'regiment of women' whom theatre critics saw as Dane's already established fans were middle-class women who identified with the characters in her hit novel. The phrase 'bobbed young women' alludes to the new generation of independent young women – the female voters of the future – who apparently identified with Sydney Fairfield, the heroine of *A Bill of Divorcement*. The critics, mostly male Oxbridge graduates, betrayed their fear that theatres were being overrun with young women and even expressed the anxiety that female leads were becoming more prevalent in new plays than males. In the wake of women's fight for suffrage before the war and their increased presence within the labour economy during the war, came real and measurable cultural anxiety about women's enfranchisement and how this would change social agendas and institutions.[12]

Theatre critics read Dane's first play through the lens of her notorious 'lesbian vamp' novel, and reviewed *A Bill of Divorcement* in the context of her identity as a *feminist* celebrity.[13] The ideological messages in the play are, however, complex (and very problematic for contemporary cultural historians): whilst *A Bill* posits the liberalisation of the divorce laws it also represents a young, independent and 'free-thinking' woman as enslaved by her sense of duty to the nation: she must not produce children if she knows that they will inherit a disease. At this time, eugenics was a discourse espoused by many leading intellectuals of the day. Dane's play needs to be seen as part of an emerging tradition of polemical plays by playwrights such as Cicely Hamilton (1872–1952) and Elizabeth Baker (1876–1962). According to your politics at the time, Dane was either a champion of women's rights or a monstrous threat to the status quo.[14]

Will Shakespeare and the shaping of public personae

By the mid-1920s, cinema was already a more popular form of entertainment than the theatre. Industry papers such as the *Era* make it clear that film provided many opportunities for work and Dane exploited the possibilities provided by this growing industry. Performers who crossed over into film, such as Fay Compton, Ivor Novello and Ruby Miller, had greater press machines at their disposal, but theatre celebrities continued to hold an important place in the public imagination.

In many ways Dane strategically capitalised on her early celebrity status as a controversial figure. Born into a middle-class family and educated beyond the levels of many women of her generation, Dane still had to work for a living, and after the success of *A Bill of Divorcement* she began to write newspaper columns, often introduced as 'the author of *A Bill of Divorcement*', or as the author of *Will Shakespeare* (1921), her next play, written in verse and far more experimental in form.[15] If *A Bill of Divorcement* had appealed to the uneducated masses (as certain critics claimed) *Will Shakespeare* certainly did not: it examined Shakespeare's creative anxiety, his love life and his relationship with Elizabeth I. Dane presented Shakespeare as a man whose artistic duty to his Queen had to be placed before any personal desires. She explored the question of patronage and suggested that Shakespeare, far from being free to exercise his creative genius, was burdened by his obligations to Elizabeth.

Dane's decision to write about Shakespeare after the controversy of *A Bill of Divorcement* is very significant: she could at once claim respectability and guarantee interest in a dramatisation of England's greatest theatrical celebrity, and she could also afford to construct her subject unconventionally – indeed, audiences would expect as much. Moreover, whilst avoiding accusations of sensationalism, Dane shrewdly pursued her preoccupation with women and power. She was fascinated by the phenomenon of unseen women inspiring men and contributing to their achievements as well as being preoccupied by the gender inequalities which characterised the reception and celebration of a creative artist. Dane consistently returned to these themes (though often less overtly) in her plays *Granite* (1926), *Wild Decembers* (1933) and *Cousin Muriel* (1940).[16]

Will Shakespeare, produced by ReandeaN company, attracted widespread critical attention for both its subject matter and its form. It interfaced with critical debates about the alleged lack of experiment and risk-taking in theatre production in England at the time and seemed to answer critics' pleas for a play which did not pander to commercial tastes (though its subject matter was of course mainstream). Though critics commented on the 'weakly drawn' men in the play and balked at Dane's harsh interrogation of Shakespeare's status as a cultural hero, *Will Shakespeare* had a lasting impact and was rewritten for television in 1938 with Margaret Rawlings as Mary Fitton in the romantic lead.[17] Dane never again earned as much from a play as she had from *A Bill of Divorcement*, but she still consistently found success.

Contemporary comments on Dane herself could be biting and bigoted. Wrongly described by critic St John Ervine as a 'oncer',[18] her plays actually often ran for over 50 performances. *Cousin Muriel* (1940), for instance, ran for 75 performances and was, according to Judy Campbell, written by Dane for Edith Evans on Coward's suggestion that Dane wrote an accessible play in which 'someone said pass me the salt'.[19] Dane, according to Gay Wachman, was one of a handful of women writers who broke the 'rules of silence and propriety that muffled middle-class discourse – and above all, the discourse of women – about class, "race", gender and sexual differences'.[20] She points to Dane's middle-class upbringing and her emergence from a Victorian and Edwardian society through the 'dislocations and losses of the war, and then the increased tolerance of gender and sexual difference in postwar London'.[21] Just as Dane's career spanned two world wars, so it crossed from the public world of the stage through to the higher echelons of literary life: she was a member of the Society for Women Journalists and one time president of PEN; she wrote film scripts in the 1930s and 1940s, winning an Oscar for *Perfect Strangers* (1947) and was still being commissioned to write plays for radio and television well into her late sixties.[22]

Dane consistently engaged with cultural debate through publications such as *The Women's Side* (1926),[23] as well as in journalism and radio broadcasting. She took over J. B. Priestley's famous wartime radio broadcasts when the BBC and the War Ministry took him off air because of his controversial stance on the war.[24] Dane carefully eschewed the notoriety she had attracted with her first play and by the Second World War had reinvented herself – for a radio public at least – as a respected cultural commentator. Remarkably, she achieved this at the same time as she surrounded herself (as always) with a coterie of sexually controversial celebrities, including as Radcliffe Hall, Katherine Cornell, Noël Coward, Ivor Novello, Binkie Beaumont and others, but Dane never spoke publicly about her lesbianism and she had developed a variety of public personae to deal with a variety of audiences. If, as Rojek suggests, the public self (or in the case of Dane, a range of public *selves*) is always 'staged', then Dane's public personae shifted between controversial author, serious playwright and popular journalist by the 1930s.[25] By this point she was being commissioned to write plays for leading actresses from both Britain and the US, including Sybil Thorndyke and Katherine Cornell.[26] She was also a sought-after scriptwriter in England and Hollywood, working on films such as *Anna Karenina* (1935).[27] Dane could be relied on to write outstandingly well for specific actresses and her talent for writing plays which could be deployed as vehicles for star actresses did much to ensure the longevity of her celebrity.

Without doubt Dane associated with other celebrities in order to enhance her own status. Never writing or performing under her real name, her public persona as Clemence Dane was multilayered, and she used her theatrical celebrity to facilitate her status as a social commentator. Yet in her journalism she adopted a persona of supposed ordinariness, as 'one of the people writing for the people', capitalising on her versatility and her ability to shift the writer's voice to fit the context.

Information on Dane's private life can be gleaned from the anecdotes and descriptions by those with whom she worked and socialised.[28] The nearest Dane ever came to writing an autobiography is *London has a Garden*, published in 1964, and although it appears to contain little about her working life, it is significant because it focuses on a investigation of the history and geography of Covent Garden as a location integrally linked to the development of the London theatre – a place where Dane lived most of her life.[29] Published a year before she died, the book is dominated by theatrical celebrities both historical and contemporary. Just as Dane's career, covering some fifty years, happened at a time when, as Leo Braudy points out 'the nature of fame changed more decisively and more quickly' than it had over the previous centuries, so Covent Garden had begun to lose its theatrical identity as part of postwar urban reconstruction.[30] *London has a Garden* provides a fascinating window on Dane's extraordinary gift to create theatrical coteries and to circulate at the centre of celebrity cultures.

Women and fame

As early as 1926, Dane was arguing that genius was a term almost exclusively applied to men and that no 'genius' has ever worked in isolation.[31] Plays such as *Will Shakespeare* and *Wild Decembers* focus on the collaborative nature of creativity and on the women who provide crucial support to their male counterparts, whether domestic or artistic.[32] Interestingly, Dane's long-term companion and secretary, Olwen Bowen, herself a writer, gets very little mention – almost certainly a deliberate strategy aimed at disguising the nature of their relationship and her own sexuality. But neglect of Dane by theatre historians is much more baffling: for someone who wrote so much for and about the theatre (including her epic novels of theatre life such as *Broome Stages* in 1931)[33] her presence in explorations of twentieth-century British theatre is that of a shadow or a ghost.[34]

Like Coward, Dane was wary of how fame could affect creativity and alert to the ways in which the trappings of celebrity could destabilise private life.

Her play *Gooseberry Fool*, written in collaboration with Helen Simpson, mocks attitudes to commercial writing and the desire or ability of a writer to be 'popular'. Dane also makes reference to prevalent critical prejudices that women cannot 'write men' and to critics' accusations aimed at her own work that she would never be a 'great' playwright because her male characters were 'weak'. Thus the writer Larch, wife to Constantine Cornely, a well-known popular novelist, points out that her critics accuse her of writing weak men, who are so 'undignified ... greedy ... so vain', and goes on to laugh at the irony that she has based all her male characterisations on the manly and 'robust' Constantine himself.[35] Very much a comedy about the tensions in a marital relationship where both partners are celebrated writers, *Gooseberry Fool* seems to allude to Dane's private life, but also hints, as Jacky Bratton's recent assessment suggests, at her experiences as an experimental writer.[36]

Eighty in the Shade, written in 1959 for and starring the legendary performers Sybil Thorndike and Lewis Casson, and running in the West End for 179 performances, is a direct comment on the effect of celebrity culture on the veridical self. The play centres on Dame Sophia Carrell's eightieth birthday celebrations. The opening scene introduces Sophia's errant son, who has left the London arts scene for the sunshine of southern Italy where he and his wife run an exclusive hotel for the London *literati*. Sophia's daughter, Blanche, middle-aged and unmarried, rules her mother with an iron rod and imposes strict domestic rules on the household. The play is a very witty portrayal of an actress at the end of her life, but also explores the emotional and practical investments made by others in supporting and caring for a retired celebrity. Arguably, the familial relationships in the play bear a strong resemblance to those of Ellen Terry and her two artistic children Edith and Edward Gordon Craig. In her biography of Craig, Katherine Cockin asserts that Dane's overriding intent was to present Blanche as 'deadly' and as a stereotype of a 'deviant and immature' lesbian; certainly Blanche's cold and tense personality is contrasted with Sophia's wit, sensuality and warmth.[37] One wonders, however, at the portrayal of Kevin, a loosely drawn portrait of Edward Gordon Craig. Kevin continually requires his mother to bail him out financially and creates very little of any substance: he writes a celebrated and provocative *Prologue* and *Epilogue* to a play that has never, and will never, be written.

> KEVIN: *Prologue to a Play* was a stunt ... And *Epilogue to a Play* was a stunt ... but ... they sold so well – ... The play got to be a sort of – legend – ... I believed it myself ... But I've got it clear at last. There isn't a play in me ... if I'm not a genius, at least I'll be a good liar ...[38]

Kevin understands publicity and sees it as more important than the artistic integrity of his play; here Dane appears to be critiquing publicity and hype as ends in themselves. She also asserts that a celebrity lifestyle may be ruinous for children who want the rewards of fame but do not have the talent to win it in their own right. Dane seems to be suggesting that the life of a female celebrity may conflict with the role of mother; in Act I Blanche accuses her mother of 'putting on an act' of caring when she was a child:

> You were doing then what you did this afternoon. Out you came ... to a meet a crowd that was watching you, admiring you, wanting to touch you, and instantly – the change ... You moved about the lawn entertaining people, open-air stage – giving out, giving out. So *they* thought. But you weren't giving out. You were drawing in, drawing everything to a centre, your centre. You were hypnotising your audience into surrendering its vitality ... All the great actors have done it, and orators too. You have to get your power from somewhere.[39]

Sophia tries to explain herself:

> But it is not like that ... However tired I am, or confused, or unhappy, when I face the occasion, then the power comes, then I can do anything ... I can pass the power on – drench it upon people in the theatre with me, or in a room with me ... the power feeds them, and me ...[40]

For Cockin this encounter indicates that Blanche finds her mother predatory and manipulative. Sophia's speech is, on the contrary, that of a *sexualised* older woman who has no fear of her public. Dane creates a scenario of a dysfunctional celebrity family: the children have had to negotiate emotionally between the celebrity and the private personalities of famous parents – between the star actress and playwright and the mother and father. Equally, Dane is commenting on the nature of performance and celebrity itself: that personae, both private and public, are beholden to and mediated by the fluctuations of celebrity. The performer is as emotionally nourished by the adulation of the audience as the audience is fed by the fantasy of celebrity and imagined celebrity lifestyles. Written for an actress approaching the end of her professional career, about a fictional woman at the end of hers, by a playwright at the end of her own career (Dane was in her seventies when she wrote the play), it is difficult not to read the *Eighty in the Shade* in the context of Dane's own experience of being a celebrity in an age that had seen vast changes in the way fame was mediated and in the ways celebrities could shape public opinion.[41]

Clemence Dane's salon

By the early 1930s Dane had become part of Coward's inner circle of friends and professional colleagues:

> In public he consorted with the stars. In private, he surrounded himself with a small coterie of like-minded souls ... At the family's heart were four

women – Lorn Lorraine ... Gladys Calthrop ... Joyce Carey ... Clemence Dane ...[42]

Terry Castle has argued that Coward modelled the character of Madame Arcati in *Blithe Spirit* (1941) in part on Dane, and has paid tribute to 'that Lesbian Muse who – in her many different guises – was so much a part of Coward's professional and imaginative life'.[43] Interestingly, Castle alludes to the many public personae Dane adopted depending on her surroundings. The relationship between Dane and Coward was more than a celebrity friendship: rather, it was an artistic liaison which provided emotional ballast for them both. In particular, Coward relied on Dane's powers of criticism and her knowledge of theatre, literature and the arts.

Clemence Dane ran her small flat at 20 Tavistock Street in London's Covent Garden as a modern version of a theatrical salon. She chose the flat for its vicinity to the new generation of theatrical and literary agents and for its setting amongst the ghosts and living legends of the London theatre scene: 'I thought to myself that to live in or near it [Bedford Street] would be the luckiest thing that could ever happen to anyone who wanted the life literary, the life artistic or the life theatrical. I had had a taste of three, and longed for more.'[44] The flat, most unsuitable as living accommodation, was in fact advertised to let as office space:

> The eighteenth century rooms were in a desolate state, with soot and a long dead fire spilling out over the dirty oaken floorboards ... I had no front door ... [but] a stall front row in the best theatre of all – the Garden [Covent] itself.[45]

Thus Dane placed herself strategically at the centre of the powerhouses behind the emerging syndicate managements of the West End. To say that she had acquired a taste for the 'artistic' life by this point is an understatement: the early notoriety and subsequent successes of her work ensured that she was the subject of interviews and articles, but they also catapulted Dane into the celebrity circles of theatre industry – and at a level far above those in which Coward circulated in the early years of his career before the success of *The Vortex* in 1924. It was to this flat in Covent Garden that Coward gravitated, bringing with him a cohort of celebrities. Here Dane could construct herself as a bohemian intellectual at the heart of London's theatre world.

Dane had a number of 'domestic lives' and the one played out in London was inextricably linked to her professional life and her celebrity status. Binkie Beaumont, the power behind the monopolising H. M. Tennant production company, allegedly told Dane that she was the 'Lady Blessington and Madame de Sevigné of Covent Garden'. Beaumont clearly understood the kind of cultural marker which Dane represented in what was fast becoming the cultural elite of the commercial theatre.[46] Dane's flat became an essential place for writers, artists and sculptors to gather, discuss their work and others', and be seen: with 'musical evenings, poetry recitals, play-readings and film conferences ... Winifred's circle laughed at everybody and everything and actually got things done. Plays were written, novels completed, poems published, paintings finished and production deals finalised. Winifred's friends were real artists. They didn't just talk about doing it, they *did* it.'[47] This is remarkable testimony to Dane's centrality to artistic creativity in London.

Coward's reminiscences of the flat in Tavistock Street evoke an exciting and exuberant meeting place maintained and renewed by Dane's capacity for mixing work with pleasure:

> From 1930 onwards, whenever I have returned from abroad, or even from the wilds of Manchester, I have always winged my way, like a homing pigeon, to that cosy, long suffering room on the first floor overlooking the market ... the poor place has to put up with a great deal ... it has been barked in, sung in, shouted in ... It has also had to stand firm ... against the impact of violent personalities both alive and dead.[48]

Thus, the geography of their friendship had at its centre Dane's office and home. Despite the representations of certain biographers who portray Dane as eccentric, for ever making verbal 'bloomers' and using *double entendres* frequently without seemingly meaning to – hence the 'Junoesque' model for Madame Arcati[49] – she clearly galvanised artistic creativity. In particular, Dane influenced Coward's reading, and later in his career helped him with his film scripts.[50] Coward, for example, documents his annoyance at her criticism over the failure of *Pacific 1860*:

> She told me that for the last three years I had been becoming so unbearably arrogant that it's grotesque; that everyone is laughing at me; that I am surrounded by yes men ... that I have no longer any touch or contact with the people and events on account of my overweening conceit ...[51]

When Dane died, Coward wrote that he felt in her debt: she was someone whose opinions he sought and absorbed and who had influenced his creative life in a variety of ways.[52] Indeed, Dane's salon stimulated artistic debate and industry for over thirty years – a remarkable achievement in itself and one which theatre historians have ignored.

Being remembered

Obituaries of Clemence Dane often pay unwilling tribute to her achievements. Extraordinarily, the label 'oncer', applied to Dane in the 1920s endures, despite the fact that she enjoyed high-profile successes in theatre and film throughout her life. Critics like W. A. Darlington mistakenly frame Dane as someone who never quite achieved what she wanted in theatre. He ignores her Oscar and her film work and makes little reference to her numerous and best-selling novels. Her list of film credits is also remarkable, including work for Alfred Hitchcock (*Murder*, 1930), David O. Selznick (*A Bill of Divorcement* and *Anna Karenina*), Erich Pommer (*Fire Over England*, 1936 and *St Martin's Lane*, 1938) and Alexander Korda (*Perfect Strangers*, 1947). Dane worked for key directors and film-makers of the day in both England and America.[53] When she began her theatre career, film had not yet become a dominant cultural force. The newspaper industry also grew in size and influence during her lifetime. The means of circulating celebrity multiplied, as did the locations in which artists could place their work. Dane was astonishingly adept at reinventing herself as a writer and public speaker. From the 1920s to the 1940s she often responded to the media's requests for her opinions on a variety of social and domestic issues of the day, and thus erased the memory of her early notoriety.

Celebrity is subject to its age and no more so than in the twentieth century where the means of identifying and distributing celebrity as a concept and commodity transformed and expanded so dramatically. As a woman Clemence Dane was not fashionably beautiful in the sense of the other boyish, sylphlike female celebrities of the day – she was no Fay Compton or Valerie Taylor (Figure 4.1). She preferred classical clothes designed for her by Victor Stiebel, and often wore long flowing dresses and a big straw hat. She was stylish but not fashionable – a strategy she found useful in making her a talking point. Later in her life Dane was often portrayed as homely and old-fashioned, a construction she encouraged because it made her seem a trustworthy public figure.[54]

After the arrival of the new wave of theatre writers in the 1950s, including John Osborne and Harold Pinter, Dane found it difficult to maintain her theatrical status. She still wrote and had plays produced, but she could not be categorised as an 'angry young man' and, like Coward's, her work was marginalised. Dane admired Pinter's work, but knew she was of a different generation of playwrights.[55] She argued that theatre was important for its direct engagement of audiences, and expressed her doubts about the political passivity that television and film might encourage. But she continued to write for both media and was still being commissioned to write television dramas until a few years before she died.[56]

Virginia Woolf's observation that few plays by women could be found on the shelves of the British Library offers little by way of recognition of the many woman playwrights of the era in which Dane was working.[57] Although Dane is far from the only female playwright to suffer the fate of oblivion, one wonders how someone so driven and so prolific, so witty and so central to artistic circles could have become so thoroughly invisible. Perhaps her brilliance at adopting different masks and different personae paradoxically

Figure 4.1 Photograph of Clemence Dane. Courtesy of the Mander and Mitchenson Theatre Collection.

served her too well. Dane was a legend to those who knew her, but this legendary character did not give her a place in history. She lived and worked for some three decades just around the corner from what is now the Theatre Museum, but there is as yet no blue heritage plaque to attest to this fact.

Notes

1. Dane wrote over twenty plays and some eleven novels as well as numerous critical essays, poems and film scripts.
2. Clemence Dane, *A Bill of Divorcement* (London: Heinemann, 1961).
3. J. C. Trewin, *The Gay Twenties: A Decade of the Theatre* (London: MacDonald, 1958), p. 58. Quoted in Rebecca Cameron, 'Irreconcilable Differences: Divorce and Women's Drama before 1945', in *Modern Drama*, 44:4 (2001), 476–90, 480.
4. Archibald Haddon, 'What the Public Wants', *Sunday Express*, 5 March 1922.
5. Clemence Dane, 'What I Think about Divorce', unmarked cutting, 14 December 1921, British Library *Daily Express* obituary file.
6. See Donald Childs, *Modernism and Eugenics: Woolf, Eliot, Yeats, and the Culture of Degeneration* (Cambridge: Cambridge University Press, 2001).
7. Dane, 'What I Think about Divorce'.
8. Clemence Dane, *Regiment of Women* (London: Virago, Reprint, 1995).

9 Mitchell A. Leaska and John Phillips, *Violet to Vita: The Letters of Violet Trefusis to Vita Sackville-West, 1910–1921* (London: Mandarin, 1991).
10 *Daily Express* obituary file: Clemence Dane, British Library, unassigned review, 4 March 1921.
11 *Daily Express* obituary file: Clemence Dane, British Library, unassigned review, 27 March 1921.
12 See Billie Melman, *Women and the Popular Imagination in the Twenties: Flappers and Nymphs* (London: Macmillan, 1988).
13 Gay Wachman, *Lesbian Empire* (New Brunswick, NJ: Rutgers University Press, 2001), p. 54.
14 Joanna Alberti, *Beyond Suffrage* (London: Macmillan, 1989).
15 Clemence Dane, *Will Shakespeare*, in *Recapture: A Clemence Dane Omnibus* (London: Heinemann, 1932). The play ran in the West End for 62 performances.
16 Clemence Dane, *Granite* and *Wild Decembers*, in *Recapture: A Clemence Dane Omnibus* and *Cousin Muriel* (London: Heinemann, 1940).
17 *Will Shakespeare* was broadcast on 4 April 1938.
18 St John Ervine, *The Theatre in My Time* (London: Rich and Cowan, 1933), pp. 137–9.
19 See unpublished manuscript of interview between author and the late Judy Campbell, who worked with Coward and for Dane on her expressionistic play about the effects of War on marital relationships, *Call Home the Heart* (1947). For published excerpts see 'Interview: Judy Campbell', in Joel H. Kaplan and Sheila Stowell, *Look Back in Pleasure: Noël Coward Reconsidered* (London: Methuen, 2000), pp. 194–9.
20 Wachman, *Lesbian Empire*, p. 3.
21 Wachman, *Lesbian Empire*, p. 3.
22 *Perfect Strangers*, directed by Alexander Korda in 1947, had the US title *Vacation from Marriage* and starred Robert Donat and Deborah Kerr.
23 Clemence Dane, *The Women's Side* (London: Jenkins, 1926).
24 See Judith Cook, *Priestley* (London: Bloomsbury, 1997).
25 Chris Rojek, *Celebrity* (London: Reaktion Books, 2001), p. 11.
26 Katherine Cornell commissioned Dane's examination of the private world of Charlotte Brontë, *Wild Decembers* (1933).
27 *Anna Karenina*, directed by David O. Selznick in 1935, starred Greta Garbo and Basil Rathbone.
28 Dane features in a number of autobiographies of those working in mainstream theatre from the 1920s to the 1950s, for examples see Katherine Cornell, *I Wanted to Be an Actress* (New York: Random House, 1938); Basil Dean, *Seven Ages* (London: Hutchinson, 1970); and Nancy Price, *Into An Hourglass* (London: Museum Press Ltd, 1953).
29 Clemence Dane, *London has a Garden* (London: Michael Joseph, 1964).
30 Leo Braudy, *The Frenzy of Renown: Fame and Its History* (London: Vintage, 1986; repr. 1997), p. 584.
31 Clemence Dane, *The Women's Side* (London: Herbert Jenkins, 1926), p. 138.
32 See Rebecca Cameron, 'Women Playwrights and the Modernist Conception of Genius: Clemence Dane's *Will Shakespeare* (1921); and Gordon Daviot's *The Laughing Woman* (1934)', *Essays in Theatre*, 18:2 (May 2000), 161–78.
33 Clemence Dane, *Broome Stages* (London: Heinemann, 1931).
34 See Maggie B. Gale, 'From Fame to Obscurity: In Search of Clemence Dane', in Maggie B. Gale and Viv Gardner, *Women, Theatre and Performance: New Histories,*

New Historiographies (Manchester: Manchester University Press, 2000), pp. 121–41. For a brief and rather reticent critical biography of Dane's work, see David Waldron Smithers, *Therefore Imagine: The Works of Clemence Dane* (Tunbridge Wells: The Dragonfly Press, 1988).

35 Clemence Dane and Helen Simpson, *Gooseberry Fool* (unpublished typescript in the Theatre Museum, London), pp. 48–51.
36 Jacky Bratton, *New Readings in Theatre History* (Cambridge: Cambridge University Press, 2003), pp. 198–9.
37 Katherine Cockin, *Edith Craig (1869–1947): Dramatic Lives* (London: Cassell 1998), p. 11.
38 Clemence Dane, *Eighty in the Shade* (London: Samuel French, 1958), pp. 55–6.
39 *Eighty in the Shade*, p. 21.
40 *Eighty in the Shade*, p. 21.
41 See Sheila Jeffreys, *The Spinster and Her Enemies: Feminism and Sexuality 1880–1930* (London: Pandora, 1985).
42 Gyles Brandreth, 'My Life with Noël', *Daily Telegraph*, 21 November 1999.
43 Terry Castle, *Noël Coward and Radcliffe Hall: Kindred Spirits* (New York: Columbia University Press, 1996), p. 101.
44 Dane, *London has A Garden*, p. 41.
45 Dane, *London has A Garden*, p. 43.
46 Richard Huggett, *Binkie Beaumont: Eminence Grise of the West End Theatre 1933–1979* (London: Hodder and Stoughton, 1989), p. 139.
47 Huggett, *Binkie Beaumont*, p. 139.
48 Noël Coward, *The Autobiography of Noël Coward: Future Indefinite* (London: Methuen, 1986 edition), pp. 349–40.
49 See Cole Lesley, *Remembered Laughter: The Life of Noël Coward* (New York: Alfred A. Knopf, 1977), pp. 227–9.
50 See 'Interview: Judy Campbell'.
51 Graham Payn and Sheridan Morley, *The Noël Coward Diaries* (London: Weidenfeld and Nicolson, 1982), pp. 71–2.
52 *The Noël Coward Diaries*, p. 596.
53 There is now an archive of Dane's film scripts in the Theatre Museum, London.
54 See for example Erica Beth Weintraub, 'Clemence Dane', in Stanley Weintraub, *Modern British Dramatists 1900–1945* (Detroit, MI: Gale Research Corp. 1982), pp. 133–8.
55 Clemence Dane, *Approaches to Drama* (London: The English Association, 1961), p. 11.
56 Clemence Dane, 'The Writer's Partner', in Dane, *Recapture: A Clemence Dane Omnibus*.
57 Virginia Woolf, *A Room of One's Own* and *Three Guineas* (London: Hogarth Press, 1984), pp. 43–7.

Part II
Notoriety

There is one thing in the world worse than being talked about, and that is not being talked about.

Oscar Wilde

5
Stolen Identities: Character, Mimicry and the Invention of Samuel Foote

Jane Moody

> On Saturday Noon, exactly at Twelve o'clock, at the New Theatre in the Haymarket, Mr. Foote begs the Favour of his Friends to come and drink a Dish of Chocolate with him, and 'tis hoped there will be a great deal of good Company, and some Joyous Spirits; he will endeavour to make the Morning as Diverting as possible. – Tickets for this Entertainment to be had at George's Coffee-House, Temple-bar, without which no Person will be admitted. – N.B. Sir Dilberry Diddle will be there; and Lady Betty Frisk has absolutely promis'd.[1]

Samuel Foote (1720–77), actor, playwright and manager of the Haymarket Theatre, was one of the most celebrated personages in mid-eighteenth-century British culture. Fashionable people collected his witticisms and *bons mots*; men crowded into coffee-houses like the Grecian and the Bedford to listen to his sparkling wit; spectators jostled to secure the best seats at the Haymarket for the latest topical hit. During the late 1740s, this short, podgy actor began to make his name selling characters; by 1766 he had acquired a royal patent to perform plays at the Haymarket. This essay explores the distinctive position of the 'modern Aristophanes' in the history of theatrical fame. At the same time, my argument seeks to reveal Foote's theatre as a notable place for the production, consumption and deformation of celebrity.[2]

Foote became famous because of his extraordinary powers as a mimic. The subjects of mimicry, of course, are those individuals whose speech, gestures and manner can be instantly recognised by an audience. Unlike the other actors and playwrights discussed in this book, Foote used the celebrity of other people as the artistic raw material for the creation of his own fame. This essay therefore explores a number of questions about the theatrical manufacture of celebrity in mid-eighteenth-century Britain, and about the intermediaries who become involved in its creative production.

Figure 5.1 Samuel Foote by William Greatbach, after Joshua Reynolds. By kind permission of the Victoria Art Gallery, Bath and North East Somerset Council.

Foote, who was always keen to display his knowledge of classical and modern theatre, traced the origins of his craft to the Roman dramatist Menander, who introduced 'the Method of exposing real Vices by the Assistance of feigned Characters'.[3] In the wake of the Licensing Act of 1737, however, the legality of 'metonymic' satire based on recognisable individuals remained uncertain.[4] Foote was skilled in presenting his performances as occupying a pivotal position between legitimacy and illegitimacy, respectability and transgression. Whilst successfully promoting himself as an Aristophanic reformer intent on exposing hypocrisy and dissimulation, his self-aggrandising rhetoric conveniently masked a mixture of less glorious motives: money, malice and a desire for power.[5]

Like David Garrick, with whom he was often paired for purposes of contrast and comparison, Foote mixed in fashionable circles. Men of high rank eagerly sought his acquaintance, and the extravagance of his dinner-table was renowned. In the course of his life Foote inherited three fortunes, all of which he managed to fritter away on the pleasures of food, vintage Burgundy wines and gambling; despite the substantial sums he earned from his productions, he was often desperate for money and seems to have been arrested for debt on a number of occasions. Such was Foote's popularity with the Duke of York that when the playwright lost his leg after a riding accident, he was presented with a patent for operating the Haymarket Theatre as a form of compensation. But whereas Garrick assiduously cultivated social respectability and moral domesticity, Foote liked to present himself as a showman – albeit a showman well versed in Aristophanes and Tully – or, as Garrick called him, an 'exotic': a mischievous, devilish, entrepreneurial shape-shifter, a man whose sheer variousness always held a hint of danger and deviance. As Samuel Johnson ruefully reflected, 'Foote is the most incompressible fellow that I ever knew: when you have driven him into a corner, and think you are sure of him, he runs through between your legs, or jumps over your head, and makes his escape.'[6]

Foote's innovation was to make a theatre of character from the celebrities of metropolitan life. Character is a peculiarly mobile term in this period, connoting both the distinctiveness and singularity of particular individuals and, increasingly, the imaginary personages of fiction and drama.[7] As we shall see, Foote's satires skilfully exploit the equivocal position of character. Crowds flocked to his shows to witness these uproarious exhibitions, albeit under fictional identities, of well-known public figures, not to mention his ingenious reinventions of himself. Some of his subjects, like Catherine Macaulay (who appears as Margaret Maxwell, the redoubtable champion of rights for women, in *The Devil upon Two Sticks*), came to laugh at their portraits; others lent him their clothes to make the character look as authentic as possible.[8] But whilst certain individuals regarded mimicry as a means by which to enhance their own fame, others saw Foote's imitations as a threat to the integrity of their public identities. Several victims regarded the prospect with such dread that they threatened, appeased and even bribed Foote to suppress his spitting images: Samuel Johnson declared his determination to beat the actor with an oak stick, purchased for that very purpose, if Foote dared to introduce him into *The Orators*.[9] On several occasions, the Lord Chamberlain responded to injured protests from and on behalf of Foote's satirical subjects and prevented further performances of the play in question. As these very different reactions attest, mimicry occupied a position on a knife-edge between fame and defamation.

Critics often invoked the language of murder, sacrifice and physical destruction to describe Foote's exhibition of public characters. As the playwright Charles Dibdin remarked, Foote 'knew no quality of satire but personality, who would sacrifice his best friend for the gratification of tormenting him'.[10] The malicious nature of these stage portraits certainly confirms that violence which seems to lie at the heart of celebrity culture.[11] Moreover, Foote actively cultivated the impression of his own criminality by advertising his caricatures or 'stage exposures' as acts of robbery and versions of forgery. Demur, the prosecuting lawyer in *The Trial of Samuel Foote* (a skit on the actor's trial and conviction for libel in Dublin at the suit of the printer, George Faulkner), demands to know 'what kind of right now this Fot has to be any body at all but himself' and suggests that the defendant should be indicted for forgery.[12] As his victims would discover, the capacity of Foote's characters to usurp their originals did produce a kind of identity theft.

As we shall see, Foote's caricatures gave a new and disturbing prominence to the body. What is more, he responded to the amputation of his leg by exhibiting his disability in newly created characters like Sir Luke Limp in *The Lame Lover* (who 'very humorously attempts to prove, that the loss of a leg is no kind of disadvantage')[13] and *The Devil upon Two Sticks*. Huge and curious crowds came to the Haymarket to watch these disabled performances. One spectator admitted that his principal reason for going to see *The Minor* was 'to see Mr Foote's left Leg exhibited under Mother Cole's petticoats ... Is it not strange that ten men would go to see Foote now he has but one leg, for one that went when he had two?' This voyeuristic playgoer even speculated whether the company at the Bedford Coffee House might now start 'stumping around the room with their wooden legs, in hopes of being as witty as Foote'.[14] A devastating accident was turned to extraordinary effect as Foote cleverly reinvented his old characters (Mother Cole now walked with a limp, Foote declared, because of her rheumatism) and transposed old jokes about artificial acting into novel forms (exhibitions of the 'woodenness' of well-known performers). Never before had a physical disability become such a versatile comic weapon.

Diversions

Foote's first production, *The Diversions of the Morning*, opened at the Haymarket in April 1747. The ban on acting for hire, gain or reward in

London other than at the Theatres Royal had produced a glut of unemployed actors in the metropolis during the 1740s. Performances like the *Diversions of the Morning*, using a scratch cast, provided an important source of income for actors like Foote; only in 1762 would the actor manage to form a company with whom to perform. In order to avoid the provisions of the Licensing Act, audiences were invited not to a theatrical performance, but rather to a concert of music, with the *Diversions* – a series of imitations of metropolitan personalities including the oculist Dr Taylor and Christopher Cock, the auctioneer, and well-known performers. In its original form, however, the show lasted only a few days before constables stopped Foote and his fellow actors in mid-performance and sent the audience home. Whether the Theatres Royal had decided to tip off local magistrates about Foote's performances or whether the offended performers had elected to take their own revenge on this new satirist remains unknown.[15] In any case, Foote simply changed his strategy: the next morning he inserted in the *General Advertiser* the chirpy and ebullient paragraph which appears at the beginning of this essay. Audiences were invited to the Haymarket to drink a dish of chocolate (in subsequent performances tea was substituted): Foote predicted 'a great deal of good Company' and promised to make 'the *Morning* as *Diverting* as possible'. This ruse seems to have kept the authorities away, and the show – warmly patronised by 'many of the principal nobility' – soon became extremely popular.[16] As Tate Wilkinson remembers, the 'manoeuvre' of presenting imitations under the guise of instructing young actors whilst the tea was being prepared was 'highly relished' and 'it became the universal fashion every noon to drink a dish of Mr. Foote's Tea'.[17] Next year, Foote repeated the formula in a similar show entitled *Auction of Pictures* (1748).

The practice of imitating the singularities of contemporary performers on stage was not itself a novelty. Garrick's adaptation of Buckingham's burlesque, *The Rehearsal*, had included various parodies of his fellow actors; indeed, Garrick was sharply upbraided for continuing to perform these savage caricatures in private for his friends.[18] In a variety of ways, however, *Tea* (as the piece came to be known) marks the emergence of a new cultural form, and especially a new form for making individuals public; moreover, Foote's imitations gave a distinct inflection to contemporary debates about the identity of the actor. In particular, his satires on performers capitalised on a distinct ambivalence in metropolitan society about the emergence of the actor as a modern hero who dared to 'ape the pride of kings'.[19]

'It is amazing', remarked James Boswell (a man both thrilled and made uneasy by the phenomenon of Foote), 'how a mimic can not only give you the gestures and voice of a person whom he represents, but even what a person would say on any particular subject.'[20] Mimics, of course, were not the only individuals selling characters in eighteenth-century culture. Print-sellers, caricaturists, puppeteers, china manufacturers and solo performers such as George Alexander Stevens (who invented the celebrated *Lecture Upon Heads* featuring characters made out of wood and *papier mâché*),[21] not to mention novelists, all competed in the marketplace of character. But Foote's imitations differed from those of his competitors, and indeed from his predecessors, by embodying the eccentricities and even the physical deformities of celebrated performers. In *The Diversions*, the deep sonorous tones and 'weighty manner' of James Quin became those of a night watchman ('Past twelve o'clock, and a cloudy morning'); the shrill, 'half-strangled' tones of the tragedian Lacy Ryan were converted into those of a razor grinder ('Razors to grind, scissors to grind, penknives to grind'); Peg Woffington's voice inspired Foote to portray her as an orange woman ('Would you have some oranges – have some orange-chips, ladies and gentlemen, – would you have some nonpareils, –would you have a bill of the play?') and one-eyed Dennis Delane appeared as a blind beggar in St Paul's churchyard.[22] That convention by which the audience accepts the singular features of a performer's own body as part and parcel of a particular role is here rudely disrupted: that body now becomes the object of vulgar scrutiny and acquires a disturbingly plebeian character.

The exhibition of physical peculiarities and disabilities on stage shocked Foote's subjects and theatrical critics alike: the production and its revival in 1758 (starring Foote's protégé, Tate Wilkinson), engendered 'fixed hatred' and made Foote enemies for life.[23] A disgusted Peg Woffington promptly marched off to the manager of Covent Garden, John Rich, and ordered him not to engage the mimic;[24] other anecdotes about the episode hint at a pervasive sense of distaste and anxiety. Tate Wilkinson recalls receiving an anonymous letter about his own imitation of Foote which criticised as 'very wrong' the gesture of 'twitching your chin with tweezers'.[25] Mimicry seemed to have crossed an invisible line dividing legitimate from illegitimate subjects of laughter. An anonymous writer published a miniature drama in which a playwright, who has called on Foote hoping to persuade him to accept his play, leaves declaring, 'I am determined neither to prostitute my own pen to personal abuse, nor encourage it in others'.[26] From beyond the theatre, too, print satirists like Charles Churchill and Robert Lloyd condemned the art of Foote and his friends for these violations of satiric decorum:

> Doth a man stutter, look a-squint, or halt?
> Mimics draw humour out of Nature's fault:
> With personal defects their mirth adorn,
> And hang misfortunes out to public scorn.[27]

Foote, of course, mocked the idea that mimicry could actually damage a performer's reputation (though he was clearly perturbed when Tate Wilkinson mimicked him on stage). On hearing that one of his offended victims had taken to his bed and was dangerously ill, the playwright swiftly rebutted what he saw as this pretence of injured malaise, observing to the great amusement of the green room that he had just met the man's wife buying 'two pounds of mutton-chops on a skewer' for her husband's dinner.[28]

Foote's *Diversions* mark the creation of a new kind of theatrical celebrity based on the mimicry of famous performers and other public figures. The hostility about this innovation and the imitations it spawned was widespread and unprecedented. Critics condemned the meanness and malice of this 'mimic race' and ridiculed the 'low audacity' of Foote in particular:

> See him invade the boundaries of sense,
> Break thro' the rules of genius and taste,
> And lay, with ridicule, their kingdoms waste.[29]

The mixture of disgust and condescension in these satires tells us a great deal about the transgressive position of mimicry in this period. Foote's imitations seemed to break the boundaries of polite sociability (many of these attacks refer to his willingness to expose 'his dearest friends'). The language of class is frequently invoked: the author of *Momus* presents mimicry as '... a crafty snare, / To catch the vulgar, and to make 'em stare'.[30] Such a claim is thoroughly misleading: what is remarkable about Foote's career is the breadth of his social appeal. But such attempts to dismiss mimicry as 'a blockhead's cause' hint at a pervasive fear about the disturbing power of imitation to overturn established social categories, judgements and even kingdoms.

Foote's exhibition of the body as a satiric subject anticipates our own contemporary fascination with minute details of and variations in celebrity bodies.[31] But whereas the bodies of today's celebrities must be ideal and unblemished, Foote successfully exploited both his own and his subjects' physical imperfections. Most importantly, these imitations fuelled performers' fears about the commercial value and the vulnerability of their public faces. For imitations challenged the presumption of originality by demonstrating just how easily that originality could be reproduced. Such tactics seem to have exploited in clever and unexpected ways an underlying anxiety in eighteenth-century culture about the emergence of the actor as a celebrity. The commercial power of mimicry, I am suggesting, was double edged: audiences revelled in the comic reproduction of celebrated performers but also enjoyed watching celebrity being distorted and even deformed.

Publicity

How did Foote produce and sell this theatre of character? Technology – from telephoto lenses and 24-hour news channels to the internet – has underpinned the exponential growth in global celebrity culture over the last two or three decades. Foote by contrast created his reputation, and a great deal of money (including annual profits of over £3,000 whilst manager at the Haymarket), through his relentless exploitation of the publicity latent in two key eighteenth-century institutions: the coffee-house and the newspaper.[32] Ironically, it was the libellous world of the latter which would eventually unleash its most savage forms of rhetoric on the playwright himself.

In the growing literature about the coffee-house as a place of metropolitan sociability and conversation, almost nothing has been said about the coffee-house as a theatrical institution.[33] But actors and spectators were regular patrons of coffee-houses such as the Bedford (a celebrated haunt of metropolitan wits) and Wright's in York Street, Covent Garden. Such establishments provided a convenient forum for the exchange of theatrical gossip and for the 'ratification' of judgements on the night's performances at the playhouses: at the Bedford in particular, 'dramatic affairs' became 'the affairs of state'.[34] The opinions of coffee-house patrons clearly mattered: it is significant that one of Garrick's detractors accuses him of sending his 'adulators' to puff the actor's performance at the local coffee-houses.[35] Foote successfully extended 'the theatre of the Bedford' (a phrase connoting both the thespian interests of its patrons and the notorious skirmishes between them) by appropriating the Bedford Coffee House as a place of performance.

The Bedford played an important role in the extensive publicity for Foote's shows. The provision of box seats made possible the creation of an informal stage: Foote's friends, gathered in the box, comprised the internal audience for his rehearsal whilst curious admirers were able to eavesdrop from adjoining boxes.[36] Indeed, the sense of intimacy with this extraordinary performer must have been part of the attraction of this improvised performance space (in our own culture, by contrast, celebrity promises only the illusion of intimacy). During the evening, Foote would hint at the characters to be satirised in his next play and perform mischievous imitations. These occasions, a novel fusion of sociability and theatricality, craftily presented the satirical subjects of his latest production as an open secret. Moreover, Foote's performances both invoked and realised the coffee-house as a leading institution in the production of celebrity. The epilogue for *Tea*, written 'by the B—d—d Coffee House' and performed by Foote, celebrates and indeed embodies this reciprocal relationship by including parodies of the House's most celebrated personalities including the eccentric preacher, Orator Henley, and the auctioneer Christopher Cock.

By the mid-eighteenth century, newspapers had become 'the vehicles of knowledge'. 'Every man who steps out of the crowd,' remarked David Williams, 'has his character inserted in them; and is held out to public observation, generally with more wit than truth, and with more ill-nature than either.'[37] The newspaper, in tandem with Foote's theatre, was emerging as a crucial site for the construction and destruction of reputations; theatres and newspapers also began to exploit their mutual interests in the production of publicity. Garrick, who owned shares in the *Public Advertiser*, the *Gazeteer*, the *Morning Post* and the *St James's Chronicle*, was famous for the frequent insertion of outrageously self-congratulatory puffs. Foote also delighted in forms of witty, ironic and often oblique self-advertisement. To 'prevent confusion' at performances of *Tea*, he requests that 'the Gentlemen and Ladies would pay for their Chocolate going in'; on another occasion, he 'begs leave to inform his Friends, that the Breakfasting in the Hay-Market is deferr'd to Saturday'.[38] Such advertisements cleverly fuse the language of polite invitation and the subject of satire: in a puff for *The Knights*, which featured a cat duet satirising the Italian opera, he advised that 'Ladies and Gentlemen are desired to leave their *Lap Dogs* and *Spaniels* at Home because of the *Cats*.'[39] Foote even created puffs purportedly composed by his satiric victims. In a paragraph entitled 'Foote a Fool', Orator Henley defiantly announced, 'Whoever attacks my Reputation, or Livelihood, is a mad Bull to me, and ought to be knock'd down, prosecuted, &c. &c. &c. ... I hear that I am to be hung up on Wednesday by one Foote, a Fool.'[40] The language of physical assault here is characteristic: violence and deformation of both bodies and characters became central to Foote's treatment of celebrity. In addition, newspapers provided Foote with raw material for new plays (a spat in the *Public Advertiser* between the politicians John Horne Tooke and John Wilkes over the whereabouts of a colourful suit collection inspired the hit scene in *The Maid of Bath*);[41] and, in the case of his victims, notably the Duchess of Kingston, a place of consummate self-exposure.

Foote prided himself on the topicality of his shows, incorporating new information sometimes even on a daily basis.[42] Many of his publicity techniques had much in common with the forms of self-presentation characteristic of contemporary newspapers. The rise of paragraph journalism (in which individuals paid for the insertion of puffs and the rebuttal of scandalous accusations) was transforming the newspaper from a text largely concerned with verifiable information to an institution where truthfulness could no longer be guaranteed. Foote's originality lay in his creation of an ironic performativity which exhibited in a variety of media the convergence between his personality and his stage roles.[43] In particular, through shows like *Taste* and *Auction* – and long before Sheridan's *The Critic* (1779) – Foote comically foregrounded the production of publicity in eighteenth-century culture by introducing the figure of Puff as a dramatic character in his own right.

Foote's plays occupy that equivocal contemporary arena between publicity and libel, 'harmless humour' and 'scandalous abuse'.[44] Just as newspapers routinely accepted hush money to suppress offensive paragraphs, so mimics like Foote and Wilkinson received various inducements to suppress or modify their caricatures.[45] Like the modern tabloid press, Foote also relished his power to bring the mighty low, to disgrace the famous: one pamphleteer identified him as the 'Inspector General of Grubstreet Bunters', in other words, the 'Detractor general of *Great Britain*'.[46] Foote often defended his satirical theatre through his characters. As Puff declares in *The Patron* (Haymarket, 1764), the public is no longer interested in panegyric: ' 'tis quite and clean out of nature'. What it hungers for is 'good sousing satire ... well powdered with personal pepper ... that demolishes a conspicuous character, and sinks him below their own level'.[47] There is something thoroughly disingenuous about this eighteenth-century defence of public interest. But the speech is notable for its acknowledgement of a violent pleasure amongst the Haymarket audiences: that of watching fame being exposed and even dismantled.

Sabotage

In 1753, the celebrated Shakespearean actor Charles Macklin leased rooms under the Great Piazza at Covent Garden and proceeded to announce, with a great deal of pomp and ceremony, the opening of a new establishment called the British Institution. The venture aimed to capitalise on both the vogue for coffee-houses (the actor, dressed in black and wearing an earnestly solemn expression, helped waiters to serve refreshments) and the fashion for elocution and oratory: Macklin gave a series of extravagantly verbose lectures on subjects ranging from 'Whether Women or Men are best qualified by Nature for Eloquence and Politicks' or the utility of having plays 'read in the Inquisition before they are exhibited on the Stage' to the 'Moral and Physical Nature of Elizabeth Canning's Story' (a reference to the alleged kidnapping of a London maidservant).[48] Macklin shrewdly recognised the desire of audiences for a new kind of intimacy with famous performers, not to mention the profits to be made from marketing the actor as an urban personality. What he created was a hybrid performance space which blended the conventions, the rhetoric and the sociability of the playhouse and the coffee-house.

But Macklin had reckoned without the exertions of his former pupil, Foote, who arrived bent on sabotaging the show with his own mischievous interruptions: when Macklin boasted about his powers of memory, Foote produced an utterly nonsensical story (featuring a woman, a cabbage leaf, a bear and a barber) which the hapless performer was quite unable to repeat. Next year, Foote staged a series of rival one-man lectures at the Haymarket, featuring the trial of Sam Smatter, 'alias Would-be, alias Mimic, alias Buffoon, alias Critt, alias Wit, alias Beau, alias fine Gentleman, and vulgarly called Esquire, for a public Cheat, and Imposter ... . The whole Public are summoned to be on the Jury, Common Sense their Foreman ...'.[49] As the language of the alias confirms, Foote set out to expose Macklin's manufacture of his own celebrity. The satire, in which Foote portrayed Macklin sitting in his armchair, examining a pupil in the classics and boasting of his own rhetorical superiority to Aristophanes, Cicero and Roscius, gaily lampooned the actor's egotistical and convoluted style of oratory and his extraordinary intellectual vanity.[50]

The Inquisition became a great success: Macklin came to see the show and was deeply hurt by the cruelty of Foote's portrait; retaliation and further mud-slinging followed. Meanwhile, the theatrical coffee house rapidly lost custom: Foote's show seems to have precipitated this financial collapse, though Macklin's waiters also embezzled the funds.[51] Not long afterwards, Macklin gave up and locked his doors, 'all animosity was laid aside' and the two celebrated actors came to shake hands at the Bedford.[52] But whilst Foote managed to profit from the controversy to the tune of £500, Macklin was declared a bankrupt two years later. Again, Foote's comic trial of Macklin's monarchical pretensions seems to have capitalised on contemporary anxieties about the burgeoning democratisation of fame.

What is unprecedented about fame in mid-eighteenth-century culture is the determination of audiences to define and participate in the making and unmaking of idols.[53] The frequent references to Foote and Garrick which pepper Boswell's *Life of Johnson* (1791) exemplify the significance of performers in this transformation.[54] By the 1760s, the construction and authenticity of Garrick's fame was coming under increasing scrutiny. In a string of letters first published in the *Craftsman*, Thaddeus Fitzpatrick argued that 'the too indulgent public' had enabled Garrick to acquire 'a large stock of fame, upon the credit of theatrical science, which you never possessed'. Fitzpatrick goes on to list Garrick's various 'histrionic blemishes' in a range of characters. But the letters – purportedly sent from coffee-houses including the Bedford and George's in Temple Bar – also expose Garrick's active manipulation of his own reputation. Fitzpatrick accuses Garrick of dismissing his rivals, jealously avoiding the performance of stock plays starring Mrs Cibber, and promoting himself through a claque of 'trusty and well-beloved adulators' paid to clap on cue at Drury Lane and then to talk up Garrick's interpretations at the coffee-houses. By summoning the nation's most famous actor 'before the tribunal of reason', Fitzpatrick set out to make this 'theatrical idol' accountable to his public.[55]

In *A Treatise on the Passions* (1747), Foote had criticised Garrick's portrayal of King Lear, notably his 'unmanly Sniveling' during the curse at the end of Act I.[56] The controversy generated by this attack[57] revealed the commercial and ideological power of Garrick as a subject for satire. At rehearsals and in company, Foote delighted in upstaging Garrick with his own witty repartee; he also liked to expose aspects of the actor's private life, especially his alleged parsimony. At the end of rehearsals, Foote would enquire whether the Garricks might have sufficient food to invite him for dinner that night 'without infringing on your servants generosity, for I know they are on board wages? Besides, the kitchen fire may be gone out if it be one of your cold meat days ...'.[58]

The relationship between the two men was an unstable one which veered between friendship, rivalry and intense hostility. As Tate Wilkinson remarked: 'Foote never was in awe of Garrick, but ever treated him with the most cutting satire, and well knew the way to profit from Garrick, was by always acting on his fears.'[59] An envious man with a sadistic streak, Foote enjoyed challenging Garrick's power, as well as exploiting the actor's intense vulnerability to ridicule. As he pointedly remarked, 'My friend David is like a man without a skin, the least touch in the world makes him wince.'[60] Foote also represented – and, more importantly, threatened to represent – Garrick on stage. In *Auction of Pictures*, Foote laughed at his rival's fame by associating his character with the sale of dead meat. Rather than simply parodying Garrick's acting, Foote allegedly persuaded a butcher from Clare-Market, who resembled the actor, to appear on stage dressed as a poet, in order to burlesque Garrick's farce, *Lethe*. The substitution of butcher for theatrical idol is wonderfully succinct in its destructive exchange of vulgarity and bloody animal products for genius and social respectability. The stunt represents a classic example of Foote's malicious desire to 'serve up' his rival actor as 'the maimed, not perfect Garrick'.[61]

Foote's mockery exploited a current of suspicion and hostility about the cult of Garrick[62] for his own commercial advantage; Garrick, meanwhile, began to discover some of the perils of life as a celebrity. Foote advertised, but never performed, a skit called the 'Drugger's Jubilee' (a burlesque parody of Garrick's Stratford Jubilee celebrations in 1769): the rain which made a mockery of the occasion represented, in Foote's view, God's revenge against Garrick's grasping desire for money and his egregious vanity.[63] The 'Devil's Definition' of the Jubilee (incorporated into *The Devil upon Two Sticks*), gives some clues about the kind of exposure planned by Foote: the Devil describes the entertainments as a series of duplicitous illusions, including 'a masquerade where half the people appeared bare-faced ... and a gingerbread amphitheatre, which, like a house of cards, tumbled to pieces as soon as it was finished'.[64] Though Garrick's friends seem to have persuaded him to abandon this show, Foote did respond to the Shakespearean pageant (mounted by Garrick in the hope of recouping the losses from the Jubilee) with an acerbic Prologue in which he accused his rival of having '... sunk a people's taste / Chill'd their fine fires, their solid sense debased'.[65]

A few years later, Foote let it be known that Garrick was to have a starring role in his new entertainment, the Primitive Puppet Show. A lady of fashion was alleged to have asked the playwright, 'Pray, Sir, are your puppets to be as large as life?' 'Oh dear, Madam, no,' Foote replied, 'not much above the size of Garrick!'[66] On this occasion, Garrick seems to have intervened, perhaps with an offer of money to buy himself immunity from this humiliation; the offending puppet never actually appeared.[67] But Foote's publicity served its purpose: so excited was the crowd outside the Haymarket on the first night that spectators actually broke down the doors to get into the theatre, scattering hats, swords, canes and cloaks across the house.[68] The disorder vividly evokes the audience's desire – a desire bordering on violence – to participate in the buying and selling of character. But do we also hear in the clattering of canes and swords a desire to witness the destruction of a theatrical icon?

Enter Mrs Coles

Actors, however, were only one of the kinds of public personalities represented by Samuel Foote. Eccentric orators, quack doctors, antiquaries and bluestockings like Catherine Macaulay, not to mention a huge number of modern profiteers from nabobs to marriage brokers, found themselves being exhibited on Foote's stage. The controversy surrounding *The Author* (Drury Lane, 1757) and *The Minor* (Haymarket, 1760) reminds us just how unprecedented were Foote's satiric exhibitions of public characters.

The seed for *The Author* was sown when a naïve but affable man named Apreece approached Foote and asked to be represented on stage. Like those individuals who volunteer to participate in reality television shows, Apreece clearly believed that the resulting publicity would enhance his reputation and political career. Indeed, so determined was the man to be identified in Foote's character that he apparently lent the actor a suit of his clothes.[69] The result was a highly successful play called *The Author* featuring the inimitable Mr Cadwallader (played by Foote), an inarticulate and supremely vulgar character obsessed with his prodigious family pedigree, and his illiterate and ignorant wife, Becky (played by Kitty Clive). Foote's caricature brilliantly captured the oddities of this corpulent individual, notably his habit of constantly moving his head towards his shoulder. The identity of the latest Haymarket victim quickly began to circulate in assembly rooms and at the coffee-houses. The play's catchphrases soon passed into fashionable conversation: '*Becky – my dear Becky*, was a constant phrase from all ranks of people both high and low, as they walked the streets of London'.[70] As Apreece discovered, Foote's play had stolen his identity only to replace it with a new character called Cadwallader. By the next season, Apreece was determined to destroy his own stage character. Having failed to persuade Foote to withdraw the play, Apreece turned up uninvited at a Drury Lane rehearsal and a lively altercation (later continued at the Rose Tavern) ensued. Eventually, the Lord Chamberlain complied with Apreece's request and *The Author* was withdrawn from the stage. But Foote successfully revived the piece after Apreece's death: 84 performances took place in London between 1769 and 1776.

Whereas *The Author* was a play created to mock a man's insatiable desire for fame, *The Minor* marks a new kind of savage iconoclasm in Foote's satires. The controversy stirred up by the play also made it one of Foote's most profitable works: 140 performances in London alone between 1760 and 1777, with rival versions being played at Drury Lane and Covent Garden Theatres in the autumn of 1760. *The Minor* departs from Foote's previous works in its controversial choice of subject matter (religious oratory) and in its technique of exhibiting a public character (Jennie Douglas, the notorious London bawd)[71] as satirical intermediary for the main target of Foote's mimicry (the Methodist preacher, George Whitefield). This process of comic substitution or satirical metonymy gave Foote a new kind of licence to shock and entertain his spectators. It is sometimes pointed out that Foote's play simply recycles familiar conventions of anti-Methodist satire, but such an argument misses the point: what made this play so outrageous was Foote's blasphemous conflation of the rhetoric of Methodism and the business of prostitution.[72]

To have exhibited George Whitefield as a character on the Haymarket stage would have incurred a charge of libel or have led to the play's suppression by the Lord Chamberlain. Instead, Foote satirises the language of Methodist reformation by embodying its rhetoric through a character who clearly has no reputation to defend. The result is a wonderfully humorous piece of ventriloquism. Foote presents Mrs Coles as a rheumatic old bawd who has been piloted 'into the harbour of grace' during her most recent illness by Mr Squintum (a well-known nickname for Whitefield). Despite her attraction to the language of spiritual reformation, Mrs Cole is still in the business of selling sex. Indeed, much of the satire on Whitefield in this play arises from the farcical disjunction between Mrs Cole's ostensible piety and her determination to clinch a deal with young George for one of her girls. In the original production, the epilogue to *The Minor* featured a miniature sermon, performed by Foote in the manner of Whitefield, in which the preacher attacked the immorality of the Haymarket Theatre and predicted that the audience would end up in hell 'for Satan's benefit'. But in the autumn of 1760, this epilogue was suppressed after the Lord Chamberlain's intervention.

When Foote revised the play for the Haymarket (the first production in Dublin had been unsuccessful), he cast himself as Mrs Coles and also took the part of a mimic named Shift. In the introduction, the prompter explains that the part of the bawd will be taken by Foote: an actress called Mrs O-Shochnesy has refused the role on the grounds of gentility. Despite this air of contingency, the revised play deliberately exploits the simultaneous presence – in the protean body of the celebrated Samuel Foote – of bawd, mimic, actor-manager, auctioneer and Methodist preacher. Moreover, so successful was Foote's imitation of Jennie Douglas that metropolitan bawds soon began to be referred to as Mrs Coles.

Foote's multiple roles in this play represent an act of self-conscious virtuosity: the protean transformations characteristic of shows like *Tea* and *Auction* now migrate into the genre of comedy. The overlaying and conflation of characters both real and fictional is compounded by Foote's decision to play the new character of Shift in imitation of his celebrated fellow mimic, Tate Wilkinson.[73] The presence of a mimic among the play's *dramatis personae* is particularly telling because Foote deploys this character to exhibit the mutual interdependence of mimicry and celebrity. Shift is employed by Sir William Wealthy to help expose a group of sharpers who are preying on his son, George. Mimicry, Shift explains, is a practice which knows no limits of person (Foote himself liked to emphasise the egalitarian character

Figure 5.2 Mr. Foote as Mrs. Cole in *The Minor* (1777). Engraving published by T. Lowndes and Partners. Courtesy of the Victorian and Albert Picture Library.

of mimicry), an art which 'makes meals' on fame and celebrity:

> Hum, – hum – Oh, Wednesday at Mr. Gammuit's near Hanover-square; there, there, I shall make a meal upon the Mingotti, for her ladyship is in the opera interest ... Thursday I dine upon the actors, with ten templers, at the Mitre in Fleet-Street ... in short ... there is not a buck or a turtle devoured within the bills of mortality, but there, I may, if I please, stick a napkin under my chin. (24)

This description cleverly fuses literal and metaphorical kinds of consumption: the eating of bucks and turtles and the consumption of celebrity. Shift presents his imitations as a form of sociable barter in which he dines upon his originals as well as on the desires of fashionable people to participate in the business of fame. Moreover, Shift's commercial acumen mirrors that of Mrs Coles: both these entrepreneurs deal in metropolitan bodies for sale.

The Minor generated a pamphlet war unprecedented in the history of the theatre because it seemed to violate implicit conventions about the 'proper objects of playhouse ridicule'.[74] According to Martin Madan, Foote had moved from 'scurrilous reflections' (*The Author*) into the arena of 'direct blasphemy'. Foote, he alleged, jumbles together 'things the most holy and profane ... putting the most sacred expressions in to the mouths of the most profligate and vile'; to add insult to injury, the Epilogue 'attempts to bring divine worship into ridicule, by turning his audience into a congregation, and preaching them a sermon'.[75] As such pamphlets confirm, the production of *The Minor* seemed to mark a new offensiveness in Foote's career. The play's success enhanced Foote's notoriety, filled his pockets and convinced him of spectators' appetite for the defamation of public figures.

Sexual scandal

Foote's public image, it has been argued, changed markedly in the years following his acquisition of the Haymarket patent. But I would dispute the idea that Foote abandoned his Aristophanic identity to become 'part of the theatrical establishment'.[76] Rather, he began to exploit the power of his institutional position as a licensed mimic to stage even more daring representations of celebrated figures in late eighteenth-century society. Sexual transgression – already a profitable and controversial undercurrent in *The Minor* – now returned to the Haymarket stage in striking forms. The two plays discussed here take as their targets women whose celebrity was being forged in the crucible of sexual scandal. Indeed, Foote compounded his audacity by depicting the crimes of these notorious women, albeit obliquely, before their trials had taken place. These scandalous exhibitions mark the pinnacle, and the threatened disintegration, of Foote's celebrity.

Foote's production of plays starring characters notorious for a specific action, rather than for their singularity or eccentricity as individuals, is notable. Physical features and mannerisms (a squint, a particular movement of the head) had dominated his satirical stage during the 1750s and 1760s. But the exhibition of women, let alone women charged with forgery or bigamy, raised different questions about character. The theatrical body, in these plays, is no longer presented as a 'telltale transcript' of a well-known human being. Rather, in both *The Cozeners* and *A Trip to Paris*, Foote starts to highlight the motives of his protagonists. To adapt the language used by Deidre Lynch, Foote begins to 'flesh out' his theatre of celebrity.[77]

In exposing women like the celebrated forger Caroline Rudd and the bigamous Duchess of Kingston, Foote capitalised on his subjects' extraordinary notoriety and their reputation for unbridled passion, 'consummate artifice' and deceit.[78] But these plays also participate in the unprecedented media frenzy surrounding the indictment and trial of these women. Ironically, Foote's only attempt to represent an aristocrat on the Haymarket stage led to his own disgrace. The editor William Jackson exploited the controversy surrounding the Duchess by embarking on a vicious smear campaign against Foote, involving accusations of blackmail and attempted homosexual assault, which ended up in the courts and arguably broke Foote's health and spirits in the final years of his life.[79] The story of that disgrace offers some fascinating insights into the proximity of celebrity and libel in this period. What I want to explore here, however, is Foote's reinvention of himself as the satirist of celebrity scandal.

The Cozeners (Haymarket, 1774, revised version 1775) and *The Trip to Calais* (1775, not performed)[80] present women whose crimes seemed to undermine society's most fundamental assumptions about the nature of femininity. Both Mrs Rudd and the Duchess were adulteresses; both had used sexual charisma to deceive and manipulate the opposite sex. The crimes of Kingston and Rudd seemed to undermine the integrity of marriage as an institution and to threaten the stability of the nation's financial systems; their trials created excitement and controversy (courts packed with fashionable spectators, dozens of column inches in the newspapers) on a scale which matches that produced by global media trials in our own culture.[81] Foote's plays exploit the moral panic which surrounded these women's crimes; in particular, they delight in exposing the private lives of notorious suspects.

In 1774, Foote produced *The Cozeners*, a play of roguery and chicanery, full of topical references to contemporary scandals and recent events. The main protagonist here is a character called Mrs Fleece'em, based on the notorious matchmaker Mrs Grieve who had duped Charles James Fox by promising him a West Indian woman with a fortune of £150,000. Foote incorporates the most notorious details of Mrs Grieve's exploits as reported in contemporary newspapers, notably her shrewd decision to pay the porters and coachmen of famous men like Lord North to stand outside her door as publicity for her business. Whereas earlier plays had simply tried to reproduce the clothes, gestures and mannerisms of a particular character, *The Cozeners* invites audiences to witness Mrs Grieve's ingenious duplicity in action; the physiognomic exhibition of character gives way to a more psychological approach featuring the theatrical reinvention of real-life events. A good example of this phenomenon is the play's virtual transcription of Grieve's method of duping Fox in which Mrs Fleece'em arranges for the delivery of a black girl from America as a match for a young man named Toby Aircastle.

By the next year, Foote's portrait of a female adventurer preying upon the gullibility of men had acquired new connotations as a symbol of contemporary moral disorder. In the spring of 1775, London society was awaiting what would become one of the most celebrated trials of the late eighteenth century. The defendants, identical twins called Robert and Daniel Perreau, had been imprisoned pending trial on charges of forgery: at their trial, however, the brothers would insist that they had been the victims of an elaborate trap laid by Daniel's lover, Margaret Caroline Rudd, a beautiful and famously extravagant courtesan with an insatiable desire to belong to the fashionable world. Mrs Rudd, however, was acquitted and the brothers were hanged the following year. Although Garrick would refuse to stage a play by Hugh Kelly which included a character resembling Mrs Rudd,[82] Foote had no such qualms. On the contrary, he delighted in the Haymarket's position as the capital's stage of celebrity. In particular, he relished his unique power, through an idiosyncratic blend of living characters and fictional identities, to triumph over rival organs of personality by exhibiting Mrs Rudd on stage.

Rather than risk prosecution by dealing with the forgery charge directly, Foote exhibits his subject's notorious duplicity through the character of Mrs Fleece'em: Grieve and Rudd are thereby reconfigured as a single, composite character. In the scene added to the play (and based, like the original script, on contemporary report), Mrs Fleece'em dupes a silk mercer named Paul Prig in Ludgate Hill.[83] Having purchased several hundred pounds worth of silks, Mrs Fleece'em tells the shopkeeper that she has left her purse on the table at home. She offers to take the mercer in her coach to her attorney's in order to have the bill paid, but actually delivers him to a celebrated doctor named Hellebore. Here, she presents Prig as her uncle and explains that he is subject to 'distractions': 'Last week he supposed himself a young nestling crow'; now 'he supposes himself a mercer on Ludgate Hill' who has sold her a parcel of silks. After a wonderfully nonsensical discussion with the hapless Prig, in which the most innocent responses are construed as irrefutable evidence of the man's delusions, the doctor decides that he should be confined immediately in a Chelsea madhouse: 'And, as you see he is violent, let him have the back room, with the barrr'd windows, up two pair of stairs.'

We can glimpse in this scene a significant change in Foote's representation of celebrity. The scene is notable for its spectacular amorality: here is an individual prepared to send a man to a madhouse in order to fulfil her desire for fashionable clothes. Indeed, Foote is clearly fascinated by this brilliant piece of criminal improvisation. The play hints at a certain pleasurable complicity, as if to acknowledge the playwright's sneaking regard for his notorious subject. But Foote's exhibition of Rudd differs markedly from his portrayal of characters such as Apreece or Whitefield. What the spectators watch is the reconstruction on stage of an episode from life, shaped so as to reveal the workings of a criminal personality. The silk-stealing anecdote succinctly proves Rudd's brilliance as a manipulator of other people, but it also reveals the psychological lens of Foote's late theatre. Moreover, this scene must surely have been interpreted as an oblique commentary on Rudd's presumed guilt. Such was Foote's conviction about the immunity of his satires in the eyes of the law that he now dared to anticipate the judgment of the courts.

The satirical target of Foote's next play had become one of the most talked about individuals in late eighteenth-century Britain. As a young woman, Elizabeth Chudleigh had scandalised society by appearing at a Ranelagh masquerade dressed as Iphigenia in a largely diaphanous costume (Foote apparently complimented her on being the most perfect Venus de Medici he had ever seen in public, whereupon she turned on her heel, declaring him to be 'the most impudent wretch upon earth');[84] by 1774, as the Duchess of Kingston, she had been indicted on the charge of having contracted a bigamous marriage.[85] Her trial in April 1776 became one of the social events of the decade. Tickets, which started at the extraordinary price of 20 guineas, changed hands for vast sums on the black market; 4,000 fashionable spectators, including Hannah More and Mrs Garrick, queued to watch the drama unfold in Westminster Hall.[86] After six days of evidence, the Lords found the Duchess guilty: she escaped branding on the hand only by invoking the privilege of the peerage and then managed to flee to the continent.

In the early summer of 1775, Foote began his publicity campaign for a new play initially entitled *The Siege of Calais*. Advertisements prepared the way for the theatrical exposure of the Duchess by announcing that 'the groundwork of the piece is to be the *dénouement* of a certain *Double Marriage*, that has lately made so much noise in the polite world, and among the lawyers'.[87] But the newspapers were soon declaring that the Lord Chamberlain would refuse permission to perform the play; it emerged that the Duchess had seen a copy and demanded its suppression. The interdiction produced tremendous controversy 'and furnished matter for much conversation in the dramatic and polite world'.[88] Infuriated by his loss of profit, Foote threatened to publish *The Trip* and dedicate it to the Duchess. She responded by calling a private meeting with Foote at which she offered to pay him not to produce the play: Foote defiantly refused. It was later claimed that he demanded £3,000 to prevent publication.[89] The playwright then proceeded to publish his correspondence with the Duchess in the *Evening Post*. His letters, shrewd, acerbic and utterly callous, contrast with her agitated desperation, unwitting self-exposure and (to Foote, at least) her unconvincing assumption of pathetic femininity.

Foote's satire on Elizabeth Chudleigh is a piece of psychological caricature in farcical form. Again, he circumvents the legal problem of representing the Duchess's crime by making his notorious heroine an advocate of bigamy rather than a bigamist herself. The tyrannical Lady Kitty therefore adjudicates the dilemma faced by a young woman called Jenny by suggesting that she might reconcile everyone by agreeing to marry two men.[90] As in *The Cozeners*, Foote exploits theatre's metonymic power to tell a story which both rehearses and avoids the charge of libel. At the same time, Foote trumps gossipy publications like the *Town and Country* by allowing his spectators the voyeuristic pleasure of eavesdropping on the Duchess's private life. Lady Kitty's hyperbolic transports of grief for her departed husband, elaborately staged in the Chamber of Tears, reveal her as a sophisticated self-publicist driven by a voracious sexual appetite and an insatiable hunger for power.

The Trip confirms the transition in Foote's work from the physiognomy to the psychology of character. This is a show which sets out to offer the audience a farcical interpretation of the criminal action which has made the Duchess a celebrity. It is a cruel and vindictive portrait devoid of the playfulness which characterised some of the earlier satires. Indeed, by fuelling suspicions about his own sexuality, Foote's misogyny may well have contributed to his own disgracing at the hands of Jackson. Again, performance has become a form of legal theatre. Foote's exhibition of his society's most notorious women marks the Haymarket's position as another kind of courtroom, a comic place of prosecution.[91]

According to a contemporary, Samuel Foote 'was without doubt the dramatic comet of his time'.[92] This unaccountable wit and mimic, steeped in the traditions of Greek and Roman comedy, created a new kind of celebrity satire in Britain. He capitalised on an intense uncertainty in eighteenth-century culture about the ability of public figures to create their own celebrity through the agency of the media and by their control and manipulation of images, institutions and performances. Through the medium of satire, Foote exploited the public's willingness to scrutinise celebrated individuals and to adjudicate on the authenticity of their fame.

At the same time, Foote cashed in on the public's seemingly inexhaustible desire – then as now – for the exhibition of fame. His living portraits were distinctive not simply for their ingenuity and physical likeness, but for their clever, self-conscious blending of real and fictional identities: his originality lay in the liberties he took with character, liberties both ethical and imaginative. As we have seen, the ethical status of these stage characters – their daring proximity to defamation, ridicule, abuse and even libel – became a matter of heated controversy. From a variety of perspectives, then, his life and works dramatise the intricate and scandalous relationships between theatre, celebrity and the print marketplace in the mid-eighteenth century.

Notes

1. *General Advertiser*, 24 April 1747.
2. For invaluable advice on an earlier draft of this essay, I am most grateful to Tracy C. Davis, Mary Luckhurst, Shearer West and Peter Thomson.
3. *The Roman and English Comedy Consider'd and Compar'd* ... (London: T. Waller, 1747), p. 7.
4. See further, Matthew Kinservik, *Disciplining Satire: The Censorship of Satiric Comedy on the Eighteenth-Century London Stage* (Lewisburg, PA: Bucknell University Press, 2002), especially chapters 3 and 4.
5. On Foote's delight in his own power, see *An Additional Scene to the Comedy of the Minor* (London: J. Williams, 1761), p. 10, where Dapperwit (clearly based on Foote) declares, 'I have the town under my thumb; – I can take 'em thus and twirl them about like a top'. Various commentators in this period refer to Foote as Aristophanes; the mimic George Saville Carey also exhibited a character called Aristophanes in his *Lecture on Mimicry* at the Great Room, Panton Street, in the Haymarket during the summer of 1774.
6. *Journal of a Tour to the Hebrides* ed. Frederick A. Pottle and Charles H. Bennett (London: William Heinemann, 1963), pp. 382–3.
7. See Deidre Lynch's magisterial study, *The Economy of Character: Novels, Market Culture, and the Business of Inner Meaning* (Chicago, IL: University of Chicago Press, 1998), especially chapter 1.
8. Horace Walpole, who saw the play from a box shared with Macaulay, remarked that she 'goes to see herself represented, and I suppose figures herself very like Socrates'. See *The Letters of Horace Walpole, fourth Earl of Oxford*, ed. Peter Cunningham, 9 vols (Edinburgh: John Grant, 1906), V, 108. Foote seems to have obtained some cast-off wigs from the composer Dr Thomas Arne and then introduced him on the stage in his play, *The Commissary*. See Joseph Cradock, *Literary and Miscellaneous Memoirs*, 4 vols (London: J. B. Nichols, 1828), I, p. 33.
9. James Boswell, *The Life of Samuel Johnson*, first published 1791 (London: Oxford University Press, new edition, 1953), p. 580.
10. *A Complete History of the Stage*, 5 vols (London: printed for the author, 1797–1800), V, p. 143.
11. See 'The Cult of Celebrity', in Jacqueline Rose, *On Not Being Able to Sleep: Psychoanalysis and the Modern World* (London: Vintage, 2004), p. 211.
12. *The Trial of Samuel Foote* (1763), printed in Tate Wilkinson, *The Wandering Patentee; or, A History of the Yorkshire Theatres*, 4 vols (York, 1795), IV, p. 253. Damages of £300 were awarded against Foote, but the actor jumped bail without paying the fine and returned to England.
13. Review in *Town and Country Magazine; or, Universal Repository of Knowledge, Instruction and Entertainment* (June 1770), p. 294.
14. 'Bipes', letter printed in *Universal Museum and Complete Magazine*, June 1776, pp. 294–5, cited Simon Trefnam, *Sam. Foote, Comedian, 1720–1777* (New York: New York University Press, 1971), p. 161.
15. See Tate Wilkinson's comments about Foote's show rousing 'the indignation and resentment of all the performers' in *Memoirs of his Own Life*, 4 vols (London: G. G. J. and J. Robinson, 1790), I, p. 23.

16 David Erskine Baker, *Biographia Dramatica; or, A Companion to the Playhouse* ... 2 vols, revised edition (London, 1782), pp. 167–8.
17 Wilkinson, *Memoirs of his Own Life*, I, p. 24.
18 [David Williams], *A Letter to David Garrick Esq. on his conduct as principal manager and actor at Drury-lane* (London: J. Williams, first published 1772, 2nd edition, 1776), pp. 8–9. Players like Kitty Clive also imitated foreign performers such as Mingotti, the Italian operatic star. See Tate Wilkinson, *Memoirs of his Own Life*, II, p. 29, on Clive's defence of this practice.
19 Charles Churchill, *The Rosciad* (London, 1761), p. 7.
20 Boswell, *The Life of Samuel Johnson*, p. 465.
21 The *Lecture on Heads* was first produced in 1764 and featured caricatures of well-known satirical types like the fop, presented through a selection of caricature heads accompanied by topical patter. Notably, the same decade saw a significant expansion in the circulation of 'heads' when Josiah Wedgewood began to sell his images of modern public figures.
22 Wilkinson, *Memoirs of his Own Life*, I, p. 25.
23 Wilkinson, *Memoirs of his Own Life*, II, p. 20. Wilkinson performed memorable imitations of Foote in some of his most celebrated parts including Lady Pentweazle (*Taste*) and Mr Cadwallader (*The Author*).
24 Peg Woffington made strenuous attempts to avoid being caricatured on stage. In 1758, one of her admirers, Colonel Caesar, waited on Garrick, relating his objections 'in point of delicacy and honour' and suggesting that Garrick would be 'called upon as a gentleman' in the event of her appearance. Garrick subsequently instructed Foote and Wilkinson that the character of Peg Woffington was now out of bounds in their satires and that Wilkinson 'should not take the liberty to make any line, speech, or manner, relative to Mrs. Woffington, or presume to offer or occasion any surmise of likeness, so as to give the least shadow of offence ...' See Wilkinson, *Memoirs of his Own Life*, II, pp. 14–15.
25 The letter may have been written by Wilkinson's fellow dramatist, Arthur Murphy. Cf. Fielding's attack on Foote's practice of 'suffering private Characters to be ridiculed by Mimickry and Buffoonery upon his Stage' in the *Jacobite's Journal*, 6 February 1748. But this may be simply a case of the pot calling the kettle black.
26 *An Additional Scene to the Comedy of the Minor*, p. 19.
27 Churchill, *The Rosciad*, p. 14; cf. Robert Lloyd, *The Actor. A Poetical Epistle* (London: R. and J. Dodsley, 1760).
28 Wilkinson, *Memoirs of his Own Life*, II, p. 19. Cp. the introduction to *The Minor* where Foote acknowledges that performers do indeed have the best ground for complaint about caricature, precisely because 'by rendering them ridiculous in their profession, you, at the same time, injure their pockets'. *The Plays of Samuel Foote*, ed. Paula R. Backscheider and Douglas Howard, 3 vols (New York: Garland, 1983), II. All references will be to this edition, hereafter cited as *Plays*.
29 [George Saville Carey], *Momus, a poem: or a critical examination of the performers, and comic pieces, at the Theatre-Royal in the Hay-Market* (London: printed for the author, 1767), p. 17.
30 [Carey], *Momus*, p. 17.
31 Cf. Catherine Lumby, *Gotcha: Life in a Tabloid World* (London: Allen and Unwin, 1999), p. 129.
32 On Foote's profits, see further, William J. Burling, *Summer Theatre in London, 1661–1820, and the Rise of the Haymarket Theatre* (Madison, NJ: Fairleigh Dickinson University Press, 2000), p. 121 and, more generally, chapter 4.

33 The most recent study of this crucial institution is Markman Ellis, *The Coffee House: A Cultural History* (London: Weidenfeld and Nicolson, 2004).
34 Genius, *Memoirs of the Bedford Coffee-House* (London: J. Single, 1763), p. 5.
35 [Thaddeus Fitzpatrick], *Enquiry into the Real Merit of a Certain Popular Performer* (London: M. Thrush, 1760), pp. 35–6.
36 William Cooke, *Memoirs of Charles Macklin, Comedian* (London: James Asperne, 1804), p. 206.
37 [Williams], *A Letter to David Garrick*, p. 2.
38 *General Advertiser*, 28 April and 1 May 1747.
39 *General Advertiser*, 28 March 1749.
40 *General Advertiser*, 21 April 1747.
41 Act II, scene i in *Plays*, vol. III. Horne Tooke responded in good part, admitting in a letter to Junius (*Public Advertiser*, 13 July 1771) that 'my Clothes were lawful Game'.
42 [Benjamin] Victor, *The History of the Theatres of London. From the Year 1760 to the Present Time* (London: T. Becket, 1771), pp. 192–3 remarks on the topicality of *The Devil upon Two Sticks*. At the end of the play, Foote 'always gave some humorous Stroke of Satire, upon the Pleasures, or Circumstances of the Day – the *Bal paree* at Ranelagh – the *Ridotto al Fresco*, at Vauxhall – the *Disputes of the Covent-Garden Managers* – and, above all, the *Stratford Jubilee*, and its *Author*'.
43 For a groundbreaking discussion about the relationships between theatricality and performativity, see *Theatricality*, ed. Tracy C. Davis and Thomas Postlewait (Cambridge: Cambridge University Press, 2003), especially the editors' superb introduction.
44 On the increasing number of libel cases brought by leading politicians in the 1770s and 1780s, see Lucyle Werkmeister, *The London Daily Press, 1772–1792* (Lincoln, NE: University of Nebraska, 1963).
45 Wilkinson, *Memoirs of his Own Life*, II, p. 50, claims that he was offered money and 'genteel presents not to be too free as an imitator'.
46 *Whipping Rods, for trifling, scurrhill, scriblers; as F-t on taste...* (London: M. Cooper, 1752), p. 1.
47 *The Patron,* Act I, in *Plays*, II, p. 17.
48 See *Public Advertiser*, 3 and 10 December 1754. On Macklin's innovation producing a distinct interruption in 'the reign of wit' at the Bedford, see *Memoirs of the Bedford Coffee-House*, p. 73.
49 *Public Advertiser*, 14 December 1754.
50 John Bernard, *Retrospections of the Stage*, 2 vols (London: Colburn and Bentley, 1830), II, pp. 122–4.
51 See *Public Advertiser*, 10 December 1754: 'Mr. Macklin humbly desires that those Gentlemen who shall call for any Thing in the Coffee-room will pay at the Bar, and not to the Waiters.'
52 *Memoirs of the Bedford Coffee-House*, p. 75.
53 Leo Braudy, *The Frenzy of Renown: Fame and its History* (New York: Vintage, 1986), p. 381.
54 Boswell, *The Life of Samuel Johnson*, pp. 417–19, 465, 580, 686, 768–9, 925, 1237.
55 The letters were then published in a pamphlet. See [Thaddeus Fitzpatrick], *Enquiry into the Real Merit of a Certain Popular Performer*, op. cit. Fitzpatrick would apparently stand up in the pit and whinny in protest at the most heartrending moments of Garrick's performances as King Lear.

56 *A Treatise on the Passions, so far as they regard the stage* ... (London: C. Corbett [1747]), p. 17.
57 On the objections he received for 'impeaching' Garrick's performance see *The Roman and English Comedy Consider'd and Compar'd* ... , p. 4.
58 Wilkinson, *Memoirs of his Own Life*, II, p. 22. Wilkinson also burlesqued Garrick in his pirated production of *The Minor*. In his memoirs, he recalls the audience's echoing murmurs of 'O Garrick! Garrick!' when he imitated the actor's interpretation of Macbeth. From that night on until the day of his death, Wilkinson alleges, Garrick never spoke to him again. See Tate Wilkinson, *Memoirs of his Own Life*, III, p. 27.
59 On Garrick's obsession with image making, see further Leigh Woods, *Garrick Claims the Stage: Acting as Social Emblem in Eighteenth-Century England* (Westport, CT: Greenwood Press, 1984).
60 *Aristophanes, being a classic collection of true attic wit, containing the jests, gibes, bonmots, witticisms, and most extraordinary anecdotes of Samuel Foote, Esq. ... by a Gentleman, who was a constant Companion to the Wits of his Time* (London: Robert Baldwin, 1778), p. xi.
61 Wilkinson, *Memoirs of his Own Life*, II, p. 23.
62 See [David Williams], *A Letter to David Garrick* which accuses the actor of buying fame through the purchase of newspaper shares and of miscasting other actors in order to enhance his own stardom.
63 William Cooke, *Memoirs of Samuel Foote, Esq. with a Collection of his Genuine Bon-Mots, Anecdotes, Opinions, &c. Mostly Original*, 3 vols (London: Richard Phillips, 1805), II, pp. 85–6.
64 *Town and Country* (September 1769), p. 477.
65 *Town and Country* (May 1770), pp. 229–30. This produced a sharp attack from Philo-Technicus Miso-Mimides (pseudonym of Dr Paul Hiffernan?) in a broadside entitled *Foote's Prologue Detected; with a miniature-prose epilogue of his manner of speaking it* (London: J. Williams [1770]).
66 William Cooke, *Memoirs of Samuel Foote*, II, 58; on Foote's puppets, see also *The New Theatre of Fun; or, the modern Aristophanes in high glee. Being a genuine collection of the jest, gibes, witticisms ... of Samuel Foote, Esq.* (London: R Durfey, 1778), p. 5. The show was entitled *Piety in Pattens; or, The Handsome Housemaid*.
67 In a letter to the Countess of Ossory of 11 February 1773, Walpole remarked that 'Garrick, by the negotiation of a Secretary of State has made peace with Foote, and by the secret article of the treaty is to be left out of the puppet-show'. *The Letters of Horace Walpole*, V, p. 434.
68 *Gentleman's Magazine* 43 (February 1773), p. 101. Interestingly, some members of the audience were so disappointed by the show that 'a scene of disorder ensured' in which parts of the auditorium were destroyed.
69 Letter to the editor, *Town and Country Magazine* (November 1777), p. 600.
70 Tate Wilkinson, *Memoirs of his Own Life*, I, p. 146.
71 Mother Douglas appears in several engravings by William Hogarth including *Enthusiasm Delineated, Industry and Idleness* (plate ix) and *The March to Finchley*.
72 On the pamphlet war generated by *The Minor*, see M. M. Belden, *The Dramatic Work of Samuel Foote* (New Haven, CT: Yale University Press, 1929), chapter 3.
73 The *Gentleman's Magazine* 30 (June 1760), p. 326, remarked that this imitation of Wilkinson's 'quaint and pert loquacity of affectation and self conceit' was performed 'with inimitable humour'.
74 *Monthly Review* (July 1760), p. 83.

75 [Martin Madan], *Christian and critical remarks on a droll, or interlude, called The Minor. Now acting by a company of stage players in the Hay-market; and said to be acted by authority. In which the blasphemy, falsehood, and scurrility of that piece is properly considered, answered, and exposed* (London: Mr. Keith, 1760), pp. 21, 26–7.
76 See Kinservik, *Disciplining Satire*, p. 156.
77 Lynch, *The Economy of Character*, chapter 1.
78 The significance of this trial is skilfully presented by Donna T. Andrew and Randall McGowen in *The Perreaus and Mrs. Rudd: Forgery and Betrayal in Eighteenth-Century London* (Berkeley, CA: University of California Press, 2001).
79 The case is considered in detail in Matthew Kinservik's trenchant essay, 'Satire, Censorship, and Sodomy in Samuel Foote's *The Capuchin* (1776)', *Review of English Studies*, n.s. 54 (November 2003), 639–60.
80 Foote made major revisions to the play and then produced it at the Haymarket in August 1776 under the title of *The Capuchin*.
81 Public disagreement over the innocence or guilt of the Perreau brothers and Mrs Rudd mirrors in some respects the dominance of 'public opinion' in the trial of O. J. Simpson. On the latter as a defining event in modern mass media, see Catherine Lumby, *Gotcha: Life in a Tabloid World*, pp. 20–1. On the concept of 'tabloid justice', see further Richard L. Fox and Robert W. Van Sickel, *Tabloid Justice: Criminal Justice in an Age of Media Frenzy* (Boulder, CO: Lynne Rienner Publishers, 2001).
82 See his letter to Kelly, 16 October 1775, in *The Letters of David Garrick*, ed. David M. Little and George M. Kahrl, 3 vols (London: Oxford University Press, 1963), III, pp. 1039–40.
83 *The Cozeners*, Act III, scene i, in *Plays*, III.
84 William Cooke, *Memoirs of Samuel Foote*, II, p. 599.
85 Chudleigh was found to have embarked on a clandestine marriage to Captain Augustus Hervey, heir to the Earl of Bristol.
86 Cindy McCreery, *The Satirical Gaze: Prints of Women in Late Eighteenth-Century England* (Oxford: Clarendon, 2004).
87 *Town and Country* (May 1775), p. 259.
88 *Town and Country* (August 1775), p. 412.
89 For an account of the débâcle, including the correspondence, see *The Case of the Duchess of Kingston* (London: J. Wheble, 1775).
90 Act III, p. 84 in *Plays*, III.
91 Cp. the current popularity of legal docudramas including 'tribunal' plays, such as Richard Norton-Taylor, *Justifying the War* (Tricycle Theatre, 2003); and *Guantanamo: 'Honour Bound to Defend Freedom'* by Victoria Brittain and Gillian Slovo (Tricycle Theatre, 2004).
92 *Aristophanes*, p. xxxix.

6
The Celebrity of Edmund Kean: An Institutional Story
Jacky Bratton

Cultural analysis has begun to suggest that the period 1789–1830 staged crucial moments in the emergence of modern identities. It is not a new idea that the age of revolutions was the first act of the psychological drama of modernity; but now we are beginning to understand that the emergent modern self was literally as well as symbolically theatricalised – played out, explored and contested publicly in the theatres of late Georgian London. The celebrity of the great Romantic actor Edmund Kean is a fruitful case in point.

Kean occupied a significant symbolic position in late Georgian society. In theatrical terms, his remarkable rise was only the latest triumph of the 'natural' newcomer who suddenly exposes the theatrical establishment as stylised and old-fashioned. Kean undercut the formal grandeur of the Kemble school, which appeared patrician beside his revolutionary manner. The western acting tradition, posited on revealing truth, renews itself regularly by such re-concealments of its artifice. Like the previous natural genius of the stage, David Garrick, Kean was physically a small, unimpressive man who actually achieved his intensely moving 'spontaneous' stage effects by hard work and careful preparation; unlike Garrick the businessman, but like many stage celebrities before and after him, Kean's heady success carried him into a self-destructive cycle of excess so that by the time he died of drink only ingrained technical mastery was keeping him upright on the stage.

Kean further differed from the arch-bourgeois Garrick in that his celebrity marked a political as well as a theatrical extreme: *his* return to nature was read as an aspect of political and philosophical revolution. His contemporaries, whether radical or reactionary themselves, seized on him as the symbol of Romantic inspiration. His Victorian biographer, Thomas Colley Grattan, lined up Kean, Byron and Napoleon as three similarly reckless men, 'brain-fevered by success', 'straining for the world's applause'.[1] In understanding Kean as part of this constellation, it is important to see him as the lowest in the line, the merely symbolic celebrity – the potential scapegoat. Napoleon Bonaparte, whatever his origins, was the conqueror of the world, a towering presence even in defeat; Lord Byron, aristocrat as well as poetic genius, was more open to criticism but still ultimately his own (gentle)man; but Kean, a bastard child of players, a cockney pretender to greatness, was the creation of middle-class critical esteem, and completely vulnerable to its withdrawal. Vindictive reactionaries and disappointed radicals alike would come to punish Kean's transgression and mark in his fall their defeat of, or turning away from, Romantic idealism.

Generations of biographers have attempted to sort out the true story of the origins and rise of Edmund Kean.[2] I shall instead explore his fall. My interest here is in his celebrity as a function of the evolution of modern middle-class identities, as exemplified in the status-stripping catastrophe of the Cox vs. Kean prosecution in 1825, and the actor's ritual humiliation upon his reappearance on the legitimate stage at Drury Lane. The shifting contract between audience and players defines how public performance and spectatorship shape class and national identity. As we explore this relationship, the crises of theatrical management in the early nineteenth century emerge as markers of changing class self-definition and, moreover, issues of female agency and spectatorship are foregrounded as tools of that hegemonic negotiation. In twenty-first-century terms, we understand the possibility of the idol's rejection and humiliation as part of the contract between the celebrity and the fans, and Kean's fall conforms to the model in that it was partly self-induced, partly created by the sensation-seeking media and was focused upon the body.[3] But it also had institutional and class-political meanings. This essay focuses on Kean's handling as a celebrity by the nascent press, as part of the battle for control of the medium of theatre and its public influence and voice. Residual and emergent institutions contend here. On the one hand is the declining Drury Lane, representing the patent system, which in turn is a figure for patronage and its allied powers. Emergent forces are embodied in Robert Elliston, a stage professional who came to the management of Drury Lane from success at the illegitimate Surrey and the Birmingham Theatre Royal and tried to operate middle-class, business-oriented conceptions of contractual and financial relationships; and *The Times* newspaper, as the voice of public opinion in the process of articulation and rise to ascendancy. In the drama of the Cox/Kean affair, Romantic ideas about human aspiration come under attack by the next move in the formation of modern consciousness, the proto-Victorian conception and institutionalisation of the British public.

An earlier crisis point in the appropriation of the voice of the theatre for middle-class self-expression was, as Marc Baer has shown, the protracted battle of the Old Price (O.P.) riots at Covent Garden in 1809, when John Philip Kemble was forced by a concerted rebellion of the audience to back down from a re-organisation of the auditorium and reassignment of the rights of admission to its various parts. This moment has been represented, within the hegemonic theatre history that originated in the 1830s, as linked to 'the Decline of the Drama', evidence of the swamping of the patent houses by 'the mob' of lower-class uneducated sensation-seekers. Baer shows that, on the contrary, the O.P. rioters were led by rational and determined members of the literate classes asserting rights of possession in a symbolically important space of performance that, they believed, belonged to the playgoing public rather than to the immoral/exclusive box patrons, the prostitutes who served them, and the always temporary manager of the day.[4] Such an assertion of the power of rectitude and intellect was part of the rising radical tide, the sweep of events that would culminate in the Reform Acts of 1832.[5] I want to suggest that the Cox/Kean riots at Drury Lane were a further step in the appropriation of the theatre to the new hegemonic voice, and show a significant change – a class narrowing – in the audiences' self-definition. Since the Covent Garden confrontation, Drury Lane had also burnt down and been rebuilt, financed by a limited company that self-consciously positioned the theatre as a domain not of aristocratic patronage, but of the public sphere. It aimed at the 'revival' of the classic stage, figured as the expression of public opinion and civic virtue. Its Committee of Management, however, failed effectively to contest (or understand) the weight of custom and practice by which a patent theatre lived. It was not until the professional managerial expertise of Robert Elliston and his assistant James Winston took the house in 1819 and exploited the quasi-providential celebrity drawing-power of Edmund Kean that Drury Lane began to return to profit. I would suggest that by 1825 this reassertion of theatrical pragmatics, where the Committee's high-minded manipulation of the medium of theatre had failed, began to threaten the hegemonic ascendancy of the newly self-aware British public. It was contested by their self-appointed champion and voice, *The Times*, and its editor Thomas Barnes. I shall focus a discussion of this contestation through Barnes's long article of 1 February 1825 but begin with a background sketch.

The night of 31 January 1825, reported in Barnes's article (see Appendix to this chapter), was Edmund Kean's third appearance at Drury Lane after his appearance at the Court of King's Bench, in the City, to answer a charge of 'criminal conversation' – that is, seduction, the theft from another man of the affections of his wife – brought by Alderman Cox, who had demanded damages of £2,000. The jury, after ten minutes' deliberation, had awarded Cox £800. Complex changes in sexual morality are flagged by the prosecution and its outcome. The seduction of the eager City wife by the gentleman rake is a staple of comedy from the Restoration and the involvement of the stage and its stars in that sport was previously accepted. But when the cockney actor Kean performed the role of rake, in the real world of the 1820s, the response was different. Disdain for the usual butt, the Alderman, was signalled by the court's contemptuous devaluation of his broken heart; but the actor was also an offender. He had taken on himself the part of a gentleman, and had appropriated even the sacred words of Shakespeare in his letters and sex games; class outrage fuelled the backlash against his presumption. Kean reappeared at Drury Lane in his signature role of Richard III seven days later, and the nights of confrontation began.[6] The battle was short-lived: after 7 February it ceased, and on 26 March Kean made his final appearance, as Othello, to a reasonable (first price) house of £404 before departing on a provincial tour.

The importance of this confrontation was clear to contemporaries, and went well beyond partisanship for or reaction against an idolised actor. On 22 January, two days before Kean's first appearance after the trial, Winston recorded[7] that Sir Richard Birnie, the Bow Street magistrate who dealt with the theatres, had heard from the Secretary of State Robert Peel that Kean should not appear, presumably for fear of serious rioting. Nothing was done about this warning – according to Barnes's account, there were not even more police or soldiers present than usual; the bills warn that nobody will be admitted free, but this was always the case at Kean's expensive and well-attended appearances, so cannot be construed as intended to exclude elements who might cause trouble. In any case, such people obviously were let in. Press interest in the affair included the usual uses to which theatrical events were put – gleeful cashing in on a juicy topic in bawdy prints and broadsides; but it went much further. All the daily papers had opinions for or against Kean; and his most recent biographer, Raymond Fitzsimons, suggests that *The Times* was responsible for setting the opposition on foot.[8] Certainly, Thomas Barnes, its editor from 1817 to 1841, and the man whose vision shaped the paper's Victorian pre-eminence, was by no means a neutral reporter of a confrontation that he recorded in obsessive and tendentious detail. His leaders appeared for several days, denouncing 'That obscene little personage (Mr KEAN)' and spelling out his offence: 'It is of little consequence to the nation whether the character of King Richard or Othello be well or ill acted; but it is of importance that public feeling be not shocked, and public decency be not outraged.'[9]

The central issue, in Barnes's rhetorical construction, is not simply Kean's sexual activities nor Elliston's management. As in 1809, it is the patent, and the special, publicly owned space created by the patent:[10] 'a monopoly, supported by Royal or Parliamentary favour, is bound, as long as it is supported, to furnish means of entertainment suitable to the tastes and habits of the moral and decent part of the community'. Rather than stay away, Barnes suggests that 'decent visiters [sic]'[11] should go and demand obedience to their will, or see to it that Drury Lane suffer the withdrawal of the licence, as would happen to a disorderly public house. He is calling the ascendant classes to another battle in the war for control of the dominant theatrical voice.

The journalist's abjection of Kean in this assault is the more striking in that his had been one of the leading media voices in the creation of the actor's celebrity status. It was the dramatic criticism written by Barnes and Hazlitt for *The Examiner* that had hailed and helped create the astonishing success of Kean in his first season at Drury Lane in 1814. To Barnes, for example, we owe the description of Kean's legendary business as Richard III, when he stood sketching with his sword-point in the sand before the final battle. The article in which this is described begins with the exclamation of an enthusiast: 'We know no greater pleasure than to hail the triumph of genius, and to watch over the progress of a growing fame.'[12] But by 1825 Barnes was no longer a young writer for a radical paper; he was exercising the authority of *The Times*. In a culture where every journal was automatically the organ of some party or faction, Barnes had sought to establish his paper as an independent and therefore, ultimately, an extremely powerful voice, which spoke for what he defined as the British public, without fear or favour. The awe which greeted the pronouncements of his paper – dubbed 'The Thunderer' – during the political debates of the 1830s was founded on such defining moments as his abjection here of the celebrity he had helped to create. What happened at Drury Lane during Kean's stardom to change Barnes's interpretation of him from dawning genius to an obscene threat to the public? The answer is, ultimately, connected with the birth of modern celebrity culture: the commercial exploitation and the mediatised framing of individual fame.

To the modern eye the most obvious and extraordinary thing about Drury Lane on 31 January 1825, as described by Barnes in his long article next morning is the interaction of all elements of theatre and theatre-going within the moment – the event's intertheatricality.[13] In this performance the least important elements are the written plays named on the playbill, Massinger's *A New Way to Pay Old Debts*, the afterpiece *Old and Young* written by Poole for Drury Lane in 1822 and still playing with its original cast, and the annual pantomime by the house arranger W. Barrymore called *Harlequin and the Talking Bird, the Singing Trees and the Golden Waters*, which concluded the bill, though Barnes does not even mention it. The comedy was full length, and the farce played at over an hour;[14] the elaborately scenic Christmas pantomime played at least two hours,[15] protracting the evening for the performers to well past midnight. Barnes says nothing about the plays, beyond their titles, for three-quarters of the piece. The first stage business described is a little pantomime enacted by Kean, Smithson, the manager Elliston and two men from the boxes, who play out an improvised dumb show on the subject of respect for women, with a part-eaten orange and a stick. When the advertised dramas are mentioned, it is to note the way in which Massinger's lines were re-read and their meaning changed by the audience and the performers, in a competitive appropriation of the text to the script of their own performance in the theatre. The report finishes rather oddly with a reversion to 'normal' dramatic reviewing, when 'our little favourite, Miss C. Fisher' is said to have 'sustained with great effect' her quick-change role as a little girl who impersonates three boy cousins, which 'went off very quietly'. Like the panto playing in the early hours, this is almost impossible to imagine, given the foregoing events; but it was in any case not what the evening was about. The contest in the auditorium was the main piece of the night.

This performance is reported in detail, and its drama derives from outside events. The back story is Kean's huge reputation and fame as a tragic actor, and alongside that the rumours of his wild behaviour off stage. His status was that of a Romantic icon, a celebrity linked with figures ranging far above him in the social scale, Byron and Napoleon himself.[16] His fame had reached the point of notoriety in the trial, the letters there read out, the language and behaviour there revealed. All this was now brought to the theatre for gladiatorial contestation, the physical playing-out of a cultural and moral debate about the values of British society.

As was the case in the O.P. riots, the rival spectators had come prepared with lines and business of their own. They displayed written texts to influence the course of events, turning Drury Lane into something like the lowest illegitimate stages at the period, where spoken dialogue was forbidden and statements vital to the plot had to be written on banners. Barnes takes trouble to demolish their statements, especially where they have laid claim to texts he regards as legitimate, belonging to his side of the dispute: the 'fellow' in the two-shilling gallery who quotes *Hamlet* has 'prostituted Shakespeare', though Barnes himself is at liberty to quote the same text with off-hand familiarity (' "set down" ', below, is a fleeting reference to Hamlet's rebuke to the clowns). He is equally determined to deny Kean's defenders their appeal to the 'British liberality' of 'a British audience'. '[B]eastly' 'professors of a hedonistic art' are not to claim such liberality; the people supporting them are not a representative 'British audience'. He goes out of his way to prove this in his descriptions of them, especially his elaborately insulting account of the 'Jew bruiser' Abraham Belasco, whose offence of hauling a slight young gentlemen out of his seat and depositing him in the lobby seems scarcely more heinous than his own mere inappropriate presence in a box.[17]

The class topography of the auditorium is stressed throughout the account: people are judged by their fit place in the two-shilling gallery, their outrageous presence in a box, their 'sturdy' occupation of the standing room at the back of the pit. Drury Lane had been rebuilt to accommodate a complex hierarchy of active spectators, and to facilitate their bringing together in a controlled way for the mutual experience of the theatre. A good house, however, could still be a promiscuous experience. On 24 January, when Kean had first returned to the stage after the trial, Winston recorded that an immense crowd assembled long before the doors opened at 6 o'clock, and the rush into the boxes left three times as many people outside to make do with the surrounding theatres: at Covent Garden they interrupted *Hamlet* to cheer or hiss when the lines Kean had quoted in his letters to Mrs Cox were spoken.[18]

But the theatre was not often so full, even for Kean's performances, after his first few triumphant seasons. It can be argued, from the Cox/Kean contestation, that the consensus that brought the O.P. rioters together successfully to countermand Kemble's innovations was breaking down, and that some influential parts of the audience were no long contesting for shared possession of the space, but were rather removing themselves from it entirely, or demanding that if *they* were to continue, others must decamp.

In 1822 Elliston, after three years of relatively successful tenure as manager, had stripped out the interior in the hope of increasing the house's attraction by reorganising it not only back stage, where he made provision for more spectacular productions to be created, but in the auditorium. He cut back the apron by six feet and moved the boxes forward ten feet, removed the stage doors, greatly increased the number of 'family' and private boxes – the self-same exclusive spaces that the O.P. rioters had scouted – and enforced the concept of 'dress boxes' on the first tier.[19] He provided alternate rows of the pit benches with backs, deterring men from striding from seat to seat.[20] Casual and promiscuous mixing were beginning to be discouraged. Despite such efforts at control, the mingling of ranks in one social space was beginning to have a deterrent effect upon parts of the audience. They were offended by the violations of the interior boundaries which inevitably occurred when the interlocking systems of free admissions or the pressure of special events allowed the 'wrong' people into the various zones. Barnes's article clearly reflects the anxiety that arose as class confrontations began to take place, and to extend into disputes between auditorium and stage, as well as between the shareholders' Committee and the hired managers.

And Edmund Kean was not Lord Byron: his class inferiority meant that he was the vulnerable back-marker of the trio of great men. Had Byron bedded a City wife, he would have been enacting the long-established role of the rake, and Barnes could hardly have made so much of it; but Kean was a player, technically one of His Majesty's servants, and not only was the behaviour and presumptions he now paraded in the playhouse offensive to middle-class morality, but the individual in whom these values were embodied was within its regulatory reach. Barnes hits out at him, to enforce his view of good order and its violation, in a rhetoric that combines the discourses of both class and gender.

From the first line the article invokes a discourse of sexual purity. The personal life of celebrities is always an aspect of their fascination to the public, and potentially the means of their degradation; Barnes works to deploy that response, and ensure that Napoleon's unspeakable mastery and Byron's aristocratic transgression become Edmund Kean's disgusting presumption. Not only Kean's offence, but also the rhetorical tactics employed in Barnes's article, are about sexuality and the gender crimes committed by Kean and by his supporters. This is not incidental. The sexualised power strategies of eighteenth-century sentimentality and its representation of women had been deployed as a conservative weapon since Edmund Burke's *Reflections on the Revolution in France*. As Betsy Bolton has it, 'Burke's moral imagination placed a radical reliance on the spectacle of female vulnerability.'[21] Between 1809 and 1825 the philosophical and ideological contest had come to focus upon the role of women in the artistic and commercial life of London, and its public manifestation in the theatre. A mounting tension existed: in the modern theatre, women, from the monumental Mrs Siddons to the accomplished Madame Vestris, were active and visible, and often powerful; while in an ideal social organisation, they would be powerless, retiring and in need of protection.

Barnes's rhetoric is pervasively and tendentiously sexualised. Beginning his attack by linking 'Muses' and 'Modesty', he denounces the 'unblushing impudence' which has usurped their realm, the theatre. His central justification for the persecution of Kean is that the actor should not have presented himself, to the outrage of women's modesty, after his filthy letters had been made public. In his leading article on the same day as this theatre report Barnes speaks of the theatre in general as about to be abandoned by decent people, allowed to become 'a kind of cess-pool for every thing that is impure in the nation'. He refuses to accept this; despite the difficulties, he is eager to reclaim the stage from degradation and turn it, with the help of his vision of the social function appropriate to women, into a place of instruction and good example. In the leader he attacks those who frequent Drury Lane as it is, and support it by their own immoral lives: he ends with threats to a 'Whig member' who has been attending and defending Kean. 'He sometimes has his middle-aged *Thais* with him. He had better not provoke us.'[22]

This set of links – the identification of modesty with women, their exemplary virtue and therefore the exemplary evil of their corruption, actual or potential – was not a new set of thoughts for Barnes. The dumb-show about the outrageous orange and its danger to Harriet Smithson fed his long-held misgivings about the position of actresses. In an 1814 dramatic review in *The Examiner*, he had made it clear that he regarded 'female delicacy' as at risk on the stage, objecting to an afterpiece in which Fanny Kelly, disguised as a page in a Sultan's seraglio, was roughly handled and thrown about.[23] On stage and off the present moral atmosphere of the theatre was degrading; it had little impact, he suggested, on 'public morals' generally, but that was no reason why efforts should not be made to reclaim it in the name of decency, and for this purpose he was prepared to use women – ladies in the audience – as his stalking-horse. One of the more unpleasant rhetorical tropes of the article above is the section in which he browbeats ladies with his description of the women whom he observed in the boxes, hoping they were brought there by men against their will, assuring us all that he is quite certain that 'our countrywomen in general will not so far violate the pure delicacy of their sex and the dignity of their characters, as to be present at scenes which are repugnant and degrading to both'.

If lady theatre-goers should be a litmus-test for the purity of a performance and a safeguard for the actresses, there was a third category of women present, who were part of the problem rather than of its solution. Barnes is very outspoken about the 'poor girls who infest the lobbies', his pity not preventing him from using their 'indecent applause' as a stick with which to beat Kean. Earlier articles in the campaign were particularly melodramatic about these prostitutes. On 25 January he described two of the 'scarcely fifty women' who were present the night before: 'in the slips, one of those who are falsely denominated *filles de joie* – (poor creature! her roarings and writhings will, for many days to come, be severely answered by exhaustion and sickness), and a lady in the dress circle, clothed in *scarlet* and *black*, – fit colours for the character she assumed. She was accompanied by a young man ... attached to one of the police offices.'[24] The decent women on stage are placed in an impossible position by Kean and his female supporters: on 29 January Barnes pitied 'the imploring looks of Mrs Bunn' and 'the up-turned eyes of Mrs West', while he poured scorn on a 'fat woman, of the Cyprian order, in the upper boxes' who 'waved a once-white handkerchief, and clapped, and cried "Bravo!" most indefatigably'.[25] Barnes's tangle of attitudes to women displays one of the cruces of early nineteenth-century theatre.

The association of the theatre and prostitution is culturally deep-rooted, and has been explored as it touched both actresses and female writers in Britain from their appearance at the Restoration onwards. Barnes's rhetoric explicitly links performance to the material presence of the sex trade in the theatre of the time.[26] There was a growing perception of incompatibility between respectable femininity and professional stage work. This problem of self-definition on the part of middle- and upper-class women was exacerbated by the coexistence of sex and theatre work, their occupation of the same spaces. The intersection of the roles of performer and sex worker was most obvious at the Opera House, where it was completely institutionalised. Protectors and keepers of varying degrees of generosity were part of the career pattern of most women singers as well as dancers. The same set of transactions on a social rather than an overtly commercial basis was expected in the boxes, which were recognised as a courting ground for upper-class young ladies and their admirers, who saw them to advantage in full evening dress, the box a sumptuous picture frame that offered semi-naked bodies in a quasi-private space in full view of an admiring audience. Drury Lane was a less fashionable follower of the Opera House in this as in other things. Sex back-stage between performers and with outsiders was taken for granted, as Winston's diaries make clear.[27] But the acknowledged commercial sexual traffic of the house took place not back-stage but in the circulation spaces, partly in the auditorium, but especially in the lobbies and saloons, where provision was deliberately made for the meeting of sex workers from outside the establishment with their customers.[28] Wyatt, the architect of the 1811 building, acknowledged that the trade could not be excluded, and only attempted to segregate them from 'rational and respectable' patrons in his design.[29] Refurbishments in 1817 created a 'grand Chinese promenade' especially for 'visitors who purpose waiting for the time of half price' and bills at the beginning of the season direct them thither, and promise more lights soon, 'in proportion to the new colours'. The levels of lighting in house and lobbies were of concern partly because lamps enabled patrons to see with whom they were associating, while extra illumination in the second tier of boxes was not a wholly desirable idea for the modesty of the rest of the house. Winston's Drury Lane papers[30] include a note dated 1818 which criticises excess lighting because it caused the prostitutes to prefer Covent Garden and so cost the house their entrance money.

The Cox/Kean affair and *The Times'* construction and ideological use of it could be said to mark the end of such a pragmatically open view of the sex trade in the theatre. Thomas Barnes exposes the theatre as a sexual threat to the bourgeois woman, and thereby undermines the freedom and power of working women – of all trades – within the London theatre. Indeed, one might say that the mob he whipped up were expressing hostility to Kean not simply as a transgressor, but as a *feminised* offender; and thence a representative of the unacceptability of the feminised power of the theatre. Barnes stresses that Kean's supporters include unchaste women and their frightening lower-class men, and the actor's own presence upon the stage puts possibly innocent actresses in bodily danger. But more than that, Kean is an actor, therefore in Straub's phrase a 'sexual suspect', who by exhibiting himself on stage takes up the feminine position of one who is paid to be looked at.[31] Now he was himself a convicted sexual sinner, and such sinners are identified as feminised, that is, as other than virtuous and manly. It is notable that the most shocking aspect of his trangression cited in the trial was his writing of a note to Alderman Cox explicitly denying his affair with the man's wife on the same day that he wrote a love-letter to her planning their next meeting. His crime was thus the female one of duplicity, in his deceiving of the husband, who was his friend – a homosocial betrayal that put him on the level of a bad woman. Hence the fury at his effrontery in exhibiting himself on stage, again assuming his feminine relation to the public, and asking for its approbation, when he is in effect no more than a 'fallen woman'.

Kean was not totally destroyed by the events of 1825, and went on to fulfil his engagement with Elliston and to work again, collapsing eventually only from his abuse of his own body. Whether or not Barnes had really beaten him, the moral ascendancy which he wished to represent and to lead in *The Times* eventually came to tell the story, and, in their books, the actor was firmly put in his place. But something else, something very equivocal and far-reaching in its consequences, had also changed: and Elliston pointed it out to the audience in his speech on 28 January. He began the first full-scale managerial 'explanation' of what was going on with the statement that 'The engagement which Mr Kean is now endeavouring to fulfil was made in

July last ... The engagement was for a period of 20 nights, at 50l. a night.' He went on to the effort and expense he had been at to enable his star 'to enjoy the full tide of popularity'[32] – he had had a play written to display his talents, and entirely suspended the free list. He hoped the public would make their decision whether or not they wanted what he offered them with this legal and, especially, financial commitment in mind. In this speech the commodification of the theatrical product, the celebrity, is the overriding issue. Fifty pounds a night was a colossal salary. Previously, patent house contracts had been for so many nights during each week of the season, often, as in Kean's case when he first came to Drury Lane, involving commitment to several further seasons at a slowly climbing figure: a contract not unlike those of stars made by Hollywood studios, and subject to the same pressures and resentments when performers proved successful and felt themselves worth more. Moreover, there had been something of a cartel between the two patent houses, whereby they offered comparable salaries and undertook not to employ any actor who defected from the other house. Performers like Charles Mathews Senior who could command big audiences felt themselves limited by this practice but were unwilling to break out of it and risk loss of status by appearing as celebrities at the minors; they had begun to rely upon making their fortunes by provincial and American tours outside the London season. But there was obviously a crack in the system that would eventually cause it to fall apart; and Elliston, needing to revive Drury Lane in 1819 and coming straight from management in the more cash-based, less traditional and less constrained minors, where comparatively few people were employed at individually negotiated salaries not based on custom and practice, was the one who first allowed it to gape open, and peered into its depths.

The consequences are most vividly described by Alfred Bunn. Bunn was a lesser Elliston and had been his disciple and follower in his provincial managements; to Winston's annoyance he was brought into the Drury Lane management team at the beginning of the 1823 season. He became acting manager there for the gentleman amateur Frederick Polhill in 1831, and began the first of four tenancies in his own name in 1834. In 1840 he published a self-justifying account of his managerial career. His analysis of his difficulties focuses obsessively upon the selfishness of the performers, their grotesque pride – and their financial demands. He is infuriated by their power: 'An actor, who from his peculiar position has the power, will sometimes bind down his employer by an article of engagement, that renders the very opening of the doors almost a personal favour on his part.' He was observing the rise of the celebrity. Throughout the book he records the ever-increasing sums demanded and paid for the services of stars, especially a diva like Malibran, who gave him some of his major operatic successes, but also Macready, whose pride, and deadly enmity with Bunn himself, Bunn claims was rooted in greed and the exercise of power, despite his artistic pretensions. He maintains that it is the actors' fault, the inflated 'scale of their emoluments' that 'will sooner or later close the doors of the two large theatres' and adds illustrations: Kean leapt from an initial contract of £8 per week to £50 per night, and was followed by many others, so that Charles Young had a weekly salary of £20 at Covent Garden in 1821–2, and a nightly fee of the same amount at Drury Lane in the following year.[33] Bunn does not point out that this particular change was brought about not by the actor, but by Elliston, who was pursuing a policy of buying in talent in order to fill the house, and to give himself the weapon of strong alternative attractions against Kean's soaring demands and increasing unreliability. It was Elliston who broke the gentleman's agreement between the houses, and his modern biographer squarely blames his short-termist policy, artistically and financially successful by 1825, for the ruin of both theatres by the mid-1830s.[34]

The rise and fall of Edmund Kean as a celebrity is imbricated with the institutional battles over the establishment of the radical agenda in Britain, and the hegemony of the (Victorian) British public. Class and gender disputes were bringing about a shift in the financial and cultural basis of entertainment that would bring down the whole patent institution, and this was chiefly a matter of class. Between the O.P. riots and the Cox vs. Kean affair the invocation of class antagonisms, the mishandling and ossification of ancient customary practices, the loss of consensus about cultural values, all harden and widen into fissures in the institution. In the O.P. riots, the crowd in the auditorium was largely united against the injustice they thought had taken place, and the victory was a source of satisfaction to the majority of theatre-goers, if not to the already struggling management. During the later disorders there were serious fights between audience factions. To put the opposition in another way, the earlier confrontation saw the middling sort flexing their muscles in opposition to what they perceived as oppression from a decaying aristocratic class and its lackeys; in 1825 the voice of the middle classes, *The Times*, turns on the abjected groups below them, the bruisers, prostitutes and 'beastly hedonistic actors', the cockneyism of Kean and the flash audience. Barnes wished to see the theatre people not emancipated from control, but brought back into submission, no longer the offhand, arrogant 'His Majesty's servants' but the servants of the British public. This transformation would be consonant with the intentions of the Drury Lane shareholders; but the cockney public and the cockney player refuse to play their part. For them the heady, dangerous interplay between the celebrity and his public was more exciting than any classic drama on the stage. The mob, the Kraken in the depths of the ocean of social change, was wakened, and commodity culture entered the field of theatrical power negotiations through Elliston's managerial innovations.

Appendix

The Times, 1 February 1825

DRURY-LANE THEATRE

We have again to describe a scene of riot and confusion. Where the Muses and their attendant, Modesty, ought to preside, violence and unblushing impudence bear sway. The comedy of *A New Way to Pay Old Debts* was last night performed; the part of *Sir Giles Overreach* (a name not ill suited to the performer) by Mr Kean. The house was very full, and there was a greater portion of females, though not of decent appearance, than we observed on the two previous appearances of Mr Kean. His friends were very numerous, especially in the pit; but a hardy band of opponents stationed themselves in the rear of that part of the house, from which all the efforts of 'the wolves' could not eject them. As on the former occasions, the dress circle took but a slight part in the contest. In the other ranges of boxes, in the pit, and in the galleries, the friends of the actor had greatly the preponderance. We are not surprised at this, for we know of our own knowledge, that a regular corps of bravoes and blackguards was organised on Saturday, for the purpose of supporting the moral tragedian and his moral cause. The fellows whom we last night saw waving their hats when Mr Kean appeared, and beating those who expressed their disapprobation, may be very excellent representatives of St. Giles's; but they are not the representatives of the London public. Many placards were hoisted on this occasion. One was placed in the front of the two-shilling gallery, with a quotation from *Hamlet* – 'if every man had his deserts who should escape whipping?' We apprehend the fellow who thus prostituted Shakespeare would not. A placard, exhibited in the pit, contained these words – 'Kean has made an apology, and a British audience is satisfied.' Each of these pronouncements is false. Kean has made no apology, and the audience last night proved that they were not satisfied. A third placard was displayed, with the words – 'British liberality, and no cant.' British liberality, we suppose, means a *carte blanche* for the professors of the histrionic art, who are, however, too beastly in their behaviour, when off the stage, to be tolerated and applauded when on it; and as to the allusion to 'cant,' we fear the 'satirical rogue' who drew up the placard meant to call the attention of the audience to Mr Kean's letters, where 'cant' is to be found in abundance. The uproar, which was very great before, became trebly violent when the curtain rose. The hooting, howling and hissing – the cries of 'Turn him out' 'Kean for ever!' 'Off, off;' and others which decency will not allow us to 'set down,' were terrific. The fights were numerous. One individual in the pit we saw shamefully beaten by a regular knot of ruffians, armed with sticks. He was forced from his seat, thrown down, and, in that situation, repeatedly struck by some of these doughty heroes. Such company as this do not, we should imagine, enrich Mr Elliston's treasury, while they utterly destroy the respectability of the theatre. The noise was incessant during the three first acts; and whenever Mr Kean appeared, it reached a deafening height. In vain did those who were at the head of the supporters, called out to their friends 'to be silent'. The moment the anti-Keanites set up a cry of opposition, his friends expressed their indignation with a degree of violence which proved the excellent state of their lungs. The poor girls who infest the saloons 'fit advocates in virtue's cause,' showed a becoming zeal on occasion they rivalled their male associates in loudness and perseverance.

In the first circle some opposition was manifested from the commencement of the play; and the persons by whom it was expressed were pointed at by the Keanites of the pit, who loudly called to have them thrown over. These exhortations, or his zeal for Mr Kean, or some other consideration which it is not worth while to inquire into, induced a Jew boxer, Abraham Belasco, to seize on a young man who had committed the heinous offence of hissing, and he dragged him with great brutality and violence out of the box into the lobby. The youth was surrounded by friends who witnessed this outrage, and even those persons who had been loudly calling 'Turn him out' could not bear to see their own decrees executed by such hands. The Jew carried his violence no further than dragging the stripling, who was not half his weight or size, out of the box, but he did not venture to prevent his returning to it. This affair will of course be investigated before some fitting tribunal, and we therefore refrain from any further observations upon it, excepting this – that the manager will find it difficult to account, in any honest or satisfactory manner, for such persons as this Jew bruiser being in the boxes of his theatre, or to persuade a rational audience to enter it when the consequence of their expressed disapprobation must, in all probability, be to receive the discipline of the prize-ring. Out of doors, and in their own haunts, the practices of these vermin are sufficiently disgusting and disgraceful; but the nuisance becomes absolutely past endurance when we find them intruding into decent society, and taking a part like that we have described in a question which they can by no possibility either feel or understand. The howling of the 'wolves', and the indecent applause of the women of the town, speak very plainly as to the merits of any cause which they can be found unanimously to support; but if a doubt remained in any man's mind upon the subject, it must surely be removed when he finds that it is attempted to silence the opposition to that cause by the unanswerable arguments of prize-fighting bullies, and the ruffians of the ring. Unfortunately, no peace-officers could be obtained, so that the Jew was permitted to sit out the remainder of the play, in the presence of the persons he had insulted. In the upper circle, there were fewer women than in the dress-boxes, and all of them, we think, without any exception, were of the most unequivocal description. The ladies of the dress-circle were evidently brought to give a countenance to the attempt which is made to outrage public decency; and, as might be guessed from the men by whom they were accompanied, were not of that class by which this part of the theatre is usually filled. Some of them quitted the theatre; the rest, induced as we would willingly believe by the persuasions, perhaps by the authority of others, sat to the end, and endured the noise and indecencies which assailed their ears almost without intermission. We had doubted whether any English women of character could be brought, after the filthy exposure of Mr Kean's correspondence, to visit the theatre in which he played; and although some have been found to do so, we are not the less certain that our opinion was in the main well-founded, and that our countrywomen in general will not so far violate the pure delicacy of their sex and the dignity of their characters, as to be present at scenes which are repugnant and degrading to both.

Uproar lorded it during the whole night. When Mr Kean appeared with Miss Smithson, who performed the character of *Margaret*, several pieces of orange-peel, and an orange nearly whole, were thrown at him, from a box on the right hand of the stage. This excited a terrible commotion; and the look and gesture of Mr Kean, who pointed to the lady, and seemed to ask – 'Is this fit treatment for a woman?' drew down very general applause. At this period, Mr Elliston came forward, and endeavoured, but ineffectually, to obtain a hearing. He continued bowing to the audience for several minutes, Mr Kean all the while standing behind him; but the clamour of the two parties rendered all hope of addressing the audience vain. At this moment a young man, armed with a stick, scrambled from one of the boxes to the stage, and threatened the parties who, he supposed, had flung the orange-peels; but this chivalric hero speedily made his retreat, Mr Elliston again advanced to the front of the stage, took up the orange which had been flung upon it, and pointed very significantly to Miss Smithson. This piece of pantomime was received with great approbation. The manager then retired. Mr Kean put on a forced smile, and proceeded with his part; but it was still all dumb show. The only words we heard Mr Kean utter during these three acts, were those with which the third act concludes, viz. – 'what men report I care not'; which he gave in a very triumphant tone, and which were received with a tumult of applause and disapprobation. A little of the second and third acts was audible, and some points of the text were marked by the auditors, according to their opinion of Mr Kean's conduct. When *Sir Giles* says to his daughter – 'You will have marriage first, and lawful pleasure afterwards. What more can you desire?' – when after the negotiation for his daughter's marriage with *Lord Lovell* is concluded, he explains 'Now all's cock-sure!' And when, addressing *Lady Allworth*, he sneeringly observes, 'Conspire with your husband, Lady!' The uproar was most vehement. Nor was it less so when *Marrall* observes to *Sir Giles*, 'I have a conscience not seared up like yours.' This expression was most triumphantly received by Mr Kean's opponents. When the curtain fell, the call for Mr Kean was violent and general. The afterpiece of *Young and Old* commenced, but still the call was unabated. Mr Kean at length came forward, amidst every species of note of which the human voice is susceptible. After a considerable time, silence was obtained, and Mr Kean said: –

'I have made as much concession to an English audience as an English actor ought (A tremendous uproar; one would have supposed that the inhabitants of Bedlam were enjoying a holiday.) My hope,' continued Mr Kean, 'for the honour of my country – as after twenty nights I shall leave you for ever – (deafening cries of No! no!) – I hope, for the honour of my country, that this persecution may never reach foreign annals.'

He then bowed, and retired. ' 'Tis a vain hope.' Mr Kean's fame is chronicled here; and it must of necessity find its way into 'foreign annals'. The afterpiece in which our little favourite, Miss C Fisher, sustained with great effect the characters of the four *Mowbrays*, went off very quietly.

Notes

1 Thomas Colley Grattan, *Beaten Paths and Those Who Trod Them*, 2 vols (London: Chapman and Hall, 1862), II, pp. 195–6. See Jane Moody, *Illegitimate Theatre in London, 1770–1840* (Cambridge: Cambridge University Press, 2000), p. 229, for the significance of this linking and Kean's 'illegitimate celebrity'.
2 See Leigh Woods, 'Actors' Biography and Mythmaking, the Example of Edmund Kean', in *Interpreting the Theatrical Past* ed. Thomas Postlewait and Bruce A. McConachie (Iowa, IA: University of Iowa Press, 1989) pp. 230–47.

3 On the potential for humiliation, see Jacqueline Rose, *On Not being Able to Sleep: Psychoanalysis and the Modern World* (London: Chatto and Windus, 2003), p. 4; on status-stripping and the body, see Chris Rojek, *Celebrity* (London: Reaktion Books, 2001), p. 82.
4 Marc Baer, *Theatre and Disorder in Late Georgian London* (Oxford: Clarendon Press, 1992).
5 See Jacky Bratton, *New Readings in Theatre History* (Cambridge: Cambridge University Press, 2003).
6 He was almost always pictured as Richard III – in the most famous print, by George Cruickshank (May 1814) bearing Drury Lane on his hump; even in the bawdy prints of him with Charlotte Cox he (or she) tends to wear the trunk hose of the Shakespearean character.
7 *Drury Lane Journal: Selections from James Winston's Diaries 1819–1827* ed. Alfred L. Nelson and Gilbert B. Cross (London: Society for Theatre Research, 1974), p. 105.
8 Raymond Fitzsimons, *Edmund Kean: Fire from Heaven* (London: Hamish Hamilton, 1976), pp. 192–201.
9 *Times*, 28 January 1825, p. 2 and 18 January 1825, p. 2.
10 See Gillian Russell, 'Theatre', in *An Oxford Companion to the Romantic Age* ed. Iain McCalman (Oxford: Oxford University Press, 1999), pp. 223–31, p. 223.
11 *Times*, 28 January 1825, p. 2.
12 *Examiner*, No. 322, 27 February 1814, p. 138.
13 See Bratton, *New Reading in Theatre History*, pp. 36–8.
14 *Drury Lane Journal*, p. 59: on the first night it played for 1 hour and 23 minutes; subsequent performances were shortened by 15 minutes.
15 *Drury Lane Journal*, p. 103; 27 December 1824.
16 Moody, *Illegitimate Theatre*, pp. 228–41.
17 This withering scorn of the prize-ring and its 'vermin' comes from a gentleman who, according to the official *Times* biography, was proud of his own boxing ability and once inadvertently challenged Tom Cribb to fight because the champion did not step quickly enough out of the young gownsman's way in a Cambridge street; Cribb was polite enough to enlighten the five-foot student boxer as to who he was, rather than knocking him down. Kean was a small man, too.
18 *Drury Lane Journal*, p. 105.
19 See *Survey of London* ed. F. H. W. Sheppard, 42 vols (London: Athlone Press for the GLC, 1970), 35, p. 64.
20 Winston's Drury Lane papers in 23 volumes, BL C.120.h.l, volume for 1821–2, unidentified cutting dated 13 October – 'we cannot decide whether this is an improvement, you certainly cannot remove from one seat to another with such ease, as before.'
21 Betsy Bolton, *Women, Nationalism and the Romantic Stage* (Cambridge: Cambridge University Press, 2001), p. 23.
22 *The Times*, 1 February 1825, p. 2.
23 *Examiner*, 18 December 1814.
24 *The Times*, 25 January 1825, p. 2.
25 *The Times*, 29 January 1825, p. 3.
26 It was also pervasively present in the surrounding streets. See Tracy Davis, 'The Actress in Victorian Pornography', in *Victorian Scandals: Representations of Gender and Class* ed. Kristine Ottesen Garrigan (Athens, OH: Ohio University Press, 1992), pp. 99–133; and see Dewey Ganzel, 'Patent Wrongs and Patent Theatres: Drama and the Law in the Early Nineteenth Century', *PMLA* 76:4 (1961), pp. 384–96, p. 391,

where he demonstrates from the evidence to the Select Committee of 1832 that the reason speculators continued to pour money into Covent Garden, despite its constant losses from productions, was that they were buying into the proceeds of prostitution, carried on in a neighbouring brothel owned by the theatre.
27 See *Drury Lane Journal*, p. 4, where he records Kean's habit of lining up women back stage, having two more waiting while he 'served' the first.
28 *Survey of London*, 35, p. 61.
29 *Survey of London*, 35, p. 60.
30 BL C.120.h.l.
31 Kristina Straub, *Sexual Suspects: Eighteenth-Century Players and Sexual Ideology* (Princeton, NJ: Princeton University Press, 1991), pp. 27–28, 40.
32 *The Times*, 29 January 1825, p. 3.
33 Alfred Bunn, *The Stage: Both before and behind the Curtain, from Observations Taken on the Spot*, 3 vols (London: Richard Bentley, 1840), I, pp. 54–66.
34 Christopher Murray, *Robert William Elliston, Manager* (London: Society for Theatre Research, 1975), p. 150.

# 7
Infamy and Dying Young: Sarah Kane, 1971–1999

Mary Luckhurst

Blast-off

If there is one thing that commentators on Sarah Kane's celebrity agree on it is the suddenness of its advent. Before the Royal Court opening of her first play, *Blasted*, on 12 January 1995, few had heard of her; the morning after the press night she was on the front page of the tabloids and by the end of the run her reputation as a theatrical *enfant terrible* was established.[1] When she died unexpectedly in 1999 *The Times* claimed that *Blasted* had 'shot her from nowhere to notoriety', the *Guardian* described her debut 'as the most controversial of recent times', and the *Independent* portrayed her as the woman who 'shot to notoriety and front-page prominence at the age of 23'.[2] From the moment Kane came to public attention she provoked outrage at her raw depiction of sex and violence, and though she later tried to redefine herself, she never shook off the inflammatory rhetoric that accompanied her abrupt ascent to fame.

Blasted scarcely has a conventional plot and is best summarised as a series of actions. It is set in a hotel in Leeds during a war: Ian, a middle-aged journalist and an agent for an unnamed right-wing faction, has befriended Cate, a backward young woman with a stammer, who suffers hysterical fits and black-outs. Their relationship is never explained psychologically – they appear mutually dependent on each other, seesawing between love and hate, tenderness and sadism. During the night Ian rapes Cate. The hotel is hit by a bomb and extensively damaged. The next morning a soldier forces his way into the room: he sodomises Ian, sucks out and eats his eyes then blows out his own brains. In the meantime Cate has been handed a baby for safekeeping, but the baby dies and she 'buries' it beneath the floorboards. The ending is elliptical and figured predominantly through stage directions, but the main actions represent Ian's slow death from hunger, illness and injury: he masturbates, defecates, urinates, eats the baby, waits for death, dies and is apparently resurrected. Cate cowers close by and tries to feed him.

British critics mostly expressed repugnance at the relentless catalogue of brutality.[3] Michael Coveney admired it and John Peter defended *Blasted* vigorously, arguing that its flaws were due to Kane's inexperience, that it required spectators to undergo a necessary 'moral ordeal' and that theatre 'is only alive if it is kicking'.[4] Peter's advocacy had no effect on curbing the tide of critical vitriol and Kane found herself at the centre of a storm of protest. Critics were assortedly overtaken by their own physical reactions, Paul Taylor describing how:

> Sitting through *Blasted* is a little like having your face rammed into an overflowing ash tray, just for starters, and then having your whole head held down in a bucket of offal.[5]

Nick Curtis's response was similarly visceral:

> I do not think I've yet seen a play which can beat Sarah Kane's sustained onslaught on the sensibilities for sheer, unadulterated brutalism. Heaping shock upon shock, *Blasted* is a powerful experience in the same way that being mugged is a powerful experience.[6]

Charles Spencer observed that 'hardened theatre critics looked in danger of parting company with their suppers', and was so revolted that he wrote reviews on consecutive days to allow himself sufficient space to castigate what he called 'this nauseating dog's breakfast of a play'.[7] Most sensational of all was Jack Tinker's review in the *Daily Mail*, now as infamous as the production it attacked:

> Until last night I thought I was immune from shock in any theatre. I am not. Finally I have been driven into the arms of Disgusted of Tunbridge Wells. For utterly and entirely disgusted I was by a play which appears to know no bounds of decency, yet has no message to convey by way of excuse. Why the 23-year-old Sarah Kane chose to write it is her affair. Presumably because she was given a grant by the hitherto admirable Jerwood Foundation in their quest to help new talent. Some will undoubtedly say the money might have been better spent on a course in remedial therapy. But the real question is why, with the cooperation of our Royal National Theatre, the Royal Court saw fit to stage it. As a piece of drama it is utterly without dramatic merit.
>
> Ms Kane merely creates her own lawless environment, and then allows her three characters to behave with utmost bestiality to each other as a result of it. We begin with a journalist indulging in all manner of graphic sexual activity with an under-aged and mentally retarded girl in his hotel room somewhere in England. Then we regress, by various implausible stages, from mere unlawful indecency to vividly enacted male rape,

through to a barbaric cannibalism of a dead baby and on to simple defecation on stage. Just for those academics who seek to justify any stage violence with the example of Gloucester having his eyes put out in *King Lear*, Ms Kane has stern news for them. Here our hero not only loses his eyes after being severely raped, his torturer munches them before our own eyes. Only one person left the arena during all these gratuitous acts, which must say a great deal for the politeness or stoicism of British audiences.

Controversy is naturally always part of the deal when pushing forward the boundaries of art. But with the hounds of repression snapping at the heels of sex and violence whenever they sniff it out, the Royal Court have surely fed them a feast of it with this. Luckily, for all of us, the play becomes so risible the only thing to do is laugh.[8]

Tinker's assault is extraordinary not just for its aesthetic conservatism but also for its expression of personal prejudices. Tinker declares war on Kane's youth, talent, intelligence, sanity (linked by implication with her sex) and morality; he criticises the play's failure to adhere to realist conventions and finally condemns it as utterly worthless. As an outburst it is extreme for the way it pathologises the playwright, yet was matched in tone by other attackers, who became much more obsessed with passing judgements on the author than on the play. Kane's intelligence in particular was derided and patronised, the play dismissed for its 'abject puerility', as 'naive tosh', 'very silly' and 'devoid of intellectual and artistic merit'.[9] Her youth was frequently held against her ('dramatist Sarah Kane puts one in mind of the naughtiest girl in the class');[10] her mental health was stigmatised; and the play pilloried as 'the prurient psycho-fantasies of a profoundly disturbed mind'.[11] There was overwhelming reluctance to treat the play as a serious artistic experiment, most critics viewing it as gratuitous in its brutality and as an exercise in shock for shock's sake.[12]

Two female critics point to the complex sets of prejudices evoked in many establishment male critics by the fact that a young woman had written the most violent new play seen on a British stage in living memory: Jane Edwardes mistakenly read *Blasted* as Kane's strategy to beat male playwrights at their own game, but Louise Doughty was more trenchant, insisting that:

> If your name is Seneca or Shakespeare and you've been dead for centuries ... you can pop as many eyeballs you like as long as it is in the service of Art. But if you are a 23-year-old woman playwright on your first outing, then forget it.[13]

Uncomfortable as the thought is, there is every reason to wonder whether Kane's meteoric rise would have happened at all had she been a man or her career shaped in the same way.[14] Sheridan Morley's invective was disturbing

110 *Mary Luckhurst*

in itself: 'Even if no other new play had been sent to them in the last decade, they [the Royal Court] would have been better off not doing this one.'[15] The tabloids spun stories about both Kane and the Royal Court's play selection procedures with headlines such as 'Rape Play Girl in Hiding' and 'Cash Fury at Vilest Play Ever'.[16] In their defence, Graham Saunders has argued that the tabloid reviewers were indulging in a performance of 'mock outrage' to create a story, and Taylor has speculated that some of his fellow critics were motivated 'not by malice, but by an almost childish sense of journalistic fun – they thought it would be a wheeze to drag the theatre out of the ghetto of the theatre pages and into mainstream public attention'.[17] But it is hard to read most comments as unintended in their ferocity or as 'fun'. Taylor's retrospective construction seeks to make an apology on behalf of certain peers, but burks the probable truth – that Kane and her play made excellent material for right-wing ideologues.[18] Richard Eyre and Nicholas Wright are certainly not inclined to be forgiving of the press, arguing that 'Most inflammatory, as far as the press was concerned, was the fact that Kane was a well-mannered and attractive young woman.'[19] Kane later expressed bemusement at the media and was disturbed that 'while the corpse of Yugoslavia was rotting on our doorstep, the press chose to get angry, not about the corpse, but about the cultural event that drew attention to it', and wondered whether the frenzy was in part revenge for her representation of a barbarous, middle-aged male journalist.[20] Later still she wondered about 'pseudo-moral outrage', but concluded that offence might have been due to the play being experiential rather than speculative.[21]

What really distinguishes Kane's notoriety as a post-war British playwright is the sheer intensity of the hostility directed towards her as a dramatist, and the concerted attempt to marginalise her play. She caused major controversy, but in reviewing *Blasted* very few critics asserted that she could write well, and none argued for her theatrical genius. This makes the gradual iconisation of her after her death all the more troubling.

Branding and re-branding Sarah Kane

For the executive of the Royal Court the furore over *Blasted* could be usefully invoked to demonstrate the institution's controversial, anti-establishment tradition of new writing which had supposedly been invented at the time of John Osborne's *Look Back in Anger* in 1956.[22] This tradition is constructed to incorporate Edward Bond, particularly the sensation caused by *Saved* in 1965, which infamously represented a baby's death by stoning. The public consensus was certainly that *Saved* was provocative, but social shifts in morality and attitudes to the representation of sex and violence meant that outcries of protest backfired and the end of censorship was actually hastened. None the less the controversy over *Saved* gave the Royal Court unprecedented media attention and powerfully reinforced its image as a politically oppositional force. While Osborne and Bond are the usual touchstones of the Royal Court's post-war construction of itself, playwrights such as Howard Brenton and Howard Barker can be included. Until Kane's enlistment the tradition had been male, but with *Blasted* the Royal Court directorate could argue that they had discovered a 1990s version of Bond and Osborne – the genuinely new take was that Kane was female. It was even better that Kane admired Bond and had looked to *Saved* as a model play.[23] As a woman playwright, Elaine Aston has argued, 'Kane, exceptionally, was presented as included, not excluded from, the male-dominated circles of the young and the angry.'[24] There is little doubt that this was because, like Osborne and Bond, she could be marketed for her violence and thereby treated as 'an honorary male'[25] – even the publicity for *Blasted* had militaristic appeal: a soldier waving a gun in a desert.

Director James Macdonald, also an associate director at the theatre, was delighted that the smaller studio space, the Theatre Upstairs, had attracted such attention. He pointed out that no more than 1,200 people had seen *Blasted* during its run, and argued that it was 'perhaps the least seen and most talked about play in recent memory'.[26] Given extensive media criticism of the Royal Court for choosing to fund *Blasted* at all, Macdonald did, however, feel obliged to justify its selection. Macdonald and the executive were caught off-guard by the notoriety Kane acquired overnight (her agent Mel Kenyon, it seems, may have had an inkling that the content of *Blasted* might offend, but it never occurred to her that the writing would be condemned).[27] Unlike the critics, Macdonald located Kane firmly at the centre of cultural debate, argued that she discussed 'the central issues of our time' and pitched the Royal Court as the obvious site for artistic debate at a national level:

> So why should anyone pay to be shocked? Because theatre is a forum for debate, and if it is to remain central to our culture, needs to debate the central issues of our time. If what seems to be happening in our culture is an increased fascination with and glamorisation of violence, then we should address that. *Blasted* does this. It also talks eloquently and with passion about nationalism, racism, emotional and physical abuse, sexual fantasy and the male urge to self-destruct. It is the first play of great heart and skill by a 23-year-old. If this isn't what the experimental arm of the country's major new writing theatre should be doing, I don't know what is.[28]

Macdonald's words are the beginning of the naturalisation of Kane into the Royal Court tradition, but they also mark the birth of a rhetoric which nationalises her and seeks to construct her as a representative voice for Britain. Kane certainly contributed to the mythologisation of the première of *Blasted* by claiming later that the Royal Court executive was 'embarrassed about it', programming it in January in the hope that few would go.[29] This hardly seems likely, and while Kenyon felt that there was 'dissent in the building' she does not exaggerate its consequences.[30] Kane, on the other hand, appeared to want to play up her rebel image by suggesting that the Royal Court regarded her as too dangerous even for their tastes.

Riding on the media interest and alert to a major publicity opportunity, the Artistic Director of the Royal Court, Stephen Daldry, and his associates saw a way of exploiting Kane's notoriety and began to develop a repertoire that included playwrights moulded in her fashion. Daldry's inauguration in 1993 had initiated him into the close relations that Royal Court managers had with the press, and he had an excellent sense of what would work on the market.[31] Jez Butterworth's *Mojo*, a Tarantino-inspired gangster play, came shortly after *Blasted* in July 1995. Mark Ravenhill's infamous *Shopping and Fucking* secured high-profile publicity because of its sexual content and above all its title (which was censored in certain parts of the country), and played in London in September 1996, touring nationally in October 1996. The following year Anthony Neilson's *The Censor*, containing explicit language and sexual fantasy, was produced at the Royal Court. Though Daldry resigned in 1996 to pursue a career in film, he had kept the Royal Court in the news[32] and helped to propagate an idea that Kane had initiated a new movement of sensational, experiential drama designed to shock. The movement was identified as 'in-yer-face theatre' or 'New Brutalism'.[33] Sierz's 'in-yer-face theatre' was the label that stuck, his book of the same name ensuring its memorialisation. His claim that Kane inspired a renaissance in new writing and 'the nasty nineties' is still widely discussed.[34] The identification of Kane as the inspiration for a new movement, however doubtful the definition and existence of that movement might be, was definitely one of the factors that ensured her theatrical and academic canonisation. If the question of a 'movement' is moot, the gradual spread of a set of sensation-filled, publicity-grabbing productions in the late 1990s and early twenty-first century at both mainstream and fringe theatres is not, perhaps, the most obvious bid to outdo Kane for blood and guts being Martin McDonagh's *The Lieutenant of Inishmore*, performed by the Royal Shakespeare Company in 2001.

Kane's next project after *Blasted* was *Phaedra's Love*, which she wrote and directed at the Gate Theatre, London in May 1996. It was a free and contemporary interpretation of the Phaedra myth, inspired by a single reading of Seneca's play, and topical in its depiction of a sexually corrupt royal family. Hippolytus' nihilism removes any erotic charge from the moment of sexual consummation with his stepmother, but the concluding scenes depict a mob attacking and killing Hippolytus, Theseus raping and slaughtering his stepdaughter Strophe, the mutilation, desecration and cannibalism of Hippolytus' body (his genitals are thrown onto a barbecue), and Theseus' suicide. The final poetic image is of vultures descending to consume Hippolytus' body parts.[35] The production was given very mixed reviews, critics reacting to the high 'atrocity-count', but largely finding the play and production flawed. Michael Billington complained that Kane still insisted on shocking the audience into submission rather than persuading them of her vision.[36] If Kane's intention was to explore the conventions of off-stage violence and bring the brutality of classical plays to the fore, she succeeded, but there seemed little else to say about her experiment.

In April 1998 Kane returned to the Royal Court, and to the main stage, with *Cleansed*. Supposedly set in a university, both play and production gave the impression that events unfolded in a concentration camp (and Kane had certainly immersed herself in Holocaust literature).[37] *Cleansed* is bleaker even than *Blasted*, and the prisoners of this satanic institution, Grace, Carl, Robin and Rod, suffer repeated torture from their sadistic 'doctor', Tinker.[38] Bodily mutilation figures heavily, including the amputation of limbs, the severing of a tongue, anal abuse and the grafting of male genitalia onto Grace's body. Carl is slowly cut up, his lover Rod is slaughtered before his eyes, Robin is driven to suicide and Grace is anatomically and emotionally transformed into her dead brother Graham.

Cleansed certainly provoked an extreme physical response in many critics: De Jongh described it 'as one of the most repellent experiences of my theatre going life', Hagerty dismissed it as 'one of the worst plays I have seen', and Gore-Langton advised would-be spectators to 'take a sick bag and enjoy the ride'.[39] Peter, a Kane admirer, left 'feeling bruised to the bone' and interpreted *Cleansed* as a poetic nightmare, compelling as well as 'incomprehensible and vile'.[40] But this time critics accused both Kane and the Royal Court of exploiting her notoriety and peddling extreme violence purely as a publicity stunt. Spencer conceded that James Macdonald directed 'with panache' and produced 'some fine stage effects' and 'some clever tricks', but thought the play itself very impoverished.

> Kane clearly believes she is a serious writer with important things to say. What saddens me is that the Royal Court encourages her in this delusion in what looks like a cynical attempt to retain its cutting edge theatre.[41]

Morley was of a similar opinion:

> *Cleansed* is in every sense a shocker, but the greatest shock of all has to do with neither drugs nor rats nor restitched genitals; it is that anyone at the Court thought Kane a playwright worth staging, let alone staging twice.
> *Cleansed* will doubtless live on its own publicity as the most violent play of the season, but that alone is hardly enough; it is also a tacky, tawdry apology for a play in which any real skill of characterisation or plotting is simply replaced by yet another bloody amputation.[42]

Billington, hyper-aware of critics' over-reaction to *Blasted*, penned a cautiously positive review, making it clear that Kane's notoriety interfered with his ability to assess her work clearly. Gross was more cynical and indicated that he thought Kane was tapping a market for violence for its own sake, and had found a way of securing her celebrity; as Coveney phrased it, Kane 'so wants to be the Bad Girl of our stage'. Macdonald's stylised direction was highly praised, but it also led to accusations that the Royal Court was simply dressing violence in 'designer chic'.[43] Macdonald argued that he had 'focused the audience on why these things are being done rather than the mechanics',[44] but in practice his Brechtian theorisation did not work. Publicity for the production certainly traded on resonances with concentration camp victims, the image showing two shaven-headed men up to their eyes in water, possibly about to drown, staring through a barbed wire fence. A reputation for glamorising brutality dogged the Royal Court for a number of years afterwards, and to some extent still does – playwright David Greig decrying the theatre's 'bullet-hole chic' in 2002.[45]

As Christopher Innes has pointed out, there is a relation between *Blasted* and *Cleansed* and the work of modern British artists like Damian Hirst and Tracey Emin presented by Charles Saatchi for the infamous 'Sensation' exhibition at the Royal Academy of Art in 1997.[46] Hirst became notorious for his preservation and presentation of animals as art – especially for his sheep in formaldehyde; Emin has specialised in quarrying her own life and produced 'Everyone I have ever Slept With' in 1995, a tent with dedications inside to her lovers, relatives, a teddy bear and an aborted foetus. Like Kane, Hirst and Emin were preoccupied with sex and death and believed in delivering extreme shocks to the spectator. But the theatre industry had a great deal to learn about packaging from fine art aficionados, and from the Young British Artists, 'YBA' as they came to be known. Aggressive marketing strategies by artists and dealers in the 1990s sought to publicise products to the mass media, particularly through newspapers and television, and created the concept of 'Britart', allegedly cutting-edge, confrontational art by YBA.[47] The brand-name and selling concept became a big commercial hit, and an idea first targeted at a domestic market suddenly provoked global demand.

At the time the Labour Party were promoting a re-branding of Britain under unhappy labels such as 'Cool Britannia', which, as Chris Smith, Secretary of State for Culture, Media and Sport, explained in his manifesto book on arts policy, was meant to signify 'the "new identity" of Britain as a hotbed of interesting creativity and modernity'.[48] In brief, the idea involved harnessing the best creative minds in the country to refashion Britain's image, whilst ensuring that these artistic talents could also be relied on to stoke the domestic economy and be exported. Ideologically, Cool Britannia was intended to create the impression that Britain had shaken off old post-war ghosts and overcome its imperial past, class divisions, racism and infrastructural problems in health and education. Theatre, argued David Edgar, was with pop, fashion, fine art and food, part of the 'new swinging London'.[49] Robert Hewison imagined he could perceive the rebirth of a nation and named Stephen Daldry next to Damian Hirst as part of a potential 'cultural renaissance'.[50] Spin and hype gained new importance in the re-branding exercise,[51] and Kane was easy to align with ideas of modernity, youth, vigorous energy and the shock of the new. As 'theatre's bad girl' she had exactly the right profile,[52] she was the Damian Hirst or Liam Gallagher of the stage and along with Butterworth and Ravenhill she was promoted as a full member of the 'Britpack'. As exportable product Kane offered the British Council exactly what they wanted in their task to market re-branded Britain: they promoted her work in their new catalogue, funded visits abroad, and ran seminars in Russia promoting her and Ravenhill in translation.[53] Their endeavours unquestionably aided the spread of Kane's work and fame in Germany, Poland, Italy, France and other European countries, where there was an 'extraordinary curiosity' about her work and what it was perceived as saying about contemporary Britain.[54]

It is worth setting the nature of Kane's celebrity in other countries against her notoriety in Britain. In Germany, for example, Kane's influence has been particularly significant. Away from a sexist English press, her celebrity is based on her writing, not on her representation of violence or any notion of her constructing herself as an *enfant terrible* for pure publicity appeal. Nils Tabert, who worked on literal translations of *Cleansed* and *Crave*, reported that:

> ... in Germany she's considered to be the most important British playwright of the 1990s, definitely the most radical, and also the most well known which started at an early stage in her career.

Tabert's remarks were made after Kane's death, which presents another complex perspective, but even so, it is clear that German theatres went to extensive efforts to frame *Blasted* 'as a drama about war, about gender and a dysfunctional society'.[55] In Poland Kane's plays have generated impassioned debate in the public arena, and Kyzysztof Warlikowski's production of *Cleansed* in 2002 has been perceived as potentially 'giving birth to a new style of Polish theatre'. In a country which has a dearth of its own new writers in the wake of communism, Kane's dramas are seen as offering investigations into the nature of existence as opposed to analysing state politics – a theme that has recently dominated the Polish stage. Gruszczynski has even argued that Kane could be described as 'Poland's national writer'.[56] The excessive nature of British reviewers' reaction to the première of *Blasted* does, therefore, enormously complicate the picture of Kane's celebrity in Britain, and paradoxically her very marketability to the sensational tastes of the British public further confounds analysis.

A craving for change

There is little before the première of *Blasted* to suggest that Kane was heading for a career in either playwriting or infamy. Evidence of her immediate response to her sudden notoriety is sparse and contradictory. In an early interview about *Blasted* Kane was dismissive of critics who made surmises about her yet knew nothing about her or her life and claimed that their response made her laugh. She disguised a thinly veiled contempt for the anti-intellectual traditions of reviewing in England:

> There's been a failure by the critical establishment to develop an adequate language with which to discuss drama. A list of contents is not a review, but that is, almost without fail, what new plays receive ... I regret that they [critics] don't take their jobs as seriously as the writers they so frequently and casually try to destroy.[57]

She also made it clear that she was 'very well protected' from the tabloids by the Royal Court and by her agent, Mel Kenyon.[58] Daldry registered his concern that the *Daily Express* 'continued to hound Sarah Kane' to the Royal Court Board nearly three weeks after *Blasted* had opened.[59] Kenyon recalls that Kane was 'very exhausted and upset' after *Blasted* and that her time spent working on *Phaedra's Love* at the Gate theatre was a way of lying low.[60] After *Cleansed*, however, Kane radically changed the style of her writing and all the indications are that she did so in order to try to rid herself of a celebrity persona that linked her to violence and sensation, and to such tags as 'New Brutalism'.[61]

Her next play, *Crave*, was a co-production between the Royal Court and Paines Plough, a new writing company where Kane was writer-in-residence, a position partly secured through Mark Ravenhill, their Literary Manager. It was directed by Vicky Featherstone, Artistic Director of Paines Plough and premièred at the Traverse Theatre, Edinburgh in August 1998, transferring to the Royal Court the following month. Evidently feeling trapped by the expectations she felt readers might impose on her work, Kane decided, in consultation with Feathersone, that she would air the script under the pseudonym Marie Kelvedon at the Paines Plough script meeting where it was under discussion for development and possible production. Featherstone later verified the story that Kane wanted to try to escape the connotations associated with her name:

> In one way, she thought it was funny. Marie was her middle name, Kelvedon was a town near where she was born. But, in another way, it was deadly serious. She had spent a lot of time shaking off the negative effects of *Blasted*. She really wanted to write something that could be judged for what it was, rather than for the fact that it had been written by Sarah Kane.[62]

Crave is a poetic performance text much more than a play: four voices interweave to create a rich musical landscape. In comparison with earlier plays, stage directions are few and they all relate to delivery and silences – and emphatically not to stage action. Themes are love, death, desire and fear. Narratives are fragmented and relations between the voices unclear, but the effect in performance is strangely riveting: snapshots of intense interior worlds vie with each other, haunting the spectator. Featherstone directed it simply and the actors sat in a row. Such was Kane's anxiety to escape her sensational image that she was resistant to engaging with publicity, and her response to Ravenhill when he asked her for ideas was: 'I'm not a brand name, I'm a person.'[63] This certainly implies that Kane had been disquieted about the Royal Court's use of publicity, and the Methuen volume of *Blasted & Phaedra's Love* (published in 1996) may have added to her displeasure: it depicted an image from the production of *Blasted* showing Ian's head in close-up, blood streaming from his eyes – the blurb on the back emphasising the play's 'sheer unadulterated brutalism'.

The critical reaction to *Crave* was overwhelmingly positive. Kane apparently demonstrated a 'uniquely experimental voice', was 'born again as a playwright' and presented an experience that was 'shockingly unsensational'.[64] Reviewers noted resonances with T. S. Eliot, Samuel Beckett, Harold Pinter and Virginia Woolf, and Kane's deployment of self-consciously literary allusions to the high canon doubtlessly helped in the reappraisal of her and her work. A good number of critics referred to the attempt to break with the past and rightly identified Kane's deliberate bid for a celebrity associated with literary respectability: *Crave* was, claimed Macaulay, 'designed to draw attention to its author's technical virtuosity'.[65] Billington romanticised Kane's experiment and admired her escape from 'media pigeon-holing', imagining that the play would allow her to 'walk free'. Others disagreed, Coveney arguing that *Crave* merely 'marked time after the shock tactics of the earlier plays'.[66] Kane herself was determined to change public perceptions of her: in a telephone call from Edinburgh to Nils Tabert in Germany she confessed:

> I'm past violence – I'm really sick of it. It's become like *Trainspotting* with film – so marketable and boring and I don't want to deal with it anymore.[67]

Kane was fiercely intelligent. Growing up with a father who was a tabloid journalist, she must have had considerable insight into what sort of stories sell to the public and how. While I have no doubt that Kane's early aesthetic agenda to push the limits of naturalism to an extreme was genuine, this remark implies that she also understood, and came to resent, the saleability of violence. Whatever her feelings about reviewers, tabloid readerships and the ferocity of consumerist publicity machinery, she also knew she was unavoidably complicit in the very things she despised about them. If Greig has argued that 'for the press Kane was redeemed by *Crave*', I doubt its author saw it quite so neatly.[68] In Britain her notoriety over *Blasted* was still the touchstone for her fame, and since she died only seven months after *Crave* it is impossible to know whether her attempt at reinvention would eventually have outshone what came before.

Death and afterlife

On 20 February 1999, at the age of 27, Sarah Kane committed suicide in King's College hospital, hanging herself on a toilet door with her shoelaces. Only a few days before she had been resuscitated after an overdose. Her death was widely reported and the shock in the theatre industry was palpable. Those close to her had known of her struggle with clinical depression throughout her twenties and had observed that each bout was worse than the last. Given the brutality, bleakness and despair manifest in her plays, it was predictable that her suicide would be retrospectively used to interpret her work. Taylor's crude headline, 'Sarah Kane was a writer of shocking and angry talent. At the age of 27 she took her own life. Did her plays foreshadow her death?', was symptomatic of a gut instinct to read her life into her work.[69] Kane had, of course, represented suicide in *Blasted*, *Phaedra's Love* and *Cleansed* and she had once quite reasonably claimed that 'in some ways all my characters are me'.[70] She had also spoken about her despair of the world many times and linked it with her belief in theatre:

> If we can experience something through art then we might be able to change the future, because experience engraves lessons on our hearts through suffering ... I'd rather risk defensive screams than passively become part of a civilisation that has committed suicide.[71]

Those comments and others like them were then literalised to create a narrative of inevitability. In fact, her suicide gave her a tragically inflected notoriety, Gottlieb, for example, retrospectively reading *Crave* as Kane's retreat into herself rather than a willed decision to engage in a new artistic experiment.[72]

The blurring of her life and work entirely characterised responses to her posthumously performed play, *4.48 Psychosis*, directed by Macdonald at the Royal Court Theatre Upstairs in June 2000. The play dispenses with characterisation altogether, and is an extraordinarily penetrating series of fragments detailing the experience of psychosis and its treatments. Its preoccupation is suicide, and the voice/s of the patient/s is/are mingled with the voices of doctors and lovers, at one point appearing to be merged into one person. *4.48 Psychosis* is as striking for its bursts of hallucinogenic writing as it is for its moments of solid rationality. The ending was especially moving in the light of Kane's death five months earlier:

I have no desire for death
no suicide ever had

watch me vanish
watch me

    vanish

watch me

watch me

    watch

It is myself I have never met, whose face is pasted on the underside of my mind.

    please open the curtains

       _ _ _ _ _[73]

Reviewers argued that it was impossible to disentangle Kane's life from her writing, but ironically chose to interpret *4.48 Psychosis* as a 'suicide note' or 'a unique obituary, compelling and macabre'. Gore-Langton felt that the event was 'beyond review'. Yet Kane's suicide was the beginning of her iconisation as Sheridan Morley noted:

> But I was, I have to say, also quite shocked by the way in which the tragic manner of her death seemed to elevate her early work: suddenly she was being described posthumously as one of the major Court dramatists, a verdict on which I think the jury would still have been out, had she not preempted any such decision. [... Over *4.48 Psychosis*] still hangs the question: would we find this as powerful and moving a play about suicide, did we not know it to have been written by a young, gifted but deeply disturbed woman who was just about to take her own life?[74]

Kane's sainted status was enhanced by the endorsement of celebrities such as Harold Pinter, who, like Edward Bond, had come out in support of her during *Blasted*. Pinter had no qualms in claiming that 'She was her work. It was one thing.'[75] Similarly, Bond's statement at the end of Saunders' book argues that Kane confronted the implacable both in life and art.[76] She has been compared to Sylvia Plath and to Buzz Goodbody, both great creative minds who took their lives at an early age.[77] These comparisons are interesting, but confuse the picture further – Kane's suicide was deployed as evidence that she was a 'great' writer but she is still remembered more for her iconoclasm than for her artistic credentials and whether her fame will endure in Britain is rather doubtful. Not surprisingly Kenyon does place her among the theatrical giants, but acknowledges that her suicide obscures much:

> There's a mythology being built up around everything. The mythology that's often associated with suicide. Either that the work is more symptomatic of a psychological illness, and I don't believe that, or there's the romantic mythology that her work is more profound because she committed suicide. I don't believe that either.[78]

More disturbingly, there are those who see Kane's suicide as a confirmation of her supposed greatness. Tabert argues that her death 'verified that she was absolutely serious, and that it wasn't just effects for effects' sake but a disquieting reflection of society and life'. Daniel Evans, who acted in *Cleansed* and in *4.48 Psychosis*, thought that her death authenticated her writing and 'just shows up the banality of a lot of the younger playwrights coming along'.[79] It is rare for male suicides to be heroised in this fashion, common for female suicides to be represented as tragic icons. It is an offensive and pathological stance which has a tradition attached to it and is well documented by feminist historians.[80] Kane's death was shocking but also exploitable. As Kenyon reported: 'Someone said to me, "well, of course everyone loves a dead girl, especially if she was talented".'[81]

The timing of Kane's suicide at the end of the second millennium also seemed iconic as Eyre and Wright have pointed out, and academics like Innes and Rabey have tended to invent and romanticise her fin-de-siècle qualities.[82] It is a gross exaggeration to claim that she 'rewrote the theatrical map',[83] but she certainly found fame through tapping the zeitgeist of 1990s Britain. It will be many years before Kane can be more accurately assessed, though her brother wonders whether, like Plath, his Kane's plays will ever be properly appraised in Britain: 'I don't think that her work and her life will be separated. Not while I'm alive anyway.'[84] Sarah Kane once said:

> When people talk about me as a writer, that's what I am, and that's how I want my work to be judged – on its quality, not on the basis of my age, gender, class, sexuality or race. I don't want to be a representative of any biological or social group of which I happen to be a member. I am what I am. Not what other people want me to be.[85]

Sadly the very nature of celebrity and its dependence on a sexist media machine makes this impossible – as Kane herself came to appreciate.

Notes

1. See Tom Sellar, 'Truth and Dare: Sarah Kane's *Blasted*', in *Theater* 27 (1997), 29–34.
2. Anonymous, *Times* obituary, 23 February 1999; Anonymous, *Guardian* obituary, 23 February 1999; Paul Taylor, in the *Independent*, 23 February 1999.
3. Though one or two affected an air of nonchalance and wondered why she had not gone further. See Jane Edwardes, *Time Out*, 25 January 1995; and Jonathan Miller, *Sunday Times*, 22 January 1995.
4. Michael Coveney, *Observer*, 5 February 1995; John Peter, *Sunday Times*, 29 January 1995.
5. Paul Taylor, *Independent*, 20 January 1995.
6. Nick Curtis, *Evening Standard*, 19 January 1995.
7. Charles Spencer, *Daily Telegraph*, 19 and 20 January 1995.
8. Jack Tinker, *Daily Mail*, 19 January 1995.
9. Paul Taylor, *Independent*, 20 January 1995; Michael Billington, *Guardian*, 20 January 1995; Robert Hewison, *Sunday Times*, 22 January 1995; and Charles Spencer, *Daily Telegraph*, 20 January 1995.
10. Charles Spencer, 20 January 1995; see, for example, John Gross, *Sunday Telegraph*, 22 January 1995; Nick Curtis, *Evening Standard*, 19 January 1995; John Peter, *Sunday Times*, 29 January 1995.
11. Roger Foss, *What's On*, 25 January 1995.
12. For example, Jane Edwardes, *Time Out*, 25 January 1995; David Nathan, *Jewish Chronicle*, 27 January 1995; Charles Spencer, *Daily Telegraph*, 20 January 1995 – 'a lazy, tawdry piece of work without an idea in its head beyond an adolescent desire to shock'; Nick Curtis, *Evening Standard*, 19 January 1995 – 'an artful chamber of horrors designed to shock and nothing more'; Sheridan Morley, *Spectator*, 28 January 1995 – 'To shock in the theatre is perfectly forgivable, but it is not enough: you also have to have something you want to say.'

13 Louise Doughty, *Mail on Sunday*, 29 January 1995.
14 I have made this point before. See Mary Luckhurst, 'An Embarrassment of Riches: Women Dramatists in 1990s Britain', in *British Drama of the 1990s*, ed. A. Knapp, E. Otto, G. Stratmann and M. Tönnies (Heidelberg: Universitätsverlag C. Winter, 2002), p. 73. Vera Gottlieb is of the same view; see 'Lukewarm Britannia', in *Theatre in a Cool Climate*, ed. Vera Gottlieb and Colin Chambers (Oxford: Amber Lane, 1999), p. 211. Gottlieb also wonders whether the press reaction contributed to Kane's death. Aleks Sierz has no doubt that 'the main reason for the outrage ... seemed to be that Kane, the author of such horrors, was young (twenty-three at the time) and a woman', but his conviction that if 'they [critics] had not overreacted, the play would have been a quiet success, perhaps playing to half-full houses of Royal Court regulars' cannot be proved. See 'The Element that Most Outrages: Morality, Censorship and Sarah Kane's *Blasted*', in *Morality and Justice: The Challenge of European Theatre* ed. Edward Batley and David Bradby (Amsterdam and New York: Rodopi, 2001), p. 235.
15 Sheridan Morley, *Spectator*, 28 January 1995.
16 *Daily Express*, 20 January 1995; and *Daily Mirror*, 20 January 1995.
17 See Graham Saunders, *'Love Me or Kill Me': Sarah Kane and the Theatre of Extremes* (Manchester: Manchester University Press, 2002), p. 3. See also Graham Saunders, 'The Apocalyptic Theatre of Sarah Kane', in *British Drama of the 1990s*, ed. A. Knapp, E. Otto, G. Stratmann and M. Tönnies, pp. 123–35.
18 Sarah Kane's father was a tabloid journalist at the time, so there may have been other agendas too.
19 Richard Eyre and Nicholas Wright, *Changing Stages: A View of British Theatre in the Twentieth Century* (London: Bloomsbury, 2000), p. 375.
20 See *Rage and Reason: Women Playwrights on Playwriting*, ed. Heidi Stephenson and Natasha Langridge (London: Methuen, 1997), pp. 130–1.
21 Aleks Sierz, *In-yer-face Theatre: British Drama Today* (London: Faber and Faber, 2000), p. 98.
22 This alleged counter-culture was doubted as early as 1960 by Caryl Churchill: ' ... already the working-class intellectual cracking at his wife's caricatured Daddy is a stock character. We know the English are still snobbish about accents, we're not happy about the British Empire, suburban life is often dull and many middle-aged men are unfulfilled. We can't communicate with each other, have a lot of illusions and we don't know what if anything life is about. All right. Where do we go from here?' Cited in Philip Roberts, *The Royal Court Theatre and the Modern Stage* (Cambridge: Cambridge University Press, 1999), p. 78. See also Dan Rebellato's analysis, *1956 and All That: The Making of Modern British Drama* (London: Routledge, 1999).
23 Saunders, *'Love Me or Kill Me'*, p. 24.
24 See Elaine Aston, *Feminist Views on the English Stage: Women Playwrights, 1990–2000* (Cambridge: Cambridge University Press, 2003), p. 79.
25 Aston, *Feminist Views on the English Stage*, p. 79.
26 *Observer* (Review Section), 28 February 1999.
27 See *Observer*, 22 January 1995; Saunders, *'Love Me or Kill Me'*, p. 146.
28 *Observer*, 22 January 1995.
29 Sierz, *In-yer-face Theatre*, p. 94.
30 Saunders, *'Love Me or Kill Me'*, p. 146.
31 In his negotiations for the position of Artistic Director, Daldry reported: 'Once I understood the political game playing I thought I'd just do the same. If this is

going to be played this way in the newspapers, I'll start ringing up the newspapers if they all are. ... I thought this is a playpen. I'll get in the playpen and start throwing a bit of sand about and see what happens.' Cited in Philip Roberts, *The Royal Court Theatre and the Modern Stage*, p. 215.
32   His successor was Ian Rickson.
33   See Saunders, *'Love Me or Kill Me'*, p. 7.
34   See Sierz, *In-yer-face Theatre*, p. 30. The main problem with Sierz's thesis is the difficulty he has in providing sufficiently distinctive common features for a very large number of playwrights.
35   Sarah Kane, *Complete Plays* (London: Methuen, 2001), pp. 98–103.
36   Paul Taylor, *Independent*, 23 May 1996; Michael Billington, *Guardian*, 21 May 1996.
37   See Saunders, *'Love Me or Kill Me'*, p. 94.
38   The significance of the name was noted.
39   Nicholas de Jongh, *Evening Standard*, 7 May 1998; Bill Hagerty, *News of the World*, 17 May 1998; Robert Gore-Langton, *Express*, 10 May 1998.
40   John Peter, *Sunday Times*, 10 May 1998.
41   Charles Spencer, *Daily Telegraph*, 7 May 1998.
42   Sheridan Morley, *Spectator*, 16 May 1998.
43   Michael Billington, *Guardian*, 7 May 1998; John Gross, *Sunday Telegraph*, 10 May 1998; Michael Coveney, *Daily Mail*, 7 May 1998; Georgina Brown, *Mail on Sunday*, 24 May 1998.
44   See Saunders, *'Love Me or Kill Me'*, p. 89.
45   David Greig, in a paper on 'Political Theatre' at the conference 'British Drama in the 1990s' held at the University of the West of England, 7 September 2002. Greig is an unequivocal admirer of Kane's work, as is evident in his introduction to her *Complete Plays*, pp. i–xviii. It was the Court's publicity machine and production values to which he was objecting.
46   Christopher Innes, *Modern British Drama: The Twentieth Century* (Cambridge: Cambridge University Press, 2002), p. 530. Interestingly, Kane herself had mixed feelings about the exhibition: see Saunders, *'Love Me or Kill Me'*, p. 28.
47   See Julian Stallabrass, *High Art Lite* (London: Verso, 1999).
48   Chris Smith, *Creative Britain* (London: Faber and Faber, 1998), p. 9. The cover showed two of Damian Hirst's paintings.
49   *State of Play: Playwrights on Playwriting* ed. David Edgar (London: Faber and Faber, 1999), p. 28.
50   Robert Hewison, *The Times*, 19 May 1996.
51   Michael Kustow argues that 'managing and marketing had become the end of public arts activity, not just its means' in the 1980s. See Michael Kustow, *theatre@risk* (London: Methuen, 2000), p. 165.
52   Georgina Brown, *Mail on Sunday*, 23 August 1998.
53   For details on the British Council's repositioning of itself, see Jen Harvie, 'Nationalising the "Creative Industries" ', in *Contemporary Theatre Review*, 13:1 (2003), 15–32.
54   Anonymous, *Daily Telegraph* obituary, 24 February 1999.
55   Nils Tabert interviewed in Saunders, *'Love Me or Kill Me'*, pp. 134–5.
56   See Piotr Gruszczynski, *American Theatre* (May/June, 2002), p. 41.
57   See *Rage and Reason*, p. 132.
58   *Rage and Reason*, p. 130.
59   See Roberts, *The Royal Court Theatre and the Modern Stage*, p. 222.
60   Saunders, *'Love Me or Kill Me'*, p. 149.

61 Kane was adamant that movements were media inventions and of no interest to the writers concerned. See Graham Saunders, 'Love Me or Kill Me', p. 7.
62 Simon Hattenstone, Guardian (Weekend), 1 July 2000. For the actual production she reverted to her own name.
63 Mark Ravenhill, Independent obituary, 23 February 1999.
64 Dominic Cavendish, Independent, 15 August 1998; Nicholas de Jongh, Evening Standard, 24 August 1998; Georgina Brown, Mail on Sunday, 23 August 1998.
65 See, for example, Alastair Macaulay, Financial Times, 22 August 1998; Nicholas de Jongh, Evening Standard, 24 August 1998; and Michael Billington, Guardian, 15 August 1998.
66 Michael Billington, Guardian, 15 August 1998; Michael Coveney, Daily Mail, 18 August 1998.
67 Saunders, 'Love Me or Kill Me', p. 135.
68 Greig, paper on 'Political Theatre'.
69 Paul Taylor, Independent, 23 February 1999. Taylor is wrong about her age.
70 Rage and Reason, p. 133
71 Rage and Reason, p. 133.
72 See Theatre in a Cool Climate, p. 211.
73 Sarah Kane, 4.48 Psychosis in Complete Plays, p. 244.
74 Michael Billington, Guardian, 30 June 2000; Stephen Fay, Independent on Sunday, 2 July 2000; Robert Gore-Langton, Express, 30 June 2000; Sheridan Morley, Spectator, 8 July 2000.
75 See Simon Hattenstone, Guardian (Weekend), 1 July 2000.
76 See Saunders, 'Love Me or Kill Me', pp. 189–91.
77 James Macdonald likened Kane to Sylvia Plath, and was very wary of any reading of her work through her suicide. Buzz Goodbody was a brilliant director at the Royal Shakespeare Company who took her own life just as her pioneering production of Hamlet was opening in 1975. See Sally Beauman, The Royal Shakespeare Company: A History of Ten Decades (Oxford: Oxford University Press, 1982), p. 330.
78 See Simon Hattenstone, Guardian (Weekend), 1 July 2000.
79 See Saunders, 'Love Me or Kill Me', pp. 135 and 173.
80 See, for example, Elisabeth Bronfen, Over Her Dead Body: Death, Femininity and the Aesthetic (Manchester: Manchester University Press, 1992). Bronfen examines representations of women's death in art and literature and concludes that the female corpse is a site where cultural anxiety about death can locate itself.
81 Saunders, 'Love Me or Kill Me', p. 144.
82 Eyre and Wright, Changing Stages, p. 376. Innes, Modern British Drama, p. 529, argues unconvincingly that Kane's work marks a new departure in feminist drama. David Ian Rabey writes interestingly on Kane's confrontational experiments with spectatorship, but concludes his book with a very sentimental panegyric, see British Drama since 1940 (London: Longman, 2003), pp. 207–9. Merle Tönnies fruitfully compares Kane's endeavours with the nineteenth-century fin-de-siècle; see 'The "Sensationalist Theatre of Cruelty" in 1990s Britain', in (Dis)Continuities: Trends and Traditions in Contemporary Theatre and Drama in English, ed. M. Rubik and E. Mettinger-Schartmann (Trier: Wissenschaftlicher Verlag, 2002), pp. 57–71.
83 Eyre and Wright, Changing Stages, p. 374.
84 Simon Kane, see Simon Hattenstone, Guardian (Weekend), 1 July 2000.
85 See Rage and Reason, pp. 134–5.

Part III
Markets

I wonder if he'll be a cigarette one day?
Laurence Olivier, commenting on the young British actor,
Nicol Williamson

8
Celebrity and Rivalry: David [Garrick] and Goliath [Quin]

Peter Thomson

The theatre has always been a happy hunting-ground for scandalmongers, but the story that surfaced quietly in the spring of 1772 was an uncommonly juicy one. The *Daily Advertiser* of 30 April carried the following enigmatic notice at the foot of its second page:

> *Whereas* on Tuesday Night last, between the Hours of Eight and Ten, a Gentleman left with a Centinel belonging to Whitehall Guard, a Guinea and a Half, and a Metal Watch with two Seals, the one a Cypher, the other a Coat of Arms, a Locket, and a Pistol Hook. The Owner may have it again by applying to the Adjutant of the first Battalion of the first Regiment of Foot-Guards at the Savoy Barracks, and paying for this Advertisement.

It was not enigmatic to the gentleman concerned. Having failed (or succeeded – the difference is immaterial) in his seduction of a soldier, he had attempted to buy the soldier's silence with money and gifts. The notice was at best a covert blackmail, and at worst a veiled threat of criminal proceedings. The gentleman fled to France, leaving his belongings at the Savoy Barracks. He was Isaac Bickerstaffe, by some way the most successful playwright of his generation, and a major influence in the development of a distinctively English style of music theatre. His major hits in that style, *Love in a Village* (1763) and *The Maid of the Mill* (1765), had enriched the manager of Covent Garden, but *The Padlock* (1768) and *Daphne and Amintor* (1765) were among David Garrick's reliable stand-bys at Drury Lane.

The Bickerstaffe scandal spurred into action one of Garrick's most persistent adversaries, William Kenrick.[1] On 18 June 1772, there appeared in the *Public Ledger* Kenrick's 'anonymous' couplets under the title 'Leap Frog', in which Garrick was implicitly linked with Bickerstaffe's unspeakable perversion:

> A Dapper Davy & his favourite Bick
> Gambol'd from sport to sport, from trick to trick.
> Davy in glee his Sooty Bick ajog
> They play'd at length that hateful game *leap frog*.

On 22 June, the *St James's Chronicle* advertised the imminent publication of Kenrick's 'Town Eclogue', *Love in the Suds*; on 24 June, Garrick received a pathetic letter, written in French, from the disgraced playwright, and endorsed it 'from that poor wretch Bickerstaffe – I could not answer it' (he knew only too well what was in the offing); and on 27 June, *Love in the Suds* was published with the sub-title 'Being the Lamentation of Roscius for the loss of his Nyky.' There was also, in folio, a two-page prefatory 'Letter to David Garrick, Esq. from William Kenrick, LLD.'

Love in the Suds was an unabashed libel. It is a verse satire in three parts, purportedly 'spoken' by Roscius himself. The first part is addressed to the Muse who alone can bring back his Nyky ('a diminutive of Isaac Bickerstaff[e], as well as a slang term for simpleton or a half-pay officer of marines'),[2] the second is an ironic defence of homosexuality ('Can antient virtue be a modern vice?'), and the third a boastful account of his (Roscius') control of the theatrical scene. Disregarding the disingenuous question posed in Kenrick's Preface – 'Does your modesty think no man entitled to the application of Roscius but yourself?' – Garrick instituted a suit for libel on 7 July 1772. There is nothing known of Garrick's life to support Kenrick's startling claim that he, like Bickerstaffe, was a 'molly', and we have to wonder why it should have been made. Is it, perhaps, evidence of what Marjorie Garber has called 'the inherent bisexuality of celebrity'?[3] Or is it addressed more specifically to members of the acting profession? Rousseau, Garrick's near-contemporary, was evidently of the opinion that actors forfeited their claims to dignified masculinity by putting their bodies on display.[4] The Victorian obsession with manly men (and womanly women) was already foreshadowed in the late eighteenth-century urge to demarcate appropriate embodiments of sexuality.

It might certainly be argued that Garrick, small and exquisite in motion, had too much of the feminine in him to serve as a model in the eighteenth-century pursuit of the idea of essential 'maleness'. His pioneering of the small wig with five curls on each side, which came to be known as 'the Garrick cut', was designed to draw attention to himself off the stage as well as on it. Was this a feminine trait? Kenrick clearly knew what he was about, and he would have liked – such was his febrile jealousy of Garrick's power – some of the mud to stick. But the publication of *Love in the Suds*, which went through five editions during the last six months of 1772, was predicated more on Garrick's celebrity than on doubts about his sexuality. The logical supposition is that Kenrick was aiming to create rumours rather than to feed off them.

The history of London theatre in the aftermath of the Restoration brings into sharp focus the need for a clear distinction between 'celebrity' and some of the words that have at least a tabloid connection with it: 'infamy', 'notoriety', '*réclame*'. Was Nell Gwyn a celebrity? Or Moll Davies? Was Anne Oldfield? Malvolio's league-table (*Twelfth Night*, II.v.140–1) has some application here. Some, though very few and most of them royal, are celebrated from birth; some achieve celebrity; but can celebrity be thrust upon a person? It takes time for newsworthiness to settle into celebrity, an enduring status with substantial provenance. A celebrity is a person who can be relied on to furnish a topic for conversation when the supply of hot gossip has dried up. Will Kemp, Shakespeare's clown, was a celebrity before he was a nine days' wonder. His morris dance to Norwich, like the marathon walks of the cricketer Ian Botham, attracted attention because it was *his*. The clowns, more even than Edward Alleyn and Richard Burbage, were the first celebrities of the Elizabethan theatre. There is no obvious parallel in the new theatre of the 1660s. It may be that the vigorous engagement of an uncommonly articulate audience impeded the progress to supremacy of individual actors at the same time as it promoted to notoriety a number of actresses. For a man-about-town like Samuel Pepys, whose diary provides frequent evidence of the impact of scopophilia on the post-Restoration theatre, the actress Elizabeth Knipp was much more an object of curiosity than any of the leading actors of the rival companies of Duke's and King's Men; and the celebrity of Thomas Betterton at the century's end is in large part the creation in retrospect of Colley Cibber. It served Cibber's purpose in composing his *Apology* – the elevation to dignity of the raffish theatre of his youth – to create a champion who might challenge the historical authority of Jeremy Collier's (and others') assault on the immoral stage of the late seventeenth century. Betterton was respectable, free of scandal, certainly talented, and on this rock Cibber would build his church. Cibber was nearly 70 (and Garrick's London debut only a year in the future) when his *Apology* (1740) was published. By then, he had been Poet Laureate for ten years and had not yet been publicly ridiculed by Alexander Pope in the revised *Dunciad* (1743). However negligible his poetic gift, Cibber was a success. It was he who had set the standard for a new kind of theatrical celebrity, based on social acceptability.

Given his paternity of such scandal-sucking children as Theophilus and Charlotte,[5] Cibber's social climbing was astonishingly successful. Poet Laureate he became, but it was his shrewd exploitation of the moral ambiguity of acting that carried him into the social frame. He was the first to define the route open to an actor:

> If he excells on the Stage, and is irreproachable in his Personal Morals and Behaviour, his Profession is so far from being an Impediment, that it will be oftner a just reason for his being receiv'd among People of Condition with Favor.[6]

Cibber, most famous for his portrayal of such sexually ambiguous fops as his own Sir Novelty Fashion (in *Love's Last Shift*) and Vanbrugh's Lord Foppington (in *The Relapse*), was a founding father *avant la lettre* of theatrical camp. This is how Aaron Hill saw him:

> There was a peeping pertness in his eye .... His attitudes were pointed and exquisite .... He was beautifully absorbed by the character, and demanded and monopolized attention; his very extravagances were colored with propriety; and affectation sat so easy about him that it was in danger of appearing amiable.[7]

It was a style that Cibber adopted in society as well as in the theatre, and few of his associates would have credited him with 'irreproachable ... Personal Morals', but he knew how to exploit the licence permitted to an actor. Because the actor lives always in apposition to his roles, his personality has (and had then) the seductive charm of elusiveness. There is kudos available to those who can claim to know what he/she is 'really like' off stage, a kudos for which the competitive society of eighteenth-century London was undeniably hungry. Some element of sexual indeterminacy, as in the fashionable interest in operatic *castrati* which just outlasted the century, may well have added a faintly lubricious *frisson* to casual encounters, so that Kenrick could have been relying on a traditional prejudice when undertaking to smear Garrick.

No one would have taken the same kind of risk with James Quin, who was known to have killed a fellow-actor in an unruly duel, and who declined a challenge from Theophilus Cibber only because fighting that outrageous little man would be 'like shitting on a toad'.[8] Quin (b. 1693) was 24 years older than Garrick, and established as England's leading actor when Garrick made his extraordinary London debut as Richard III in 1741. There was nothing exquisite or sexually ambiguous about Quin, whose characteristic 'sawing' gesture was likened by Tobias Smollett to 'the heaving of ballast into the hold of a ship'.[9] In William Hogarth's portrait of *c*. 1740, though, watchful in full wig and double chin, he is every inch a gentleman, finely dressed in a braided coat and silk cravat (Figure 8.1). His gaze is well off-centre, addressed perhaps to one of his many admirers in a stage-box. As an enthusiastic adherent of the fashion for gourmandising, Quin was never less than bulky, but he had a Gielgud of a voice and the deserved reputation of a wit to

Celebrity and Rivalry: David [Garrick] and Goliath [Quin] 131

Figure 8.1   William Hogarth, Portrait of Quin (c. 1739), Tate Gallery, London.

endear him to the noble ladies who cultivated him. It is normally, and somewhat approximately, argued that Quin sustained the artful rhetorical tradition he had inherited from Betterton and Barton Booth until that tradition was swamped by the more 'natural' style of Garrick. Such polarising of art and nature has bedevilled all general histories of western acting since critics (Aristophanes was the earliest) first tried to come to grips with the distinction between Aeschylus and Euripides. It would be truer to say that Quin, like Betterton, built his reputation by doing well what came naturally to him. He could manage *gravitas* in tragedy – Addison's Cato became his by adoption and he reconfigured Shakespeare's volatile Coriolanus in the likeness of Cato – and he could delight audiences by turning *gravitas* on its head as Falstaff or Vanbrugh's Sir John Brute (in *The Provok'd Wife*). It was only in the last of those roles that Garrick ever challenged him. John Zoffany's wonderful painting of Garrick as the beskirted Sir John laying about him with a staff captures the zest of his performance of Brute as an old reprobate whose misbehaviour was seductively softened by the actor's own tell-tale charm. That was not how Quin played him, as Charles Churchill's *Rosciad* records in one of theatre history's greatest back-handed compliments:

> In Brute, he shone unequall'd; – all agree,
> Garrick's not half so great a brute as he.

But then, as Churchill goes on to say:

> In whate'er cast his character was laid,
> Self still, like oil, upon the surface play'd.
> Nature, in spite of all his skill, crept in,
> Horatio, Dorax, Falstaff – still was Quin.[10]

The image is of an actor who can reproduce himself in various guises, but who lacks Garrick's access to an *other*:

> 'Tis true when he drank freely, which was often the case, he forgot himself, and there was a sediment of brutality in him when you shook the bottle [Quin in his two most famous comic roles]; but he made you ample amends by his pleasantry and good sense when he was sober [Quin in tragedy].[11]

Drunk or sober, comic or tragic, he was a force to be reckoned with.

A serious biography of Quin would need to take account of a confused childhood and an unworldly father who seems to have entered unknowingly into a bigamous marriage. The actor's grandfather had been Lord Mayor of Dublin in 1667 and, to add to the skeletons in the family cupboard, a suicide seven years later. Unlike Garrick, who was in close touch with his siblings throughout his life, Quin was an only child who, again unlike Garrick, spent much of his adult life in solitude. He sought society when he chose, whereas Garrick lived mostly in society whether he chose it or not. The temperamental contrast is extreme. Accusations of surliness and indolence were fired at Quin, never at Garrick, whom Samuel Johnson aptly summarised as 'the cheerfullest man of his age'.[12] Quin never married, perhaps because he found himself more and more unattractive as his gourmandising (comfort-eating?) led to increasing weight: in retirement in Bath, he rounded off at about 20 stone. One visual image to be borne in mind here is Hogarth's ingenious double-sketch of Garrick and Quin through which the artist set out to prove that, although Garrick was much shorter, he was, owing to the exquisite configuration of his body, *proportionally* taller.[13] Another is of the occasion when, during the season of their playing together at Covent Garden (1746–7), Quin as Falstaff shouldered the dead body of little Hotspur/Garrick off stage, asking audibly as he left, 'Well then – Where shall we sup tonight?'[14] The significant point here is that, in stage silhouette, they would have looked more like Laurel and Hardy than serious rivals for the dramatic crown. It is to the credit of both men that they came to rest in a convivial friendship, but they remained utterly unlike each other.

It was both an accident of history and the pervasiveness of media hype that brought Garrick into competition with Quin. The older actor had been recently mortified when playing Antonio to Charles Macklin's iconoclastic Shylock at Drury Lane in February 1741, and it may have been in pique that he began his regular Dublin engagement in June 1741. He was not in London for Garrick's October debut at Goodman's Fields. He heard about it, of course, and he stayed in Dublin until February 1742. In similar circumstances, Garrick would have rushed to the quay to book his passage home, but Quin had never striven for celebrity, merely allowed it to settle on him. Fame allowed him to speak his mind and to make his own terms with John Rich, the long-serving patentee of Covent Garden. He was, quite simply, unavailable for the 1741–2 season, though he played Addison's Cato at Drury Lane in March for the benefit of the widow and children of the recently dead William Milward.

John Rich was no mug, though. He is often misrepresented by theatre historians as an illiterate oaf who struck it lucky when he bought *The Beggar's Opera* from John Gay in 1728, but whose only real interest was in pantomime. Rich was quirky certainly,[15] but he was a shrewd judge of the public taste, so that it can only have been a foolhardy complacence on Quin's part that allowed his manager to manoeuvre him into opening as Richard III at Covent Garden on 13 October 1742, since Rich at least (and Quin perhaps too late) was well aware that Garrick was making his season's debut at Drury Lane in the same part, *his* part, on the same night. An anonymous pamphleteer was quick to pounce. *A Clear Stage and no Favour, or Tragedy and Comedy at War, occasioned by the Emulation of the two Theatrick Heroes, David and Goliath* was rushed through the press. Although Garrick was fully capable of stimulating interest through anonymous authorship, there is no likelihood that he did so on this occasion. It was the beginning of a long campaign to bring Quin and Garrick to perform together. It was not, however, the first indication of rivalry. If Thomas Davies is to be believed – and he was not inveterately a fabricator – Quin had already made his famous observation that 'if the young fellow was right, he, and the rest of the players, had been all wrong', as well as suggesting that the taste for Garrick was as faddish (and, by implication, as unhealthy) as the taste for the evangelical preaching of George Whitefield. Davies has Quin saying that 'Garrick was a new religion; Whitfield [sic] was followed for a time; but they would all come to church again.'[16] This was not the only time that Garrick was paired with the charismatic Whitefield, but it stung him into one of the near-impromptu verses at which he excelled:

> Pope Quin, who damns all churches but his own,
> Complains that heresy infects the town;
> That Whitfield–Garrick has misled the age,
> And taints the sound religion of the stage:
> Schism, he cries, has turn'd the nation's brain;
> But eyes will open, and to church again!
> Thou great infallible, forbear to roar,
> Thy bulls and errors are rever'd no more;
> When doctrines meet with gen'ral approbation,
> It is not heresy, but reformation.[17]

There is an intriguing whiff of something more than theatrical disagreement here. There were diehards in the Tory Party who remained loyal to the Catholic Stuarts (the Jacobite uprising of 1745 was not far in the future), and 'Pope' Quin is implicitly linked with them. Garrick's own political interests – though he was too careful of his reputation to insist on them outside the ranks of the converted – were Whiggish. Drury Lane under Colley Cibber and the rest of the triumvirate had declared itself for the Whig Robert Walpole, whilst, as if by default (though with the 1728 triumph of the anti-Walpole *Beggar's Opera* in Rich's political portfolio), Covent Garden leaned towards the Tory opposition. I have found no evidence that Quin was a Tory, but this riposte of Garrick's suggests that he thought it convenient, in the heady days of his early success, to align his rival with the Jacobite reactionaries.[18] What is certain is that there is more work to be done on the political affiliations of the two patent theatres in the eighteenth century. Their rivalry seems often to have been more than merely theatrical.

Publicity thrives on partisanship as surely as journalism thrives on controversy. The Quin or Garrick debate was kept simmering in the coffee-house discourse of the 1740s, fuelled by anecdotal gossip and green-room banter. It was almost always Garrick who broke the public silence first. Exaggeratedly afraid throughout his life of being made to appear ridiculous, he was on edge when playing Shakespeare's more warlike heroes, knowing that his lack of inches might count against him. His homework on the text before playing Macbeth (7 January 1744) was particularly intense, and he aimed to forestall hostile criticism by accompanying his performance with an aggressively titled sixpenny pamphlet: *An Essay on Acting, in Which Will Be Considered the Mimical Behaviour of a Certain Fashionable, Faulty Actor*. The title-page carries two telling mottoes – 'O Macbeth has murder'd G-----k' and 'So have I seen a Pygmie strut, mouth and rant, in a Giant's robe' – and the text confirms prejudice at the same time as it points a mocking finger at Quin by confessing that Macbeth should be played by

> a person of near six feet high, corpulently graceful, a round visage, a large hazel eye, aquiline nose, prominent chest, and a well-carved leg, rather inclined to that which is called an Irish leg.[19]

The pamphlet is an example of a tactic Garrick would use quite regularly: in order to fend off ridicule from others, he ridicules himself. The style of performance he ironically recommends is the style of Quin, which he himself has every intention of flouting. Quin is hardly to be blamed for his later reaction to Garrick's playing of Othello (7 March 1745): 'There was a little black boy, like Pompey, attending with a tea-kettle, fretting and fuming about the stage, but I saw no Othello.'[20] The allusion to the second plate of Hogarth's *Harlot's Progress*[21] exemplifies the magisterial wit of Quin when riled.

Rivalry, and in particular the *public* controversy generated by it, is a great stimulus to stage celebrity. The competing managers of Drury Lane and Covent Garden constantly provoked it during the eighteenth century, and the activities of hired or self-appointed claques reinforced it. The fact that a preference was fought for was persuasive evidence that it was *worth* fighting for, and the worthiness of *this* struggle was essential grist to the emerging body of stage-centred journalists throughout the 1740s. *Plus ça change*. Few reviewers can resist comparisons, and they thrive on contrast. Describing the new sensation Edmund Kean, Hazlitt and Leigh Hunt discovered the shortcomings of the old pretender, John Philip Kemble. James Agate rarely wrote better than when setting the flamboyant Sarah Bernhardt against the lymphatic Eleonora Duse. If Olivier and Gielgud had been essentially similar, they would have been less often paired. Comparing like with like is after all comparatively unrewarding for a journalist in search of the kind of copy that stirs readers. Because of the way in which the theatrical discourse of the 1740s was framed, the quarrel has appeared to modern historians to be between the conservative advocates of Quin and the radical advocates of Garrick, and it is not difficult to produce evidence in support of this convenient polarity. Let us take a case in point. In early February 1745, Covent Garden revived *King John* – in Colley Cibber's mended version as *Papal Tyranny in the Reign of King John* – with Quin in the title role and the

73-year-old Cibber himself as Pandulph. On 20 February Drury Lane put up the same play, in a version that conserved more of Shakespeare, with Garrick as the King and Macklin as Pandulph. Quin, who must have taken time off to visit the rival theatre, was critical of Garrick's mannered performance (as he saw it) and contemptuous of Macklin's playing of Pandulph as if he had formerly been a parish clerk.[22] From the facts that the Covent Garden production closed on 26 February and that Colley Cibber never acted again, Macklin's modern biographer concludes that 'audiences left no doubt that they preferred the more naturalistic style of Garrick and Macklin to the stylized manner of Quin and Cibber'.[23] Perhaps, but I have found no conclusive evidence; and the Covent Garden production had lasted for a respectable ten nights. We might, with equal justice, decide that the rival managers were exploiting to good effect the drawing power of two (or four) towering personalities.

It was at this point in the journalistically fuelled rivalry that a new, and potentially emollient, force attempted an intervention. Susannah Cibber was 31 in 1745. Born into the musical Arne family, she had had the misfortune to become the second wife of Colley Cibber's son Theophilus in 1734. David Erskine Baker, the first compiler of *Biographia Dramatica* in 1764, gives a wonderfully tongue-in-cheek account of Theophilus Cibber, in the course of which he grants his subject an overriding quality of *effronterie* whilst conceding that '[h]is person was far from pleasing, the features of his face were rather disgusting'.[24] But it was Theo's financial recklessness above all that had wrecked the marriage by 1737, and it was to one of his creditors that he virtually offered his wife as a temporary sop. William Sloper was a moderately wealthy, moderately married man of about 30 when he fell in love with Susannah Cibber, whose children he fathered and to whom he remained devoted until her death in 1766. The liaison, which began with Theo's blessing, might have been concealed from the public gaze had it not been for Theo himself. Dismissed from a *ménage à trois* of his own devising, he resolved to bring a charge of criminal conversation against William Sloper, and it was probably to advertise his plight as suffering husband in advance of the court case that he kidnapped Susannah from Sloper at gunpoint in September 1738. At the subsequent hearing (December 1738), Cibber as plaintiff was awarded £10 instead of the £5,000 he had demanded. Here if ever was a theatrical scandal to set tongues wagging, and it says much about the personalities of both Theophilus and Susannah that, once the storm had subsided, Susannah's adulterous return to Sloper was greeted with silence. By 1745, she was established as a tragic actress of unique sensitivity, delicate of feature and physique, but with the voice of a trained singer. Theophilus took his effrontery elsewhere.

It was an intelligent recognition of the drawing power of Quin, Garrick and herself that provided the motive for Susannah Cibber's scheming during the summer of 1745. She had played opposite Quin, whose early concern for her had been generous and not at all predatory, and Garrick, whose fiery liaison with the Irish actress Peg Woffington came to its fiery end in June of that year, and she admired both of them as actors. Knowing (everyone did) that Drury Lane was in financial straits, Susannah Cibber would like to have proposed to these two leaders of the stage a new management triumvirate to outshine the one in which her father-in-law had been famously involved at Drury Lane. There was nothing outlandish to her about the idea – she, after all, knew London's theatres from the inside – of Quin and Garrick acting together. Her problem was arranging a meeting with either. Quin had already established a social and professional routine which Garrick would soon emulate. During the London season, he would attend occasional *levées* and regular society dinners on nights when he was not due to perform. After the season was over, he would either fulfil an engagement in Dublin or wile away the time as a guest of one or other member of the nobility (probably at the behest of the lady of the house). Sometimes he would manage both, but he was not in Ireland in 1745. As the *Daily Gazeteer* reported on 5 September, 'Temperate Jack is swilling Hogsheads of Claret in Boeotia.' As for Garrick, he was playing hard to get for everyone, including Susannah. It was a summer of feverish negotiation. James Lacy, engaged in a holding operation at Drury Lane, was trying to secure the services of Garrick and Susannah Cibber, but, for different reasons, neither would make a commitment, and Garrick persisted in deflecting Susannah's requests for a meeting onto his business friend, Somerset Draper. It may well be that her vision of a triumvirate, with herself as leading lady to the two acknowledged giants of the London stage, was a pipe-dream. Quin had little stomach for the burdens of management, and Garrick – worried now by Peg Woffington's possession of his letters – was mistrustful of women, particularly of one whose business partnership would introduce the threat of interference from her obnoxious husband. It might be inferred from the surviving correspondence that he chose to pretend ignorance of Susannah's proposition. Finally, and only after the shock of the rout of the English army by Charles Stuart's Highlanders at Prestonpans on 21 September, she wrote to Garrick with a concrete plan. Now clearly in a corner, he turned again to Somerset Draper, writing on 26 October 1745:

> I should not have troubled you so soon again, was it not to tell you I have received a letter from Mrs. Cibber, who proposes a scheme for our acting with Mr. Quin, gratis, in the Haymarket; in order to raise a sum of money to enlist men for his Majesty's service.
> Now, although I imagine this proposal merely chimerical and womanish; yet, as I would not give my opinion too hastily upon such an affair, I must desire you to wait upon her; and to be sure if I can, in any way, contribute to the general good, I shall be ready, upon the first notice, to come and give my assistance ....

> Mr. Quin, she tells me, is in the country, and knows nothing of it yet; for until I give my consent, she thinks it will signify nothing to speak to him. I beg you will see her as soon as possible, and give me your opinion upon it.[25]

It should be remembered that, up to this point, Quin and Garrick had avoided acting together, and it was beginning to look as though they never would.

It is a credit to Susannah Cibber's perspicacity that she was not blinded by the journalistic impulse to segregate the 'old' school and the 'new', and equally to her credit that she persisted in her scheme despite Garrick's prevarication which, by January 1746, had toppled over into equivocation. Whilst voicing his doubts to Draper at the end of December 1745 – 'how can she be a joint patentee? Her husband will interfere, or somebody must act for her, which would be equally disagreeable'[26] – he was not prepared to close off Susannah's interest. That, unless Draper was playing a double game on his own account, is clear from her new year letter to Garrick:

> Mr Draper called upon me a day or two before I had your letter and told me you proposed Mr Quin should be one of the triumvirate; that you were studying parts in a different cast and that you were willing to make everything easy to him ... I did not know whether you would give up any of your parts and if it was likely you could live in friendship playing them alternately. He is an honest, worthy man, and besides being a great actor he is a very useful one and will make the under actors mind their business.[27]

Garrick would purchase a share of the Drury Lane patent on his own account in 1747 without the 'womanish' burden of Susannah Cibber, but it is she who emerges from their exchanges more agreeably.

And she was right. Before 1746 was over, Garrick and Quin were acting together at Covent Garden, thereby initiating a friendship that would last until Quin's death in 1766, which came in the immediate aftermath of a sojourn with the Garricks in their fashionably tasteful country house in Hampton. Although much has been made of the eventual confrontation of the two great actors in Rowe's *The Fair Penitent* on 14 November 1746, usually by way of quoting Richard Cumberland's recollection of the impression it made on him as a fourteen-year-old, the celebrity contest was effectively over once Quin and Garrick had performed on the same stage. Garrick had without doubt been the beneficiary, less certainly the victor: his career was in its early stages; Quin's was approaching its end. There was a brief locking of horns when Garrick contrived, by a clever choice of plays, to keep Quin out of the Covent Garden audience's sight for most of a month, but the 1747–8 season marked the beginning of Garrick's long reign at Drury Lane.

He was, in effect and perhaps intentionally, conceding Covent Garden to Quin, whilst Quin, by determining to spend more and more of his time in Bath, was making reciprocal concessions to Garrick.

By reducing the histrionic battlefield to two contestants, the theatre's publicity machine – which by now included actors, managers, journalists and print-shop proprietors – had served its master well. But the on-stage collision of Quin and Garrick has more to tell us about the evolution of the eighteenth-century stage. A re-evaluation of Cumberland's famous verdict will provide a tolerable guide. This is how Cumberland presents Quin in the character of Horatio that November evening:

> ... in a green velvet coat embroidered down the seams, an enormous full-bottomed periwig, rolled stockings and high-heeled, square-toed shoes. With very little variation of cadence, and in a deep, full tone, accompanied by a sawing kind of action, which had more of the senate than the stage in it, he rolled out his heroics with an air of dignified indifference, that seemed to disdain the plaudits that were bestowed upon him.

This is not, of course, an objective recollection; it is a summing-up for the prosecution, carried over into the description of Garrick's entrance as Lothario:

> [W]hen, after long and eager expectation I first beheld little Garrick, then young and light and alive in every muscle and in every feature, come bounding on the stage, and pointing at the wittol Altamont and heavy-paced Horatio, it seemed a whole century had been stepped over in the transition of a single scene.[28]

As presented by Cumberland, this is a rehearsal of the age-old struggle for stage supremacy between the aural and the visual, with Quin beside the sonorous Gielgud and Garrick beside the spectacular Olivier. This is, of course, too stark, but not without substance. Quin was never at ease with his body, but always proud of his voice. It was not on grounds of age that, in 1754, he declined the invitation to perform for his old friend Lacy Ryan's benefit, but because he had lost teeth: 'I'll whistle Falstaff for no man.'[29] Garrick was always sufficiently self-aware to know that he was beautiful in action. His management of Drury Lane would bring about significant improvements in the furnishing and illumination of the stage, something of which Quin was careless. (His Falstaff, exhausted by his exertions at Shrewsbury, 'sank into a crimson velvet *fauteuil*, with gilt claws and blue fringe, pitched conveniently on the battlefield'.[30]) Sensitive to the age's increasing fascination with the appearance of things, Garrick was sufficiently an entrepreneur to ensure and prolong his own supremacy. That becomes clearer if the visual theme is further pursued.

We know that Garrick's facial features were uncommonly mobile, and that a spectacularly rapid visible transition from passion to passion was his party trick. Hogarth was not the only portraitist to find him a tricky subject because his expression changed so quickly. Nevertheless, as Shearer West has conclusively demonstrated,[31] it was above all Garrick who presided over the cultural shift that made actors a particularly appealing subject for painters. Reconfiguring sensibility for his contemporaries, Laurence Sterne has Tristram Shandy argue that '[a] man's body and his mind ... are exactly like a jerkin, and a jerkin's lining; – rumple the one – you rumple the other'.[32] Who better than an actor to illustrate Sterne's simile? Garrick's cultivation of painters was richly rewarded in the circulation of his image through prints. He was the first actor fully to exploit the publicity value of the studio portrait. In his detailed suggestions to Francis Hayman for a painting of himself as King Lear (October 1745), he combines the functions of director and easel artist:

> Suppose Lear Mad upon the Ground with Edgar by him; His Attitude Should be leaning upon one hand & pointing Wildly towards the Heavens with his Other, Kent & Fool attend him & Glocester comes to him with a Torch; the real Madness of Lear, the Frantick Affectation of Edgar, and the different looks of Concern in the three other Characters will have a fine Effect.[33]

What Garrick has in mind here is the lofty style of history painting, which stood where tragedy stood in the esteem of connoisseurs, on the topmost rung of artistic achievement. But, unable to contain his eagerness to see Hayman's portrait of him as Richard III, he adds, 'Have You finish'd My Picture Yet?' Garrick had presumably had a sight of Hayman's unfinished canvas, which portrays a heroically defiant Richard, his fallen helmet between his splayed feet, his sword erect, his sword arm bare and his horse lying dead behind him. ('A horse! A horse! My kingdom for a horse!') But he was at least equally anxious to see the completion of Hogarth's better-known 'history' painting of his Richard, starting from his couch at the sight of the first of the spectral visitors to his tent before the battle of Bosworth. In a letter to Somerset Draper, sent from Dublin on 1 December 1745, he moves without so much as a paragraph break from Mrs Draper's illness to Hogarth's progress on the massive canvas:

> I am very sorry poor Mrs Draper continues ill, and am afraid she must wait for the spring to recover her. Pray, does Hogarth go on with my picture, and does he intend a print from it? Pray, when you see him, give my services.[34]

Prints were much more functional than the painting itself. Not until 1760, when Hayman's *Richard III* was exhibited at the Society of Artists, was any portrait of Garrick put on public display, but prints could become Garrick's visiting cards. In Paris in 1764, he found himself so pressed for pictorial representations of his greatest roles that he urged his brother George (20 November) to send him prints of Reynolds' 'Mr. Garrick between Tragedy and Comedy' (six copies), Benjamin Wilson's portraits of him as Lear and as Hamlet, Zoffany's Jaffier and Belvidera (two to three copies), anything else of Zoffany's that may be available, and two or three copies of prints from James McArdell's engraving of Jean Liotard's pastel portrait. Two years later, also from Paris, George Colman wrote to tell him that 'There hangs out here in every street, pirated prints of Reynolds' picture of you, which are underwritten "L'Homme entre le Vice et la Vertu".'[35] Garrick had travelled a long way since the day in September 1749 when, walking in the Strand, he was ingenuously delighted to discover that the sign being erected outside a bookseller's shop was his own portrait '& My Name written about it, in Letters as tall as Myself'.[36] However incalculable the precise contribution of the visual arts to Garrick's celebrity may be, there can be no doubting its significance. By contrast, Quin, so deeply disadvantaged historically by the much reproduced image of his Coriolanus (in a breastplate and stiff skirt that make him look like a grotesque drag-queen in a liberty bodice and a tutu), was indifferently served, but then, in a later age, he would have been considered less photogenic.

The idea of celebrity, like the idea of performance, raises issues of authenticity. Does the person match the reputation? The celebrated actor, as a professional imitator of persons not himself, is, then, either liable to double scrutiny or protected by a riveting ambiguity. As was evident in his reception in Paris and elsewhere in Europe during his grand tour of 1763–5, Garrick was often viewed as a representative Englishman. There are signs, particularly in his conscious self-refashioning at the end of the 1740s, that he prepared himself for just such a representative role. Having kicked over the traces of Peg Woffington, he set himself for a society marriage to Eva Marie Violetti, an Austrian dancer, whose London residence was as a ward of the wealthy Earl of Burlington. Through Burlington, Garrick gained access to London's artistic élite and, most significantly, to the Cavendish family (Dukes of Devonshire) into which Burlington's daughter had married. For the rest of his life he performed the dual role of protean genius and exemplary husband, and he and his wife were amply rewarded by high society. 'It is my utmost pride and ambition', he wrote in his maturity, 'to deserve the kind thoughts of the great and good.'[37] The wall between authenticity and obsequiousness may sometimes have been paper-thin, but it was a wall. The Garricks gave good value in return for their acceptance. Her natural charm was enhanced by a physical grace that matched his and by the quirkily Austrian inflection of her spoken English, and his social energy was always prodigious. If Garrick can be legitimately charged with a self-serving cultivation of aristocratic friendships, it should also be recorded that he worked hard to entertain his high-society friends to their mutual advantage.

Even so, the price Garrick paid for his celebrity was, as it so often is, anxiety ('To be thus is nothing, but to be safely thus'). The man who understood him best was not Samuel Johnson but Joshua Reynolds. There are, I suspect, few better commentaries on celebrity than Reynolds' imaginary conversation between Dr Johnson and Edward Gibbon, in which Johnson takes on the role of Garrick's advocate:

> No man, however high in rank or literature, but was proud to know Garrick, and was glad to have him at his table .... [He], by paying due respect to rank respected himself; what he gave was returned, and what was returned he kept for ever .... [T]hat Garrick husbanded his fame, the fame which he had justly acquired both at the theatre and at the table, is not denied; but where is the blame either in the one or the other, of leaving as little as he could to chance? .... [H]e possessed a power over other men's minds approaching to fascination.[38]

Reynolds is all the better qualified to encapsulate Garrick's qualities by virtue of the fact that their relationship was an uneasy one. Whereas Thomas Gainsborough called Garrick 'my sprightly genius' and thought him, quite simply, 'the greatest creature living in every respect',[39] Reynolds recognised in Garrick the doubleness of human nature that fascinated him. 'If I was to judge from my own experience', he wrote, 'the mind always desires to double, to entertain two objects at a time',[40] and of the mind's two modes of receiving pleasure, Reynolds upheld that one approaches the divine and the other sinks to sensuality. Garrick, perhaps because he perceived in him a simmering sexuality, served Reynolds as an object lesson in duality. He saw him as the victim of a passion for fame, which 'however proper when within due bounds as a link in the social chain, as a spur to our exertions to acquire and deserve the affections of our brethren, yet when this passion is carried to excess it becomes a vice, either ridiculous, or odious, or sometimes criminal'. It is a pen-portrait that lacks entirely the mellowness of the summative imaginary conversation, and it concludes grimly by placing Garrick among those who, '[f]rom having no great principle ... live in perpetual anxiety what conduct to take on every occasion to insure this petty praise'.[41]

Garrick seems to have been wholly unaware of the extent to which Reynolds carried his character study into the image of the actor between Tragedy and Comedy: the man desiring 'to entertain two objects at a time', and yet surely acknowledging with a self-excusing shrug to 'divine' tragedy

Celebrity and Rivalry: David [Garrick] and Goliath [Quin] 143

Figure 8.2 Joshua Reynolds, *Garrick between Tragedy and Comedy* (1761), courtesy of the Garrick Club, London.

that it is 'sensual' comedy that has ensnared him (Figure 8.2). It seems to me less significantly a portrait of Garrick than an image of anxiety. Reynolds' Garrick is diminished by the unending desire to please. It was Fanny Burney's observation that 'Garrick never enters a room but he regards himself as the object of general attention, from whom the entertainment of the company is expected.'[42] Reynolds has a gloss on this: 'He never came into company but with a plot how to get out of it. He was forever receiving messages of his being wanted in another place. It was a rule with him never to leave any company saturated.'[43] This is unfair. Reynolds, like most people, lived a much less busy life than Garrick – and Reynolds signalled his acknowledgement of the unfairness in his imaginary conversation by displacing the judgement onto the hostile Gibbon (who ascribes it to the playwright George Colman). But the anxiety of a man pulled in two ways remains in the picture. It is an oddly androgynous actor who stands there in the middle; a flirtatious figure beside the masculine sturdiness of

Tragedy. Very soon, Comedy will take him behind the trees on the left and seduce him.

Anxiety to excel and the fear of ridicule were Garrick's constant companions. Did it never occur to him that, by placing him in this portrait within the classic frame of 'The Choice of Hercules', Reynolds was carrying the diminutive Garrick to the brink of the ridiculous? Quin's was neither the first nor the last rivalry to trouble him. As early as 23 June 1742, he wrote from Dublin that '[Dennis] Delane has played against me, but wanting allies has quitted the field.'[44] Much more formidably, the acerbic actor, writer and wit Samuel Foote competed socially and mimically, but Garrick generally had the good sense to keep his distance from Foote. The handsome actor Spranger Barry, six feet tall and blessed with a voice that lilted, was a less easily avoided threat. But Garrick had learned from that initial confrontation with Quin that sheer manliness would not necessarily command the stage. Quin was, in the street slang of the time, a 'top diver': a lover of women, but fundamentally a man's man. The tender passions were outside his dramatic range. Teasing him for his unwillingness to play lovers, the Duchess of Queensberry once asked, 'Pray, Mr. Quin, do you ever make love?' 'No, Madam', answered Quin, 'I always buy it ready made.'[45] Garrick, who was a ready sharer of bawdy talk with men, would never have made such a boast in mixed company, even if it had been true. Celebrity entrenched his fastidiousness. By comparison with 'top divers' like Quin or Barry, Garrick was, partly in appearance but more in the grace and detail of his carriage, a 'twiddle poop',[46] an effeminate man. It was on this recognition that William Kenrick had dared to launch his libel. He may have read the bisexuality of celebrity in Reynolds' troubled and troublesome portrait of duality, or he may have stumbled accidentally on the theatre as a lively site for sexual speculation. Because he traded so much on his body, Garrick was vulnerable to insinuators like Kenrick. There has been much recent work on cultural shifts in attitudes to the commerce of sex in the eighteenth century,[47] but not much of it has focused on the theatre. If we keep the precedent of *Love in the Suds* in mind, the publication almost exactly four years later of William Jackson's *Sodom and Onan* further enforces the link between theatrical celebrity and sexual vulnerability. Jackson's satire unequivocally accused Samuel Foote of sodomy. In the subsequent trial, Foote was found not guilty, but, because the fire around Foote burned more fiercely than Garrick's, the smoke has never dissipated.

Notes

1 The 1812 edition of *Biographia Dramatica* (vol. 1, part 2, pp. 430–1) reports of Kenrick that his life was passed 'in a state of warfare', and that '[f]ew persons were ever less respected by the world; still fewer have created so many enemies, or dropped into the grave so little regretted by their contemporaries'. But that is a

partisan view. Kenrick certainly tended to overrate the literary talents he undoubtedly possessed, and that led him to cross swords with Garrick over the relegation of his *Falstaff's Wedding* (1766) to a single benefit performance and again over his share of the take for his *The Widow'd Wife* (1767). More particularly, in the early summer of 1772, he was riled by Garrick's rejection of his latest play, *The Duellist*.

2 See Michal Kobialka, 'Words and Bodies: A Discourse on Male Sexuality in Late Eighteenth-Century English Representational Practices', *Theatre Research International*, 28:1 (March 2003), 5. Bickerstaffe had been, perhaps still was at the time of the incident, a half-pay marine officer.

3 As quoted by Paul Franklin, 'The Terpsichorean Tramp: Unmanly Movement in the Early Films of Charlie Chaplin', in *Dancing Desires: Choreographing Sexualities on and off the Stage* ed. Jane Desmond (Madison, WI: University of Wisconsin Press, 2001), p. 63. The argument touched on here is illuminated by Laurence Senelick, 'Mollies or Men of Mode? Sodomy and the Eighteenth-Century London Stage', *Journal of the History of Sexuality*, 1:1 (July 1990), 33–67, and fully explored in Kristina Straub, *Sexual Suspects: Eighteenth-Century Players and Sexual Ideology* (Princeton, NJ: Princeton University Press, 1992).

4 See Jean-Jacques Rousseau, *Politics and the Arts: Letter to M. D'Alembert on the Theatre* (1758; repr. Ithaca, NY: Cornell University Press, 1993), pp. 75–92.

5 Theophilus Cibber's marriage to Susannah Arne is treated later in this essay. His extraordinary sister, Charlotte (1713–60), was notoriously given to transvestism. Her *Narrative of the Life of Mrs Charlotte Charke* was published in 1755. In it, as *Biographia Dramatica* records (1812 edn., vol. 1, part 1, p. 103), 'from infancy she owns she had more of the male than female in her inclinations'.

6 *An Apology for the Life of Mr. Colley Cibber*, 2 vols, ed. R. W. Lowe (London: John C. Nimmo, 1889), I, pp. 82–3.

7 Aaron Hill, *The Prompter*, ed. W. W. Appleton and Kalman Burnim (New York: Blom, 1966), pp. 7–8.

8 In the 1887 republication of the anonymous *Life of Mr. James Quin* (London, 1760), this is bowdlerised as 'Quarrelling with such a fellow is like – (using an indecent expression)', p. 31.

9 From *Peregrine Pickle* (1751). Quoted in Mrs. Clement Parsons, *Garrick and His Circle* (London: Methuen, 1906), p. 44.

10 *The Rosciad* was much revised before and after its original publication in 1761. Churchill's account of Quin, as Quin himself might have read it, appears on pp. 92–3 of the 1887 edition of the *Life of Mr. James Quin*.

11 Unattributed quotation from a contemporary commentator in the 1887 edition of the *Life of Mr. James Quin*, p. 93.

12 James Boswell, *Life of Johnson*, ed. R. W. Chapman (Oxford: Oxford University Press, 1970), p. 1021.

13 The double-sketch is in the Queen's Collection. It is excellently reproduced in Alan Kendall, *David Garrick* (New York: St. Martin's Press, 1985), p. 36. For an account of its provenance, see Ronald Paulson, *Hogarth*, 3 vols (New Brunswick, NJ: Rutgers University Press, 1992), II, p. 257.

14 This anecdote appears variously in contemporary sources and has probably solidified into truth through repetition.

15 Anyone who visited Rich at his home would have to clear away two or three of his dozens of cats before sitting down in one of his tastefully upholstered chairs.

16 Thomas Davies, *Memoirs of the Life of David Garrick*, 2 vols (London, 1780), I, pp. 44–5.
17 Arthur Murphy, *The Life of David Garrick*, 2 vols (London: J. Wright, 1801), I, p. 32.
18 I am here developing a point made by Jean Benedetti in his *David Garrick and the Birth of the Modern Theatre* (London: Methuen, 2001), p. 63.
19 David Garrick, *An Essay on Acting* (London: W. Bickerton, 1744), p. 11.
20 Reported in William Cooke, *Memoirs of Charles Macklin* (London: James Asperne, 1804), p. 114.
21 In Plate 2 of *A Harlot's Progress*, a tiny black houseboy, wearing a turban with an incongruous feather, is bringing in a kettle just as the over-exuberant harlot is kicking over the table of her first keeper.
22 Cooke, *Memoirs of Charles Macklin*, p. 19.
23 William W. Appleton, *Charles Macklin* (Cambridge, MA: Harvard University Press, 1961), p. 74.
24 See *Biographia Dramatica* (1812 edn.), vol. 1, part 1, pp. 125–8.
25 *The Letters of David Garrick*, 3 vols, ed. David M. Little and George M. Kahrl (Cambridge, MA: Harvard University Press, 1963), I, p. 66.
26 *The Letters of David Garrick*, I, p. 74.
27 *The Private Correspondence of David Garrick*, 2 vols, ed. James Boaden (London: Henry Colburn and Richard Bentley, 1831–2), I, pp. 48–9.
28 Richard Cumberland, *Memoirs* (London: Lackington, Allen and Co, 1806), pp. 59–60.
29 See *Life of Mr. James Quin*, p. 93 for a version of this widely reported excuse.
30 Mrs Clement Parsons, *Garrick and His Circle*, p. 105.
31 See Shearer West, *The Image of the Actor* (London: Pinter, 1991), *passim*.
32 Laurence Sterne, *The Life and Opinions of Tristram Shandy, Gentleman*, ed. Ian Campbell Ross (Oxford: Clarendon Press, 1983), p. 127.
33 *The Letters of David Garrick*, I, p. 53.
34 *The Letters of David Garrick*, I, p. 70.
35 *The Private Correspondence of David Garrick*, ed. James Boaden, I, p. 232. The prints were, of course, pirated from Reynolds' 'Mr. Garrick between Tragedy and Comedy'.
36 *The Letters of David Garrick*, I, p. 124.
37 *The Letters of David Garrick*, II, p. 765.
38 Reynolds' imaginary conversations about Garrick are reproduced in Mrs Clement Parsons' often underrated *Garrick and His Circle*, pp. 394–405.
39 Quoted in Isabelle Worman, *Thomas Gainsborough* (Lavenham: Terence Dalton, 1976), pp. 58–9.
40 *Reynolds' Portraits*, ed. Frederick W. Hilles (London: Heinemann, 1952), p. 119.
41 *Reynolds' Portraits*, pp. 87–8.
42 *Early Diary of Fanny Burney*, 2 vols, ed. Annie Raine (London: George Bell, 1889), II, pp. 159–60.
43 *Reynolds' Portraits*, p. 87.
44 *The Letters of David Garrick*, I, p. 40.
45 The exchange, recorded by Lady Mary Coke, is cited in Mary Nash's excellent biography of Susannah Cibber, *The Provoked Wife* (London: Hutchinson, 1977), p. 196n.
46 Eighteenth-century street slang has literary high points at one end in Ned Ward's *The London Spy* (1703) and at the other in Pierce Egan's *Life in London* (1820). 'Top

diver' and 'twiddle-poop' are recorded in Francis Grose's 'dictionary of the vulgar tongue', *Lexicon Balatronicum* (1785).
47 See, for example, *Sexual Underworlds of the Enlightenment*, ed. G. S. Rousseau and Roy Porter (Chapel Hill, NC: University of North Carolina Press, 1988); and Victor Norton, *Mother Clap's Molly House: The Gay Subculture in England, 1700–1830* (London: GMP Publishers, 1992).

9
Actresses and the Economics of Celebrity, 1700–1800
Felicity Nussbaum

> I am the Famous She, Whose moving Arts
> Give Life to Poetry, to Poets Fame:
> I Charm Spectators Eyes, and chain their Hearts,
> 'Till their Applause and Love are but the same.
> Thomas Otway, 'Under Mrs. B---[arry]'s Picture' (1689)

The theatre stands at the crux of urban life in eighteenth-century England, and women figured at its very centre. Women played crucial roles as actresses, playwrights, dramatic characters, orange girls and pawnbrokers, as well as costume-makers and vendors. Star players such as Elizabeth Barry, the subject of the epigraph above, linked public fame to romantic affection through the magnetic theatrical appeal of a palpable female presence. She and other actresses openly violated the conventional injunction to women of this historical period: 'Your sex's glory,' enjoined Edward Young in *Love of Fame* (1725–8), ''tis, to shine unknown; / Of all applause be fondest of your own'.[1] Ranging in reputation from prostitutes to socially respectable ladies, early actresses offer a dynamic cultural site for examining unequivocally public women in a period that ostensibly fostered domesticity as an ideal. In the critical change from a land economy to a mercantile one, from an aristocracy to an increasingly urban landscape dominated by trades people, actors became public commodities whose worth fluctuated depending upon public demand.[2] The expansion of print culture in the eighteenth century, along with the rise of mercantilism, the lessening power of the aristocracy, the secularisation of society and the increase in leisure gave rise to a media apparatus that was essential to the construction of celebrity. Yet the economic realities of the theatre, as I will argue, disrupted any simple staging of femininity. The concepts of 'woman' and 'actor' were often at odds in this formative period. By what definition were these first actresses to be regarded as women? How could one reconcile 'the rarity and beauty of their talents' with 'the discredit of employing them'?[3]

It has long been acknowledged that the eighteenth century was an age of the actor rather than of the play. Through the course of the Restoration and the eighteenth century women on stage began to emerge as celebrities, a process that culminated by the century's end in the staggering popularity of Sarah Siddons, whose avid fans breakfasted near the playhouse to claim coveted tickets. She and other actresses negotiated a kind of public femininity that had not been displayed before. At first women engaging in theatrical activity seem to have been regarded, especially by the Puritans, as curiosities in the same aberrant category as the exotics – the hog-faced woman, hairy wench or baboon – exhibited in public places for commercial return in the seventeenth century. Women acting in women's roles seemed to some observers to be even more unnatural than boys playing at being women had seemed in earlier periods.

Women participated in court entertainments, public theatricality, popular festival rituals and guild performances throughout the seventeenth century, but no women appeared in the legitimate theatre until the Restoration in 1660. The Puritans, of course, had abruptly closed the theatres during the Interregnum beginning in 1642. Male actors had earlier interpreted the roles of Cleopatra and Desdemona, Kate and Ophelia, in the eroticised parts that Shakespeare created with boys in mind. Partly as a response to the shortage of experienced boy actors caused by the closing of the theatres for nearly two decades, the prohibition against women performing was lifted with the restoration of Charles II; yet Thomas Kynaston of Davenant's Company ('the prettiest woman in the whole house'),[4] as well as James Nokes and Charles Hart of Killigrew's Company, continued to perform as women, particularly in their favoured roles as bawds or sentimental heroines. Yet perhaps the most compelling reason for preventing women from acting on the stage was the economic competition they would bring.[5] Simultaneously roles for real women were for the first time invented and expanded, and Restoration theatre became more rooted in the actual female body. While boys had been the gender-benders in the Renaissance, cross-dressed women thespians were the gender-benders in the Restoration and eighteenth century. In addition, female dramatists (most significantly Susannah Centlivre, Susannah Cibber, Hannah Cowley, Frances Burney, Elizabeth Griffith and Elizabeth Inchbald) were attracted to the burgeoning business of writing for the newly feminised stage. In short, women's indispensability to the commercial theatre was firmly established during the eighteenth century.

Intense debates, dating from the early seventeenth-century misogynist anti-theatrical tracts, charged that women, often taken to be metonyms for the theatre itself, were at once responsible for the theatre's corrupting influence and more susceptible to it. In fact, troupes of French women performing at the Blackfriars as early as 1629 were termed by Thomas Brand to be 'monsters rather'; and Jeremy Collier voiced the extreme anti-theatrical view that allowing immodest women on stage 'is to make Monsters of them, and throw them out of their Kind'.[6] Male playgoers preyed on the early actresses, sometimes paying a fee to visit them backstage in the hope of gaining sexual favours. The boundary between theatre and life, public and private, was remarkably supple, especially in regard to women's sexuality. The very vagueness of the demarcation between public and intimate knowledge often heightened the actresses' marketability as the audience held both together in their imagination. The actress's private life, from her first appearance on the stage, was fair game for gossip in a way that was never the case for male actors.[7] Creating 'public intimacy' involved performing within the public realm with the express intent to expose private matters and to generate affect around their own persons in order to kindle celebrity.[8] For actresses whose 'virtue' was always at issue, the boundaries between life and role could be manipulated at the stage's edge. It is not so much that the women became more important than the roles they played, but rather that Restoration and eighteenth-century actresses allowed the two enticingly to merge. Where in fact did a woman player's commercial value lie – in her dramatic roles, in her character as a private person, or in some fusing of the two, especially when these identities may have been discontinuous? At the same time, the actress's theatrical genius, sometimes overshadowed by her sexual behaviour, frequently went unrewarded. While virulent satires attacked her as 'that mercenary Prostituted Dame', even the extremely popular Elizabeth Barry was at first paid only 50 shillings a week, while her co-star, Thomas Betterton, received £5.[9] The audience's illusion that they possessed intimate knowledge of the actress could obscure her status as a working woman and as a professional who honed her craft.

The woman player acting on stage possessed both the imagined body of the character she represented as well as her own actual body as a person.[10] Yet these two bodies – the virtual body of the role and the real body of the actress – were not easily separated into discrete entities; their highly sexualised bodies create double trouble as spectators bring privileged knowledge to their interpretation of the actresses' roles. 'Private' information was openly, even ostentatiously displayed and circulated in the emergent public sphere. Encouraging spectators to invade their privacy and actually performing a version of that privacy on stage, the early actresses manipulated privacy into a construction of an imagined offstage personality. In its performance, privacy lost its characteristic secrecy and became a theatricalised substitute for authentic knowledge of the actress's life. The biographical publications written about these women, and the memoirs they begin for the first time to write themselves, also create the illusion of public intimacy with readers and audiences. These include memoirs about Lavinia Fenton (1728), Anne Oldfield (1730, 1731 and 1741), Eleanor Gwyn (1752), Peg Woffington (1760), George Anne Bellamy (1785), Frances Sheridan (1824) and Sarah Siddons (1831); the memoirs explore the ways that women players' lives contradict or merge with their dramatic roles to offer scripts for private life as well as public performance. Actresses' memoirs written by others (during the eighteenth century almost always by men) attempt to suture together the ruptures between public appearance and private life into a coherent whole, while actresses' autobiographical narratives tend to expose their instability of identity. Perhaps the rise of a credit economy based on speculation and paper credit contributed to their fluctuating sense of self both on and off stage.[11] In helping to produce a recognisable and consistent public identity, the memoirs often closely linked the women with their stage characters, publicised personal scandals, intensified quarrels between players, and thus stimulated the patronage of the commercial theatre.

Casting for new plays usually occurred *before* the plays were drafted, and playwrights began to create parts especially for specific celebrated actresses. The actresses' character on stage was often confused with the woman herself who was known, not by her own name, but by her most famous role, such as Roxalana (Hester Davenport), Lady Betty Modish (Anne Oldfield), Polly (Lavinia Fenton), Sir Harry Wildair (Peg Woffington), Perdita (Mary Robinson) or Lady Teazle (Frances Abington). The first autobiographical narrative by an actress in her own person is Charlotte Charke's account (1755), which describes her transgressively dressing as a man in life, as Mr Brown with her partner Mrs Brown, thus imitating her travesty role as Scrub (in George Farquhar's *Beaux Stratagem*), or, more notoriously, mimicking the foppish roles made famous by her father, the theatre manager and actor Colley Cibber. When the Irish actress Peg Woffington debuted as Polly, Macheath's moll, in Gay's *Beggar's Opera*, in spite of being not yet twelve years old, her memoirist claims that 'she appeared to be the very Character she personated'.[12] For Anne Bracegirdle, after Lord Mohun's attempt to abduct her, her reputation was revived when she portrayed Fulvia (in *The Richmond Heiress*), a character who, like her, triumphs over several abduction attempts. In another example of the elision between theatre and life, Kitty Clive created the principal role of Mrs Hazard for herself in *The Rehearsal* (1750) in which her character (who has ostensibly written a play in which Clive stars) plays on the confusion between role and actress by joking about whether Hazard's costume will fit Clive. The characters Mr Cross and Mrs Hazard affect to await Clive (obviously already present on stage), who sends word that she cannot come 'as she's oblig'd to go to some Ladies about her Benefit'.[13] Celebrity thus adhered both to the actress and to the part.

Eighteenth-century actresses also delighted in being assigned prologues and epilogues in which they teased the audience with public intimacy as a way of increasing their popularity or notoriety. This practice of engaging the private identities of the actresses on stage, and conflating their own bodies with their roles, was an effective means of complicating the celebrity's identity while stimulating the playgoer and creating the illusion of shared secrets. Actors' memoirs often include the prologues and epilogues they recited as lending themselves to recounting their life story. But there was also dissonance between life and stage. The popular actress Jane Rogers played virtuous tragic heroines (such as Imoinda in Thomas Southerne's *Oroonoko*) while she engaged in a notorious affair with actor Robert Wilks. To defend herself from maligning critics, she scurried to the stage's edge to protest her virtue, speaking as 'herself', thus attempting to make her person and her roles less discordant and to cultivate the audience's favour.[14] Peg Woffington flirted from the stage, as did Kitty Clive, 'a mixture of combustibles', who amused herself by breaking character and identifying patrons in the audience: 'Mrs. Clive would suffer her eyes sometimes to wander from the stage into the boxes in search of her great acquaintance, and now and then give them a comedy nod or curtsy.'[15] Patronage was, after all, a common means of support for artists in the eighteenth century, and engaging in coquetry with audience members was an inventive way to solicit potential benefactors and to increase receipts.

Public intimacy also wielded the potential to afford women an avenue to class mobility in a way previously unavailable to either sex, but especially to women. The variable and often indeterminate social class of actresses, made more opaque through the class variation of the roles they played, could sometimes empower them. From the days of the King's Protestant whore, Nell Gwyn, 'actress' in the Restoration period was often synonymous with 'prostitute', though it is too simple to say with Elizabeth Howe that 'society assumed that a woman who displayed herself on the public stage was probably a whore'.[16] The uncertain class position of the newly professionalised actress brought into play the sign of the 'actress-as-whore', if not the actuality of trading money for sex. Seeming to be unmoored from the fathers and husbands who determined their status, the social class of women players was more malleable than for most women. Laura Rosenthal has argued that the Restoration actress, as 'an untitled and unmonied professional ... theatricalised an emergent instability of class identity' and destabilised real gender relations because male audience members 'forgot' that actresses playing aristocratic ladies were simply inhabiting a role and were not properly marriageable in their own person.[17] That actresses often wore the cast-off clothing of noblewomen may well have exacerbated the tensions concerning their ability to attract libertine aristocrats. Yet it is also true that the practice of ladies giving their discarded dresses to inferiors was not confined to actresses: servants often appeared on the street wearing such clothing, and class instability came into consideration on stage and off.[18]

The highest praise for a star actress in eighteenth-century commentaries was that she consistently became the person she impersonated, alleviating the strain between public and private identity but more significantly between uncertain rank and recognisable status. The new celebrity of actresses made many of them, if not equivalent to royalty, the sought-after imitation of it.

Actresses moving through the classes in drama and in life while mastering the etiquette of nobility, revealed the performative nature of social class to audiences consisting of kings, citizens and servants. The memoirs of actresses attempted to reconcile the fact that these women were *not* queens but could convincingly impersonate them. Anne Oldfield's memoirist writes of her role in Colley Cibber's sentimental comedy *The Careless Husband* that the real woman was totally absorbed into the dramatic role, making her appear to be the woman of quality that she portrayed: 'It was not the Part of Lady *Betty Modish*, represented by Mrs. *Oldfield*; but it was the real Mrs. *Oldfield* who appeared in the Character of Lady *Betty Modish*.'[19] Cibber himself suggested that the relationship between stage and life was often reciprocal, causing ladies of quality on occasion to emulate the actress rather than the reverse: 'I have often seen [Oldfield] in private Societies, where Women of the best Rank might have borrow'd some part of her Behaviour without the least Diminution of their Sense or Dignity.'[20] He adds in his preface to John Vanbrugh's *The Provok'd Husband* (1728) that 'her natural good sense and lively turn of conversation made her way so easy to ladies of the highest rank, that it is a less wonder if on the stage she sometimes was, what might have become the finest woman in real life to have supported'.[21] And in Oldfield's 1730 memoir, 'modern Ladies of Quality' are enjoined to impersonate her, 'so infinitely did the Copy transcend the Original, and so much more amiable did they appear when represented by Mrs. *Oldfield*, than when at home with their Lords'.[22] Claiming unverified genteel origins on her mother's side, Oldfield is rumoured to have travelled to and from the theatre in a hired sedan chair accompanied by liveried footmen. As a star actress she displayed the accoutrements of a woman of quality, and a catalogue of her belongings compiled after her death testified to her accumulation of material goods, including rich tapestries, jewels, antiquarian books, valuable paintings and japanned chests.

Though she was known to be a mistress, Oldfield exemplified, then, a sign of the actress that countered the more familiar one of a prostitute. She and some of her fellow actresses were believed to possess a natural elegance, an inherent affinity to imitate people of rank, or a capacity to learn it quickly. It is a commonplace for actresses' biographers to brag about the high company that the women keep, and access to actresses, sexual and otherwise, was often regarded as an aristocratic privilege. While Oldfield conducted illicit relations with Charles Churchill (a supporter of Prime Minister Walpole) and the heavy drinking spendthrift Arthur Maynwaring, she was reportedly welcomed into the homes of women of fashion and quality, as were Frances Abington and Kitty Clive. Elizabeth Barry under Davenant's patronage was invited into the best company where she became 'soon Mistress of that Behaviour which sets off the well-bred Gentlewoman'; she was even said to have powerfully influenced the Countesses of Rutland and Nottingham.[23] For the first time in history, celebrity created real as well as feigned social mobility for women and allowed sought-after actresses to defy the restrictions of rank.

In other words, the celebrity of the acting profession was manifest in a variety of ways that extended well beyond actresses carrying the tenacious residue of the whore. Women players who acted aristocratic parts could assume the position of a woman of quality by becoming the mistress of an admiring aristocrat, or in rare cases, marrying such men.[24] Lavinia Fenton, a stunning success as Polly in Gay's *Beggar's Opera*, lived with the Duke of Bolton for over two decades until she became the Duchess upon the death of his wife. William Cooke writes of the event:

> The last century has not produced, perhaps, a greater instance of the change of fortune in an individual, than in the character before us ... *no body's daughter*, bred up, in the early part of her life, at the bar of a public coffee-house; afterwards introduced upon the stage; with a handsome person, and attractive accomplishments; and yet with all these links to seduction, conducting herself with that propriety and conduct, as to attain the first rank in the country, with the esteem and approbation of the public.[25]

It is not the frequency of their bypassing traditional standards of chastity and class limitations that is remarkable, I am arguing, but the fact that it could *ever* happen in real life that made the star actress such a threat and a curiosity.

The earning power among star actresses was primary among the factors that threatened the status quo. Dependent on the theatre for a living wage, many were heads of households responsible for supplying the family income. Yet more than one theatrical pamphlet registered a complaint against actors who believed that gaining fame should merit them very substantial remuneration. One such tract, *Theatrical Correspondence in Death*, complains about 'the Servants, [an actress's] high Salary enabled her to keep' and her insisting 'upon an annual Income superior to those of many private gentlemen, equal to those of some ennobled'.[26] In addition, actresses' entitlement to social privilege was often complicated by their true circumstances as the daughters of families of substantial means who had lost their fortunes.[27] Not only did they effectively impersonate quality, many actresses *might have been* women of quality, save for the misfortune of their families. Though happenstance or luck is often part of the narrative as to why women are recruited into the theatre, it also seems possible that placing themselves within listening range of well-known playwrights, managers or other actors may well have been not an accident, but a clever young woman taking an opportunity to audition for a potentially lucrative position in order to support herself and, incidentally, regain the status her family had lost. A considerable number of actresses were 'discovered' in relatively public places. Peg Woffington, the daughter of a journeyman bricklayer and washerwoman in Dublin, was apprenticed at the age of twelve to Mademoiselle Violante after the Italian gymnast and equilibrist (rope dancer) spotted her natural talent. Charles Taylor insisted that George Farquhar was totally responsible for Oldfield becoming an actress rather than attributing that fact to her initiative when she, speaking from behind the bar, impressed him as a potential patron with an eloquent dramatic reading at the Mitre Tavern in St. James's Market.[28] Oldfield's 1741 biography maintains that her lover Maynwaring's instructions contributed heavily to her success as a player.[29] Kitty Clive's fortuitous singing within hearing of the Beef-steak Club at the Bell Tavern may have led to her promotion to the stage by Club members, Mr Beard and Mr Dunstall, though William Chetwood maintains an alternative story that he and Theophilus Cibber recommended her to Colley Cibber upon hearing her sing.[30] Perhaps Woffington, Oldfield and Clive had firmly planted themselves within hearing in order to ascend to the stage.

In the eighteenth-century theatre, the budding star system promoted large disparities between major and minor actresses.[31] The difference between the ordinary actor and the celebrated or notorious star only increased during the century.[32] Though early actresses were underpaid and earned significantly less than men, it has not been pointed out that the most celebrated women players in the eighteenth century could make more money from acting than many male thespians, more than men who laboured in other trades, and – most significantly – more than any other working women up to that point in history. Women novelists with their erratic incomes generally earned less than well-placed actresses and could seldom reach even the middling ranks by their writing. Fees paid for fiction manuscripts ranged from about 5 guineas to 10 guineas by the end of the century: 'The average copyright fee from one novel was roughly equivalent to the annual wages of a laundry, scullery, or dairy maid, and therefore entirely inadequate for anyone attempting to maintain middle-class status.'[33] To enter the middle ranks, one would have to bring in at least £50 a year, a sum that would require writing about ten novels.[34] Even the renowned Frances Burney was paid only £25 for *Evelina* (1778), though she commanded £250 for *Cecilia* (1782). Charlotte Smith's ability to earn £50 per volume was thought to be a significant sum. By the early nineteenth century Elizabeth Inchbald eventually received an annual income of about £260 from writing novels and plays. Still, the most celebrated actresses were paid considerably more than women writers and many male writers. This includes women playwrights, who could not survive on their earnings until a new compensation system that was no longer based on benefit nights was introduced in 1794. From the few records extant for plays written by women before 1760, it seems that none could gain a sufficient income until late in the century. The average fee earned by a woman playwright between 1776 and 1794 was £74, though eventually Inchbald, Hannah Cowley, Frances Sheridan and Elizabeth Griffith were able to garner substantial sums from their writing.[35]

In fact, then, the most talented and savvy actresses could compete with eminent actors in the theatrical economy. To cite only a few examples, Kitty Clive bettered Charles Macklin in the 1742–3 season by about £40; later in the century Dora Jordan earned £31 10s a week, the same fee given to John Philip Kemble, while Sarah Siddons was paid an equivalent sum *per night* for a season of about 30 weeks.[36] Peg Woffington often made more than Charles Mill. The actresses who were in greatest demand could actually accumulate wealth. With their disposable income they became patrons of the arts, philanthropists or benefactors to their relatives and heirs; they loaned money, made wagers and investments, extended credit, borrowed substantial funds and even entertained the possibility of purchasing a theatre patent.[37] They cunningly and adeptly negotiated contracts, and several rose to become managers or co-managers.[38] On occasion they purchased country estates.[39] Yet actresses, especially the best actresses, often complained about having their contractual obligations slighted or having their salaries falling into arrears. While women players such as Oldfield, Barry, Clive and Woffington were sometimes chided for their headstrong nature or greed, one wonders if these epithets are unfairly applied, and whether the women were simply insisting on being granted equity along with their just deserts for hard work.

In short, by trading on their celebrity, many actresses managed to gain power and influence through a kind of financial independence that was unprecedented except for upper-class women. Economic freedom combined with sexual confidence may have spilled over into professional competence. Pepys, visiting Nell Gwyn and Beck Marshall backstage, remarked that the actresses oozed confidence: 'But, Lord! Their confidence! And how many men do hover about them as soon as they come off the stage, and how confident they are in their talk!'[40] This easy access of the public to their private lives may have given actresses practice in fending off admirers, lewdly or otherwise, and toughened them up to become the feisty, bold women who could compete, even physically, with managers and with other actresses for the most coveted and lucrative parts. Beginning with a weekly salary of 15 shillings, Anne Oldfield soon earned as much as two or three times the annual salary required for living a modest but comfortable middling life;[41] in the 1708–9 season she disputed the house charges that Rich deducted from her benefit before paying her remainder. For Oldfield as for other players, a benefit allowed an actor to garner the profits from her chosen programme on a single night, less the overhead expenses. Because actors sold many of their own tickets, the benefit often amounted to a popularity contest enhanced by social connections. Though Oldfield began as a financial partner at Drury Lane, Colley Cibber reports, management reneged on its commitment and instead increased her salary to £200, rising to 300 guineas, along with the promise of a benefit free of deductions. In 1703 her earnings of £70–£80 per annum put her in the mid-range of actresses in the company, and in 1706 she earned £120 a year at the Haymarket, advancing to well over

£500 in 1728–9.[42] An army officer would have earned less than £100, while Jane Rogers was promised a guaranteed salary of £100 in 1711–12. In 1707 Anne Bracegirdle was sufficiently wealthy to retire with a good living, supplemented by gifts and bequests from admirers such as the Earl of Scarsdale, William Congreve and Edward Porter. Yet a husband could control his wife's money and claim at least half of it. Susannah Cibber's salary was purportedly the sole family income during the 1740s:

> This Lady's Salary, I am credibly informed, is 600 Guineas for playing three times a Week only part of the Season with Mr. F---, besides a benefit clear of Charges; and between 3 or 400l. more for singing about twenty times with Mr. H---; so that her Income, (without reckoning any Presents, or Gratuities, from any Particular Friends, for her Extraordinary Performances) may, by a moderate Computation, be reckon'd at 1200l. for less than six Months Labour; while her Husband (who made her and Actress) and his Daughters (her children in Law) have yearly---0l. 0s. 0d.

Her substantial salary supported her non-working husband and children.[43] Theophilus Cibber, who arranged for his wife Susannah's adultery and then subjected her to a trial, took her clothes, linen, half her salary and the £50 Charles Fleetwood had given her after her performance in *Zara*.[44]

Achieving the professional status to command a benefit night was a critical turning point for an actress, who could subsequently manipulate celebrity and thus capitalise on her loyal following to elevate her salary.[45] Most important to our consideration of celebrity was Elizabeth Barry's groundbreaking move in 1708 when, according to Colley Cibber, she was the first woman to negotiate and demand such an opportunity. Once an actress earned a benefit night, she could increase her salary not only by gaining public acclaim for her talent, but also by reaping personal rewards from her efforts at cultivating celebrity. Actresses personally sold tickets and reserved places from their homes, often collecting substantial gratuities.

From the 1720s to the 1760s, three Drury Lane actresses – Catherine Clive, Susannah Cibber and Hannah Pritchard – earned between a third and a half of their annual incomes from benefit nights, and each cultivated a devoted following. The most celebrated stars could bargain for acting in their drama of choice, and each of these actresses further enhanced the theatre's receipts by asking David Garrick to co-star with them. Increased popularity meant that their fans and friends would turn out for the benefit night, so boosting the night's profits. Mrs Cibber, for example, made £100 during the 1734–5 season, doubling her salary in the next two seasons, tripling her benefit earnings by 1747–8, and doubling them yet again to make a total of £700 in the 1755–6 season. Near the end of the century Sarah Siddons negotiated two benefit nights each season, and even in retirement Elizabeth Barry earned £100 annually and was given profits from benefit nights in her honour.

In short, benefit nights could be enormously lucrative and their success depended heavily on sustaining a visible celebrity and popularity.[46]

In addition, many actresses cultivated the patronage of the aristocracy they emulated on stage and off. For the most famous, salary and benefits were regularly supplemented by gifts, bribes and offers of living accommodation from wealthy male and female playgoers.[47] The prevailing resentment over the fact that actresses consequently became women of means was sometimes justified by recounting their philanthropic and charitable acts. Mrs Oldfield, writes William Chetwood, was 'made up of benevolent Charity, affable and good-natur'd to all that deserv'd it'.[48] The 'celebrated virgin' Anne Bracegirdle granted alms to the poor unemployed basket women in Clare Market 'so that she could not pass ... without the thankful Acclamations of People of all Degrees'.[49] Lavinia Fenton contributed a maintenance to her stepfather, and her biography touts her 'Humanity to the Distressed'. Peg Woffington not only settled a pension on her mother but also a bequest to support her sister Mary (Polly) Cholmondeley, consisting of stage jewels which originally belonged to Queen Margaret. She also endowed almshouses near her estate at Teddington.[50] Similarly, in 'An Epistle to Mrs. Clive', Henry Fielding hints at the bitterness Kitty Clive's financial success aroused when he excuses her ambition and apparent greed by detailing her charitable acts to family and fellow actors:

> But as great a Favourite as you at present are with the Audience, you would be much more so, were they acquainted with your private Character; cou'd they see you laying out great part of the Profits which arise from entertaining them so well, in the Support of an aged Father; did they see you who can charm them on the Stage with personating the foolish and vicious Characters of your Sex, acting in real Life the Part of the best Wife, the best Daughter, the best Sister, and the best Friend.[51]

Clive, protesting against low salaries, also supported her fellow actors when they were caught in the dispute between players and patentees after Theophilus Cibber absconded to the Haymarket with part of the Drury Lane company: 'You have been so far from endeavouring to exact an exorbitant Reward from Persons little able to afford it, that I have known you offer to act for nothing, rather than the Patentees should be injur'd by the Dismission of the Audience.'[52] These accounts of charitable private behaviour insert the actress within conventional expectations of women of quality, while seeking to define the parameters of an acceptable public femininity that depends upon the performance of an interior sensibility and natural generosity.

To heighten their fame and marketability, actresses also found themselves to be represented by goods or articles of trade. Colley Cibber, actor, manager and playwright, openly acknowledged the actresses' commodity status when he compared them to 'Bawbles' for purchase in a 'Toy-shop'.[53] Anne Oldfield's memoirs describe her as a spectacle to be consumed by the playgoers: 'How have I seen the crouded Audience ... devour her with their Eyes, whenever She appear'd!'[54] Women players were literally commodified as admirers eagerly purchased portraits, fans, playing cards, chinaware and screens emblazoned with the likenesses of popular actresses such as Lavinia Fenton as Polly in Gay's *Beggar's Opera*.[55] An engraving of the older Kitty Clive as Mrs Riot in *Lethe* holding a pug dog (1750) appeared on Bow and Chelsea porcelain; the image of Peg Woffington as a sphinx from a painting by Pond became a china statue (Figure 9.1); Mary Ann Yates was immortalised on Delftware tiles, as was Susannah Cibber as Monimia. Staffordshire figurines of Mrs Siddons represented her as Lady Macbeth, and 130 Wedgewood chess sets featuring Siddons as the Queen sold between 1785 and 1795.[56] Such representations of actresses' faces, bodies and characteristic clothing both defined and extended their celebrity. Actresses too served as arbiters of fashion and displayed, especially after mid-century, their own modish variations on classical or historical costumes.[57] Frances Abington parlayed her fashion flair into an early trademark, the 'Abington cap', and supplemented her stage income as an adviser for elegant social events. The point of dressing with style on stage was to establish a current vogue: to set fashion and even to act as fashion consultants to women of rank who sometimes donated their clothing to actresses who were, in turn, known to reciprocate by offering their costumes to noblewomen. Anne Oldfield purportedly wore the same dress that she had dined in to the theatre later in the evening. Celebrity circulated via clothing and costume from stage to court and back again. For example, Maria Beatrice of Modena, the second wife of James II, loaned Elizabeth Barry her wedding suit and coronation robes, while Sarah Siddons mentions in her correspondence that 'Lady B.' borrowed her Lady Macbeth banquet dress for a masquerade where 'many of these beauties will appear in my stage finery'.[58]

Actresses also heightened their commercial appeal by catapulting their rivalries to centre stage, sometimes at the instigation of the managers. The women's public rivalries were catfights enacted for an audience hungry for celebrity fodder (Figure 9.2). Others have emphasised the sexual competition symbolised in these contests, but I wish to stress instead the economic stakes involved. Public quarrels between actresses were instrumental in building celebrity, stimulating interest in the theatre and increasing attendance and receipts on benefit nights. Recognising that other women in the troupe were her principal competition, George Anne Bellamy stipulated in her contract that she 'was to have a larger salary than any other female performer at that theatre', amounting to 500 guineas.[59] Actresses' battles throughout the eighteenth century erupted over pay and roles, not over men; in contrast, similar accounts of male actors' public quarrels are very scarce. These contests in the eighteenth-century theatre often involved the active engagement

Figure 9.1 China statue of Peg Woffington. By courtesy of the Trustees, Fitzwilliam Museum, Cambridge.

Actresses and the Economics of Celebrity, 1700–1800 161

Figure 9.2 *The Rival Queens of Covent Garden and Drury Lane Theatres, at a Gymnastic Rehearsal* (BM 6126). By kind permission of the Trustees of the British Museum.

of the audience on behalf of an actress who sought ownership of a leading role, profits and celebrity. In a well-known example, a quarrel erupted between Oldfield and Bracegirdle in 1707 concerning which actress should perform the title role in Thomas Betterton's *The Amorous Widow; or, The Wanton Wife* (1670). When Oldfield's performance outshone Bracegirdle's after each acted the part in turn, legend has it that Bracegirdle retired.

In another example, Susannah Cibber competed with Kitty Clive in 1736 for the coveted part of Polly in *The Beggar's Opera*.[60] Fleetwood, the new manager of Drury Lane, favoured Cibber over Clive, who had been assigned the inferior role of Lucy. Both actresses engaged the press, including *Fog's Journal*, *The Grub-Street Journal*, *The Daily Journal* and *The Town*, and the media attention competed with the play itself. The paper wars that circulated within the coffee-house culture of the 1730s created the equivalent of modern tabloid rumour and innuendo. A character from *The Historical Register* complains, 'I find that by our theatrical squabbles and altercations we make as much amusement to the town in a morning as by our performance in an evening.'[61] The public disagreement reached mock-epic proportion in the ballad in *The Beggar's Pantomime* in which duelling prima donnas named

Madam Squall and Madam Squeak, scratching and tearing at each other's clothes, were anything but silent, as the lyric composed on the occasion conveys:

> Cibber, the Syren of the Stage,
> A Vow to Heav'n did make,
> Full Twenty Nights in Polly's Part,
> She'd make the Play-house shake.
> When as these Tidings came to Clive,
> Fierce Amazonian Dame;
> Who is it thus, in Rage she cries,
> Dares rob me of my Claim.[62]

The result was increased receipts and heightened gossip. In a purported dialogue with Clive regarding the theatre dispute, the attorney Dash protests that the manager 'certainly encreased Kitty's salary so extravagantly as made it much above any Woman's now upon the Stage', though she protests that her pay was in arrears.[63] After the stormy public fight had continued for three months, the flinty Kitty Clive proposed a radical amendment to theatre practice as Letitia Cross had attempted before her – that a dramatic part should become the legitimate property of the person accustomed to playing it: 'That no Actor or Actress shall be depriv'd of a Part in which they have been well receiv'd, until they are render'd incapable of performing it either by Age or Sickness.'[64] The irate actress indicated that she feared a larger conspiracy was afoot to steal her principal parts in order 'to make me so little useful to the Stage, as not to deserve the Sallary I now have, which is much inferior to that of several other Performers'. Salary, and the reputation upon which it was based, motivated Clive to protect her roles and the public's perception of her. We might think of Clive and other eighteenth-century actresses like her not as annoying harridans, but indefatigable campaigners for their own equitable treatment as professionals and more generally as advocates for the rights of actors. Clive's activities, aimed squarely at protecting her income and reputation, are among a significant number (including timely payments, accurate playbills and proper notice of dismissal) that she supported throughout her career to strengthen working conditions for her guild, especially for women.

Another series of battles and even violent acts surrounded the performance of Nathaniel Lee's popular tragedy, *The Rival Queens* (1677), its title a reflection of the staged competition between its principals. Elizabeth Barry (as Roxana), arguing with actress Mrs Bowtell (also known as Boutel) (as Statira) over a veil, a bit of costuming that she coveted, actually stabbed her nemesis during the performance: 'They were so violent in performing their Parts, and acted with such Vivacity ... on which *Roxana* hastening the designed Blow, struck with such Force, that ... [the dagger] made way through

Mrs. *Boutel*'s Stayes, and entered about a Quarter of an Inch in the Flesh.'[65] Later acting in these same roles, Peg Woffington literally stabbed George Anne Bellamy. Bellamy's account of her quarrel with Woffington may not be wholly accurate, but even if it is only partly true, it provides further evidence that actresses' negotiation of celebrity is embedded in competition with other actresses. Seeking elegant costumes to wear as the Persian heroine, Bellamy charged her emissary to Paris, who was embarking 'upon an affair of such momentous consequence', to choose chic gowns that would reflect the most modish taste.[66] While Bellamy was contracted to purchase her own new clothing, the manager Rich had obtained for Woffington merely a castoff inferior dress from the Princess Dowager of Wales which 'seemed to be a dirty white by candle-light'.[67] Taken aback by the richness of Bellamy's deep-yellow gown and purple mantua, Woffington jealously demanded that the rival actress change her clothing: 'The sight of my pompous attire created more real envy in the heart of the actress, than it was possible the real Roxana could feel for the loss of the Macedonian hero.'[68] The next night Bellamy, wearing another splendid Parisian gown, continued to taunt Woffington, who 'imperiously questioned me [Bellamy], how I dared to dress again in the manner she had so strictly prohibited. The only return I made to this insolent interrogation, was by a smile of contempt.'[69] Bellamy reports that Woffington 'drove me off the carpet [and] gave me the *coup de grâce* almost behind the scenes'.[70] These infamous ruptures demonstrate (in addition to the fierce tempers of these audacious actresses) the high stakes involved regarding the conditions of celebrity, including allowance for clothing, salary and benefit nights. It also shows the kind of public shenanigans that women were willing to perform in order to attract attention and gain new devotees. Similar examples of actresses' quarrels, publicly displayed, could be endlessly multiplied, including Sarah Siddons' battles with Frances Abington, Dorothy Jordan and Mary Ann Yates regarding roles, costumes and other vital circumstances of performance.[71]

In sum, celebrity for the first and second generation of actresses in the British theatre was not merely an accident of circumstance. The economic gain for these women players paradoxically depended on their construction of a private space that was regularly and purposefully violated by an emergent media apparatus, sometimes at the actress's own instigation. The actress, excessively sexualised in the eighteenth century and subsequently by later commentators, crafted an apparent transparency, an intimate familiarity, which helped to define a public femininity compatible with wealth, authority and fame. She manipulated the very vagueness of the demarcation between public and private information to demand the recognition of her skills and to highlight the competitive aspects of theatrical stardom. Celebrity, allowing patrons to feel that they 'knew' the actress, was fuelled by memoir and gossip. The 'character' of an eighteenth-century actress was inextricably bound up with her private actions and public reputation – with her rivalries, costuming and roles. An actress's private passions often tainted her theatrical identity or added lustre to it, but her hard-won ability to advance her interests increased her commercial appeal, her earnings and her celebrity. Fame and infamy capitalised on women's bodies on stage, playing with the difference or similarity between actress and part, enticing both patrons and lovers, increasing the possibility of class mobility, enhancing receipts and making possible the accumulation of substantial wealth and power. On the negative side, however, public intimacy sometimes distracted the audience from recognising the expertise involved in acting, obscured the intense labour of the theatrical space, and veiled an actress's need to compete with other actors in order to make a living wage.

The task of a good actress continues to be precisely to make her transformation into a dramatic character seem to be wholly effortless. Dramatically constructing new definitions of womanhood at the stage's edge, these early actresses demonstrated the difficult and arbitrary nature of embodying a recognisable femininity in public space. These notorious players quarrelled with theatre managers and competed with other actresses. They defied class strictures, assumed the character of women of rank, supported themselves and their dependants, acted as agents of their own celebrity, and came to exemplify an unprecedented kind of femininity. Complicating their propensity to act up, the most celebrated of them began to lay claim to status as tough negotiators on their own terms: in other words, they became legitimate professionals.

Notes

1 Edward Young, *Love of Fame, the Universal Passion in Seven Characteristical Satires*, in *Poetical Works of Edward Young* (1833; repr. Westport, CT: Greenwood Press, 1970), p. 113.
2 For example, in a well-known public competition for the role of Lady Lurewell in *The Trip to the Jubilee* Anne Oldfield's brilliant performance led to Jane Rogers' withdrawal from the contest and her subsequent suspension for organising a claque to taunt Oldfield.
3 This contradiction is noted in the entry for 'actress' in *Encyclopaedia Britannica; or, a Dictionary of Arts, Sciences, and Miscellaneous Literature*, 3rd edn., Vol. I (Edinburgh, 1797), p. 103.
4 *The Diary of Samuel Pepys*, ed. Henry B. Wheatley (London: Bell, 1946), 18 August 1660, quoted in *The Restoration Stage*, ed. John I. McCollum, Jr. (Boston, MA: Houghton Mifflin, 1961), p. 127.
5 Michael Shapiro, 'The Introduction of Actresses in England: Delay or Defensiveness', in *Enacting Gender on the English Renaissance Stage*, ed. Viviana Comensole and Anne Russell (Urbana and Chicago, IL: University of Illinois Press, 1999), p. 185.
6 Cited in Henry Wysham Lanier, *The First English Actresses from the Initial Appearance of Women on the Stage in 1660 till 1700* (New York: The Players, 1930), p. 28; Jeremy Collier, *A Short View of the Immorality, and Profaneness of the English Stage* (1698) (London: Routledge/Thoemmes, rptd. 1996), p. 9.

7 For a related discussion, see Cheryl Wanko's fine study, *Roles of Authority: Thespian Biography and Celebrity in Eighteenth-Century Britain* (Lubbock, TX: Texas Tech University Press, 2003) to which I am indebted. See also Kristina Straub, *Sexual Suspects: Eighteenth-Century Players and Sexual Ideology* (Princeton, NJ: Princeton University Press, 1996); and James Thompson, *Models of Value: Eighteenth-Century Political Economy and the Novel* (Durham, NC: Duke University Press, 1996).

8 Invoking this memorable phrase, Joseph Roach in 'Celebrity Erotics: Pepys, Performance, and Painted Ladies', *The Yale Journal of Criticism*, 16:1 (2003), 213, sardonically remarks that public intimacy is 'the sexy version of the worthy but stolid bourgeois public sphere described by Jürgen Habermas'.

9 Elizabeth Howe, *The First English Actresses: Women and Drama 1660–1700* (Cambridge: Cambridge University Press, 1992), pp. 27, 31.

10 Thomas A. King, ' "As if (she) were made on purpose to put the whole world into good Humour": Reconstructing the First English Actresses', *The Drama Review*, 36:3 (Fall 1992), 78–102.

11 Colin Nicolson, *Writing and the Rise of Finance: Capital Satires of the Early Eighteenth Century* (Cambridge: Cambridge University Press, 1994), p. 7, has linked the rise of credit to fractured selves: 'The emergence of classes whose property consisted not of lands or goods or even bullion, but of paper promises to repay in an undefined future, was seen as entailing the emergence of new types of personality, unprecedentedly dangerous and unstable.' See Wanko, *Roles of Authority*, p. 163.

12 *Memoirs of the Celebrated Mrs. Woffington, Interspersed with several theatrical Anecdotes; the Amours of many Persons of the First Rank; and some interesting Characters drawn from real Life* (London: Lowe, 1760), p. 12.

13 *The Rehearsal: or, Bays in Petticoats. A Comedy in two acts. As it is performed at the Theatre Royal in Drury-Lane. Written by Mrs. Clive* (Dublin: J. Exshaw and M. Williamson, 1753), p. 22.

14 Colley Cibber, *An Apology for the Life of Colley Cibber* (1740), ed. B. R. S. Fone (Mineola, NY: Dover Publications, 1968), p. 79.

15 Thomas Davies, *Memoirs of the Life of David Garrick, Esq. Interspersed with Characters and Anecdotes of his Theatrical Contemporaries*, 2 vols (London, 1780), II, p. 191.

16 Elizabeth Howe articulates the case for the Restoration actress as prostitute in *The First English Actresses*, pp. 32–6. See also John Harold Wilson, *All the King's Ladies: Actresses of the Restoration* (Chicago, IL: University of Chicago Press, 1958), who claims that actresses helped playwrights 'to "heap the steaming ordure of the stage" ', p. 107.

17 Laura Rosenthal, ' "Counterfeit Scrubbado": Women Actors in the Restoration', *The Eighteenth Century: Theory and Interpretation*, 34 (1993), 3–22 has helpfully suggested that 'this tension between an actress's own social position and the position of the characters she played ... brought the actress as whore sign into play' (p. 8), though I argue instead that actresses' upward mobility is not merely illusory. Deborah C. Payne contends that the actress is a supplicant and intermediary more than a sexual object in 'Reified Object or Emergent Professional? Retheorizing the Restoration Actress', in *Cultural Readings of Restoration and Eighteenth-Century Theatre*, ed. J. Douglas Canfield and Deborah Payne (Athens, GA: University of Georgia Press, 1995), pp. 13–38. We might usefully distinguish the nuances among prostitutes, mistresses and courtesans, and actresses who simply enjoyed unorthodox sex lives.

18 Anne Buck, *Dress in Eighteenth-Century England* (New York: Holmes and Meier Publications, 1979).

19 William Egerton [Edmund Curll], *Memoirs of Mrs. Anne Oldfield* (London, 1731), p. 3. An abridged version was published as an addendum to *The History of the English Stage, from the Restauration to the Present Time* (London, 1741) ostensibly from the papers of Thomas Betterton by Edmund Curll and Colley Cibber.
20 Cibber, *An Apology for the Life of Colley Cibber*, p. 167.
21 Colley Cibber, 'Preface' to Sir John Vanbrugh and Colley Cibber, *The Provoked Husband* [1728], ed. Peter Dixon (Lincoln, NE: University of Nebraska Press, 1973), p. 9. Capitalisation is modernised in this edition.
22 *Authentick Memoirs of the Life of that Celebrated Actress Mrs. Ann Oldfield. Containing a Genuine Account of her Transactions from her Infancy to the Time of her Decease. Third Edition, with Large Additions and Amendments* (London, 1730), p. 38.
23 *The History of the English Stage from the Restauration to the Present Time. By Dr. Thomas Betterton. Written really by Edmund Curll* (London, 1741), p. 14.
24 Terry Castle, *Masquerade and Civilization: The Carnivalesque in Eighteenth-Century English Culture and Fiction* (Stanford, CA: Stanford University Press, 1986); Jessica Munns and Penny Richards, 'Introduction', *The Clothes that Wear Us: Essays on Dressing and Transgressing in Eighteenth-Century Culture* (Newark, DE: University of Delaware Press, 1999); and Cynthia Lowenthal, *Performing Identities on the Restoration Stage* (Carbondale, IL: Southern Illinois University Press, 2003) also discuss the class instability provoked by actresses mimicking aristocrats on stage. I suggest here that actresses actually *were* socially mobile, and that the aristocracy also emulates *them*.
25 *Memoirs of Charles Macklin, Comedian* (London: James Asperne, 1804), pp. 41–2.
26 *Theatrical Correspondence in Death. An Epistle from Mrs. Oldfield, in the Shades to Mrs Br---ceg---dle, upon Earth* (London: Jacob Robinson, 1743), pp. 7, 12.
27 Examples include Frances Abington, Elizabeth Bowtell, Kitty Clive and Mary (Davies) Sumbel. Elizabeth Barry was probably raised in the home of Lady Davenant. See also Sandra Richards, *The Rise of the English Actress* (London: St. Martin's Press, 1993).
28 William Egerton [Edmund Curll], *Memoirs of Mrs. Anne Oldfield*, p. 56.
29 *Memoirs of Mrs. Anne Oldfield*, p. 4.
30 William Rufus Chetwood, *A General History of the Stage, from its Origins in Greece Down to the Present Time ... Collected and Digested by W. R. Chetwood* (London: W. Owen, 1749), p. 127; and *The London Stage*, 8 vols, ed. William Van Lennep (Carbondale, IL: Southern Illinois University Press, 1963), IV, p. 342.
31 Cheryl Wanko, 'Contracts for Two Drury Lane Actresses in 1822', *Harvard Library Bulletin Series* 2. 5 (1994), 53–67. Some salary lists divide players into four ranks, according to Edward A. Langhans, 'Tough Actresses to Follow', in *Curtain Calls: British and American Women and the Theater, 1660–1820*, ed. Mary Anne Schofield and Cecilia Macheski (Athens, OH: Ohio University Press, 1991), p. 4. Percy Fitzgerald, *A New History of the Stage*, 2 vols (London: Tinsley Brothers, 1882), II, p. 445, cites an agreement regarding actors' benefits that divides them into those making £4, £2 10s and £2 per week respectively. The better-paid actor managers may have constituted a fourth category.
32 Judith Milhous, 'United Company Finances, 1682–1692', *Theatre Research International*, 7 (Winter 1981/2), 45–50, notes that actors earned more than most trades, and more than actresses. My point is that a few celebrated and influential actresses earned more than most men.
33 A common labourer earned about £25 per year, a curate about £40, while £400 per year allowed a family and household supporting two servants to attain a

genteel life in the 1790s. See Edward Copeland, *Women Writing about Money: Women's Fiction in England, 1790–1820* (Cambridge: Cambridge University Press, 1995), p. 29.
34 Cheryl Turner, *Living by the Pen: Women Writers in the Eighteenth Century* (London and New York: Routledge, 1992), pp. 111–16.
35 Judith Milhous and Robert D. Hume, 'Playwrights' Remuneration in Eighteenth-Century London', *Harvard Library Bulletin*, 10 (Summer–Fall 1999), 3–90.
36 Langhans, 'Tough Actresses to Follow', p. 3; Sandra Richards, *The Rise of the English Actress*, pp. 56, 78, and *A Biographical Dictionary of Actors, Actresses ... and Other Stage Personnel in London*, 16 vols, ed. Philip H. Highfill Jr., Kalman A. Burnim and Edward A. Langhans (Carbondale, IL: Southern Illinois University Press, 1980), XIV, pp. 22–3.
37 For example, Elizabeth Barry loaned Alexander Davenant £400 in exchange for a share in the United Company, and Anne Oldfield is believed to have settled £50 per year on the poet Richard Savage.
38 Langhans, 'Tough Actresses to Follow', p. 5.
39 Kimberly Crouch, 'The Public Life of Actresses: Prostitutes or Ladies?', in *Gender in Eighteenth-Century England: Roles, Representations and Responsibilities*, ed. Hannah Barker and Elaine Chalus (London and New York: Longman, 1997), pp. 58–78, notes that Woffington bought a home in Teddington for herself and her sister Polly. In addition, Pritchard purchased a place in Twickenham; Oldfield bequeathed her house on Grosvenor Street to her son; and Frances Abington, after leasing a house in Hammersmith near the Thames, later sold it to fellow actress Sophia Baddeley. Horace Walpole gave Kitty Clive a small house dubbed 'Clive's-den' at Strawberry Hill, which she occupied from around 1753.
40 *The Diary of Samuel Pepys*, ed. Henry B. Wheatley, 7 May 1667–8, in *The Restoration Stage*, ed. John I. McCollum, Jr, p. 165.
41 Edward Copeland, *Women Writing about Money*, cited in Wanko, *Roles of Authority*, pp. 166–7. This amount would be a typical wage for actors performing near the time of the 1737 Licensing Act.
42 Joanne Lafler, *The Celebrated Mrs. Oldfield: The Life and Art of an Augustan Actress* (Carbondale, IL: Southern Illinois University Press, 1989), provides the statistics for the Haymarket, p. 51.
43 Mr Neither-Side (pseud.), *An Impartial Examen of the Present Contests Between the Town and the Manager of the Theatre with Some Proposals for accommodating the Present Misunderstandings between the Town and the Manager, Offered to the Consideration of Both Parties* (London, 1744), p. 9.
44 *A Biographical Dictionary of Actors, Actresses ... & other stage personnel in London*, ed. Philip H. Highfill, Jr., Kalman Burnim and Edward Langhans, III, p. 267.
45 Matthew J. Kinservik, 'Benefit Play Selection at Drury Lane in 1729–1769: The Cases of Mrs. Cibber, Mrs. Clive, and Mrs. Pritchard', *Theatre Notebook*, 50:1 (1996), 17, provides helpful statistics from which I have drawn.
46 For this reason, I think that Straub, *Sexual Suspects*, pp. 103ff. underestimates the potential agency available to actresses when she stresses their victimisation and 'rape', both ocular and literal.
47 Crouch, 'The Public Life of Actresses', p. 71.
48 Chetwood, *A General History of the Stage*, p. 202.
49 Antony Aston, *A Brief Supplement to Colley Cibber, Esq. His Lives of the Late Famous Actors and Actresses* (London, 1747), p. 10.
50 Murphy cited in *Dictionary of National Biography*. See also Tate Wilkinson.

51 Henry Fielding, 'An Epistle to Mrs. Clive', in *The Intriguing Chambermaid. A Comedy of Two Acts* (London: J. Watts, 1734), p. 3.
52 Fielding, 'An Epistle to Mrs. Clive', p. 4.
53 Cibber, *An Apology for the Life of Colley Cibber*, p. 303.
54 Dedication, *Authentick Memoirs of the Life of that Celebrated Actress Mrs. Ann Oldfield*, p. vii.
55 See Charles E. Pearce, *'Polly Peachum': Being the Story of Lavinia Fenton ... and the Beggar's Opera* (New York: Brentano's, 1913).
56 See Iain Mackintosh assisted by Geoffrey Ashton, *The Georgian Playhouse: Actors, Artists, Audiences, and Architecture, 1730–1830* (London: Arts Council of Great Britain, 1975), Entry 112.
57 Aileen Ribeiro, 'Costuming the Part: A Discourse of Fashion and Fiction in the Image of the Actress in England, 1776–1812', in *Notorious Muse: The Actress in British Art and Culture*, ed. Robyn Asleson (New Haven, CT: Yale University Press, 2003), p. 122.
58 Letter from Sarah Siddons to Mrs FitzHugh, 12 July 1819, in Thomas Campbell, *The Life of Mrs. Siddons*, 2 vols (London: E. Wilson, 1834), II, p. 366.
59 George Anne Bellamy, *An Apology for the life of George Anne Bellamy*, 5 vols (London: J. Bell, 1786), III, p. 12.
60 In turn Clive later fought with Peg Woffington which sparked 'The Green-Room Scuffle: Or Drury-Lane in an Uproar', an unpublished play.
61 Henry Fielding, cited in Percy Fitzgerald, *The Life of Catherine Clive* (1888; repr. New York: Benjamin Blom, 1969), p. 19.
62 Mr Lun, Jr [Henry Woodward], *The Beggar's Pantomime; Or, the Contending Columbines ... Dedicated to Mrs. Clive and Mrs. Cibber*, 3rd edition (London: C. Corbett and W. Warner, 1736), Prologue.
63 William Rufus Chetwood, *Dramatic Congress. A Short State of the Stage Under the Present Management* (London: M. Cooper, 1743), p. 21.
64 Letter to *London Daily Post and General Advertiser*, 19 November 1736. For Cross, see Judith Milhous and Robert Hume, 'Theatrical Politics at Drury Lane: New Light on Letitia Cross, Jane Rogers, and Anne Oldfield', *Bulletin of Research in the Humanities*, 85:4 (Winter 1982), 412–29.
65 *The History of the English Stage from the Restauration to the Present Time*, p. 21.
66 George Anne Bellamy, *An Apology for the life of George Anne Bellamy*, II, p. 216.
67 Bellamy, *An Apology*, II, p. 217.
68 Bellamy, *An Apology*, II, p. 217.
69 Bellamy, *An Apology*, II, p. 219.
70 Bellamy, *An Apology*, II, p. 218. The dispute was immortalised in Samuel Foote's theatre-piece, *Green-room Squabble, or a Battle-Royal between the Queen of Babylon and the Daughter of Darius*.
71 For other descriptions of actresses' rivalries, see Sandra Richards, *The Rise of the English Actress*.

10
Private Lives and Public Spaces: Reputation, Celebrity and the Late Victorian Actress

Sos Eltis

Of all late Victorian actresses, it was Sarah Bernhardt (1844–1923) who embraced celebrity with the greatest enthusiasm. Building her career on a reputation both on and off stage for illicit and unbridled passion, power and danger, Bernhardt had, as Henry James observed, 'in a supreme degree what the French call the *génie de la réclame* – the advertising genius; she may, indeed, be called the muse of the newspaper'.[1] Though she had begun her career under the auspices of the Comédie Française, performing in classical plays by Victor Hugo and Jean Racine, she broke free to control her own career and repertoire, soon displaying a marked preference for scandalous roles as courtesans, adulteresses and murderers in contemporary boulevard dramas by Victorien Sardou and Alexandre Dumas *fils*. The 156 performances she gave in her 1880 tour of the United States, for example, included 65 of *La Dame aux Camélias*, 41 of *Frou-frou*, 17 of *Adrienne Lecouvreur* and 6 of *Phèdre*. As William Archer was moved to observe in 1895, 'Someone to cajole and someone to murder are the two necessities of artistic existence for Madame Sarah Bernhardt', accompanying his comment with an explanatory table, listing the victims and lovers in each of her recent plays.[2]

Bernhardt's off-stage flamboyance – buying pet leopards and tigers, for example – projected a passionate personality to match her repertoire, while earning her the soubriquet 'Sarah Barnum' for her skill in self-advertisement.[3] Even when denying the more extravagant rumours about her behaviour, her publicity machine effectively fostered them. In 1879, while still part of the Comédie Française ensemble, Bernhardt employed Edward Jarrett as her press agent, impressed by his promise to secure her an additional income from independent appearances while on tour in England. In 1880, Jarrett put out a promotional booklet, claiming to correct false stories that Bernhardt slept in a coffin, that her favourite dishes were 'burnt cats, lizards' tails, and peacocks' brains *sautées au beurre de singe*', and that she played croquet with human skulls. While repeating these extravagances, the booklet also asserted that she kept 'the skeleton of a man who is said to have destroyed himself on account of disappointment in love'.[4] Bernhardt employed not one but two impresarios when touring in America – Jarrett and his American partner, Henry Abbey – and she was acutely aware of her public image and wished to maintain tight control over it. All publicity was not good publicity, in her view, as was demonstrated in her rage when an American entrepreneur, Henry Smith, persuaded her to visit his enormous captured whale and then released publicity claiming that she had killed it ripping out its bones for her corset, which he in turn advertised as being 'made by Mrs Lily Noë'.[5] Despite offering her a cut of his profits, Bernhardt remained unimpressed by Smith's genius for simultaneously publicising the whale, the actress and Mrs Noë's corsets. She expressed some of her fury at Smith's hijacking of her celebrity image by slapping him in the face, but she none the less had to endure being followed on her tour of the East Coast by his steadily decaying whale.

Bernhardt's flamboyant life combined with an exceptionally strong head for business to secure her large financial rewards. She formed her own production company in 1880, and toured the United States nine times, eight of which were billed as positively the last tour she would ever make. Remarkably she managed to market her appeal not only to highbrow audiences, but also to a much wider popular audience; on her 1905–6 tour, for example, she and her company filled a specially commissioned round-top 'Sarah Bernhardt' tent with 6,000 spectators.[6] Bernhardt made a considerable fortune but, as the female head of an extraordinarily successful theatrical enterprise, she had to endure a critical chorus of opprobrium, accusing her of prostituting her talents to a money-making machine and neglecting the greater challenges of classical drama simply to play herself in a series of crowd-pleasing pot-boilers.[7]

As a French woman almost permanently on tour abroad from the 1880s onwards, Bernhardt was inevitably viewed as an exotic outsider, and she embraced this image to the full, marketing herself as a glamorous and mysterious phenomenon. In response, Bernhardt tried to maintain careful control of her reputation and laid claim to her own form of integrity. In her autobiography, *Ma Double Vie*, published in 1907, she presented herself as naturally impulsive and spontaneous. While omitting to mention the circumstances surrounding, or the effects on her life, of the birth of her illegitimate son Maurice in 1864, she frequently asserted that her eccentric reputation sprang not from self-publicity but from natural exuberance and a lack of affectation.[8]

Sarah Bernhardt was undoubtedly the most committed self-publicist, but she was by no means the only actress to recognise the potential of the late nineteenth-century celebrity cult. Ellen Terry, Mrs Patrick Campbell and Lillie Langtry all exploited the mechanisms available for creating and marketing a celebrity persona: the explosion of print culture at the end of the nineteenth century and the attendant proliferation of articles, interviews and profiles; photography and its cheaply reproducible multiple portraits; the touring circuit, both in England and, more lucratively, in the United States. Like Bernhardt, they published autobiographies that projected their own carefully constructed versions of themselves. But where Bernhardt appeared insouciant about her off-stage notoriety, even encouraging it as a complement to her on-stage roles of adulteress and courtesan, Terry, Langtry and Campbell sought to balance their commercial success with a degree of social respectability, not only through their memoirs but also through their performances in the press and on stage.

Under the curious gaze of the public, celebrity actresses had to negotiate a more complex set of prejudices and assumptions than their male counterparts. Operating in a male-dominated market and using her physical attributes to please an audience, the late Victorian actress was still vulnerable to age-old assumptions of sexual looseness, to the common association of actress and prostitute.[9] Furthermore, in an age when the private domestic life was the touchstone of a woman's integrity, and female virtue was commonly figured as open, artless and sincere, an actress's public assumption of emotions she did not feel was doubly suspect.

Yet, despite these difficulties, by the late Victorian period respectability was an achievable ambition. Henry Irving's knighthood in 1895 demonstrated the higher esteem in which the acting profession was held, but actresses had to wait until 1921 for the first of their number, Geneviève Ward, to be similarly honoured. From the mid-nineteenth century onwards, a number of actresses fought to gain and retain a virtuous reputation. Madge Kendal, Marie Bancroft and Helen Faucit were prominent among them, carefully staging a private, domestic self to counterbalance their public stage persona. Through interviews and autobiographies they emphasised their private lives as daughters, sisters and happily married wives, driven to the stage reluctantly by financial necessity or drawn by the exigencies of high art. This private domestic identity could even be brought into play in the public arena, in the husband and wife acting partnerships of the Kendals and the Bancrofts, or in Marie Bancroft's transformation of the Prince of Wales's Theatre into a cushioned and carpeted extension of a Victorian drawing room.[10] But for Terry, Langtry, Campbell and Bernhardt, such tactics were not viable. They did not have conventionally respectable private lives to publicise. Often on tour, financially independent, with multiple marriages, divorces and illegitimate children between them, they could not market themselves on a dichotomy between their private/domestic and public/ professional selves. Instead they had to find more complex ways of maintaining their popularity while protecting their private lives, negotiating traditional ideas of female virtue without abandoning their personal claims to respectability.

Following the social psychologist George Herbert Mead, Chris Rojek has theorised celebrity status as implying a 'split between the *I* (the "veridical" self) and the *Me* (the self as seen by others)', where interviews and encounters with the public are often focused on how closely the public face of a celebrity accords with his or her veridical self.[11] Aware that celebrity carried the burden of public interest in their private lives, these actresses produced a private life for public consumption; accustomed to performing on the public stage, they knowingly performed a 'veridical' self to satisfy their audience.

* * *

Where Sarah Bernhardt projected an unconventional and passionate persona both on stage and off, Lillie Langtry's construction of her reputation was more intricate. Arriving in London in 1876, an unknown beauty from Jersey, Lillie Langtry (1853–1929) first came to public notice as an artist's model, sitting for John Millais and Edward Poynter amongst others. She formed an early friendship with Oscar Wilde, who educated her in the techniques and uses of publicity, simultaneously advertising himself and Lillie by celebrating her beauty in verse and walking through London with a single lily to pay homage to her.[12] Wilde was a master of self-promotion and also well aware of the need to manufacture a private persona for public consumption. Having lectured on 'The House Beautiful', he employed the designer Edward Godwin and spent thousands of pounds having his house in Tite Street redecorated to accord with his publicised theories, and lost no time in persuading Lillie to follow suit. Langtry soon became famous for more than her beauty, shooting to notoriety thanks to her affair with the Prince of Wales. By 1878 her photographs were on sale in penny-postcard stalls, pinned up underneath the prince's.[13]

Since her dress bills exceeded her income, Langtry, with Wilde's help, launched herself on a professional stage career in 1882, seeing it as a potentially lucrative solution to her debts. Wilde introduced her to Henrietta Labouchère, a former actress, who became Langtry's coach and theatrical adviser. Langtry started with a repertoire based on sentimental, domestic and inoffensive comedies, such as Tom Robertson's *Ours* and Tom Taylor's *An Unequal Match*, suggesting an attempt to establish a new theatrical reputation distinct from her celebrity status as high-class mistress. Such an attempt was doomed to failure, as critics referred repeatedly and with clear sexual implications to her status as goods for sale. Her 1880 debut as Kate Hardcastle was greeted by Clement Scott as an announcement that she had 'put herself up for hire to the highest managerial figure in the theatrical market', while a comic paper declared with snide double-meaning that it would justify her claim to be a 'Professional Beauty'.[14] When every actress was presumably paid for her appearances, Langtry's critics alluded persistently to her salary, with the attendant innuendo that she was selling herself rather than just her acting skills – an association between actress and prostitute that was to dog her entire career. So, in 1902, the American critic Henry Austin Clapp fulminated, she was 'the absurdist [sic] of actresses, whose professional stock in trade consisted of her social notoriety, her face, her figure, and the garments and jewels wherewith said figure was indued, – the garments being tagged by their "creators' " names and bearing price marks still intentionally legible'.[15] These visible price-tags suggest Langtry's vulgar concern with money, but also seem to hint darkly that it is not only the jewels that are for sale. Certainly, Langtry's scandalous celebrity constituted a powerful box-office draw and lucrative negotiating tool; as early as 1882, after playing to large audiences and very poor reviews in England, Langtry negotiated with Henry Abbey, the New York impresario, for an American tour at a fee marginally larger than Sarah Bernhardt had been paid the season before.[16]

When Henrietta Labouchère publicly broke with Langtry over the latter's scandalous and much-publicised affair with an American millionaire, Langtry thereafter took on roles that clearly exploited her sexual celebrity. One need only list the titles of her later repertoire to identify the line of marketing which lay behind it: Clement Scott's *A Wife's Peril* (1888) and Sydney Grundy's *The Degenerates* (1899); Charles Coghlan's *Lady Barter* (1891), *Gossip* (1895) by Clyde Fitch, *Mrs Deering's Divorce* (1900) by Percy Fendall, *The Sins of Society* (1911) by Cecil Raleigh and Henry Hamilton. Even when performing Shakespeare in a bid for artistic status, a distinctly non-artistic appeal was part of her marketing strategy. When she played Shakespeare's Cleopatra in 1890, publicity for the play offered photos of Lillie dripping in jewellery, which was declared to be genuine – its provenance could only add to the sexual *frisson* on which her performance was marketed. In her own production of *As You Like It* in 1889, as Rosalind, she eschewed the high boots and trunks of tradition, instead exploiting the sexual opportunity of a breeches role to the full by wearing only a short tunic and cross-gartered tights (Figure 10.1). Though she did not achieve critical acclaim for her acting skills, she did make a substantial fortune as an actress – large enough for her to purchase her own train for touring more comfortably in the United States. But, for all her flamboyance, Langtry was careful to keep her private life from view; when her illegitimate daughter Jeanne finally joined her on tour she did so in the guise of a niece. Indeed, Jeanne discovered her true parentage only when she came to marry in 1902.

Langtry's autobiography, *The Days I Knew* (1925), is a sustained performance in a similar vein; no mention is made of her affair with the Prince of Wales or any of her other lovers, nor is the existence of her daughter even acknowledged. Though the notoriety of her scandalous life presumably constituted the primary reason for purchasing her reminiscences, Langtry frustrates readers' prurient curiosity by offering a collection of harmless aristocratic gossip, comic stories and theatrical anecdotes, locating herself as a humorous and sympathetic observer of the strange worlds of society and the theatre. She unapologetically lays claim to the status of serious and celebrated actress, telling how her talents led playwrights and managers from

Figure 10.1 Lillie Langtry as *Rosalind* in Shakespeare's *As You Like It*. St. James's Theatre, London (1890), photographed by Lafayette Studios of Dublin. Photograph courtesy of the Victoria and Albert Picture Library.

Oscar Wilde to Henry Irving and George Alexander to beg her to take on roles. She also includes her own extended analysis of the character of Shakespeare's Rosalind, thereby aligning herself with Helen Faucit and Ellen Terry as a theatrical authority on Shakespeare.[17] Langtry then coolly acknowledges the surprise her autobiography may have offered to a reader familiar with the scandal which characterised her career and which she exploited in her repertoire and publicity. Apologising if any reader has found her reminiscences rather 'mild', Langtry calmly explains that 'what was considered *risqué* then would pass unnoticed in the present day', quoting as an example a shocked newspaper report of Mrs Langtry smoking in public.[18]

This whitewashing of her image offers such a confounding of readers' expectations as to seem deliberately tongue-in-cheek, rendering her autobiography a conscious and skilful performance for those in the know. Langtry implicitly defies criticism that might place her outside the smart society she portrays by deliberately blurring the line between the professional actress and 'respectable' Society women. The actresses who make fleeting appearances in Langtry's narrative are presented as spontaneous and innocent: Sarah Bernhardt is 'as natural as a child'; the famous Polish actress Helena Modjeska is a 'simple, lovable, flower-like woman'.[19] By contrast, Langtry describes her presentation at Court, the most revered ceremony in high society, as an uncomfortable and highly public production:

> At that time, the Courts were held at three o'clock in the afternoon, and it was certainly anything but agreeable to sit in full costume, with low neck and bare arms, in bright sunlight, for the edification of the surging crowd.[20]

Without any reverence for this highest of aristocratic occasions, Langtry describes herself and all the other Society ladies as revealingly and rather absurdly dressed and prominently displayed for the amusement of the public. When she subsequently narrates her entry into the theatrical profession, she presents it not as a fall from grace, but rather as a continuation of a Society woman's public display. So she explains her rather blasé attitude to her new career:

> I had never been stage-struck, and after all the adulation and social *éclat* that had fallen to my lot since my arrival in England, there was nothing strange in it for me from a publicity point of view. Indeed, to appear on the stage in the same play, speaking the same words, wearing the same gowns at the same time every evening, seemed a very dull and monotonous existence ... I had loomed so largely in the public eye that there was no novelty in facing the crowded audience, in which I knew most of the occupants of the stalls and boxes, and all in the cheaper parts knew me.[21]

In an era when becoming an actress could be seen as tantamount to entering 'the Mouth of Hell', as actress Lena Ashwell's father rather melodramatically put it, Langtry narrates it as a natural transition; the actress and the Society lady are employed in the same business, the only difference being the hard work and discipline demanded of the stage performer.[22]

The Days I Knew is a sustained and subtly complex star turn. Langtry claims that Oscar Wilde wrote the role of Mrs Erlynne in *Lady Windermere's Fan* expressly for her, and narrates a scene in which she rejects the part:

'What is my part?' I asked, not at all sure if he was joking or not.
'A woman', he replied, 'with a grown-up illegitimate daughter.'
'My dear Oscar,' I remonstrated, 'am I old enough to have a grown-up daughter of any description? Don't open the manuscript – don't attempt to read it. Put it away for twenty years.'[23]

Langtry's reasons for rejecting a part that too closely echoed her own carefully concealed private life are easily deducible, but her narrative is more ambiguous. In 1892 Jeanne was twelve, while Langtry was approaching 39 – quite old enough to play Mrs Erlynne. Yet the terms of her rejection actually echo the words of Wilde's heroine, who refuses the role of mother by asking, 'How on earth could I pose as the mother with a grown-up daughter? Margaret is twenty-one, and I have never admitted that I am more than twenty-nine, or thirty at the most.' Was Langtry's narration of this episode therefore ironically layered, offering a publicly proper version of events, while laughing privately at the proximity between the stage role and her own personal fictions?

* * *

Unlike Lillie Langtry, Mrs Patrick Campbell (1865–1940) first came to public notice in 1893 by virtue of her acting ability, shooting from relative obscurity to considerable celebrity after being cast as Paula Tanqueray, the fallen woman attempting to rehabilitate herself in Arthur Pinero's *The Second Mrs Tanqueray*. The likelihood of the public assuming that her private life accorded with her stage role was increased by the naturalistic emphasis of her acting.[24] As Shaw observed of Pinero's precision in casting, 'Mrs Pat is exactly the woman for him. He is in the position to have exactly what he likes; and naturally he is not content with mere acting ... he wants *being*'.[25] Over the next few years London's powerful actor-managers, George Alexander, Johnston Forbes Robertson, Herbert Beerbohm Tree and John Hare, offered Mrs Pat a succession of roles that echoed her performance as Paula Tanqueray. As a radical opponent of marriage in Pinero's *The Notorious Mrs Ebbsmith*, a rehabilitated prostitute in Haddon Chambers' *John-a-Dreams* and a woman ready to kill her unfaithful lover in Victorien Sardou's *Fédora*, Campbell was offered roles which effectively typecast her in a mould of passion, rebellion and sexual impropriety. Her frustration with this career trajectory was manifested in her deliberate sabotaging of her role as a potentially adulterous barmaid in Henry Arthur Jones's *The Masqueraders* (1894), and later walking out on the lead role in his *Michael and His Lost Angel* (1896), where she was cast as a rich married woman intent on seducing a clergyman.[26] Among the first roles in which Campbell cast herself after going into independent management were the ethereal heroine of Count Maeterlinck's *Pelléas et Mélisande* (1898), and a doctor torn between loyalty to her father and horror at his abuse of colonial powers in Gilbert Murray's *Carlyon Sahib* (1899). But the public still wanted to see her as Paula, and for the next twenty years her staple and lucrative touring repertoire was a trio of self-destructive 'new women': Paula Tanqueray, Agnes Ebbsmith and Hedda Gabler. Since Paula and Hedda had become favourite roles for Eleanora Duse and Sarah Bernhardt, the most celebrated actresses of the day, it remains ambiguous whether Campbell's repertoire was a bid for international celebrity status or an acceptance that these were fated to be her most profitable roles.

While achieving considerable renown for her on-stage persona, Campbell took equal care of her off-stage reputation. Proud of her friendships with Society women such as Lady Elcho, the Countess of Pembroke and Margaret Burne-Jones, she had a strong interest in establishing a private image distinct from her theatrical roles. Having turned to the stage to support herself and her two children after her husband left to seek his fortune in Australia and South Africa, she first worked under the stage name 'Miss Stella Campbell', before settling on 'Mrs Patrick Campbell', a somewhat unusual emphasis on her married status when most actresses who used their husbands' names also acted with them. When Patrick Campbell returned to England in 1894 he found himself playing the public role of husband, awkwardly accompanying Stella to social events where he was patently ill at ease. Her children regularly joined her on tour and, when they both chose acting careers, they frequently became part of her supporting cast on as well as off stage, helping to emphasise her role as wife and mother.

Yet this respectable private image was never allowed to interfere with her lucrative stage career. When her daughter Stella tried to return to the stage after her marriage, she found that few managers were interested in hiring 'Stella Mervyn Campbell', but her mother threatened her with legal proceedings were she to emphasise her origins with the stage name 'Stella Patrick Campbell'.[27] While playing fallen women might lead to unflattering assumptions about her private life, Campbell was quite ready to accept such suspicions if that meant maintaining a monopoly on such roles. In an interview given in America, she declared that fallen women made far more interesting heroines than strictly virtuous women, and asserted a clear connection between an actress's off-stage reputation and her performance:

> I have never ceased being amused at dear Mrs Kendall attempting Paula Tanqueray. Fancy that domestic soul with six children sobbing over her past misdeeds and social ostracism. The scene was flat when I remembered her own happy domesticity. It's the temperament of the actress, I may add the personality, that gives these stage women their charm.[28]

In this interview Mrs Pat deliberately treads a very fine line, emphasising the moral lessons offered by fallen woman plays, while questioning the narrow definition of female virtue as sexual continence, talking about the roles as distinct theatrical creations, while acknowledging the influence of the actress's off-stage celebrity persona.

This canny marketing of a delicate mixture of womanly domesticity plus hints of a more Bohemian and unconventional side is clearly manifest in her publication of *My Life and Some Letters* in 1922. While burying her affair with Johnston Forbes Robertson, for example, to present herself as a model of married bliss, she clashed vigorously with Shaw over her publication of his love letters to her. Shaw insisted on radically editing the letters in which he extravagantly courted her, trying desperately to keep private a flirtation that did nothing for his public dignity or reputation for rationality. Mrs Pat's image, however, could only be enhanced by letters which showed her virtuously rejecting her impassioned suitor; a public display of the ardour she had inspired could only help boost her image as a *femme fatale*, at a time when age, a thickening waist and an expensive divorce from her second husband had left her desperate for better pulling power at the box office. Shaw, himself a master of self-creation and publicity, who had scripted numerous interviews with himself, was out-manoeuvred by Mrs Pat over the publication of their correspondence, but her rewards were slight: mixed reviews and a salary of £3 a week to play Hedda Gabler.[29]

Mrs Pat maintained a careful balance, but there were limits to how effectively she could play the domestic card. In 1913 J. M. Barrie wrote *The Adored One* as a vehicle for her particular theatrical charm. It is the tale of an enchanting and devoted mother, Leonora, who pushes a man to his death from a moving train because he insists on keeping the window open despite the fact that her little daughter has a cold. Leonora is brought to trial, but so charms the judge and jury that she is let off, despite having openly confessed her crime. The play was a commercial and critical flop, largely because neither the on- nor off-stage personae of Mrs Pat meshed with the comic naivety and artless domesticity of Barrie's heroine.

The Adored One was clearly intended as an extravagant fantasy, full of absurd humour and whimsicality, despite its somewhat black theme. Yet a number of contemporary reviewers treated it with ludicrous seriousness, taking it as a tasteless comment on the violence of the suffragette movement.

As *The Illustrated London News* rather ponderously concluded:

> Possibly Sir James Barrie's play is a parable on the lawlessness of Militant Suffragism and its immunity from punishment; possibly his burlesque murder trial scenes, in which judge and counsel coquet with the fascinating prisoner, and allow her all sorts of indulgences, as in some Gilbertian opera, is meant to symbolise our law's feebleness in dealing with hunger-strikers.[30]

Such a reference appears particularly inappropriate when Leonora is presented quite specifically as the epitome of the old-fashioned woman; so the judge explains while giving Leonora her liberty: 'You are not of to-day ... [As] we look at you, we see again in their habit as they lived, those out-of-date, unreasoning, womanish creatures, our mothers and grandmothers and other dear ones long ago loved and lost ...'[31] But the key-note of Mrs Pat's career was modernity, whether playing specifically modern 'social problem' heroines such as Paula Tanqueray and Hedda Gabler, or prompting critics to re-conceive Shakespeare's Juliet or Sheridan's Lady Teazle as *fin-de-siècle* heroines through her performances.[32] The casting of Mrs Pat thus transformed Leonora in many critics' eyes from an old-fashioned woman into a militant suffragette, and Barrie's play into a contemporary social satire. Only one reviewer greeted the play as a real success, and he quite emphatically noted Mrs Pat as transcending her usual type in playing 'what we should describe as "an Ellen Terry part"'.[33] When the play opened in New York, by contrast, Maude Adams, recently famous as Peter Pan, was enthusiastically received in the role and the play greeted as 'a roundabout way of praising what it is not now popular to praise, the "old-fashioned woman"'.[34]

Mrs Pat maintained a moderate critical acclaim and financial success (though never on the scale of Bernhardt or Langtry), by creating a celebrity persona with sufficient hints of the Bohemian to claim a monopoly on social problem heroines, and enough traditional femininity to make her acceptable as Shakespeare's Juliet or Maeterlinck's Mélisande, thereby keeping her social and theatrical options open.

* * *

The extent to which an actress's off-stage persona could become an entity in itself, not her 'veridical' self but a persona that usefully complemented her on-stage repertoire, is perhaps most amply demonstrated in the celebrity career of Ellen Terry (1847–1928). Terry became famous as an icon of traditional feminine tenderness and virtue, as demonstrated by a critic's description of the old-fashioned, devotedly maternal Leonora as 'an Ellen Terry part'. Yet Terry lived the life of a Victorian Joan Collins: three marriages, the first at the age of sixteen and the last to a man many years her junior; two divorces and two illegitimate children, Edith and Edward, by the designer Edward Godwin. But, as *The Times* declared at the 1906 Jubilee celebrations of her fifty-year stage-career, Terry inspired in her audiences 'that simple, homely, yet all-powerful sentiment which the world is agreed to call love'.[35] As Max Beerbohm observed, characterising her as 'a great dear', no one could rival her ability to 'radiate such kindness and good humour' or 'her power of endearing herself across the footlights'.[36]

Ellen Terry's repertoire consisted almost exclusively of virtuous women. As the theatrical consort of Henry Irving at the Lyceum, she became famous playing a succession of Shakespearean heroines close to the Victorian public's heart: Ophelia, Cordelia, Desdemona, Portia, Beatrice and Imogen. Indeed, Ruskin offers an almost identical list as exemplars of female perfection in his essay 'Of Queens' Gardens'.[37] It was not only the roles themselves, but Terry's particular interpretation that established her stage reputation for feminine softness, generosity and enchantment. Some critics might demur – Henry James, for example, found her Portia too forward in her relations with Bassanio, 'too osculatory', as he put it – but Christopher St John's description of her interpretations of two Shakespeare heroines conveys the spirit that so attracted the public: 'For Portia, the pedant, and Portia, the decorous grand lady, she had substituted a witty and decorous being, passionately full of heart, yet always well-bred. For Beatrice, the odious termagant, she gave us as fine a lady as ever lived, a great-hearted woman, beautiful, accomplished, high-spirited, tender.'[38] Her other most popular roles similarly tended towards vulnerability, warm-heartedness and, on occasions, a childish innocence apparently preserved in aspic: she first played Olivia, the beloved daughter in W. G. Wills' adaptation of *The Vicar of Wakefield* in 1878, and was still playing her in 1897, at the age of fifty; as Ellaline in Alfred Calmour's *The Amber Heart*, she played a woman protected from the pains and education of love by a magic necklace which preserved her as a permanent emotional child.

Ellen Terry achieved considerable financial success – commanding a weekly salary of £200 at the age of 36, she was earning the highest wage of any woman in Britain.[39] But she was never viewed as grasping or even financially canny. Unlike other high-earning actresses such as Langtry and Bernhardt, Terry was not accused of greed, most obviously because for nearly twenty-five years she acted as consort to Henry Irving, allowing him to choose the repertoire and manage the finances. Indeed, she was prepared to make financial and artistic sacrifices for him, whether by allowing Irving to steal her idea for a lustrous blood-red cloak for *Macbeth* in 1888 or by halving her salary to save an insolvent Lyceum in 1902.[40] For all her personal success, Terry was figured primarily as a faithful, Ruskinian helpmeet to her theatrical partner.

The extent to which this image of the selfless actress, unmotivated by ambition, was constructed or was created by a general desire to view the woman herself as a reflection of her stage roles remains difficult to determine. In her memoirs, *The Story of My Life*, Terry narrates how, when Charles Reade found her in rural seclusion in 1874 and asked her to return to the stage, she laughingly said, 'Well, perhaps I would think of it if someone would give me forty pounds a week!' This was then the top salary for an established star – an extravagant sum for an actress who had not yet made her name – but, according to Terry, Reade took her joke seriously and declared 'Done!'[41] Later biographers tended to reproduce this version of how Terry came to secure a top salary from Reade, characterising the actress as playful or naïve rather than financially astute or ambitious.[42] A veritable conspiracy of silence – or, indeed, a collective fiction – also seems to have surrounded the facts of Terry's private life. In Walter Calvert's *Souvenir of Miss Ellen Terry* (1897), he glosses over her six-year residence in the country with Edward Godwin, during which she bore him two children; the author simply remarks: 'Into the private life of the famous actress it is not in my province to enter, more than to say she enjoys the reputation of being as charming off the stage as she is upon it.' The suggestion here that there might be something to conceal is then erased in his eliding her children's parentage by describing them as 'Miss Edith Wardell' and 'Mr. Edward Wardell', leaving the reader to assume that they were offspring of her second marriage, to Charles Wardell.[43] Charles Hiatt's *Ellen Terry and Her Impersonations* (1898) similarly leaves Terry's affair with Godwin a blank, and does not just tacitly infer that their father was Wardell by again giving them his surname, but baldly states that they were 'children of this marriage' – though Edith was born nine years earlier and Edward six years.[44]

This construction of Ellen Terry's celebrity persona in an image of old-fashioned feminine virtue in defiance of her distinctly unconventional private life catered to her audiences' desire to see her on-stage persona as real. As Shaw commented, 'she never needed to perform any remarkable feat of impersonation: the spectators would have resented it: they did not want Ellen Terry to be Olivia Primrose: they wanted Olivia Primrose to be Ellen Terry'.[45] When female virtue was figured as transparent and visible, and Terry performed virtue so convincingly, it was reassuring to interpret her performances as the manifestation of an essential inner goodness. Also at play may have been the enduring desire of fans to 'know' the object of their admiration, projecting into the blanks left in biographies their own versions of her life and character. In the absence of a publicly displayed private life, fans could best create a sense of intimacy with Terry by believing in the veracity of her stage persona.

For those who knew details of Terry's private life, interesting contortions could result. Clement Scott, a vociferous moral conservative, charted his almost reluctant suspension of disbelief as he reviewed her performances. Words like 'charm', 'enchanting', 'fascinated' and 'bewitching' echo through his reviews, as though she were casting a spell over him.[46] When reviewing her performance as Margaret in *Faust*, he narrated this very process of enchantment. Terry's first entrance was that of the celebrity:

> ... she was bound to be Miss Terry to an enthusiastic house. She could not recover Margaret in two short lines. All ideas of church, confession, surprise, innocence, and simplicity vanished. It was Ellen Terry received with enthusiasm at the expense of the play.[47]

By the second act, Scott reported, 'Miss Ellen Terry is becoming more and more the ideal Margaret', and by the end of the play Scott was in awe of the 'purity, pathos, and intensity' she projected. The transformation was complete, and disbelief suspended as Ellen Terry became the good woman: 'A suggestion of the ideas of Margaret has often been given, but here we seem to see and read the woman's very soul.'[48]

For all the freedom and lack of public scrutiny that Terry enjoyed in her private life, she experienced occasional frustration at the limitations that occasionally resulted from her enduringly virtuous reputation. She wrote to Shaw of her desire to play his seductive and petulant Cleopatra, or Mrs Warren, his robustly vulgar prostitute, but when he offered her a role it was as Lady Cicely, his 'Angel in the Atlas', a woman who can reduce men to children under her command but the secret of whose success is her selflessness and lack of sensuality.[49] Similarly, when J. M. Barrie wrote for her the title role of *Alice Sit-by-the-Fire*, a mother who cannot give up her childish playfulness, Terry ruefully commented that 'although [the role] had been made to measure, it didn't fit me. I sometimes felt that I was bursting at the seams.'[50] In her memoirs she wrote with pride and enthusiasm about her performance as Lady Macbeth, though critical opinion had tended to conclude that she was too soft, kind and yielding to play Shakespeare's harpy. When she was praised for her grace and charm as a rough old fisherwoman in *The Good Hope*, a role which she had chosen for herself, Terry was exasperated: 'It does not seem to occur to them that if I convey the impression of fairy-like grace when I am representing a fisherwoman or a washerwoman I must be a very bad actress.'[51] Like Lillie Langtry, Terry responded by emphasising the performative nature of her existence; as she put it in her note to her 1906 Jubilee programme, merging her theatrical performances and the mutable self:

> 'One man in his time plays many parts.'
> (And so does a *woman*!)

While public perception of Ellen Terry's 'veridical' self was predominantly a reflection of her on-stage persona, the evidence from her life and letters presents a woman who was as generous, impulsive and warm-hearted as her theatrical creations. But, according to Victorian conventions, she was also an amalgam of contradictions: artistically ambitious and yet often selfless; kind-hearted and compassionate with a considerable sexual appetite and scant regard for contemporary mores. She thus confounded attempts at constructing a straightforward public/private divide in her life, especially for those clinging to conventional notions of feminine virtue. This is amply demonstrated in Edward Gordon Craig's biography of his mother, *Ellen Terry and Her Secret Self* (1931). It was written in outraged response to Bernard Shaw's publication of his long correspondence with Terry, which Craig saw as an invasion of his dead mother's privacy and a malicious portrayal of her as a disreputable woman. As Terry's son and her biographer, Craig's motivation in writing also clearly included a desire to annexe Terry for himself – so he famously declared, 'I don't see how you can rock the cradle, rule the world, *and* play *Ophelia* perfectly, all in the day's work.'[52] But Craig also demonstrates the specific ways in which his mother confounded his quite conventional notions of female virtue. In his account of her life and work, he responded by quite literally splitting his mother's persona in two, separating the good woman and the ambitious celebrity into discreet identities, who engage in frequent strangely schizophrenic conversations with each other throughout their biography. The secret self of the title is 'Nell' or 'Nelly', a woman who had only one true love, Craig's father Edward Godwin, and who would have far preferred to spend the rest of her days secluded in the countryside with her children, instead of treading the boards of the Lyceum. In contrast to the secret Nelly, 'E.T.' is the famous actress, guilty of ambition, too quick to sell herself to public applause, and as a result, often an obtuse, clumsy and absent mother.

Craig was clearly troubled not only by the impossibility of Terry being a good working mother, but also by the very idea of a virtuous woman acting. Pretence, deception and transformation are so far from Craig's notion of a good woman that he presents Terry's acting as a form of childish make-believe, a product not of scholarship and training, but of unthinking instinct. He describes her playing at kings and queens like a child in performances that were 'spontaneous, genial and free'.[53] Craig effectively denies Terry agency in her own productions, while blithely ignoring the detailed character analyses she outlines in her own memoirs and her description of 'the three I's' indispensable to the actress: 'imagination, industry, and intelligence'.[54] In 'A Plea for G. B. S.', an annexe to the biography in which Craig inveighs against the publication of his mother's letters, the son grudgingly admits the possibility of Terry performing as naturally and mutably in private correspondence as on the public stage:

> But some will say that just as G. B. S. was writing with a view to publication, so was she acting – that, after all, her letters were a performance.
> It is possible .... I had never thought of that.[55]

Just as Terry herself had emphasised the performative nature of her life, so Craig finds himself forced to contemplate its possibility. The curious interactions between Ellen Terry's on- and off-stage lives and her celebrity persona, together with her natural exuberance, prompted in those close to her an awareness that all appearances may be performances, whether in public or private. In his preface to their correspondence, Shaw notes how Terry carried habits of emotional exaggeration and projection from stage into her private life, seizing on every emotion and amplifying it, and explains that in their letters she and Shaw 'were both comedians, each acting as audience to the other'.[56] Similarly, in their edition of Terry's memoirs, extended and footnoted in defiant response to Craig's biography of little Nell, Edith Craig and her partner Christopher St John explain any apparent discrepancies in Terry's character by remarking that 'it came naturally to Ellen Terry to dramatise herself. So there are hundreds of Ellen Terries, all genuine in their way, for there was in this extraordinary rich and varied nature an abundance of material for their creation'.[57] The quest for a veridical, private self is thus dismissed as essentially misguided.

* * *

Bernhardt, Langtry, Campbell and Terry negotiated their on- and off-stage celebrity reputations in varied and complex ways, belying any clear divide between public and private, and hinting at the performative nature of all aspects of their lives, and perhaps other women's lives. The notion that women's lives were most appropriately confined to a private, domestic sphere was still widespread at the end of the nineteenth century, and, indeed, formed a touchstone of anti-suffrage arguments, with opponents of female enfranchisement insisting that direct involvement in the public sphere would damage women's natural modesty, purity and selflessness. It is, therefore, unsurprising that actresses had such a significant role to play in developing suffragist tactics. The Actresses' Franchise League (AFL) was founded in 1908, putting on propaganda plays and helping to organise the vast suffrage marches in which thousands of women processed through central London. These marches included divisions of women, gathered together under the banner of their professions, the AFL adding celebrity glamour to the public visibility of working women. By training women how to stand, walk and speak in public, members of the AFL also helped ordinary women to make an effective and dignified display of themselves.[58] Having eroded distinctions between public and private in their own lives, Campbell, Langtry and Terry became involved in the campaign to give all women a role in the public sphere.

In 1909 the AFL presented *A Pageant of Great Women*, written by Cicely Hamilton and directed by Terry's daughter, Edith Craig. 'Woman', played by Adeline Bourne, argues with Prejudice (the only male role) over his

Figure 10.2 Ellen Terry as Nance Oldfield in Cicely Hamilton's *A Pageant of Great Women*. Photograph by Lena Connell, published by the Suffrage Shop (1910), courtesy of the Victoria and Albert Picture Library.

opposition to female suffrage. Fifty-two famous women are paraded across the stage to support Woman's argument, played by actresses dressed as saints, soldiers, writers, artists and rulers from St Hilda and Sappho to Joan of Arc, Rosa Bonheur and Florence Nightingale.[59] Notably, Woman introduced and spoke for all the characters, apart from Ellen Terry, who played the actress Nance Oldfield, and declared that if Prejudice had had his way, 'The stage would be as dull as now 'tis merry, / No Oldfield, Woffington, or – Ellen Terry!'[60] (Figure 10.2). The *Pageant* was a protest against women's confinement to the private sphere and a celebration of their contribution to the public life of the nation. Living exuberantly in both worlds, Ellen Terry's performance defied attempts to distinguish between them; she appeared triumphantly as Ellen Terry the private woman playing Ellen Terry the actress playing an entirely different actress singing the praises of Ellen Terry the celebrity.

Notes

1 Henry James, 'The Comédie Française in London', *The Nation*, 31 July 1879, quoted in Susan A. Glenn, *Female Spectacle: The Theatrical Roots of Modern Feminism* (Cambridge, MA: Harvard University Press, 2000), p. 9.
2 William Archer, 'Fédora', *The Theatrical World of 1895* (London: Walter Scott, 1896), 29 May 1895, p. 184.
3 Marie Columbier, for example, entitled her scurrilous fictional biography of Bernhardt *The Life and Memoirs of Sarah Barnum* (London: Crown Publishing, 1884).
4 Quoted in Glenn, *Female Spectacle*, p. 30.
5 Sarah Bernhardt, *My Double Life: The Memoirs of Sarah Bernhardt*, translated by Victoria Tietze Larson (Albany, NY: State of New York Press, 1999), p. 271.
6 Glenn, *Female Spectacle*, p. 17.
7 See, for example, William Archer, 'The Rival Queens', *The New Budget*, 20 June 1895, reprinted in Archer, *The Theatrical World of 1895*, pp. 205–6; George Bernard Shaw, 'Duse and Bernhardt', *Saturday Review*, 1 June 1895 and 15 June 1895, reprinted in Bernard Shaw, *The Drama Observed*, 4 vols, ed. Bernard F. Dukore (University Park, PA: Pennsylvania State University Press, 1993), II, pp. 357, 367–8; A. B. Walkley, 'Sarah Bernhardt' (July 1889), in *Playhouse Impressions* (London: T. Fisher Unwin, 1892), pp. 239–44.
8 Bernhardt, *My Double Life*, pp. 195–96, 222.
9 See, for example, Raymond Blathwayt, ' "Does the Theatre Make for Good?": An Interview with Mr Clement Scott', reprinted from *Great Thoughts* (London: A. W. Hall, 1898); Tracy C. Davis, *Actresses as Working Women: Their Social Identity in Victorian Culture* (London and New York: Routledge, 1991).
10 For examples of such tactics, see Mary Jean Corbett, *Representing Femininity: Middle-Class Subjectivity in Victorian and Edwardian Women's Autobiographies* (New York and Oxford: Oxford University Press, 1992), chapters 4 and 5.
11 Chris Rojek, *Celebrity* (London: Reaktion Books, 2001), p. 11.
12 Laura Beatty, *Lillie Langtry: Manners, Masks and Morals* (London: Vintage, 2000), p. 138. 'The New Helen' was first published in *Time* in July 1879.
13 Beatty, *Lillie Langtry*, p. 108.

14 Quoted in Ernest Dudley, *The Gilded Lily: The Life and Loves of the Fabulous Lillie Langtry* (London: Oldhams Press, 1958), pp. 64, 67.
15 Henry Austin Clapp, *Reminiscences of a Drama Critic* (Boston: Houghton, Mifflin and Company, 1902), p. 77, reprinted in *Victorian Actors and Actresses in Review: A Dictionary of Contemporary Views of Representative British and American Actors and Actresses, 1837–1901*, ed. by Donald Mullin (London: Greenwood Press, 1983), p. 298.
16 Beatty, *Lillie Langtry*, p. 226.
17 Lillie Langtry, *The Days I Knew* (London: Hutchinson, 1925), pp. 229–31. Ellen Terry had given a series of lectures on Shakespeare's heroines, and Helen Faucit published her study *On Some of Shakespeare's Female Characters* in 1885.
18 Langtry, *The Days I Knew*, p. 316.
19 Langtry, *The Days I Knew*, pp. 124, 180.
20 Langtry, *The Days I Knew*, p. 104.
21 Langtry, *The Days I Knew*, p. 173.
22 Lena Ashwell, *Myself a Player* (London: Michael Joseph, 1936), p. 44.
23 Langtry, *The Days I Knew*, p. 97.
24 See, for example, Joel H. Kaplan and Sheila Stowell, *Theatre and Fashion: Oscar Wilde to the Suffragettes* (Cambridge: Cambridge University Press, 1994), chapter 2; Mrs Patrick Campbell, *My Life and Some Letters* (London: Hutchinson, 1922), chapter 5.
25 Letter to Charles Charrington, quoted in Margot Peters, *Mrs Pat: The Life of Mrs Patrick Campbell* (London: Hamish Hamilton, 1984), p. 107.
26 See Peters, *Mrs Pat*, pp. 95–9, 122–5.
27 Peters, *Mrs Pat*, p. 358.
28 *The Philharmonic*, p. 38, n.d. (but mention of *Beyond Human Power* and *The Joy of Living* places it as c.1903), Harvard University, Houghton Library, Mrs Patrick Campbell Collection.
29 Peters, *Mrs Pat*, pp. 375–8. For Shaw's self-scripted interviews see, for example, *The Star* and *The New Budget*, reprinted in *The Bodley Head Bernard Shaw: Collected Plays with their Prefaces*, 7 vols (London: Bodley Head, 1979), I, pp. 122–32, 473–80, 595–9.
30 *The Illustrated London News*, 13 September 1913, p. 412. See also *The Graphic*, 13 September 1913, p. 496; *The Bookman*, December 1918, pp. 103–6.
31 *The Adored One*, first performed at the Duke of York's Theatre, London, 4 September 1913. British Library, Lord Chamberlain's Collection 1913/28. Act III, pp. 27–8. Only the first act was ever published, under the title *Seven Women*.
32 A. B. Walkley in *The Star*, for example, described her Lady Teazle as 'wholly modern, neurotic, Pinero-ish', quoted in Alan Dent, *Mrs Patrick Campbell* (London: Museum Press, 1961), p. 133.
33 *The Era*, 10 September 1913, p. 19.
34 Walter Pritchard Eaton, 'Maude Adams as a Murderess', reprinted in Carl Markgraf, *J. M. Barrie: An Annotated Secondary Bibliography* (Greensboro, NC: ELT Press, 1989), p. 99.
35 *Dublin Daily Express*, 24 March 1906, *Times*, 13 June 1906, quoted in Nina Auerbach, *Ellen Terry, Player in Her Time* (New York: W. W. Norton, 1989), pp. 5, 342.
36 Max Beerbohm, 'A Great Dear', *Saturday Review*, 24 March 1906, p. 360.
37 Noted by Susan Torrey Barstow in 'Ellen Terry and the Revolt of the Daughters', *Nineteenth Century Theatre*, 25:1 (Summer 1997), 5–32.
38 Henry James, 'The London Theatres', *Scribner's Monthly*, 21 (January 1881), reprinted in *Henry James: Essays on Art and Drama*, ed. Peter Rawlings

(Aldershot: Scolar Press, 1996), p. 335; Christopher St John, *Ellen Terry* (London: John Lane, 1907), p. 51. For Terry's own account of her performances, including her defence of her interpretation of Portia, see Ellen Terry, *Ellen Terry's Memoirs*, with Preface, Notes and Additional Biographical Chapters by Edith Craig and Christopher St John (London: Gollancz, 1933), pp. 90–1, 141–6, and *passim*.
39 Sandra Richards, *The Rise of the English Actress* (London: Macmillan, 1993), p. 131.
40 Richards, *The Rise of the English Actress*, p.127; Laurence Irving, *Henry Irving: The Actor and His World* (London: Columbus Books, 1989), pp. 501–2.
41 Ellen Terry, *The Story of My Life* (London: Hutchinson, 1908), pp. 82–3. As Thomas Postlewait has observed, Terry is here also offering a common self-effacing trope of nineteenth-century actresses' autobiographies in crediting a man with a pivotal role in making her career. See Postlewait, 'Autobiography and Theatre History', in *Interpreting the Theatrical Past: Essays in the Historiography of Performance*, ed. Thomas Postlewait and Bruce McConachie (Iowa City: University of Iowa Press, 1989), pp. 259–64.
42 See, for example, Margaret Steen, *A Pride of Terrys: Family Saga* (London: Longmans, 1962), p. 135; Irving, *Henry Irving*, p. 255.
43 Walter Calvert, *Souvenir of Miss Ellen Terry* (London: Henry J. Drane, 1897), p. 14.
44 Charles Hiatt, *Ellen Terry and Her Impersonations: An Appreciation* (London: George Bell, 1898), pp. 60–1.
45 'Preface', in *Ellen Terry and Bernard Shaw: A Correspondence*, ed. Christopher St John (London: Constable, 1931), p. xix.
46 See, for example, Clement Scott, *From 'The Bells' to 'King Arthur': A Critical Record of the First-Night Productions at the Lyceum Theatre from 1871 to 1895* (London: John Macqueen, 1896), pp. 148, 168, 271.
47 Review of Faust by W. G. Wills, 19 December 1885, reprinted in Scott, *From 'The Bells' to 'King Arthur'*, p. 288.
48 Scott, *From 'The Bells' to 'King Arthur'*, pp. 290, 295.
49 *Ellen Terry and Bernard Shaw*, ed. Christopher St John, pp. 338, 334.
50 Terry, *Ellen Terry's Memoirs*, p. 258.
51 Terry, *Ellen Terry's Memoirs*, p. 257.
52 Edward Gordon Craig, *Ellen Terry and her Secret Self* (London: Sampson Low, Marston, 1931), p. 51.
53 Craig, *Ellen Terry and her Secret Self*, pp. 23, 172, 163.
54 Terry, *Ellen Terry's Memoirs*, p. 34.
55 Craig, *Ellen Terry and her Secret Self*, Annexe, p. 12.
56 *Ellen Terry and Bernard Shaw*, ed. Christopher St John, pp. xii, xiv.
57 Terry, *Ellen Terry's Memoirs*, notes to Chapter 4, p. 74.
58 Lisa Tickner, *The Spectacle of Women: Imagery of the Suffrage Campaign, 1907–14* (London: Chatto and Windus, 1987).
59 Julie Holledge, *Innocent Flowers: Women in the Edwardian Theatre* (London: Virago, 1981), pp. 69–71.
60 Cicely Hamilton, *A Pageant of Great Women* (London: Suffrage Shop, 1910), p. 31.

Part IV
Nation

> I *am* England and England is me.
> Noël Coward

11
Siddons, Celebrity and Regality: Portraiture and the Body of the Ageing Actress
Shearer West

During the eighteenth century the concept of celebrity was in its formative stages. Although the effects and consequences of public recognition existed before this time, its by-products – including journalistic voyeurism, public obsession and image manipulation – were manifestations of a commercial culture that became especially strong in England during the latter half of the eighteenth century. Despite the ostensible differences between developing ideas of celebrity in the eighteenth century and a fully formed concept of celebrity perpetuated through the mass media of modernity, there are many continuities between Georgian London and twenty-first-century global culture. Mechanisms of publicity that were only in the process of invention in the eighteenth century remain: image-making, puffing, idolatry, the collapse of distinctions between public and private, and an obsession with the body. Furthermore, as Richard Dyer has argued, 'stars' can serve the function of either reinforcing dominant value systems or patching over often unspoken cultural problems,[1] and these ideological operations existed as strongly in the 'pre-cognitive' celebrity culture of the eighteenth century as they do today.[2] What changed in the intervening centuries was the way these ingredients gradually overturned the continuity and longevity of public 'fame' in favour of the evanescence and replaceability of 'celebrity'.[3]

Theatrical performers provide an appropriate testing ground for the development of a concept of celebrity, as they were objects of the media manipulation, audience fervour and public obsession that characterised the commercial culture of the eighteenth century. They also represented the effects of what Chris Rojek has called 'achieved' celebrity, as opposed to the 'ascribed' celebrity of the nobility and aristocracy.[4] Eighteenth-century performers had a vested interest in contributing to their own notoriety and perpetuating their popularity (and potential earnings) by manipulating the increasingly important tools of public communication available to them – especially prints, pamphlets and paintings.

These considerations are particularly relevant for the actress Sarah Siddons (1755–1831), who could be said to have been the first woman 'superstar' to appear on the English stage. I would like to probe the idea that Siddons and her audiences together constructed an image of the star that enabled her to achieve and retain a celebrity status through five decades. Her towering reputation remained stable despite changes in her body caused by pregnancy, ageing, obesity and illness, which were all too visible on the stage but were rationalised by the imaginations of her audience and critics, the skill of the artists who represented her, and her own manipulation of her image. Arguably, the continuity of her reputation, and the commemoration of her death by a vast funeral procession, monuments and other signs of public mourning gave Siddons the mantle of lasting fame rather than fleeting celebrity. However, Siddons' unwavering popularity among her publics was counterbalanced by the flexibility of her public image, and her own, as well as her audience's, ability to adapt to a changing idea of their theatrical icon. This iconic malleability is more characteristic of the modern form of celebrity than the ancient one of fame. The changes in the physical and iconic bodies of Siddons were negotiated by artists, critics and Siddons herself to create an enduring double vision of the actress as queen during a period of nationalistic royalism and political instability. The potent combination of the greater presence of the visual arts, and a public facing unprecedented political events help explain the management, perception and perpetuation of celebrity in this formative period.

Siddons' theatrical background was not unusual for an eighteenth-century actress. She was from an acting family (the Kembles), and was raised from an infant as a strolling player, performing in country barns as well as regional theatres. Her thespian family remained integral to her career, as her brother, John Philip Kemble, rose to prominence alongside her, and in later years, they promoted each other's reputations. However, there is no easy explanation for Siddons' sudden success, although this is partly accounted for by her frequent appearances in fashionable Bath, Bristol and Cheltenham at a time when there was a demand for actresses who could play a range of parts but a dearth of women with the versatility and stamina to live up to provincial expectations. Siddons' 'discovery' by David Garrick in 1775 was followed by a failure to make an impression at Drury Lane Theatre and a retreat to the provinces, where she consolidated her reputation. Her triumphant reappearance in London in 1782 came after she had already made herself a favourite among the elite audiences summering in Bath.

In the 1780s and 1790s, while she was enjoying London success, Siddons' acting style was characterised by its energy, physicality, the flexibility of her facial expressions and her ability to find fresh meaning in familiar lines. She carried Garrick's 'natural' style of performing to a deeper level, making actors of his generation appear stilted and bland by comparison. Her violent and emotional style chimed well with the expectations of audiences brought up on the idea of sensibility – which favoured a demonstrative display of feeling. They expressed their appreciation empathetically, by crying, screaming, fainting, vomiting and other extreme physical reactions. By the end of the eighteenth century, Siddons' acting style had changed dramatically, becoming more studied and statuesque and involving a more careful manipulation of visual effects such as costume and stage procession. These new techniques were adapted to suit the enlarged Drury Lane Theatre, as the loss of the intimacy that had been characteristic of earlier theatre interiors prevented audiences from mapping her expressions and movements in quite so much detail. Her audience, too, had changed, as the more intense physical responses gradually dropped away with the waning of the sensibility phenomenon.[5]

These facts about Siddons' life evince her rise to public recognition but do little to explain how she maintained her status as a celebrity throughout her life. In attempting to answer this question, it is worth noticing that Siddons is best remembered for rendering respectable a profession that had previously besmirched the name of any woman who joined it. She achieved this through a careful attention to the relationship between her public and private life. First of all, from an early age, she was associated with members of the aristocracy – initially as a teenage companion to Lady Mary Greatheed, and eventually through her acquaintance with Georgiana, Duchess of Devonshire, the Earl of Aylesbury, Fanny Burney and many others. Second, unlike many other actresses, Siddons managed to evade or divert sexual scandals. Although she lived apart from her husband after 1804, and there were rumours that she had affairs with both the artist Thomas Lawrence and a fencing master called Galindo,[6] she managed her public façade so effectively that whiffs of scandal were quickly dispelled. Third, throughout her life, she chose tragic roles that emphasised suffering virtue and self-sacrifice. Although she could and did play courtesans and fallen women, such as Elvira in Sheridan's *Pizarro* and the eponymous Jane Shore in Nicholas Rowe's tragedy, she managed to leave an impression of heroic affliction rather than lost reputation. She was particularly effective at manipulating the unconscious perceptions of audiences who tended to see the performer and the role as two sides of the same coin – what William Gruber refers to as 'the actor/character alloy'.[7] By extracting qualities of pathos, heroism, stoicism, determination and filial dedication from her characters, Siddons directed audience attention to their virtuous qualities. The establishment and effective maintenance of her celebrity was partly a result of the way Siddons managed public perceptions of both her private life and her stage presence.

As part of this self-presentation, Siddons was enthusiastically involved in cultivating her public image through portraiture.[8] Although David Garrick had been a willing subject of a huge range of visual representation, Siddons became much more closely involved in her own image-making – selecting and rejecting artists, engravers and poses.[9] In her brief *Reminiscences*, written at the end of her life, she boasted about this aspect of her publicity campaign: 'I was, as I have confess'd, an ambitious candidate for fame ... As much of my time as could now be "stol'n from imperious affairs," was employ'd in sitting for various Pictures.'[10] The implication of Siddons' reference to 'fame' is that she felt artists could provide a lasting monument that would hold her image in the public mind long after her transient stage performances were forgotten. However, there were other, more ephemeral, advantages to using portraiture as part of her image management that contributed as much to her lifetime celebrity, as to her posthumous fame. Siddons' portraits in and out of character were painted by all the top artists of the day, including Joshua Reynolds, George Romney, Thomas Gainsborough and Thomas Lawrence. These artists commanded the highest prices and had an élite clientele who frequented their studios as part of their leisure activities. By including Siddons among their sitters, they reinforced her social associations with the well born. In addition, Siddons' success coincided with the advent of major public exhibitions in London: the Royal Academy exhibitions from 1769 grew larger and more fashionable each year, with a particularly boom period between 1780 and 1800, when Siddons was at the height of her fame.[11] These changes in the London art world meant that paintings, prints and popular imagery were widely disseminated as part of the expanding commercial culture of the metropolis, enhancing Siddons' visibility and thus celebrity among her contemporary 'fans'. Siddons' public image thus came about, on the one hand, through her own agency, and, on the other, through the reception of her audience and critics – informed by changes in viewing practices fed by the greater accessibility of visual art in London.

Portraiture can serve to create a stable and enduring image of the individual represented, and thus, as Siddons saw it, contribute to their fame.[12] However, by using portraiture as part of her image management so early in her career, Siddons was in danger of consolidating an iconic view of herself that would not last the vagaries of changing theatrical fashion or withstand public awareness of inevitable alterations in her physical appearance. Siddons used visual culture to help perpetuate her celebrity, but the very visual world in which she was working was also changing, becoming more sensitively attuned to the aesthetics of acting – that is, scenography, blocking and the physical qualities of actors' bodies. Actresses were a particular focus of this attention to the body. Writers about the theatre had always commented on the beauty of actresses, sometimes making general references to the desirability of their figure. Such comments tended to be rather vague until the Siddons era when much more explicit references to the shape of actresses' bodies became common. Breeches parts became an excuse to adorn attractive actresses in tightly fitting garments, to reveal the lines of their legs and the shape of their breasts.[13] The comedy of a woman's shape in a man's costume titillated as well as amused, but it also fuelled discussion about actresses that focused on their body type. Such attention to actresses' bodies became an extension of debates about decorum: actresses were frequently maligned for being too elderly or corpulent to perform the ubiquitous role of ingenuous young beauty. The physical suitability of a performer for their role was at the heart of Charles Churchill's satiric *Rosciad* of 1761, and he made a specific reference to women's bodies in his passage on Mrs Pritchard:

> In comedy – 'Nay there,' cries critic. 'Hold.'
> Pritchard's for comedy too fat and old.
> Who can, with patience, bear the grey coquette,
> Or force a laugh with over-grown Juliet?
> Her speech, look, action, humour are all just;
> But then, her age and figure given disgust.[14]

Although Churchill went on to claim that the great actor could transcend physical imperfection, the many imitations of *The Rosciad* in succeeding decades continued to fret about clashes that could occur between an actor's histrionic ability and their physicality.[15] There was a particular disdain for heavily pregnant actresses performing virgins.[16] It was clear that audiences saw performers through a kind of double vision – observing both their real and imagined bodies and attempting either to reconcile or elide any inconsistencies. With a more focused attention on the bodies of actresses in the 1780s and 1790s, corporeal decorum – the suitability of a performer's body for the roles they played – became something of an obsession. Although ideas of decorum could be tested on men's bodies (for example, criticisms of John Henderson's pudgy Hamlet or Charles Macklin's aged Macbeth), such an emphasis was more frequently applied to women who attempted to play beautiful *ingénues* when they were approaching middle age.[17]

This concern filters through the responses to Siddons' acting. After her successful second debut in London in 1782, Siddons was seen as conforming to an ideal body type for the young actress. As one critic insisted: 'There never, perhaps, was a better stage figure than that of Mrs. Siddons. Her height is above the middle size, but not at all inclined to the *en-bon-point*.'[18] Here, 'enbonpoint' referred to a shapely and desirable body. For a very short time, Siddons' body was seen to be perfect for those roles that she performed, yet from the beginning, there were also voices of dissent within the clamorous admiration for Siddons' physical qualities. While the critic above commented on the statuesque perfection of her figure, another noted her alarmingly 'emaciated frame' when playing the scene of Jane Shore dying of hunger.[19] Also, despite her perceived ideal body type, Siddons, unlike other actresses, did not exploit the full commercial potential of her body; her disdain for breeches parts led her to adopt a hybrid dress when she played Rosalind – complete with apron to conceal her legs.[20] At a time when many young actresses were making their fortune by exposing their legs, Siddons made a public, visual point of covering hers. From early in her career, the formulaic descriptions of the actress's body ceased to be applied to Siddons for a number of reasons. First of all, both before and after her success in London in 1782, Siddons – like many actresses – performed while heavily pregnant. This irritated Garrick when he sent Henry Bate to scout the provincial theatres for new actresses in 1775. Bate noted Siddons' ability when he saw her in Cheltenham, but wrote, 'Her figure must be remarkably fine, when she is happily delivered of a big belly, which entirely mars for the present her whole shape.' Garrick replied to Bate, 'Your account of the big belly alarms me! – when shall we be in shapes again?'[21] Later in her career, Siddons' noticeable on-stage pregnancies were commented on as lacking in decorum, given the kinds of roles she was performing. Admonition at just such impropriety accompanied her performance as a woman in distress in Robert Dodsley's *Cleone* at Drury Lane Theatre, and Hester Piozzi asserted that Siddons' performance as a pregnant Lady Macbeth would merely fuel the gossip that suggested Siddons was 'covetous' and willing to do anything to earn money.[22]

Siddons' pregnancies came to an end when she reached middle age, but then a new body image began to dominate her public persona even more forcefully. After decades of pregnancy and persistent illnesses such as rheumatism and erysipelas, Siddons gained a large amount of weight – something that even her staunchest admirers found initially difficult to ignore. As early as 1789 Fanny Burney commented that Siddons 'looked too large for that shepherd's dress' in the role of Rosalind.[23] Romantic critics were particularly harsh about her increasing girth: 'the figure of MRS. SIDDONS is now too large and too matronly to represent youth', wrote Leigh Hunt.[24] Siddons' biographer Thomas Campbell found it jarring that Siddons performed both Belvidera and Hermione when, as he delicately put it, 'she was in the autumn of her beauty, large, august and matronly'.[25] When she played Isabella in 1805 after a time away from London, Siddons' husband William wrote to Hester Piozzi, 'The News papers of yesterday were all very liberal in their praise, but all agree as to the "en bon point" since her last engagement.'[26] In this context, the French term signified plumpness, rather than shapeliness. It was acknowledged by many that the perfect form that she had seemed to possess in her earliest years was gone. But even plumpness was less problematic for Siddons' admirers than her visible ageing. William Hazlitt was only one of many who lamented the public displays of the ageing actress and felt alarmed that the process of decay was so visible.[27]

The critical response to Siddons' physical changes were clearly ambivalent, and it is instructive to see how the image-conscious actress appeared in portraits that represented her as she aged and lost the body shape that was considered desirable for many of the roles she played. There is some evidence that artists at first attempted to put the best possible gloss on her ageing and weight gain. This was noticed in the rather nasty commentary of the critic 'Anthony Pasquin', who condemned William Beechey's portrait of *Mrs. Siddons with the Emblems of Tragedy* (1794, London National Portrait Gallery) as 'too thin for the original', and Thomas Lawrence's portrait of Siddons (*c.* 1797, London, Tate Britain) as unconvincingly young: 'We have here youth, flexibility of features and an attempt at the formation of beauty, to denote a lady who is ... so far from being young that her climacteric will be no more.'[28] However, the pictorial flattery of Beechey and Lawrence became less apparent by the beginning of the nineteenth century, when portraitists made no effort to evade or apologise for Siddons' matronly body. For example, the portraits of Siddons as Lady Macbeth by George Henry Harlow (*c.* 1814, Greenville, South Carolina, Bob Jones University) and Richard Westall (1800, London, Garrick Club) highlight the actress's expansive form, muscular arms and almost masculine physicality.[29] Although 'Pasquin' had accused Lawrence of flattering his sitter in the portrait of 1797, a later portrait of Siddons by the same artist is almost exaggerated in its emphasis on the uneven relationship between Siddons' small head and her large body (Figure 11.1).

There could be a number of explanations for these alterations in the representational history of Siddons. The simplest one is that she was ageing and growing larger, and artists depicting her in any other way would have been stretching credibility. Another explanation can be found in the changing nature of portraiture. At the beginning of Siddons' career, professional portraiture was dominated by the theories of Joshua Reynolds. Reynolds' exhortation that portraitists 'improve' their subjects by borrowing their effects from generalised history painting offered a theoretical justification for flattery and eschewing the 'accidents' of age and physical imperfection.[30] However, by the beginning of the nineteenth century, changes in taste and practice favoured a more probing form of portraiture, as critics such as Hazlitt attacked the falseness of idealised portraits. As Nadia Tscherny has argued, portraitists in this period were more often equated with 'biographers' than 'historians' and were expected to unlock the characters of their subjects by depicting idiosyncrasies, eccentricities, even physical imperfections.[31]

These points provide some explanation for the changing artistic representation of Siddons, but they do not wholly account for how the images of the ageing actress contributed to, and even enhanced, her celebrity. It needs to be remembered that those artists who portrayed Siddons were working with a woman known for manipulating and directing her public image. Their sometimes unflattering representations were most likely approved by the actress herself.[32] A comparison between the representational history of Siddons and that of other female performers reveals a contrast between the longevity of Siddons' image and the abrupt disappearance of other actresses from the domain of visual culture. As noted earlier, female performers whose bodies were incompatible with their roles were generally maligned. It was

Figure 11.1 Thomas Lawrence, *Mrs. Siddons* (1804). Copyright Tate London 2004.

partly due to this prejudice that both the comic actresses Dorothy Jordan and Frances Abington were frequently depicted in art when they were young, slender and lithe, but as Abington aged and Jordon's weight ballooned after bearing ten children for the Duke of Clarence, portraits of these actresses ceased appearing in public exhibitions and printshops.[33] If ageing and corpulent female performers were represented, they could become the butt of visual jokes. This was the case with Emma Hamilton, famous for her performed 'attitudes' in Naples. Hamilton's visible weight gain was seen as incongruous to her tableaux of maidens, goddesses and Christian martyrs, and she therefore became a source of public amusement. The illustrated series of Hamilton's attitudes engraved by Frederick Rehberg in 1797[34] was parodied by James Gillray in 1807 as *A New Edition Considerably Enlarged of Attitudes faithfully copied from Nature and Humbly Dedicated to all admirers of the Grand and Sublime*. Gillray's parody included all of Rehberg's illustrations, but he vastly increased Hamilton's girth, rendering her elegant attitudes ridiculous. 'Sublime', in this case, was a euphemism for fat.[35]

In contrast to the absent portraits of ageing comic actresses and the increasingly derisive attitude to Hamilton, and despite the effects of pregnancy, age and weight gain, Siddons remained a celebrity throughout her life. In order to understand her continued reputation, it is important to examine attitudes to ageing in the later part of her career. Historians of ageing have pointed out that age has different chronological, functional and cultural dimensions in different periods of history: the date at which one is considered old (chronological age) can be at odds with a person's functional age (signalled by the decay of the body) and cultural aspects of ageing (how society expects older people to appear and behave).[36] Romantic critics dwelt on these cultural manifestations of the ageing performer – the behaviour, attitudes, appearance and manner – that both reminded them of their youthful pleasure in viewing the young performer, and offered them poignant glimpses of their own mortality. As Charles Lamb put it, 'There is something strange as well as sad in seeing actors ... subjected to and suffering the common lot.'[37]

Such reflections pervaded both textual and visual responses to Siddons, after her putative retirement from the stage on 29 June 1812. Despite this official retirement date, Siddons continued to appear sporadically in London and provincial stages for another four years and kept herself in public view by open readings of Shakespeare and Milton. This prolonged retirement fuelled ambivalent and nostalgic reflections of Romantic critics, as did the coincidence of Siddons' sixtieth birthday year with the defeat of Napoleon and effectively the end of an era. Anecdotes more frequently refer to Siddons off the stage as well as on, and they take on a voyeuristic and longing quality that presages the public obsessions with celebrity of the twenty-first century. For example, Henry Crabb Robinson followed Siddons around the Louvre when she visited there in 1814, and watched her with a mixture of admiration and disgust:

> I kept as near as I could with decorum, & without appearing to be watching her; yet there was something about her that disturbed me .... She knit her brows ... on looking at the pictures, as if to assist a failing sight. But I recognised her fascinating smile with delight, though there was a line or two about her mouth which I thought coarse.[38]

The very last portrait of Siddons echoes this combination of fascination and disgust felt by Crabb Robinson. Henry Perronet Briggs' portrait of Siddons (aged 75) and her actress niece, Fanny Kemble, represents the iconic actress as a pale old woman idly turning the pages of a book that rests unsteadily on her lap (Figure 11.2). The contrast between the enfeebled Siddons and her lively and youthful niece seems to offer a poignant reminder of a living legend. But it also shows Siddons as reflective – staring into the distance as if into her own glorious past – while the vigour of Fanny Kemble signifies the strength of dynastic succession.

The Romantic fascination with the ageing actress was one possible reason for the maintenance of Siddons' celebrity long after she had lost full use of her histrionic faculties. Another pertinent contribution to her lasting celebrity was the way Siddons and her admirers used the alterations in her body to cultivate an enduring image of the actress as a queen at a time when fantasy regality carried more authority than the real thing. This regal trope was established early in Siddons' career through Reynolds' portrait of *Siddons as the Tragic Muse* (Figure 11.3). Although there are several speculations about the origins of Reynolds' portrait,[39] one unremarked aspect is the way in which the portrait configures Siddons as a queen on a throne. In a famous anecdote about the sitting for this painting, Reynolds tells Siddons to 'ascend your undisputed throne and graciously bestow upon me some idea of the Tragic Muse'.[40] Although retrospective and surely apocryphal, this story reinforces the aura of regality that permeates this image. Eighteenth-century individual and group portraits of seated women do exist, but formal frontal views of seated women such as this one were rare. This visual motif was traditionally employed for representations of popes and monarchs, and owed its origin to images of God the Father in medieval and early Renaissance art, with all the implications carried by such references.[41] This regal aura was enhanced by the fact that Reynolds' portrait of Siddons was physically as large as portraits of King George III and Queen Charlotte, and this parity of size became apparent when such works were exhibited at the Royal Academy.[42] *Siddons as the Tragic Muse* must have been in the young Thomas Lawrence's mind when he painted a seated portrait of Queen Charlotte only six years after Reynolds' iconic image (Figure 11.4).[43] However, in contrast to the confident grandeur of Siddons, Lawrence's Charlotte is slumped, unprepossessing and somewhat dishevelled. Despite the presence of Windsor

Figure 11.2 Henry Perronet Briggs, *Sarah Siddons and Fanny Kemble* (1830), courtesy of the Boston Athenaeum.

Castle in the background, and the grandiose Baroque trappings of curtains and columns, Charlotte's regality is undermined, and her chair appears more like a seat than a throne.[44]

This early visual parallel between Siddons and Queen Charlotte was complemented by continual references to royalty in Siddons' public and private

Figure 11.3 Joshua Reynolds, *Mrs. Siddons as the Tragic Muse* (1784). Courtesy of the Henry E. Huntington Library, Art Collections, and Botanical Gardens, San Marino, California.

Figure 11.4 Thomas Lawrence, *Queen Charlotte* (1789) by kind permission of the National Gallery, London.

life from the 1780s onwards. These associations were both actual and metaphorical, and were deliberately cultivated by Siddons in conjunction with her brother, John Philip Kemble. First of all, Siddons was known to the royal family, and she performed before Queen Charlotte, who allegedly praised her for conducting herself like a lady of the court.[45] Second, as she aged, Siddons more frequently specialised in playing queens. She had always performed queens, but from the 1790s she gradually relinquished the roles of young, distressed women such as Belvidera and Jane Shore for more matronly parts like Lady Macbeth and Queen Katherine from Shakespeare's *Henry VIII*. To reinforce Siddons' regal aspect, Kemble rewrote sections of *Henry VIII*. In his promptbooks for the play, Kemble notably changed Shakespeare's stage directions for the trial scene (Act II, scene 4). Where the Shakespearean text used by Kemble indicated: 'Enter the Queen preceded by Guildford with a cushion which he places; then the Queen kneels', Kemble altered this to 'When the Queen enters, all stand up and bow to her – they continue standing till the Queen rises from the cushion.'[46] The reflex of deference alluded to by Shakespeare became an obsequious show of reverence to 'Queen Siddons' in Kemble's version. Such elaboration also appears in George Henry Harlow's massive painting of Siddons in this role (1817, Sudeley Castle), which shows the actress dwarfing the combined authority of the King, Wolsey and the assembled bishops. The exhibition of this work at the Royal Academy in 1817 drew much public attention and helped maintain Siddons' celebrity when she was 62 and a year on from her absolutely final stage appearance.

This combination of Siddons' performances in society and on the stage led observers to attribute regal qualities to Siddons' private character as well. Some of these attributions were generic: Thomas Campbell, for example, commented on the 'strong moral resemblance' between Siddons and Queen Katherine.[47] Hester Piozzi claimed that 'At times, in private company, she gave one a notion of a wicked, unhappy Queen, rather than of a purely well-bred gentlewoman.'[48] Siddons' biographer, James Boaden, affirmed that she 'courted the regal attire'.[49] Among the merchandise that accompanied Siddons mania was a chess set with Siddons' head representing the queen.[50] Siddons joked in a letter when her son George was born: 'My sweet boy is so like a person of the Royal Family, that I'm rather afraid he'll bring me to disgrace.'[51] In each of these and many other instances, Siddons' queenliness was something exaggerated, larger than life, playful, fantastical or metaphorical.

Such generic or metaphorical comparisons are hardly surprising for a tragic actress noted for her queenly roles. Nevertheless, the references could also be quite specific, and it is this contemporaneity that aided Siddons's sustained celebrity. From the 1790s, for example, Siddons and Kemble were both noted for their royalist leanings, which led to the politicising of Kemble's management of Covent Garden Theatre during the Old Price riots of 1809.[52] Kemble's decision to increase space for élite spectators while raising prices and minimising the comfort of the lower classes led him to be accused of 'despotism' by the radical fringe of London society but praised for patriotism by the aristocratic faction of his audience.[53]

The patriotism of the Kemble family and their visibility on the stage led to overt parallels between the physical appearance of Kemble and past British monarchs. James Boaden claimed that Kemble's success in the character of Shakespeare's King John was largely due to his physical resemblance to the Plantagenet monarch:

> It is one of those characters in which he has in every spectator fairly substituted his own face and figure for the *picture sense* of King John ... I do not say that the *picturesque* of an actor's person will do everything – but to be externally like your object secures a welcome at the first appearance.[54]

More significantly, Kemble putatively bore an uncanny resemblance to King Charles I when he performed that character in Havard's eponymous play.[55] Kemble's use of Van Dyck's portraits of Charles I to affect this visual mimicry elicited comparisons with the similarly beheaded King Louis XVI – a common association during the period of revolution and war with France.[56] Kemble's pictorial sense of acting linked him in the public imagination with the dynastic heritage of the British royal family from the Plantagenets through to the Stuarts, as well as to the contemporary King of France. By implication, Kemble's kingliness reminded his viewers of the current royal family, without any breach of decorum.

This range of social, theatrical and metaphorical associations with royalty was also relevant to Siddons, but in her case, the principal point of reference was Queen Charlotte. Whereas Kemble was directly linked with monarchy by his alleged physical resemblance to English kings of the *past*, Siddons' parallel with the living queen was made largely by implication and through visual culture. This is hardly surprising, given that any kind of explicit comparison between Queen Charlotte and a contemporary actress (however respectable) could only have been perceived as a slur on the queen's status and virtue. As demonstrated already, the composition of Reynolds' *Siddons as the Tragic Muse* was appropriated by Lawrence in his portrait of Queen Charlotte, but later portraits of Siddons and Charlotte cultivated more subtle visual relationships. Like Siddons, Charlotte did not age gracefully but bore the marks of frequent childbirth, illness and private distress. Unlike Siddons, however, Charlotte was never considered a beauty, and her rather plain visage and austere dress sense led to some disappointment among her subjects, who craved a more publicly presentable queen.[57] Later portraits of Charlotte, like those of Siddons, did little to disguise the effects of age. Peter Eduard Stroehling's heavily allegorical portrait of the seated Charlotte of 1807 (Her Majesty the Queen) still retains an echo of the Tragic Muse, but the over-determined and contradictory imagery lacks the effective generality of Reynolds' work. The elaborately draped curtain, sculpture of Britannia and discarded crown and sceptre rest uneasily with Charlotte's informal dress and eager lapdog. Furthermore, little has been done to disguise the plainness of her face, her large body and the clear protrusion of a double chin. Even more uncompromising is the very last portrait of Charlotte engraved by L. Gahagan (Figure 11.5). As the inscription to the print indicates, this portrait was taken when Charlotte was at the spa in Bath, so there is a clear association between the portrait sitting and the declining health of the sitter. Here Charlotte is represented in sombre black clothes, her face broken and pinched by age, and her eyes looking downwards in an expression that lacks the confidence of her earlier posed works. Like Briggs' late portrait of Siddons Gahagan's work emphasises, rather than disguises, the ageing face, but Briggs' association of the actress with majesty and dynastic succession contrasts rather dramatically with the wrecked visage of the lonely and bereaved queen.

Whether visual or metaphorical, specific or general, the trope of Siddons as a queen was a persistent one, particularly in the latter part of her career, and this explicit comparison with Queen Charlotte reveals some important clues to the reasons Siddons retained and enhanced her celebrity as she aged. It is perhaps too obvious to say that an aura of regality compensated for an actress who was ageing, ill, obese and well past her prime theatrically, but this image actually served important ideological purposes.

First of all, as Linda Colley has argued so eloquently, the turn of the eighteenth century was a period in which patriotism in the wake of conflict with France led to a surge of royalism.[58] There were many different focal points for this royalism, including Queen Charlotte herself[59] and the patriotic posturing of Kemble at Covent Garden Theatre. The visual cult of Siddons further contributed to this nascent wave of demonstrative patriotism. In the 1785–6 season, she was wheeled onto the Drury Lane stage in the guise of the Tragic Muse, sitting on the obligatory prop of the throne-like chair.[60] Three years later, in 1789, there was an echo of this *tableau vivant* when she appeared at Covent Garden 'in the exact attitude of Britannia as impressed upon our copper coin'.[61] The visual slippages between Siddons as the Tragic Muse/ Queen and as Britannia, the allegory of a united nation, was particularly powerful at a time of incipient revolution in France. The Britannia tableau furthermore coincided with reports of George III's recovery from his first serious bout of madness. Siddons' pose was an indexical sign for a queen who was seen to have nursed her husband through a period of crisis; this referencing could not have failed to enhance Siddons' iconic significance for her audiences.[62] In addition, even in her later career, Siddons was more assiduous than many other 'stars' in travelling to provincial theatres in England, Scotland and Wales when the London season finished. Siddons thus became very much a British, as opposed to merely English, icon, in much the way the German Queen Charlotte had to transform herself into a British monarch and symbol of a united nation.

Figure 11.5 L. Gahagan, *Engraving of Her Most Gracious Majesty Queen Charlotte* (c. 1817), courtesy of the National Portrait Gallery, London.

In these ways, Siddons' public persona reinforced dominant ideologies – providing a comfortable vision for the growing patriotism of her audiences. But, as Richard Dyer has argued, celebrity can also act as a solace for cultural or social tensions, and Siddons' queenly persona also had this healing quality. Although patriotism grew during Siddons' career, this was also a period when the royal family was undergoing an epidemic of private and public crises, with the madness of George III, the profligacy of the Prince of Wales, the 'delicate investigation' into the Princess of Wales' infidelity and an anxiety about radical thinking in the wake of events in France. Siddons provided order amidst the chaos. At a time when, as Simon Schama points out, the royal family began to cultivate an image of domesticity which only barely disguised their deep-rooted dynastic concerns, the actress was cultivating the opposite image: one of exalted royalty.[63] Siddons also provided the British public with a confident and noble queen – a foil to the respected, but none the less rather dowdy Queen Charlotte. What Siddons managed to adopt was not an air of genuine aristocracy but a fairy-tale regality that allowed her audiences to retain a fantasy of royal power at a time of monarchical disintegration.

The signs of age and corpulence in her body offered enough physical comparison with Charlotte to make this fantasy credible on a visual, as well as purely metaphorical level. Siddons was an example of what Rojek called 'achieved' celebrity, but the maintenance of her reputation was largely due to the 'attributed' celebrity that grew from her association with the 'ascribed' celebrity of the reigning queen.[64] The delicate balance among these different aspects of celebrity helped Siddons to establish a position that would contribute to the maintenance of a theatrical dynasty that competed with the Hanoverians in its longevity. Through her self-consciousness about her own image, Siddons attempted to create a public persona, but the association with queenship was one that grew from a combination of the expectations, desires and aspirations of her audiences and her own agency.[65] The ability of an actress to be at once both herself and an iconic figure – the 'actor/character alloy' – echoed the monarchical double vision of 'body natural' and 'body politic'.[66] Siddons helped maintain the fiction of an invincible queen in a period in which the idea of aristocracy coexisted uneasily with a strengthening bourgeois culture.[67] Her physical body became the place where these various tensions were imaginatively reconciled and the means by which the celebrity of a theatrical dynasty was established.

Notes

1 Richard Dyer, *Stars* (London: British Film Institute, 1979; revised edition 1998). For a convincing application of Dyer's ideological view of stardom to a twentieth-century celebrity, see Charles Maland, *Chaplin and American Culture: The Evolution of a Star Image* (Princeton, NJ: Princeton University Press, 1989).

2 I'm borrowing here E. P. Thompson's concept of a 'pre-cognitive' working-class culture that also existed in the late eighteenth century. This concept helps reinforce the idea that 'celebrity' as we now conceive it was a reality well before the term was articulated, but in a nascent and fragmented form. See E. P. Thompson, 'Eighteenth-Century English Society: Class Struggle without Class?', *Social History*, 3 (1978), 133–65.
3 For an excellent and quite clear summary of distinctions between 'fame' and 'celebrity', see Cheryl Wanko, *Roles of Authority: Thespian Biography and Celebrity in Eighteenth-Century Britain* (Lubbock, TX: Texas Tech University Press, 2003), especially pp. 6–8.
4 Chris Rojek, *Celebrity* (London: Reaktion Books, 2001), pp. 17–20. Rojek's categories of ascribed, acquired and achieved celebrity theorise Shakespeare's quip in *Twelfth Night* (II.v): 'some men are born great, some achieve greatness, and some have greatness thrust upon them'. These are useful categories, but the slippages between these labels are also revealing.
5 For a full account of Siddons' life and reputation, see the excellent biography of Siddons by Roger Manvell, *Sarah Siddons: Portrait of an Actress* (London: Heinemann, 1970).
6 See the accusatory pamphlet from Galindo's wife: [Catherine Galindo], *Mrs. Galindo's Letter to Mrs. Siddons* (London: The Authoress, 1809).
7 William Gruber, *Comic Theaters: Studies in Performance and Audience Response*, (Athens and London: University of Georgia Press, 1986), p. 1.
8 For details and many examples, see the essays in *A Passion for Performance: Sarah Siddons and her Portraitists*, ed. Robyn Asleson (Los Angeles: J. Paul Getty Museum, 1999).
9 For the ways art worked for David Garrick, see Peter Thomson's essay in this volume. There are many examples of Siddons involving herself in commissions for portraits. See, for instance, the bad-tempered exchange of letters between Joshua Reynolds and the engraver Valentine Green regarding Siddons' wishes for the engraving of Reynolds' *Tragic Muse* portrait: *Letters of Sir Joshua Reynolds*, ed. Frederick Whiley Hilles (Cambridge: Cambridge University Press, 1929), pp. 103, 245–8 (letters of 6 May 1783; 31 May 1783; 1 June 1783). Siddons' interest in art is attested to by her spare-time activity as a sculptress.
10 *The Reminiscences of Sarah Kemble Siddons, 1773–1785*, ed. William Van Lennep (Cambridge, MA: Widener Library, 1942), p. 17.
11 The growth of art theory and art criticism consequent on the success of the RA exhibitions had an impact on critical responses to the theatre – so much so that the language of connoisseurship and decorum cultivated by Reynolds in his *Discourses* frequently found its way into critical writing about the theatre. See my argument in Shearer West, 'Body Connoisseurship', in *Notorious Muse: The Actress in British Art and Culture 1776–1812*, ed. Robyn Asleson (New Haven, CT and London: Yale University Press, 2003), pp. 151–70.
12 For the way in which portraiture can create an iconic image as well as paradoxically capture a fleeting moment, see Shearer West, *Portraiture* (Oxford: Oxford University Press, 2004).
13 James Boaden, *The Life of Mrs. Jordan*, 2 vols (London: Edward Bull, 1831), I, p. 46.
14 Charles Churchill, *The Rosciad* (Dublin, 1761), pp. 14–16.
15 For example, see *The Aesopiad* (Dublin: 1784–5), p. 45.
16 See, for example, James Boaden, *The Life of Mrs. Jordan*, I, p. 41 on Mrs. Smith performing as a young virgin in York while pregnant.

17 In fact, it was middle age rather than old age that seemed to be a more critical turning point in actresses' careers. For how middle age was conceived in the eighteenth century, see Susannah R. Ottaway, *The Decline of Life: Old Age in Eighteenth-Century England* (Cambridge: Cambridge University Press, 2004), p. 41.
18 This is from a long early review, quoted without attribution by James Boaden, *Memoirs of Mrs. Siddons*, 2 vols (London: Henry Colburn, 1827), I, p. 287.
19 *The Beauties of Mrs. Siddons* (London: John Strahan, 1786), pp. 47–8.
20 Boaden, *Memoirs of Mrs. Siddons*, II, p. 166: 'She ventured to appear upon the London stage in a dress which more strongly reminded the spectator of the sex she had laid down, than that which she had taken up. Even this ... shewed the struggle of modesty to save all unnecessary exposure.'
21 Letter from Rev. Henry Bate to David Garrick 12 August 1775, and Garrick to Bate 15 August 1775, in *The Letters of David Garrick*, ed. David M. Little and George Kahrl, 3 vols (Oxford: Oxford University Press, 1963), p. 1026 and for a discussion of these, see Manvell, *Sarah Siddons: Portrait of an Actress*, pp. 24–9.
22 Boaden, *The Life of Mrs Jordan*, I, p. 103; and *Thraliana: The Diary of Mrs. Hester Lynch Thrale 1776–1809*, ed. Katherine C. Balderston, 2 vols (Oxford: Clarendon Press, 1942), p. 876 (3 April 1794).
23 Fanny Burney, *Diary and Letters of Madame d'Arblay*, 7 vols (London: Henry Colburn, 1854), V, p. 32 (July 1789).
24 Leigh Hunt, *Critical Essays* (London: John Hunt, 1807), p. 19.
25 Thomas Campbell, *The Life of Mrs. Siddons*, 2 vols (London: Effingham Wilson, 1834), I, p. 182.
26 William Siddons to Hester Piozzi (12 October 1805), in Kalman Burnim, 'The Letters of Sarah and William Siddons to Hester Lynch Piozzi in the John Rylands Library', *Bulletin of the John Rylands Library*, 52 (1969–70), 46–95.
27 William Hazlitt, 'Mrs. Siddons's Lady Macbeth', in *The Complete Works of William Hazlitt*, 21 vols, ed. P. P. Howe (London and Toronto: J. M. Dent and Sons, 1930-34), 18: *Art and Dramatic Criticism*, 232–3.
28 Anthony Pasquin [John Williams], *A Liberal Critique on the Present Exhibition of the Royal Academy* (London: H. D. Symonds, 1794), p. 17; and John Williams, *A Critical Guide to the Present Exhibition at the Royal Academy for 1797* (London: H. D. Symonds, 1797), p. 13. The reference to the menopause here is highly unusual in public print. See Ottaway, *Decline of Life*, p. 36.
29 For discussion of Siddons' 'masculine' image, see Shearer West, 'The Public and Private Roles of Sarah Siddons', in *Passion for Performance: Sarah Siddons and her Portraitists*, ed. Robyn Asleson (Los Angeles: J. Paul Getty Museum, 1999), pp. 10–13.
30 See especially Reynolds' *Discourse IV* delivered in 1771 in Joshua Reynolds, *Discourses on Art*, ed. Robert Wark (New Haven, CT and London: Yale University Press, 1981), pp. 57–73 (for *Discourse IV*), p. 72 (for portraiture).
31 Nadia Tscherny, 'Likeness in Early Romantic Portraiture', in *Portraits: The Limitations of Likeness*, ed. Richard Brilliant, in *Art Journal*, special issue, 46:3, (1987), 193–9. See also John Kerslake, 'The Portrait of "Genius": Spearhead of Eighteenth-Century English Taste', *Eighteenth Century Life*, 11 (1987), 155–62.
32 Although we do not have evidence of Siddons' involvement with some of these portraits, it is unlikely, for example, that Lawrence – who was closely involved with the Siddons family – would have painted portraits of her without sanction. Nor is it feasible that Siddons would have renounced her involvement in her public image at the height of both her fame as an actress and her vulnerability as an ageing woman nearing retirement.

33 Abington's attempts to play young women despite her advancing years was savagely attacked when she returned to the role of Beatrice in *Much Ado About Nothing* in 1797, after seven years away from the stage and at the age of 60. See *Monthly Visitor*, October 1797, p. 352: 'her former Beatrice was a chaste, animated, unaffected and captivating performance; but her Beatrice of this night was, for the great part, languid and unattractive ... her person is too big and heavy to give any effect to the more gay and sprightly scenes. We conceive it to be the height of folly and impudence in her to come forward in the present advanced period of her existence; and that too, with a person so ill-calculated for the department, and attempt characters which demand all the vigour and activity of youth.'

34 Frederick Rehberg, *Drawings Faithfully Copied from Nature at Naples* (London: S. W. Fores, 1797).

35 For Hamilton and her attitudes, see Kirsten Gram Holmström, *Monodrama, Attitudes, Tableaux Vivants: Studies on Some Trends of Theatrical Fashion 1770–1815* (Stockholm: Almquist and Wiksells, 1967); Ulrike Ittershagen, *Lady Hamiltons Attitüden* (Mainz: Verlag Philipp von Zabern, 1999); and Shearer West, 'Romney's Theatricality', in *Those Delightful Regions of the Imagination: Essays on George Romney*, ed. Alex Kidson (New Haven, CT and London: Yale University Press, 2002), pp. 131–58.

36 See Ottaway, *Decline of Life*; and Pat Thane, *Old Age in English History* (Oxford: Oxford University Press, 2000).

37 Charles Lamb, 'On Some of the Old Actors', in *The Works in Prose and Verse of Charles and Mary Lamb*, ed. Thomas Hutchinson, 2 vols (London: Oxford University Press, 1908), I, p. 643.

38 Quoted in Yvonne Ffrench, *Mrs. Siddons: Tragic Actress* (London: Verschoyle, 1954), p. 238. Crabb Robinson made many similar observations about Siddons performing her last roles before retirement. As he put it, 'Her advancing old age is really a cause of pain to me', and his observations were undercut with nostalgia for her lost beauty and youth. See *The London Theatre 1811–1866: Selections from the Diary of Henry Crabb Robinson*, ed. Eluned Brown (London: Society for Theatre Research, 1966), p. 35.

39 For an analysis of some of these stories, see Shelley Bennett and Mark Leonard, ' "A Sublime and Masterly Performance": the Making of Sir Joshua Reynolds's *Mrs. Siddons as the Tragic Muse*', in *Passion for Performance*, ed. Robyn Asleson, pp. 97–136; and Heather McPherson, 'Picturing Tragedy: Mrs. Siddons as the Tragic Muse Revisited', *Eighteenth-Century Studies*, 33:3 (2000), 401–30.

40 *The Reminiscences of Sarah Kemble Siddons, 1773–1785*, ed. William Van Lennep, pp. 16–18.

41 For the origins of posing conventions in portraiture, see Lorne Campbell, *Renaissance Portraits: European Portrait Painting in the Fourteenth, Fifteenth and Sixteenth Centuries* (New Haven, CT and London: Yale University Press, 1990), pp. 107ff. For other conventions of regal portraiture, especially the full-length portrait, see Marianna Jenkins, *The State Portrait: Its Origin and Evolution* (New York: College Art Association, 1947).

42 Reynolds' *Siddons as the Tragic Muse* measures 239.4 × 147.6 cm, differing only negligibly from Lawrence's portrait of Queen Charlotte (239 × 147 cm). Other portraits of Siddons, such as William Beechey's portrait of *Siddons with the Emblems of Tragedy* were similarly large (245.1 × 153.7 cm). Although canvases came in standard sizes, it is notable that artists chose the largest (and most visible) canvas sizes for actors and monarchs. However, it is also worth noting that comparably sized portraits of Siddons and Queen Charlotte were not hung at the

same Royal Academy exhibitions. The effect this would have had is apparent from David Solkin's excellent *Art on the Line* exhibition at the Courtauld Institute Galleries in 2001. See *Art on the Line: The Royal Academy Exhibitions at Somerset House 1780–1836*, ed. David Solkin (New Haven, CT and London: Yale University Press, 2001). For the ways in which the hanging of portraits could affect interpretation at Royal Academy exhibitions, see Mark Hallett, 'Reading the Walls: Pictorial Dialogue at the British Royal Academy', *Eighteenth-Century Studies*, 37:4 (2004), 581–604.

43 The influence that this portrait had on Lawrence persisted until late in his career, when he delivered a eulogy to Reynolds' portrait of Siddons in one of his lectures to the students at the Royal Academy, calling it 'a work of the highest epic character, and indisputably the finest female portrait in the world'. Thomas Lawrence, *An Address to the Students of the Royal Academy delivered before the General Assembly at the Annual Distribution of Prizes* (London: W. Clowes, 1824), p. 14.

44 Later portraits of Charlotte, such as that of Joshua Reynolds and John Downman, return to the chair motif and correct the impression of ordinariness conveyed by Lawrence's portrait. But even in these works, the impact is less striking than in Reynolds' earlier portrait of Siddons as the Tragic Muse.

45 *The Reminiscences of Sarah Kemble Siddons, 1773–1785*, ed. William Van Lennep, p. 22. This interpretation was reported by Siddons herself.

46 *John Philip Kemble Promptbooks*, ed. Charles H. Shattuck, 11 vols (Charlottesville, VA: University of Virginia Press, 1974), IV, p. 31.

47 Campbell, *The Life of Mrs. Siddons*, II, pp. 135–6.

48 *Piozziana, or Recollections of the Late Mrs Piozzi*, ed. by Edward Mangin (London: Edward Moxon, 1833), pp. 85–6.

49 Boaden, *Memoirs of Mrs. Siddons*, I, p. 312.

50 This is mentioned in Michael R. Booth, John Stokes and Susan Bassnett, *Three Tragic Actresses: Siddons, Rachel, Ristori* (Cambridge: Cambridge University Press, 1996), p. 36.

51 Quoted in Manvell, *Sarah Siddons*, p. 140.

52 For the politicisation of the Old Price Riots, see Shearer West, 'Thomas Lawrence's "Half-History" Portraits and the Politics of Theatre', *Art History*, 14:2 (June 1991), 225–49; and Marc Baer, *Theatre and Disorder in Late Georgian London* (Oxford: Clarendon Press, 1992).

53 For Kemble's despotism, see, for example, *Morning Chronicle*, 20 October 1809; for his royalist inclinations, see his act of closing Covent Garden Theatre when Louis XVI was beheaded in January 1794, despite Sheridan's express wishes to the contrary. See James Boaden, *Memoirs of the Life of John Philip Kemble*, 2 vols (London: Longman et al., 1825), II, p. 77.

54 Boaden, *Memoirs of Mrs. Siddons*, II, p. 59.

55 *Memoirs of Mrs Siddons*, I, p. 17.

56 See, for example, the radical publication 'Comparison between the Disastrous Reigns of Charles I and Louis XVI', in 'A Collection of Miscellaneous Cuttings ... Relating to the French Revolution', London, British Library [1791, 1792].

57 See Michael Levey, *A Royal Subject: Portraits of Queen Charlotte*, Exhibition Catalogue (London: National Portrait Gallery, 1977).

58 Linda Colley, *Britons: Forging the Nation 1707–1837*, new edn (London: Pimlico, 2003).

59 For a discussion of Charlotte's reputation and a positive gloss on her contribution to British culture, see Clarissa Campbell Orr, 'Queen Charlotte, Scientific Queen', in *Queenship in Britain 1660–1837: Royal Patronage, Court Culture and Dynastic Politics*, ed. Clarissa Campbell Orr (Manchester: Manchester University Press, 2002), pp. 236–66.
60 *London Chronicle*, 19 November 1785, p. 485. See also Boaden, *Memoirs of the Life of John Philip Kemble*, I, pp. 299–300. This occurred on the occasion of the revival of David Garrick's *Jubilee*.
61 *Memoirs of Mrs Siddons*, II, pp. 277–8. By the beginning of the nineteenth century, it was common for women of the middling sort with royalist leanings to dress as Britannia for patriotic parades (see Colley, *Britons*, p. 227).
62 Here I am using the semiotic terminology of C. S. Peirce, 'The Icon, Index and Symbol', in *Collected Works*, ed. Charles Hartshorne and Paul Weiss, 8 vols (Cambridge, MA: Harvard University Press, 1931–58), II, pp. 156–73. In Peirce's view, the index refers to something, whereas the icon is a more direct reference to it. In Siddons' case, the indexical reference enhances her iconic status as a queenly figure.
63 Simon Schama, 'The Domestication of Majesty: Royal Family Portraiture 1500–1850', in *Art and History: Images and their Meanings*, ed. Robert Rotberg and Theodore K. Rabb (Cambridge: Cambridge University Press, 1989), p. 159.
64 Rojek, *Celebrity*, pp. 17–20.
65 For the audience's role in helping construct celebrity, see especially Leo Braudy, *The Frenzy of Renown: Fame and its History* (New York: Vintage Books, 1997), especially pp. 381–2.
66 This is the idea of the 'King's two bodies' put forward originally and most forcefully by Ernst Kantorowicz, *The King's Two Bodies: A Study in Medieval Political Ideology*, new edn (Princeton, NJ: Princeton University Press, 1997).
67 See especially, John Cannon's argument about 'the paradox of a developing capitalism within the framework of a non-capitalist order', in *Aristocratic Century: The Peerage in Eighteenth-Century England* (Cambridge: Cambridge University Press, 1987), p. ix.

12
'Some of you may have seen him': Laurence Olivier's Celebrity

Peter Holland

The action hero

Early in John McTiernan's film *Last Action Hero* (1993), young Danny Madigan, bored at school, is made to watch a clip from Olivier's *Hamlet* (1948), which is not exactly the kind of movie he enjoys, his mind, as always, fixed on his hero Jack Slater, the star of a sequence of action films he excitedly follows. Danny's teacher tries her best: 'Treachery, conspiracy, sex, swordfights, madness, ghosts. And in the end everybody dies. Shakespeare's *Hamlet* couldn't be more exciting.'[1] But her pedagogically odd choice of film version to engage her class – why not Zeffirelli's then recent 1990 version with Mel Gibson?[2] – is of course underpinned by the popular cultural assumption that the Olivier film represents the tradition of *Hamlet*, Shakespeare as high-cultural object, the dyed-blond Olivier as the central figure of the great line of theatrical Hamlets, the apotheosis of everything against which the action movie is set.

As he watches the prayer-scene and Olivier's Hamlet reaches the apogee of hesitation, Danny intervenes – 'Don't talk, just *do* it!' – and, magnificently and mysteriously, as the film cuts again to what Danny is watching, Olivier has metamorphosed into Arnold Schwarzenegger, playing Danny's hero Jack Slater, now become Hamlet: 'Hey, Claudius. You kilt my foddah.'[3] As parody of Shakespeare, of art-film and of high-culture, the next few seconds are extraordinary: as a voice-over announces 'Something is rotten in the state of Denmark ... And Hamlet's takin' out the trash', Arnold/Jack mows down the palace guards, using a skull and an Uzi, and, discarding a cigar while deciding 'To be, or not to be? Not to be', leaves Elsinore exploding behind him.

It is a strange line that journeyed in 1993 from Laurence Olivier to Arnold Schwarzenegger, from the late Baron Olivier of Brighton to the future Governor of California. But it is one that emblematises a move from the filmic traces of English theatrical celebrity that the film preserves to unquestioned contemporary American film stardom, even if, at this point in his career, Schwarzenegger was broadly considered to be a star on the wane.

Olivier, plagued all his life by accidental or intentional anglicisations of his Huguenot name into Oliver (as well as misspellings of his first name into Lawrence), the epitome of the English theatrical voice at its least lyrical and most powerful, can be set against another immigrant, mocked and sometimes self-mocked for his heavily accented, always foreign speech.

But, though *Last Action Hero* has no space for or desire to remark on it, the two also converge precisely at the point of action-hero. While Danny's teacher comments, with the desperate enthusiasm of any teacher confronted with a recalcitrant class, 'And though it may seem that he [Hamlet] is incapable of taking any action, he is in fact one of the *first action heroes*',[4] it is Olivier rather than Hamlet to whom the label most easily applies. Mel Gibson's performance had been notable for its physical restraint, far from the dash of Olivier's. No actor of the twentieth century was more celebrated than Olivier as an action hero, no one more likely to be performing dangerous actions on stage. No one else would have been able to – or would have wished to – write an introduction to William Hobbs' *Techniques of the Stage Fight* (1967) by cataloguing some of his own long list of stage- and film-related injuries.[5] Nor would it have made sense in a book collecting celebratory memories for any other actor for the introduction to use as the means to outline the actor's career that appalling passage recounting with such characteristic ostentation the pain and physical harm Olivier had undergone.[6] His film performance of Hamlet is probably now best remembered for the climactic swallow-dive, sword in hand, from the gallery of the hall on to Claudius at the film's end, a moment that would reduce risk-management assessors to a state of abject terror:

> The dangers involved in what I had conceived for this moment presented themselves to me in the light of the following five possibilities: I could kill myself; I could damage myself for life; I could hurt myself badly enough to make recovery a lengthy business; I could hurt myself only slightly; or I could get away with it without harm.[7]

In the upshot, the single take of the moment worked perfectly and Olivier got 'away with it without harm'. Olivier defines this action sequence, the actor's action more than the character's, as '[t]he one brave moment of my life'.[8] The event does not make it on to the list of injuries. But there was injury to the stuntman, standing in for Basil Sydney as Claudius, who was knocked out by Olivier's full weight landing on his chin and lost two teeth. Characteristically, the injury to others does not seem to concern Olivier at all.

Viscerally exciting as the moment is, it epitomises a cultural anxiety about Olivier and not only when he was at his most physical. As Simon Callow recalled:

> When I was at drama school, the Laurence Olivier controversy raged. Was he the greatest actor who had ever lived? Or was he simply appalling, a ham, external, tricksy, unwatchable, and so on?[9]

If a significant part of celebrity can be measured by the kind of cultural visibility consequent on controversy (often – and especially so for Olivier for lengthy periods of his career – because of domestic scandal, sometimes – as here – because of a problem of aesthetic values), then the 'Laurence Olivier controversy' is itself a sign of his celebrity, at least among drama students.

Cameras and cigarettes

But for Danny Madigan, Olivier could have had no celebrity status as theatre actor. His teacher – and the actor's delivery makes clear her mockery of the kids to whom she needs to say such things – has to find a different measure of his fame:

> What you are going to see is a scene from the film by Laurence Olivier. Some of you might have seen him in the Polaroid commercial, or as Zeus in *Clash of the Titans*.[10]

In *Saturday Night Fever* (1978) a Manhattan theatre agency receptionist is trying to impress John Travolta's character: Laurence Olivier came into her office; 'Who?' '*Who's Laurence Olivier*? You don't know who he is? He's just the greatest actor in the whole world, that's who. Oh, *come on*. You know, the guy on television, the one who did the Polaroid commercial.'[11] Holden apart, the advertisements, precisely that which conferred celebrity on Olivier to a post-1970 generation of television-watching Americans, are completely ignored by Olivier's many biographers (and no theatre actor has attracted more biographers),[12] whether the least sympathetic[13] or the most complete and glossily comprehensive[14] or by his sons.[15] Only Olivier's autobiography confronts the work, for which Olivier was paid $1 million,[16] and it does so apologetically and insecurely: 'I will never know whether I should be ashamed of the little confession that follows or not'.[17] Olivier complains of high taxes and poor state schools, his 'modest stipend' as Artistic Director of the National Theatre and the 'life-style that would seem to be expected of people in our sort of position' as an explanation for 'the occasional two- or three-day film appearances' which he 'welcomed'. There is mockery of those '[p]eople who like to think of themselves as artists' and 'are inclined to regard their profession more in the light of a vocation' and who therefore 'seem to cheapen themselves by advertising some commodity' – 'at least I fancy that is so in our lovely old country'. Olivier therefore excluded showings in the UK but 'I felt sure enough that the European countries with the US would not disapprove, but only sympathise with any guy who needed a buck'. What made Olivier unquestionably able to be known as a celebrity to the American public – and the commercials never identified him by name, the sign of celebrity lying here in the lack of any need to be named – was seen by Olivier as being potentially in awkward tension with the basis of his

British celebrity: famous theatre actors and members of the House of Lords do not appear in television advertisements, even 'for the remarkably clever camera created by the brilliant engineer, Mr Lans'.[18] Olivier's British celebrity, his cultural definition as the essence of Englishness coupled with his social status as life peer, works against precisely those aspects of his career that would most powerfully define his celebrity abroad.

Prior to the Polaroids, Olivier had made only one major commercial endorsement, agreeing to a brand of Benson and Hedges cigarettes being named Olivier. In this he was accepting a commercialisation and commodification of his status that perplexed some. Angus McBean, whose photographs of Olivier and, especially, of Vivien Leigh define him as the most brilliant celebrity photographer of his age, photographed Olivier for the campaign 'and my silhouette picture of him with a drift of smoke was even on the packet'.[19] McBean 'could never understand why he did that job. I suppose the monetary inducement was too great to refuse.'[20] Olivier probably did need the money but there may also have been an awareness of a specific celebrity honour and tradition in this transformation of actor into commodity. Only two earlier brands of cigarettes had been named after performers: De Reszkes, named after Jean de Reszke (1850–1935), principal tenor at the New York Met, and Du Mauriers, named after Gerald Du Maurier (1871–1934), the original Captain Hook in *Peter Pan*. Sir Ian McKellen was able to make the latter link when recalling that '[l]ike Gerald Du Maurier before him, my acting hero Laurence Olivier even had a cigarette brand named after him', but McKellen also noted how the brand was used as a sign of authority – or was it a joke? – under Olivier's artistic direction at the National:

> When I worked for his fledgling National Theatre Company, in the actors' greenroom ... there was a cigarette machine only ever filled with the Olivier brand, although it was capable of dispensing half a dozen different ones.[21]

Olivier cigarettes lasted fifteen years. Holden documents Olivier as 'proud to be immortalised as a cigarette' but also, when the brand was withdrawn in 1973, Olivier's commenting on Nicol Williamson, then the hero to the National's 'young spear-carriers', 'I wonder if he'll be a cigarette one day?'[22] Significantly, though, all three performer-related cigarette brands were marketed specifically to women: as early as 1920 De Reszkes were advertised with a woman offering a man a cigarette in *Vogue*; Du Mauriers were advertised in *Woman* in the 1930s; and Oliviers were marketed, also in *Woman*, in 1963 with the lines:

> Women like us like our very own things. Like fashion. Like Olivier. So beautifully cool and smooth. So elegantly packed. So sensibly priced. Our very own Olivier.[23]

Implicitly, of course, the wording encourages an application from the cigarettes to their namesake: Olivier himself might, even in his sixties, still be seen as cool, smooth, elegant and, now in his post-Vivien Leigh incarnation as the devoted husband and father, reasonably modest in his familial image, 'sensibly priced'. The actor's identity is completely subsumed into the name which can be applied to the marketing object. But the cigarette's success – and Oliviers did not last long in the market, not long enough to become, as De Reszkes and Du Mauriers had managed, disjunct from their namesake – was premised on the particular applicability of Olivier's celebrity identity to such a masculine object of female desire. Laurence Olivier was enough of a celebrity to be a fashion accessory.

Last actions and the performance of sexuality

If Danny Madigan's teacher might remember the series of commercials, Danny himself had probably never seen the Polaroid ads from twenty years earlier. It is only a little more likely that he had seen Olivier as Zeus in a television re-run in Desmond David's *Clash of the Titans* (1981). It is a performance that is also mostly ignored by biographers, with only Roger Lewis spending space on it as 'almost a parody – and yet also a direct representation – of Olivier's Olympian, Zeus-like sensibility', seeing its value – and positing that Olivier saw its value – only in the possibility 'to give strength and integrity to Zeus' understanding of paternal love'.[24] There is, of course, something ridiculously appropriate about the god of classical theatre playing the god of classical Olympus, however tacky the film. But the film was popular, not for the acting but for Ray Harryhausen's special effects, and redefined a version of Olivier's celebrity on screen, while being parasitical on his status as theatre celebrity, in exactly the way that *Saturday Night Fever* noted: the greatest actor in the world who also does adverts on the television.

The series of film roles that Olivier took in the years after he stopped acting on stage are nearly all usually treated as the aberrant embarrassments of an ageing actor who needed to work either for the money or to continue to convince himself that he could, when no longer physically or mentally able to face the rigours of a theatrical run. Like Gielgud late in his career, Olivier on film seemed to many to be doing hack-work, a jobbing actor not a star, making use of his celebrity in vehicles unworthy of him, something that was in stark contrast with Olivier's distinguished television work in this period of his life, performances that needed no such awkward apology, like his series for Granada Television, including Pinter's *The Collection* (1976), Tennessee Williams' *Cat on a Hot Tin Roof* (1976), William Inge's *Come Back, Little Sheba* (1977), Lord Marchmain in *Brideshead Revisited* (1981), as Lear (1983) or in Fowles' *The Ebony Tower* (1984) or, for Thames Television, as John Mortimer's blind father in *A Voyage Round My Father* (1982).[25] Little good has been said about his performances in, for example, *A Bridge Too*

Far (1977), *The Betsy* (1978), *A Little Romance* (1979), *Dracula* (1979), *The Jazz Singer* (1980), *Inchon* (1981) or *The Jigsaw Man* (1984), for all of which only the most sympathetic of biographers can find a good word. Theatrical celebrity is permitted by British culture to transfer to televised versions of theatrical roles or canonical novels but not to transfer to the film cameo. It seems, in a way of which high culture cannot approve, to be trading on celebrity – a conjunction of trade and celebrity which is as much anathema to concepts of high cultural celebrity as trade would have been for a nineteenth-century aristocrat.

Only Olivier's final performance in Derek Jarman's *War Requiem* (1989), released after his death, was permitted approval, its combination of his mute visible frailty and his voice-over of Wilfred Owen's 'Strange Meeting'[26] unquestionably moving as well as being dignified in the forms that the culture requires of its oldest celebrities. The film's visual narrative, framed as the memories of Olivier's character, could be acceptably seen as fulfilling the backward-looking desires of both its performer and its audiences, a record as much of what Olivier had been as what the character remembered. In addition, the cultural authority accruing to Jarman as independent filmmaker, to Owen as poet and to Britten as composer as well as to the fact that, given Olivier's death, the film's soundtrack had to be heard as the swan-song of the celebrated voice, were ample to give it the cultural kudos appropriate to the greatest actor of his time. That the combination of Jarman, Owen and Britten was, for Jarman, a deliberate statement about male homosexuality, war and art, added a certain broadly approvable liberalism to Olivier's presence, especially given the ambiguities over Olivier's own sexuality in the history of his performances and in the contradictory claims of biographers.

In the case of John Gielgud, the actor's homosexuality was cloaked in 1930s responses to his performance style by the conventionalised euphemisms of descriptions of his lyricism (the lyric voice as a queer sign). Later, his sexuality simply had to be accepted, especially in the aftermath of his prosecution for cottaging. With Olivier the aggressive masculinity of the heroic and dangerously violent performance was always in tension with his pleasure in camp (a performative mode ambiguously able to be read as queered or not) and a flirtatiousness that was always an assertion of sexuality or, as Peter Hall defined it in 1959, the 'sexiness' which was 'Olivier's most distinctive quality'.[27] Olivier's comment to Michael Billington, 'I may be rather feminine but I'm not effeminate', serves for Billington as 'a clue to part of Olivier's titanic greatness as an actor: his sexual contradictoriness'.[28] The sexual contradictoriness can also be seen as an essential component of Olivier's performative charisma and consequently of his celebrity.

From the line of the standing body to the characteristic but unusual palms-up gesture of the hands, from the frequent over-softening of the voice to the fullness of the face, Olivier was able to play on the matinée idol image, epitomised by his Heathcliff in *Wuthering Heights* (1939), probably the performance nearest to that of Hollywood star in his career. At least until the harsh reversal of Archie Rice in Osborne's *The Entertainer* (1957), though traceable in some performances thereafter, Olivier traded on the attractiveness to both genders and both sexualities of his stage presence, building his fame on the breadth of his sexual appeal. This as-it-were representation of the self, Olivier on stage or film undisguised, needs to be set against the performances as character actor, fully veiled by the mountains of make-up, clear in his early successes as, for example, Sir Toby Belch (1937) or Justice Shallow (1945) as much as in later work like Titus Andronicus (1955) or Shylock (1970).[29]

Billington, who carefully and brilliantly defines this 'ability to embrace sexual opposites' as part of Olivier's 'stage sexuality', is totally uninterested in the biographers' obsession with whether or not Olivier had a series of homosexual relationships throughout his life from his school years through the offered and declined relationship with Noël Coward to the one with Danny Kaye of which Donald Spoto writes emphatically as an active sexual affair.[30] Robert Lewis is in one sense right in his comment on 'Spoto's unsubstantiated theory that Olivier was a committed homosexual – as if that had anything to do with the price of tea',[31] but, as Tarquin Olivier notes, Olivier's 'fear of homosexuality' was also in part driving and driven by a judgement on the performances of many male actors since he defined it as a source of the 'emasculation of many male performances on stage, where an actor's sexual preference is so undisguisedly communicated to the audience'.[32]

The crucial word here is 'undisguisedly', for Olivier's stage roles are unambiguously dependent on disguise, with the endless fascination with make-up, which disguises his face into the unrecognisability consequent on nose-putty and false teeth.[33] There is a temptation here to indulge in a comic Freudian analysis of the connection between Olivier's fascination with frequent enlarging of his nose on stage and the supposedly small size of his penis. But Olivier's own account of his lack of sexual appetite, especially by comparison with Vivien Leigh's, defines that lack as an active displacement:

> It was therefore hard to make her understand ... that all *that* had gone into my acting, and that you can't be more than one kind of athlete at a time; a sexual athlete is not likely to find sufficient energy for work of another athletic kind, and the acting of great parts most definitely was and always will be athletic, depending on inner if not on visible energy.[34]

If it is a displacement of energy it is also a teetering displacement of sexuality. Billington's sharp description of Olivier's Archie Rice as 'ambisextrously comic' [*sic*] is perfectly balanced by his awareness that 'Olivier's stage-persona' is not 'one of candid bisexuality' and that '[a]cting is perhaps one way of overcoming the sexual stereotyping of conventional society'. The result is that

> Even at his butchest Olivier slips in hints of a dandified vanity: one remembers that astonishing first entrance in Othello with a red rose held gently between thumb and forefinger and with the hips rotating slightly in a manner half way between Dorothy Dandridge and Gary Sobers. Conversely Olivier's fops leave you in no doubt as to their ultimate masculinity: His Captain Brazen in the 1963 Recruiting Officer made a high-speed entrance in a chestnut wig and planted a resounding kiss on the cheeks of a male friend but the well-pitched military camp concealed a heterosexual resolve.[35]

On stage, then, Olivier's presentations of characters as teasing denials of monosexuality were always balanced by what is socially assumed to be the masculinity of heroism and physical danger in ways that were comfortingly simultaneously both expressions and denials of bisexuality. Off stage, Olivier's celebrity depended in large part and through much of his career on a balance between the ostentatious heterosexuality of his publicly private life and his delight in the social coding of theatre as a realm of camp and hence of a culturally projected homosexuality, a twinned-being most completely encoded in his double-bill in 1945–6 as Oedipus and Mr Puff in Sheridan's The Critic, a combination precisely apparent in the compression of the show's backstage nickname as 'Oedipuff'. No knighted actor and perhaps no actor so defiantly heroic has performed camp better than Olivier.

There is a further and final layering to the strata of celebrity in Last Action Hero. When John McTiernan cast the cameo role of the schoolteacher, he achieved the necessary and perfect piece of casting, for the role was played by Joan Plowright, by then visible to some of the audience only as Olivier's widow. Whatever the merits of her own performances in theatre and in minor films, as far as Hollywood was concerned she had no other identity, her – very minor – celebrity status was entirely controlled by his.[36] The joke of Lady Olivier's saying of her late husband 'Some of you might have seen him' is, of course, accessible to only a small part of the intended vast audience of Last Action Hero; comparatively few American filmgoers would have been able to name the actor playing the schoolteacher. The reversal from the previous Lady Olivier was complete: Plowright's considerable theatrical success resulted in little film work where Leigh's film stardom, however hard Leigh tried, always seemed to transpose into comparative failure on stage.

Celebrity honours

If studies of the concept of the star usually see the actor as profoundly lacking in agency, the individual weakly and unprotestingly constructed by the studio-system, by the press, by audience desire and by socially generated structures of identity, Laurence Olivier stands as a magnificent alternative. While Plowright can be seen in *Last Action Hero* as passively assenting to being only a widow, Olivier's career and his celebrity are able to be taken as acts of agency in which his choices are often visibly premised on his own ambitions for and creations of his public self. Partly through social assumptions about the nature of acting, partly through the nature of the acting that Olivier performed, partly through his pleasure in other kinds of social performance, Olivier could at times be seen as devoid of his celebrity status. It is striking that it is Olivier's personal publicist, Virginia Fairweather, herself a failed actor, who enjoys her own narration of Olivier's lack of celebrity status when drinking at a pub near Chichester in the run-up to the opening of Olivier's first season as director of the Chichester Festival Theatre. Fairweather and her husband took Olivier for a drink at a nearby village pub, 'mostly frequented by the local farm workers and nearby inhabitants' and Olivier 'entered into a learned conversation with a farm-hand about pig-breeding':

> On one occasion, when word had got around that he was Laurence Olivier, one of his pub mates retailed this to him with great solemnity and said 'I told Fred not to talk daft. After all, I said, you've seen him in here yerself, he's no fuckin' actor!' Larry gravely agreed, thanked him for the defence and bought him a pint.[37]

Fairweather, as the person employed to control and develop Olivier's public status as celebrity, clearly likes this moment that, in one sense, defines her own failure. The pleasurable idea of Olivier unrecognised is at the same time a mark of the social placing of theatre, for the actor is unknown both to the workers and to the rural locals since, with the Chichester theatre being a new project, theatre celebrity is still defiantly the prerogative of its middle-class and urban audiences. Yet the Olivier who discusses pig-breeding is also plainly an actor. The man whose genuine delight in gardening and farming at Notley Abbey, the country home he created with Vivien Leigh, is also a remarkable and theatricalised social performance as country squire.

This performance of social role extends into Olivier's becoming the first actor to be made a life peer, a crucial part of his identity as celebrity after 1970 and a sign of his unremitting social ambition earlier. This is in part Olivier's continual denial of boundaries, whether those of physical safety in performance or of the cultural placing of the actor (who could be generally accepted as a knight but not yet as a peer). It can also be seen as Olivier's own self-management of himself as imperialist, the creation of his own empires through his monarchical celebrity that combines being the king of actors and a continual self-creation as not only English but as a metonym for England. As Charles Laughton commented on Olivier's performance as Henry V on stage in 1937, 'Do you know, Larry, why you're so good in this part? Because you *are* England!'³⁸ The English edition of Fairweather's book, which closes bitterly with her account of being sacked by Olivier, is called *Cry God for Larry*, a predictable pun on Olivier's heroic status and perhaps his most celebrated Shakespeare role. Olivier's 1944 film version of *Henry V* emerged logically out of the success of his theatre performances, as *Richard III* and *Hamlet* would also do. But the film's famous dedication to the armed forces and its usefulness as wartime propaganda connect with a significant part of Olivier's frequent identification of religion with social rank and of both with a proud and determined sense of nationality.

John Osborne, in many respects antagonistic to Olivier as 'Establishment figure', defines him not as 'a simple title-hunting snob' but as someone who 'likes being a member of the English Establishment and he thinks he should be':

> He's a self-conscious man, very aware of his role in the history of the twentieth century and his place in the English hierarchy. Up to a point, I think, his attitude is that he is making history, particularly English history, apart from just appearing in historical plays.³⁹

Holden states that '[a] sizeable slice of Olivier desperately wished he had been educated at Eton and Oxbridge'⁴⁰ and that desire, amply attested throughout his career, became a part of his celebrity identity: as Roger Lewis phrases it, 'he came to embody patrician authority and achievement – to embody Englishness and a sense of glory ... He had, like the admirals and generals he played, a stern sense of duty and a respect for public honours.'⁴¹

When Leigh, in the aftermath of her affair with Peter Finch, made plain to Olivier in 1948 that their marriage had imploded, Olivier could not contemplate divorce or separation: 'My recent knighthood, bestowed just before I set out for Australia, was sacred to me too; I just could not bring myself to offer people such crude disillusionment.'⁴² In one sense it is easy to mock the clergyman's son who constructs his knighthood in quasi-medieval terms as 'sacred'. But it is intimately bound up with a sense here of public obligation, of the duties of celebrity as defined by the national honour. It took two years for Harold Wilson to persuade Olivier to accept the peerage:

> The idea of separating myself from my colleagues by the kind of class distinction this would suggest was abhorrent to me. Knighthoods were altogether different; there had been quite a generous sprinkling of these around the profession since Sir Henry Irving at the turn of the century; besides, there was something glamorous, something chivalrous about a knighthood. But about a 'lawd' there seemed only something a bit stuck-up.⁴³

Before work started on the film *Sleuth* (1972), Olivier's co-star Michael Caine received a letter from him:

> Dear Mr Caine, it suddenly occurred to me that you might be wondering how to address me as I have a title; well, I think we should introduce us by our own titles which would be Mr Caine and I would be Lord Olivier the first time we meet, forever after that I hope it will be Larry and Michael.[44]

In one light the letter would be insufferably pompous, a playing on precisely that separation that Olivier feared. Yet what is most surprising is that Caine introduces the letter by his own anxiety: 'You're stuck with "What do I call him?" I can't call him Sir Laurence because he's Lord Olivier; basically you're supposed to call him "My Lord", I suppose.'[45]

But if Olivier was, on this evidence, right to be anxious about the separation the peerage conferred, his eventual acceptance had none of the effect Wilson had intended, for the Prime Minister's laudable concept was that Olivier's presence in the House of Lords would provide 'people in the artistic professions ... [with] a forum from which to speak on behalf of their own and other artistic matters'.[46] Olivier announced, 'I accepted the title out of a sense of duty ... I shall speak in the Lords on any cause on which I can speak with authority.'[47] Introduced into the Lords in March 1971 – and Olivier's own account of the event concentrates on his failure to get the catering manageress to serve 'sausages and mash' at the lunch he gave, 'the most homespun thing I was allowed was steak and kidney pie'[48] – Olivier gave his maiden speech in July 1971 in a debate on the preservation of the Equity closed-shop for actors. His speech, a perfect example of Olivier at his most embarrassing when trying to be most winsome, with its contorted syntax and awkward coyness, was proudly reprinted as Appendix B of his autobiography with the single comment, 'It may be observed that I only exceeded the statutory ten minutes by two.'[49] Olivier, that is, makes no comment on whether his intervention in the debate had any effect; it exists as performance within the rules of the House rather than as persuasive oratory. Olivier offers it as a dramatic speech, more Thespian than Ciceronian. He never spoke in the Lords again. If the topic was one on which he could indeed have spoken 'with authority', the effect of that authority is irrelevant to him and, for all the hesitation over acceptance, his anxiety that 'an actor who is a lord' would be 'a figure of fun',[50] there may be some truth in Spoto's report that Olivier said, 'I've been working fifty years for this' and that he had told Richard Burton 'that for a very long time he had been "determined to be the first actor-peer"'.[51] Status and celebrity and pre-eminence stand over the political possibilities and the obligations of duty and the social power that the peerage might have enabled. The achievement of rank appears to be all that matters, the sign of celebrity in the prefix to the name, something that is strikingly parallel to one of the three Shakespeare roles that interested

Olivier sufficiently to warrant exploring twice in his career, the change of Caius Martius into Coriolanus.[52]

As Olivier himself admitted, Ralph Richardson's knighthood in 1947, before Olivier had gained one, resulted in 'screams of fury',[53] while Holden quotes one supposedly verbatim account of those screams:

> I should have been the fucking knight! ... I've done every bit as much as he has, look how I've carried the flag abroad ... and [had] an even fuller record in the classics – and there was a little film called *Henry V*.[54]

If Richardson's seniority in the profession delayed Olivier's knighthood (but only by six months: Olivier is still, at 39, the youngest actor to have been knighted), so too may Olivier's divorce and remarriage, an event that, while fundamental to his celebrity, was also still often unacceptable in the Honours List. But, while on tour in 1948, Olivier was infuriated by Donald Wolfit's knighthood because of a remarkably detailed knowledge of the rules of precedence: 'He already has the CBE ... and that means he takes precedence over me!'[55]

Carrying the flag abroad, doing good deeds for the nation, was something that would continue to mark Olivier's status and celebrity, whether giving a speech at a memorial service for King George VI in New York or narrating *The World at War* series for Thames in 1974. His public awards, ranging from honorary degrees from numerous British universities (starting with Oxford in 1957) to being made a Commander of the Order Dannebrog (1949) and given the Order of Yugoslavia Flag with Golden Wreath (1971), climax with national honour (Order of Merit in 1981, the only actor so honoured), film honours (special Oscar in 1979, Cecil B. de Mille Award at the Hollywood Golden Globes in 1982), and most strikingly a kind of apotheosis of a theatre honour when the annual awards from the Society of West End Theatre were named after him in 1984.[56]

Honours are of course a sign of the marketability of the celebrity. A list of primarily performance honours is available on the 'Official Web Site of Sir Laurence Olivier',[57] a site which has no truck with the peerage but does emphasise that 'CMG Worldwide is the exclusive business representative for the Estate of Laurence Olivier', working 'with companies around the world who wish to use the name or likeness of Laurence Olivier in any fashion' and reminding us that

> The words and the signature 'Laurence Olivier' are trademarks owned and protected by the Estate of Laurence Olivier ... We will consider your request to use the name, voice or image of Laurence Olivier.[58]

CMG's clients in the entertainment category are nearly all dead and, while Olivier is placed in the company of Marilyn Monroe, James Dean, Rock

Hudson, Errol Flynn and Ivana Trump, other British theatre celebrities, like, say, Gielgud and Richardson, are conspicuously absent.[59] Olivier's business representative is, in that light, more concerned with his celebrity as screen-actor in *Hamlet* and *Clash of the Titans* than his stage-work: 'read our Biography about the Impressive Screen Legend'.[60]

Global celebrity: the king on tour

Olivier may have been the finest Orlando ever in his screen performance in *As You Like It* (1936), but Olivier's early screen career was overshadowed by the success of Jill Esmond, his first wife. He may have been superb as Heathcliff in *Wuthering Heights* (1939), Maxim in *Rebecca* (1940), Darcy in *Pride and Prejudice* (1940) and Nelson in *Lady Hamilton* (1941), but this tranche of screen success was equally overshadowed by Vivien Leigh's triumph as Scarlett O'Hara in *Gone with the Wind*. Though his achievement in *Henry V* gained him a special Oscar in 1946 for 'his outstanding achievement as actor, producer and director in bringing *Henry V* to the screen' and he gained Best Actor (his only success among the ten nominations he received) and Best Picture Oscars for *Hamlet* in 1949, Leigh was always the greater Hollywood star.

Yet in the immediate post-war years, Olivier achieved a kind of celebrity that was remarkable. When the Old Vic season closed in April 1946,

> more than 2,500 people thronged outside the New Theatre and along St Martin's Lane, shouting for Olivier and Richardson. Olivier's coat was ripped and buttons were torn off as adoring crowds grabbed at him ... The public adoration was unprecedented – and it heralded the new postwar obsession with stardom.[61]

Such celebration of a theatre actor, if not really unprecedented, was certainly unusual in the era of the film star. There were similar scenes when the company performed in New York for the six weeks immediately following – significantly prior to and therefore not dependent on the New York opening of the *Henry V* film, which would, in the event, run for eleven months at the City Center Theatre[62] – with Olivier frequently pursued by autograph seekers and journalists.

But Olivier's celebrity at this time can be most powerfully measured by the accounts of the Old Vic tour to Australia and New Zealand in 1948, the point at which Olivier and Leigh were most widely perceived as being and most strenuously performed as the royal family of theatre.[63] The tour was set up by the British Council as an openly diplomatic cultural mission; it was necessary to provide some kind of cultural gesture to Australia and New Zealand, both of which were vital to the success of the Commonwealth and to the provision of food and other material supplies for Britain, still abysmally short of virtually everything in the aftermath of the war. The Old Vic, as the one major classical theatre in operation, also needed to earn money and the tour was seen as potentially a source of some profit, though no estimate anticipated the huge success and considerable income it would generate. If, in intention and retrospect, one of its major cultural results was to provide a formation for a future national theatre – and to define Olivier as the only sensible choice as its Artistic Director fifteen years later – it defined Olivier as 'surrogate monarch' who, with Leigh, performed 'many functions of royalty' including 'ship christenings, broadcasts, tours of neighbourhoods and public works, inspections of lines of troops'.[64] But it is also a crucial aspect of Olivier's status as celebrity, the actor who could best perform kingliness, perhaps rather better than King George VI. But, in part, Olivier was filling a genuine social need, a desire by Australians 'to demonstrate loyalty', a desire which the company could satisfy by being 'the King's representatives', for instance with Olivier 'taking the salute at a naval march past' in Sydney, a comic translation for the actor whose career in the Fleet Air Arm was a catalogue of failures.[65]

O'Connor's narrative of the tour is full of descriptions of the defining aspects of celebrity: the long lines queuing for tickets, the crowds outside the hotels, the meetings with local dignitaries. But what seems to me most striking about this celebrity is its essential disjunction from the normal forms of theatrical and film stardom. Though most of the audience would have seen Leigh on film, many fewer would have seen Olivier's screen roles and only the tiniest handful would have seen him on stage. Olivier's celebrity on this tour was then fundamentally likely to be disjunct from any direct perception of him. Necessarily theatre celebrity tends to be localised, restricted to a considerable extent to the geographical parameters of performance, while film makes the star a form of global phenomenon impossible for the stage-actor. Shortly after the tour reached Sydney, cinemas cashed in on the arrival of film stars so that 'there were no less than five films running in which one or other, or both, appeared – *Lady Hamilton, Waterloo Bridge, Henry V, Pride and Prejudice, Rebecca*'.[66]

Hence, there was the awkwardness over Olivier's first entrance on stage in the first performance of the tour. In Perth the company performed *The School for Scandal* with the Oliviers as the Teazles, one more step in the repeated history of Olivier performing the stresses of his own marriages that would eventually climax in Edgar in Strindberg's *The Dance of Death* in 1967. As Sir Peter Teazle Olivier had, as usual, retreated behind make-up, playing the character as elderly, with the result that his entrance was unnoticed by an audience that, desperate to applaud the star, could not know who had entered: as a reviewer commented, 'until they print programmes in phosphorous ink, or emboss them in Braille, we're likely to be pretty clueless about the identity of any heavily disguised character who totters on to the stage'. Leigh, unmistakable on her entrance, 'got a tremendous round'.[67]

When the company returned to London and opened their season at the New Theatre in January 1949, the productions were sold on fame and beauty: 'For the first time together in London, the greatest actor in the world and his wife, one of the loveliest women.'[68] The crowds, most without tickets, were enormous, the opening more like a film premiere, with the foyer full of the famous being photographed. Alan Melville's comic verse defines the fans' sense both of occasion and celebrity: whatever the discomfort of queuing for days for tickets,

> None of this marred
> Our regard
> For the Bard –
> That is, when Sir Laurence appears ....
> When He appeared,
> How we cheered!
> Mother feared
> That she'd ruptured her larynx for life.
> Though I can't say
> That the play
> Was okay –
> Old-fashioned, it all seemed to me.
> At the stage-door,
> The furore! ...
> And, what's more,
> I *touched* him – and Vivien Leigh![69]

As a moment, the opening of the New Theatre season may rank with the funeral of Garrick as the high point of the social celebrity of theatre. There is something quasi-religious about the experience of Melville's family of fans. Olivier has become a capitalised 'He' as if divine, someone to be '*touched*' like a saint. In an unexpected way, it is the reverse of the priestliness of the reader-fan-audience to whom Olivier directs his autobiography, titled *Confessions* in a fully religious sense and opening with a 'Confiteor': 'Bless me, Reader, for I have sinned. Since my last confession, which was more than fifty years ago, I have committed the following sins ...'[70]

The interaction of actor and public at these extreme moments has almost moved beyond the terrestrial. Yet what finally is most able to define Olivier's status is the label that, certainly by 1944 and for the rest of his career, became his natural cognomen, the automatised inclusion of 'the greatest actor of the world' as if part of his name. For the phrase is essentially meaningless, needing and suppressing a series of qualifiers (like 'theatre' or 'alive today' or 'anglophone' or 'that I have seen' or 'as people call him'), to become an assumption of Olivier's meaning as celebrity. Remarkably unquestioned, matched only occasionally by Gielgud's name and, for the 1940s, by

Richardson's, the title is bound to Olivier's regal status: the rightful king of the theatre world, the deserved monarch. The title carried risks and problems of succession in the arrangements for Olivier's memorial service:

> Prince Charles was unavailable but had asked Kenneth Branagh to represent him. According to Royal protocol, the representative carries the same position in etiquette as the Royal he or she represents. Therefore, as invitations stood, Mr. Branagh – as senior Royal representative – would be the last person to enter the Abbey .... Frankly, I think several surviving senior Thespians would have passed away on the spot. Moreover, those close to Larry knew him to be not entirely selfless and to have gone to the grave firmly clutching whatever laurels he had earned. The last thing he'd want at his memorial would be the apparent crowning of an heir to his throne.[71]

Branagh, who certainly would have wished to be Olivier's heir apparent, was replaced by Sir Richard Attenborough, 'a welcome, press-safe, Royal representative'.[72] Like the addition of Coriolanus to Caius Martius, the title of 'the greatest actor in the world' would not be passed on. That title, the most significant celebrity marker, dies with the body natural of the celebrity.

Notes

1 My quotations from the film are taken from Eric S. Mallin's fine article, ' "You Kilt My Foddah": or Arnold, Prince of Denmark', *Shakespeare Quarterly*, 50 (1999), 127–51 (p. 127).
2 Of course, the question makes no real sense in the context of film-production: McTiernan has no access to such a recent clip.
3 Mallin, ' "You Kilt My Foddah" ', p. 128.
4 Mallin, ' "You Kilt My Foddah" ', p. 127.
5 Quoted from Anthony Holden, *Laurence Olivier* (New York: Atheneum, 1988), p. 333.
6 See Garry O'Connor's 'Introduction' to his *Olivier: In Celebration* (New York: Dodd, Mead and Company, 1987), pp. 12–18.
7 Laurence Olivier, *Confessions of an Actor* (London: Weidenfeld and Nicolson, 1982), p. 123.
8 Olivier, *Confessions of an Actor*, p. 124.
9 Simon Callow, 'Laurence Olivier and My Generation' in Garry O'Connor, *Olivier: In Celebration*, p. 97.
10 Mallin, ' "You Kilt My Foddah" ', p. 128.
11 Quoted by Holden, *Laurence Olivier*, p. 426.
12 My certainly incomplete count reaches 26.
13 For example, Donald Spoto, *Laurence Olivier: A Biography* (New York: HarperCollins, 1992) or Roger Lewis, *The Real Life of Laurence Olivier* (London: Century Books, 1996).
14 For example, Robert L. Daniels, *Laurence Olivier: Theatre and Cinema* (London: The Tantivy Press, 1980); Jerry Vermilye, *The Complete Films of Laurence Olivier*

(New York: Citadel Press, 1992); Margaret Morley, *The Films of Laurence Olivier* (Secaucus, NJ: Citadel Press, 1977). All three of these give ostensibly complete accounts of Olivier's television work. Only Robert Tanitch notes, at the foot of his television listings, that 'In 1972 Olivier made a series of commercials for Polaroid' (see Robert Tanitch, *Olivier: The Complete Career* (New York: Abbeville Press, 1985), p. 185.

15 Tarquin Olivier, *My Father Laurence Olivier* (London: Headline Book Publishing, 1992); Richard Olivier, *Melting the Stone: A Journey Around My Father* (Woodstock, CT: Spring Publications, 1996). The latter is, incidentally, the oddest Olivier biography I have read with a lengthy bibliography including Robert Bly, Alvin Toffler and W. B. Yeats but not a single book by or about Laurence Olivier.
16 Holden, *Laurence Olivier*, p. 430.
17 Olivier, *Confessions of an Actor*, p. 249.
18 Olivier, *Confessions of an Actor*, p. 249.
19 A dull publicity photograph is reproduced in Garry O'Connor, *Olivier: In Celebration*, following p. 128.
20 O'Connor, *Olivier: In Celebration*, pp. 180–1.
21 Ian McKellen, 'Smoke Signals', *Flaunt*, December 2002. http://www.mckellen.com/writings/0212flaunt.htm [accessed September 2004].
22 Holden, *Laurence Olivier*, p. 4.
23 See Penny Tinkler, '"Red Tips for Hot Lips": Advertising Cigarettes for Young Women in Britain, 1920–70', *Women's History Review*, 10 (2001), 249–72 (p. 262).
24 Roger Lewis, *The Real Life of Laurence Olivier*, pp. 25–6.
25 The title of Richard Olivier's biography tries unsuccessfully to work off Mortimer's title of his play about his own father.
26 The film has no sound-track other than Olivier's reading of the poem and the playing of Britten's own recording of his *War Requiem*.
27 Quoted by Michael Billington, 'Lasciviously Pleasing', in O'Connor, *Olivier: In Celebration*, pp. 71–5 (p. 71).
28 Billington, 'Lasciviously Pleasing', p. 71.
29 Jonathan Miller, the director of *The Merchant of Venice*, had to work hard to persuade Olivier to remove 'rather a lot of encrustations' of directorial ideas as well as make-up 'before I could find the clean lines of the play'. The 'enormous amount of make-up' included 'false nose, ringlets, a Disraeli beard', the 'pantomime trappings' which embarrassed Miller as a Jew. See Miller, 'Aboard the Victory O', in O'Connor, *Laurence Olivier: In Celebration*, pp. 125–9 (pp. 126–7).
30 Olivier's autobiography is repeatedly and characteristically coy in its hints about his homosexuality; Spoto is equally characteristically forthright and refers frequently to an earlier draft of the autobiography which 'frankly admitted the numerous homosexual episodes of his adult life' (e.g., p. 230), while Tarquin Olivier quotes his father saying 'I've never been queer' (see Olivier, *My Father Laurence Olivier*, p. 256).
31 Lewis, *The Real Life of Laurence Olivier*, p. xii.n.
32 Olivier, *My Father Laurence Olivier*, p. 256.
33 Richard Olivier is memorably funny on his curious action of sending Dustin Hoffman, then playing Shylock, the false teeth that Olivier had worn in the role: 'I never heard from him – I'm not surprised' (See Olivier, *Melting the Stone*, p. 28).
34 Olivier, *Confessions of an Actor*, p. 229. Olivier follows this passage with a comment that 'one has often heard that the most magnificent specimens of boxers,

wrestlers, and champions in almost every branch of athletic sport prove to be disappointing upon the removal of that revered jockstrap' (p. 229)! Olivier's coy prose with that distancing 'one' produces here the strange revelation that the 'jockstrap' is 'revered' without beginning to explain by whom or why.
35 Billington, 'Lasciviously Pleasing', p. 75.
36 Compare, in an earlier incarnation, the extent to which Vivien Leigh could be identified simply as one half of 'the Oliviers' in the title of the first significant biography of Laurence Olivier, Francis Barker's *The Oliviers: A Biography* (Philadelphia: J. B. Lippincott, 1953).
37 Virginia Fairweather, *Olivier: An Informal Portrait* (New York: Coward-McCann, Inc., 1969), p. 54.
38 Quoted by Holden, *Laurence Olivier*, p. 10.
39 Interview with John Osborne in *Olivier*, ed. Logan Gourlay (New York: Stein and Day, 1975), pp. 145–56 (p. 148).
40 Holden, *Laurence Olivier*, p. 101.
41 Lewis, *The Real Life of Laurence Olivier*, p.154. Lewis elsewhere appropriately compares Olivier with John Wayne ('Olivier represented the English consciousness in the same way that John Wayne symbolised the American ideal of gun-slinging frontier heroics', p. 138) and John Betjeman ('There is a reverence for railway stations, town halls, the Brighton Belle, breakfast kippers, the details of gothic church architecture', p. 194).
42 Olivier, *Confessions of an Actor*, p. 132.
43 Olivier, *Confessions of an Actor*, p. 238.
44 Michael Caine, 'The Whirlwind', in O'Connor, *Olivier: In Celebration*, p.103.
45 Caine, 'The Whirlwind', p. 103.
46 Olivier, *Confessions of an Actor*, p. 238.
47 Quoted in Holden, *Laurence Olivier*, p. 412.
48 Olivier, *Confessions of an Actor*, p. 241.
49 Olivier, *Confessions of an Actor*, p. 286.
50 Quoted in Holden, *Laurence Olivier*, p. 412.
51 Spoto, *Laurence Olivier*, p. 354.
52 Coriolanus (1938 and 1959), Macbeth (1937 and 1955), Lear (1946 and 1983). I discount in this list those returns to roles that are, in most senses, continuations, for example Henry V (1937 and 1944) and Hamlet (1937 and 1947).
53 Olivier, *Confessions of an Actor*, p. 133.
54 Holden, *Laurence Olivier*, p. 213.
55 Quoted by Spoto, *Laurence Olivier*, p. 275.
56 I take this list as a selection from Tanitch's tabulation of 'Awards and Honours'. See Tanitch, *Olivier*, pp. 188–9.
57 http://www.laurenceolivier.com/about/awards.html [accessed September 2004].
58 http://www.laurenceolivier.com/businq/overview.html [accessed September 2004].
59 http://www.cmgmm.com/clients.html [accessed September 2004].
60 http://www.laurenceolivier.com/home.html [accessed September 2004].
61 Spoto, *Laurence Olivier*, p. 196.
62 Spoto, *Laurence Olivier*, p. 199.
63 The best account of the tour is unquestionably Garry O'Connor's in *Darlings of the Gods* (London: Hodder and Stoughton, 1984). See also Jesse Lasky, Jr. with Pat Silver, *Love Scene: The Story of Laurence Olivier and Vivien Leigh* (New York: Thomas Y. Crowell, 1978).
64 Spoto, *Laurence Olivier*, p. 212.

65 O'Connor, *Darlings of the Gods*, p. 109.
66 O'Connor, *Darlings of the Gods*, p.107.
67 O'Connor, *Darlings of the Gods*, p. 50.
68 O'Connor, *Darlings of the Gods*, p. 158.
69 Quoted in O'Connor, *Darlings of the Gods*, pp. 159–60.
70 Olivier, *Confessions of an Actor*, p. xiii, ellipsis Olivier's.
71 Olivier, *Melting the Stone*, p. 30.
72 Olivier, *Melting the Stone*, p. 30.

Select Bibliography

Aberbach, David. *Charisma in Politics, Religion and the Media: Private Trauma, Public Ideals.* London: Macmillan, 1996.
Asleson, Robyn (ed.). *Notorious Muse: The Actress in British Art and Culture.* New Haven, CT: Yale University Press, 2003.
Aston, Elaine. *Feminist Views on the English Stage: Women Playwrights, 1990–2000.* Cambridge: Cambridge University Press, 2003.
Babington, Bruce (ed.). *British Stars and Stardom.* Manchester: Manchester University Press, 2001.
Baer, Marc. *Theatre and Disorder in Late Georgian London.* Oxford: Clarendon Press, 1992.
Barstow, Susan Torrey. 'Ellen Terry and the Revolt of the Daughters', *Nineteenth Century Theatre*, 25:1 (Summer 1997), 5–32.
Barthes, Roland. *Mythologies*, trans. Annette Lavers. New York: Hill and Wang, 1972.
Benedetti, Jean. *David Garrick and the Birth of the Modern Theatre.* London: Methuen, 2001.
Bennett, Shelley and Leonard, Mark. ' "A Sublime and Masterly Performance": The Making of Sir Joshua Reynolds's *Mrs. Siddons as the Tragic Muse*' in *Passion for Performance: Sarah Siddons and her Portraitists*, ed. Robyn Asleson. Los Angeles: J. Paul Getty Museum, 1999, pp. 97–136.
Bolton, Betsy. *Women, Nationalism and the Romantic Stage.* Cambridge: Cambridge University Press, 2001.
Boorstin, Daniel J. *The Image: Or What Happened to the American Dream?* London: Weidenfeld and Nicolson, 1961.
Booth, Michael R., Stokes, John and Bassnett, Susan. *Three Tragic Actresses: Siddons, Rachel, Ristori.* Cambridge: Cambridge University Press, 1996.
Bratton, Jacky. *New Readings in Theatre History.* Cambridge: Cambridge University Press, 2003.
Braudy, Leo. *The Frenzy of Renown: Fame and its History.* New York: Vintage Books, 1997.
Bristow, Joseph (ed.). *Wilde Writings: Contextual Conditions.* Toronto: University of Toronto Press, 2003.
Bronfen, Elisabeth. *Over Her Dead Body: Death, Femininity and the Aesthetic.* Manchester: Manchester University Press, 1992.
Burling, William J. *Summer Theatre in London, 1661–1820, and the Rise of the Haymarket Theatre.* Madison, NJ: Fairleigh Dickinson University Press, 2000.
Canfield, J. Douglas and Payne, Deborah (eds.). *Cultural Readings of Restoration and Eighteenth-Century Theatre.* Athens, GA: University of Georgia Press, 1995.
Carlson, Julie. 'Forever Young: Master Betty and the Queer Stage of Youth in English Romanticism', *South Atlantic Quarterly*, 95:3 (Summer 1996), 575–602.
Crouch, Kimberly. 'The Public Life of Actresses: Prostitutes or Ladies?', in *Gender in Eighteenth-Century England: Roles, Representations and Responsibilities*, ed. Hannah Barker and Elaine Chalus. London and New York: Longman, 1997, pp. 58–78.
Daniels, Robert L. *Laurence Olivier: Theater and Cinema.* London: The Tantivy Press, 1980.
Davis, Tracy C. *Actresses as Working Women: Their Social Identity in Victorian Culture.* London and New York: Routledge, 1991.

Davis, Tracy C. *The Economics of the British Stage, 1800–1914*. Cambridge: Cambridge University Press, 2000.
Davis, Tracy C. and Postlewait, Thomas (eds.). *Theatricality*. Cambridge: Cambridge University Press, 2003.
De Leon, Charles L. Ponce. *Self-Exposure: Human-Interest Journalism and the Emergence of Celebrity in America, 1890–1940*. Chapel Hill, NC: University of North Carolina Press, 2002.
Desmond, Jane (ed.). *Dancing Desires: Choreographing Sexualities on and off the Stage*. Madison, WI: University of Wisconsin Press, 2001.
Durkheim, Emile. *The Elementary Forms of Religious Life*, trans. Karen E. Fields. New York: The Free Press, 1995.
Dyer, Richard. *Heavenly Bodies: Film Stars and Society*. London: British Film Institute, 1986.
——. 'A Star is Born and the Construction of Authenticity', in *Stardom: Industry of Desire*, ed. Christine Gledhill. London: Routledge, 1991, pp. 132–40.
——. *Stars*. London: British Film Institute, 1979, revised edition 1998.
Edwards, Owen Dudley (ed.). *The Fireworks of Oscar Wilde*. London: Barrie and Jenkins, 1989.
Eyre, Richard and Wright, Nicholas. *Changing Stages: A View of British Theatre in the Twentieth Century*. London: Bloomsbury, 2000.
Fox, Richard L. and Van Sickel, Robert W. *Tabloid Justice: Criminal Justice in an Age of Media Frenzy*. Boulder, CO: Lynne Rienner Publishers, 2001.
Gale, Maggie B. and Gardner, Viv (eds.). *Women, Theatre and Performance: New Histories, New Historiographies*. Manchester: Manchester University Press, 2000.
Garber, Marjorie. 'Greatness', in *Symptoms of Culture*. New York: Routledge, 1998.
Giles, David. *Illusions of Immortality: A Psychology of Fame and Celebrity*. Basingstoke: Macmillan, 2000.
Gledhill, Christine (ed.). *Stardom: Industry of Desire*. London: Routledge, 1991.
Glenn, Susan A. *Female Spectacle: The Theatrical Roots of Modern Feminism*. Cambridge, MA: Harvard University Press, 2000.
Gritten, David. *Fame: Stripping Celebrity Bare*. London: Allen Lane, 2002.
Gruber, William. *Comic Theaters: Studies in Performance and Audience Response*. Athens, GA and London: University of Georgia Press, 1986.
Halasz, Alexandra. ' "So beloved that men use his picture for their signs": Richard Tarlton and the Uses of Sixteenth-Century Celebrity', *Shakespeare Studies*, 23 (1995), 19–38.
Holden, Anthony. *Laurence Olivier*. New York: Atheneum, 1988.
Holledge, Julie. *Innocent Flowers: Women in the Edwardian Theatre*. London: Virago, 1981.
Howe, Elizabeth. *The First English Actresses: Women and Drama 1660–1700*. Cambridge: Cambridge University Press, 1992.
Huggett, Richard. *Binkie Beaumont: Eminence Grise of the West End Theatre 1933–1979*. London: Hodder and Stoughton, 1989.
Innes, Christopher. *Modern British Drama: The Twentieth Century*. Cambridge: Cambridge University Press, 2002.
Kaplan, Joel H. and Stowell, Sheila. *Theatre and Fashion: Oscar Wilde to the Suffragettes*. Cambridge: Cambridge University Press, 1994.
King, Thomas A. ' "As if (she) were Made on Purpose to Put the Whole World into Good Humour": Reconstructing the First English Actresses', *The Drama Review*, 36:3 (Fall 1992), 78–102.

Kinservik, Matthew. 'Benefit Play Selection at Drury Lane in 1729–1769: The Cases of Mrs. Cibber, Mrs. Clive, and Mrs. Pritchard', *Theatre Notebook*, 50:1 (1996), 15–28.
——. *Disciplining Satire: The Censorship of Satiric Comedy on the Eighteenth-Century London Stage*. Lewisburg, PA: Bucknell University Press, 2002.
——. 'Satire, Censorship, and Sodomy in Samuel Foote's *The Capuchin* (1776)', *Review of English Studies*, n. s. 54 (November 2003), 639–60.
Kobialka, Michal. 'Words and Bodies: A Discourse on Male Sexuality in Late Eighteenth-Century English Representational Practices', *Theatre Research International*, 28:1 (March 2003), 1–19.
Kustow, Michael. *theatre@risk*. London: Methuen, 2000.
Lafler, Joanne. *The Celebrated Mrs. Oldfield: The Life and Art of an Augustan Actress*. Carbondale, IL: Southern Illinois University Press, 1989.
Lanier, Henry Wysham. *The First English Actresses from the Initial Appearance of Women on the Stage in 1660 till 1700*. New York: The Players, 1930.
Leggatt, Alexander. 'Richard Burbage: A Dangerous Actor', in *Extraordinary Actors: Essays on Popular Performers* ed. Jane Milling and Martin Banham. Exeter: University of Exeter Press, 2004, pp. 8–20.
Littler, J. 'Making Fame Ordinary: Intimacy, Reflexivity and "Keeping it Real"', *Mediactive*, 2 (2003), special issue on celebrity, 8–25.
Luckhurst, Mary. 'An Embarrassment of Riches: Women Dramatists in 1990s Britain', in *British Drama of the 1990s*, ed. A. Knapp, E. Otto, G. Stratmann and M. Tönnies. Heidelberg: Universitätsverlag C. Winter, 2002, pp. 65–77.
Lumby, Catherine. *Gotcha: Life in a Tabloid World*. London: Allen and Unwin, 1999.
Maland, Charles. *Chaplin and American Culture: The Evolution of a Star Image*. Princeton, NJ: Princeton University Press, 1989.
Marshall, P.D. *Celebrity and Power: Fame in Contemporary Culture*. Minneapolis, MN: University of Minnesota Press, 1997.
McCollum, John I. Jr. (ed.). *The Restoration Stage*. Boston, Mass: Houghton Mifflin, 1961.
McCreery, Cindy. *The Satirical Gaze: Prints of Women in Late Eighteenth-Century England*. Oxford: Clarendon, 2004.
McPherson, Heather. 'Picturing Tragedy: Mrs. Siddons as the Tragic Muse Revisited', *Eighteenth-Century Studies*, 33:3 (2000), 401–30.
Moody, Jane. *Illegitimate Theatre in London, 1770–1840*. Cambridge: Cambridge University Press, 2000.
Morley, Margaret. *The Films of Laurence Olivier*. Secaucus, NJ: Citadel Press, 1977.
Mullin, Donald (ed.). *Victorian Actors and Actresses in Review: A Dictionary of Contemporary Views of Representative British and American Actors and Actresses, 1837–1901*. London: Greenwood Press, 1983.
Norton, Victor. *Mother Clap's Molly House: The Gay Subculture in England, 1700–1830*. London: GMP Publishers, 1992.
Orr, Clarissa Campbell (ed.). *Queenship in Britain 1660–1837: Royal Patronage, Court Culture and Dynastic Politics*. Manchester: Manchester University Press, 2002.
Postlewait, Thomas. 'Autobiography and Theatre History', in *Interpreting the Theatrical Past: Essays in the Historiography of Performance*, ed. Thomas Postlewait and Bruce McConachie. Iowa City: University of Iowa Press, 1989, pp. 248–72.
Postlewait, Thomas and McConachie, Bruce A. (eds.). *Interpreting the Theatrical Past*. Iowa City: University of Iowa Press, 1989.
Powell, Kerry. *Oscar Wilde and the Theatre of the 1890s*. Cambridge: Cambridge University Press, 1990.

Quinn, Michael L. 'Celebrity and the Semiotics of Acting', *New Theatre Quarterly*, 22:6 (May 1990), 154–61.
Rebellato, Dan. *1956 and All That: The Making of Modern British Drama*. London: Routledge, 1999.
Richards, Sandra. *The Rise of the English Actress*. London: St. Martin's Press, 1993.
Roach, Joseph. 'Celebrity Erotics: Pepys, Performance, and Painted Ladies', *The Yale Journal of Criticism*, 16:1 (2003), 211–30.
——. 'It', *Theatre Journal*, 56:4 (2004), 555–68.
Roberts, Philip. *The Royal Court Theatre and the Modern Stage*. Cambridge: Cambridge University Press, 1999.
Rojek, Chris. *Celebrity*. London: Reaktion Books, 2001.
Rose, Jacqueline. *On not being Able to Sleep: Psychoanalysis and the Modern World*. London: Chatto and Windus, 2003.
Rosenthal, Laura. ' "Counterfeit Scrubbado": Women Actors in the Restoration', *The Eighteenth Century: Theory and Interpretation*, 34:1 (1993), 3–22.
Saunders, Graham. *'Love Me or Kill Me': Sarah Kane and the Theatre of Extremes*. Manchester: Manchester University Press, 2002.
Schickel, Richard. *Intimate Strangers: The Culture of Celebrity*. New York: Doubleday, 1985.
Schofield, Mary Anne and Macheski, Cecilia (eds.). *Curtain Calls: British and American Women and the Theater, 1660–1820*. Athens, OH: Ohio University Press, 1991.
Senelick, Laurence. 'Mollies or Men of Mode? Sodomy and the Eighteenth-Century London Stage', *Journal of the History of Sexuality*, 1:1 (July 1990), 33–67.
Sierz, Aleks. *In-yer-face Theatre: British Drama Today*. London: Faber and Faber, 2000.
Spoto, Donald. *Laurence Olivier: A Biography*. New York: HarperCollins, 1992.
Straub, Kristina. *Sexual Suspects: Eighteenth-Century Players and Sexual Ideology*. Princeton, NJ: Princeton University Press, 1992.
Tanitch, Robert. *Olivier: The Complete Career*. New York: Abbeville Press, 1985.
Taylor, George. *The French Revolution and the London Stage, 1789–1805*. Cambridge: Cambridge University Press, 2000.
Tickner, Lisa. *The Spectacle of Women: Imagery of the Suffrage Campaign, 1907–14*. London: Chatto and Windus, 1987.
Trewin, J. C. *The Gay Twenties: A Decade of the Theatre*. London: MacDonald, 1958.
Vermilye, Jerry. *The Complete Films of Laurence Olivier*. New York: Citadel Press, 1992.
Wanko, Cheryl. *Roles of Authority: Thespian Biography and Celebrity in Eighteenth-Century Britain*. Lubbock, TX: Texas Tech University Press, 2003.
Weber, Max. *On Charisma and Institution Building*, ed. S. N. Eisenstadt. Chicago, IL: University of Chicago Press, 1968.
Weintraub, Stanley. *Modern British Dramatists 1900–1945*. Detroit, MI: Gale Research Corp., 1982.
West, Shearer. *The Image of the Actor: Verbal and Visual Representation in the Age of Garrick and Kemble*. London: Pinter, 1991.
——. *Portraiture*. Oxford: Oxford University Press, 2004.
——. 'The Public and Private Roles of Sarah Siddons', in *Passion for Performance: Sarah Siddons and her Portraitists*, ed. Robyn Asleson. Los Angeles: J. Paul Getty Museum, 1999, pp. 10–13.
——. 'Thomas Lawrence's "Half-History" Portraits and the Politics of Theatre', *Art History*, 14:2 (June 1991), 225–49.
Wilson, John Harold. *All the King's Ladies: Actresses of the Restoration*. Chicago, IL: University of Chicago Press, 1958.

Woods, Leigh. 'Actors' Biography and Mythmaking, the Example of Edmund Kean', in *Interpreting the Theatrical Past*, ed. Thomas Postlewait and Bruce A. McConachie. Iowa: University of Iowa Press, 1989, pp. 230–47.
——. *Garrick Claims the Stage: Acting as Social Emblem in Eighteenth-Century England*. Westport, CT: Greenwood Press, 1984.

Index

Aberbach, David, 29n
Abington, Frances, 151, 153, 159, 199
  Abington cap, 159, 163
Achilles, 25
acting, 149–50, 154–5, 157–8, 163–4,
    171–3, 176–7, 183–4, 192–5, 205,
    217–18, 220, 222
  and aristocracy, 18, 22
  ban on, 68
  moral ambiguity of, 129
  Noh, 17
  parody of Garrick, 76
  Quin and Garrick acting together,
    136–8
  technique, 5, 68
  western acting tradition, 90, 131
actor, 1–3, 7, 34, 36, 39, 65, 68–9, 72,
    74, 76–7, 90–3, 95, 97, 129–30,
    132–3, 138, 140–2, 144, 149, 152,
    155–6, 162, 193, 195, 215–22,
    224, 226–9
  image of, 5, 23, 25, 148
  manager, 3, 6, 8, 31, 34, 69, 78, 151,
    158, 176
  and satire, 6, 75–6
  and sexual indeterminacy, 219–21
actors, 3, 6, 8, 21–2, 25, 40, 42, 55, 65,
    69, 72, 75, 77, 80, 117, 128–9, 136,
    138–9, 148–51, 154, 156, 158–9,
    162, 164, 192, 194, 199, 205, 208,
    217, 222, 224–5
actresses, 5, 8, 16, 21, 23, 27–8, 48,
    52–3, 54–5, 78, 97–8, 99, 129,
    136–7, 148–51, 161–4, 169–73,
    175–7, 178–9, 180, 181–3, 184,
    186, 191–3, 194–7, 199, 200,
    204–6, 208
  and ageing, 196–7, 199, 200
  as arbiter of fashion, 159
  and aristocrats, 21, 23, 154, 158, 175
  being assigned prologues and
    epilogues, 151–2
  and benefit nights, 157–8
  body of, 194–5, 197

commercial power of, 8, 28, 154,
    155–7
commodity status of, 148, 158–9
as curiosity, 129, 149, 154
and 'It', 16
memoirs of, 150–1, 153, 159, 210n
and patronage, 158
philanthropic acts of, 158
and private life, 5, 8, 150, 163, 171–2,
    182–3, 193
professional identity of, 21,
    150, 193
and prostitution, 152, 171–2
public rivalries, 159, 161–3
public role of, 8, 52, 151
as public woman, 149
and regality, 200–8
in Restoration theatre, 129, 149
and sexuality, 21, 98–9, 149–50
social status, 152–4
unstable identity of, 152–4
virtue of, 8, 150
Actresses' Franchise League, the, 184
A Pageant of Great Women, 184–5
Aeschylus, 130
Alexander the Great, 2, 22
Alexandra, Princess of Wales, 19
Andrew, Donna, 89n
Archer, William, 169
Aristophanes, 65, 67, 74, 131
Arnold, Matthew, 18
Asleson, Robyn, 209n, 210n
Aston, Elaine, 111
Aston, Tony, 25
Attenborough, Sir Richard, 229
audience, 1–5, 9–10, 26, 32, 34, 41–2,
    44, 48–52, 55, 58, 65, 69–72, 74–6,
    78, 80, 82, 84, 91–2, 94–101, 109,
    113–14, 129, 132, 136, 138, 150–3,
    158–9, 161, 164, 170–3, 175, 180–1,
    184, 191–5, 205–6, 208, 219–22,
    227–8
aura, 2, 16–17, 22, 200, 206
authenticity, 84, 141

autobiography, 53, 170–1, 173, 175, 178, 181, 216, 224, 228, 230n

Baer, Marc, 91, 105n, 212n
Bagehot, Walter, 17–18, 22, 27, 29
 The English Constitution, 17–18, 27
 and visibility, 18, 22, 29
Baker, Elizabeth, 51
Banham, Martin, 10n, 11n
Barker, Howard, 111
Barrie, J. M., 178–9, 182
 The Adored One, 178–9, 182
 Alice Sit-by-the-Fire, 178–9
Barry, Elizabeth, 24, 27, 148, 153, 156, 162
 earnings, 150, 157
 loaned wedding suits and coronation robes, 159
 negotiating benefit night, 157
Barstow, Susan, 187n
Barthes, Roland, 24
Bassnett, Susan, 10n
Beaumont, Binkie, 52, 56
Beckett, Samuel, 117
Bedford Coffee House, 65, 68, 72, 75
Beerbohm, Max, 32, 34, 36, 40, 43, 45, 180
 caricature of Oscar Wilde, 32, 36, 40, 45
Beerbohm Tree, Herbert, 176
benefits, 133, 139, 158
Bernhardt, Sarah, 31, 169–73, 175, 177, 179–80, 184
 eccentric reputation of, 169–70
 Ma Double Vie, 170
 self-advertisement of, 8, 169
Betterton, Thomas, 25–6, 28, 129–30, 161
 The Amorous Widow; or, The Wanton Wife, 161
 burial of, 25, 28
 earnings, 150
 physical description of, 25
Bickerstaffe, Isaac, 127–8
Billington, Michael, 20n, 113–14, 117, 121n, 219–20, 231n
biography, 9, 54, 91, 132, 136, 155, 158, 181, 183–4, 216, 226
Bolton, Betsy, 105n
Bond, Edward, 110–11, 120

Boorstin, Daniel, 2
Booth, Michael, 10n
Boswell, James, 69, 75
Bow, Clara, 17, 20, 27–8
Bowen, Olwen, 53
Bowtell, Elizabeth, 162–3
Bracegirdle, Anne, 24, 27, 161
 attempted abduction of, 151
 charitable acts of, 149
 retirement of, 157
Branagh, Kenneth, 229
Bratton, Jacky, 61n
Braudy, Leo, 2, 53, 60n, 87n, 213n
Brenton, Howard, 111
Bristow, Joseph, 45, 46n
Bronfen, Elizabeth, 124n
Brown, Georgina, 124n
Bunn, Alfred, 100
Burbage, Richard, 129
Burke, Edmund, 17, 26, 97
Burling, William, 86n
Burton, Richard, 224
Butler, Samuel, 36–7
Butterworth, Jez, 112, 115

Caine, Michael, 224
Callow, Simon, 215, 229n
Calloway, Stephen, 11n
Calthrop, Gladys, 56
Cameron, Rebecca, 59n
Campbell, Lorne, 211n
Campbell, Mrs Patrick, 31, 170–1, 176–9, 184
 My Life and Some Letters, 178
 as 'new woman', 177
 off-stage reputation, 177
 as Paula Tanqueray, 176
 publishing Bernard Shaw's love letters, 178
 in *The Adored One*, 178–9
 threatening daughter with legal proceedings, 177
Cannon, John, 213n
Carey, Joyce, 56
Casson, Lewis, 54
Castiglione, 17
Castle, Terry, 166n
Cavendish, Dominic, 124n
celebration, 4, 51, 76, 180, 186, 226

Index

celebrity, 1–10, 16–17, 20, 23–4, 26, 31, 37, 41, 43, 45, 48, 50–8, 65, 71–4, 76, 78, 80–5, 90–5, 100–1, 107, 114–17, 121, 127–9, 133, 135, 138, 141, 144, 148, 151, 154, 156–8, 163–4, 169–73, 176–86, 191–4, 197, 199–200, 204, 206, 208, 214, 216–19, 221–9
  'achieved', 3, 25, 191, 208
  and anxiety, 142
  'ascribed', 3, 25, 191, 208
  'attributed', 3, 208
  and authenticity, 84, 141
  and autobiography, 53, 170, 173, 175, 178, 181, 216, 224, 228, 230n
  and biography, 9, 54, 91, 132, 136, 155, 158, 181, 183–4, 216, 226
  and bisexuality, 128, 144, 220–1
  culture, 54, 68, 71
  deformation of, 65, 71
  economics of, 4, 7, 10, 148, 154–64
  and eighteenth-century print culture, 140
  etymology of the word, 4
  and fashion accessories, 159
  and film, 2–4, 9, 23, 112, 117, 214–16, 218–21, 223–8
  and infamy, 107, 116, 164
  as media production, 3, 72, 148
  and monarchy, 2, 9–10, 18, 21, 24, 69, 153, 159, 162, 200–1, 204–6, 208–9, 222
  and nation, 9, 18–19, 28, 49, 50, 75, 81, 91, 93, 97, 111, 115, 134, 186, 189, 206, 225, 227
  and notoriety, 5–7, 32, 45, 50, 52, 56, 58, 63, 80–1, 95, 107, 110–18, 129, 151, 171–3, 191
  and public intimacy, 4–5, 8, 14–16, 19, 21, 23–8, 150–2, 164
  and rivalry, 7–8, 31, 74–5, 95, 127–44, 159–63
  and royalty, 18, 21, 24, 69, 152, 201, 205, 208, 229
  and satire, 33, 67–71, 73–5, 77–8, 80–1, 83–4, 85n, 128, 144, 179
  and scandal, 6, 20, 73, 80–3, 127, 129, 136, 151, 173, 175, 193, 216
  and sensation, 6–7, 49, 53, 91–2, 110, 112, 114, 116, 135
  and sexuality, 6, 80, 84, 96, 121, 128, 142, 144, 150, 171, 173, 218–19, 220–1
  and social mobility for women, 153–4
  and tabloid newspapers, 81, 86n, 89n, 107–10, 116
  and transgression, 5, 80, 99, 107–10, 114, 169–70, 172–3
censorship, 3, 85n
charisma, *charismata*, 2, 4–5, 17, 19, 24, 26, 81, 219
Charles I, 25, 205
Charles II, 20, 21, 22
  lifts restriction against women performing, 149
charm, 17, 130, 132, 141, 178, 182
Cher, 16
Childs, Donald, 59n
Chudleigh, Elizabeth, 83–4
Churchill, Caryl, 122n
Churchill, Charles, 70, 132, 153, 195
  Rosciad, 132, 195
Cibber, Colley, 129, 134–6, 151, 153, 155–7
  on actresses' commodity status, 158–9
  on Anne Oldfield's social behaviour, 153
  Apology, 129
  The Careless Husband, 153
  in *Love's Last Shift*, 130
  Poet Laureate, 129
  in *The Relapse*, 130
  and theatrical camp, 130
Cibber, Susannah, 75, 136, 149, 159
  affair with William Sloper, 136
  and earnings through benefit nights, 157
  marriage to Theophilus Cibber, 136, 157
  mocked in *The Beggar's Pantomime*, 161–2
  and rivalry with Kitty Clive, 161
  scheme to bring Quin and Garrick together on stage, 136–8
  as tragic actress, 136
Cibber, Theophilus, 129–30, 136, 158
  arranging Susannah's adultery, 136, 157
  discovery of Kitty Clive, 155
Cicero, 74

Index 241

Clive, Kitty, 77, 151, 153, 155, 159
  charitable acts of, 158
  earnings, 156
  flirting with the audience, 152
  mocked in *The Beggar's Pantomime*, 161–2
  recommended to Colley Cibber, 155
  in *The Rehearsal*, 151
  rivalry with Susannah Cibber, 161–2
Cockin, Katherine, 61n
Colley, Linda, 212n
Compton, Fay, 48, 51, 58
'Cool Britannia', 114
Corbett, Mary Jean, 186n
Cornell, Katherine, 52
Cosmopolitan, 15
Coveney, Michael, 108
Covent Garden Theatre, 53, 56, 70, 72, 74, 77, 92, 95, 99, 101, 127, 133, 135–6
  James Quin and David Garrick acting together at, 132–3, 138
  O.P. riots of 1809, 91
  and Tory opposition, 134
Coward, Noël, 48–9, 52–3, 55–8, 189, 220
  Blithe Spirit, 56
  Pacific 1860, 57
  The Vortex, 56
Cromwell, Oliver, 20
Crouch, Kimberly, 167n
Curtis, Nick, 108

Daily Express, 116
Daily Gazeteer, 137
Daily Mail, 108
Daldry, Stephen, 112, 115–16
Dane, Clemence, 5–6, 48–59
  Anna Karenina, 53, 58
  A Bill of Divorcement, 48–52, 58
  Broome Stages, 53
  Cousin Muriel, 51–2
  critical reception of, 50–1
  as cultural commentator, 52
  on divorce laws, 49
  Eighty in the Shade, 54
  and feminism, 50
  Fire Over England, 58
  Gooseberry Fool, 54
  Granite, 51
  interest in eugenics, 49
  London has a Garden, 53
  Murder, 58
  and notoriety, 5, 50, 52, 56, 58
  Perfect Strangers, 52
  private life of, 5, 53
  Regiment of Women, 49–50
  self-erasure of, 6
  St. Martin's Lane, 58
  theatrical salon of, 55–7
  Wild Decembers, 51, 53
  Will Shakespeare, 51–3
  The Women's Side, 52
danger, 67, 97, 99, 108, 130, 169, 194, 215, 221
David, Desmond, 218
Davies, Moll, 129
Davis, Tracy, 11n, 87n, 105n, 186n
De Jongh, Nicholas, 113
Dean, James, 225
Delane, Dennis, 70, 144
Dibdin, Charles, 68
domesticity, 67, 148, 178, 208
Doughty, Louise, 108
Douglas, Lord Alfred, 32, 36–7, 39, 42
Douglas, Jennie, 77–8
Downes, John, 22
  Roscius Anglicanus, 22
Draper, Somerset, 137–8, 140
  negotiations with Susannah Cibber, 137–8
Drury Lane Theatre, 75, 77, 91–5, 97–8, 100–1, 127, 133–6, 138–9, 156–8, 161, 192–3, 196, 206
Durkheim, Emile, 23–4
  The Elementary Forms of Religious Life, 23
Duse, Eleonora, 135, 177
Dyer, Richard, 10n, 191, 208, 208n

Edwardes, Jane, 108
Eliot, T. S., 117
Elizabeth I, 4
Ellis, Markman, 87n
Elliston, Robert, 91–4, 96, 99, 100–1
Ellmann, Richard, 46n
Elvis, 16
Emin, Tracey, 114
Esquire, 15
Euripides, 132

242 Index

Evans, Daniel, 120
Examiner, 94, 97
Eyre, Richard, 110, 121, 122n

Fairbanks, Douglas, 22
Fairweather, Virginia, 222
fame, 1–10, 22, 32, 43, 65, 67–8, 74–7, 80, 84, 94–5, 107, 115, 118, 120–1, 133, 142, 148, 154, 158, 163–4, 191–2, 194, 216, 220, 228
famous, 1–2, 4, 19–20, 24, 26, 34, 37, 65, 71–5, 82, 129, 132–3, 138, 172, 175, 179–81, 183, 186, 199–200, 217, 223, 228
fan, 91, 149, 157, 181, 194, 228
fashion, 8, 38, 42, 69, 74, 76, 112, 115, 120, 130, 153, 159, 194, 217–18, 225
Fay, Stephen, 124
Featherstone, Vicky, 116–17
Fenton, Lavinia, 151
  in *The Beggar's Opera*, 154–5
  charitable acts of, 158
  memoirs of, 150
film, 3–4, 9, 23, 112, 117, 214–16, 218–21, 223–8
  Anna Karenina, 53, 58
  A Bill of Divorcement, 48, 58
  Brideshead Revisited, 218
  Cat on a Hot Tin Roof, 218
  Clash of the Titans, 216, 218, 226
  Fire over England, 58
  Gone with the Wind, 226
  Hamlet, 214, 223, 226
  Henry V, 223, 225–7
  Lady Hamilton, 226–7
  Last Action Hero, 214, 221–2
  Murder, 58
  Perfect Strangers, 52
  Pride and Prejudice, 226–7
  Rebecca, 226–7
  Richard III, 223
  Saturday Night Fever, 216, 218
  St. Martin's Lane, 58
  Stage Beauty, 20
  Trainspotting, 117
  War Requiem, 219
  Wuthering Heights, 219, 226
Fitzpatrick, Thaddeus, 75
Flynn, Errol, 225

Foote, Samuel, 6, 65–84, 144
  Auction of Pictures, 69, 76
  The Author, 77, 80
  and the body, 68, 70–1, 78
  and coffee houses, 65, 72, 77
  The Cozeners, 81–2, 84
  and David Garrick, 67, 75–6, 82, 144
  The Devil upon Two Sticks, 67–8, 76
  and disability, 68
  The Diversions of the Morning, 68–71
  'The Drugger's Jubilee', 76
  and illegitimacy, 67
  and imitations, 67, 69–72, 78, 80
  The Knights, 73
  The Lame Lover, 68
  The Maid of Bath, 73
  The Minor, 68, 77–8, 80
  as Mrs Coles, 77–8, 80
  and newspapers, 72–3, 81
  and notoriety, 6, 80
  The Orators, 68
  The Patron, 73
  The Primitive Puppet Show, 76
  and satire, 67–9, 71, 73–5, 77–8, 83–4
  and sexual transgression, 80, 144
  The Siege of Calais, 83
  and stage exposures, 67–8, 76, 83
  Taste, 73
  Town and Country, 84
  A Treatise on the Passions, 75
  The Trial of Samuel Foote, 68
  The Trip to Calais, 81
Franklin, Paul, 145n

Gainsborough, Thomas, 142, 194
Gallagher, Liam, 115
Garber, Marjorie, 2, 128
Garbo, Greta, 24
Gardner, Viv, 61n
Garrick, David, 8, 24, 26, 67, 69, 72, 75–6, 90, 127–44, 157, 192–3, 196, 228
  and acting style, 130, 192
  anxiety of, 141–2, 144
  celebrity contest with James Quin, 8, 127–44
  compared to new religion by James Quin, 134
  exploiting publicity of studio portrait, 140

Garrick, David – *continued*
  the 'Garrick cut', 128
  and homosexuality, 127–8
  political interests of, 134
  purchasing a share of the Drury Lane patent, 138
  as representative Englishman, 9, 141
  as Richard III, 133
  Richard III portrait of, 140
  suit for libel, 128
  visual arts and celebrity of, 140
  Zoffany's painting of, 132
George III, 200, 206, 208
Gibson, Mel, 215
Gielgud, John, 8, 130, 135, 139, 218–19, 226, 228
Gildon, Charles, 22
  Life of Thomas Betterton, 22
Giles, David, 10n
Gledhill, Christine, 3, 10n
Glenn, Susan, 186n
Glyn, Elinor, 16–17, 19–23, 26–8
  It, 16, 21
Gore-Langton, Robert, 113, 120
Gottlieb, Vera, 122n
GQ, 15
Greig, David, 114, 118, 123n
Gritten, David, 10n
Grundy, Sydney, 38, 44, 173
  The Degenerates, 173
  The New Woman, 38, 44
Gruczczynski, Piotr, 123n
Guardian, 107
Gurr, Andrew, 11n
Gwyn, Eleanor, 150
Gwyn, Nell, 21, 23, 129, 152, 156

Hagerty, Bill, 113
Halasz, Alexandra, 12n
Hall, Radcliffe, 52
Hallett, Mark, 212n
Hamilton, Cicely, 184–5
Hare, Arnold, 29n
Hart, Charles, 22, 149
Hattenstone, Simon, 124n
Haymarket Theatre, 34, 65, 67–9, 71–4, 76–8, 80–2, 84, 137, 156, 158
Hazlitt, William, 26, 93, 135, 196–7
Henley, Orator, 72–3
Hepburn, Katherine, 48

Hewison, Robert, 115
Hichens, Robert, 32, 39–40
hierarchy, 2, 95, 223
Hirst, Damien, 114–15
Hitchcock, Alfred, 58
Hogarth, William, 139–40
  double sketch of James Quin and David Garrick, 133
  A Harlot's Progress, 135
  portrait of James Quin, 130–1
Holden, Anthony, 217
Holledge, Julie, 188n
Hollywood, 16–17, 19, 22, 27, 53, 100, 220–1, 225–6
Holroyd, Michael, 46n
homosexuality, 219
  and David Garrick, 128
  and Laurence Olivier, 219–21
Horne Tooke, John, 73
Howe, Elizabeth, 152, 165n
Hudson, Rock, 226
Hume, Robert, 167n, 168n
Hunt, Leigh, 135, 196

idol, 23, 26, 75–6, 91, 219
Independent, 107
infamy, 107, 116, 129, 164
Innes, Christopher, 114, 121, 123n
Irving, Sir Henry, 31, 171, 175, 180
  knighthood of, 223
'It', 5–6, 13, 15–21, 23, 25–9
  girl, 17, 21, 27–8

Jackson, William, 81, 84, 144
James, Henry, 32, 169
  on Ellen Terry's Portia, 180
  Guy Domville, 32
Jarman, Derek, 219
Jenkins, Marianna, 211n
Johnson, Samuel, 67–8, 132, 141–2
Jones, Henry Arthur, 177
Jordan, Dorothy, 24, 163, 199

Kane, Sarah, 107–21
  4.48 Psychosis, 118–20
  Blasted, 107–20
  Cleansed, 113–18, 120
  continental reception of, 115
  Crave, 115–18
  iconisation of, 7, 110, 120

Kane, Sarah – *continued*
  and 'in-yer-face-theatre', 112
  'Marie Kelvedon', 116
  and notoriety, 6–7, 107, 110–18
  Phaedra's Love, 112, 116–18
  and realist conventions, 109, 117
  and sensation, 7
  suicide of, 7, 118–21
  and tabloids, 107–10, 116
  and violence, 107–17
Kaplan, Joel, 60n, 187n
Kean, Edmund, 1, 7–8, 90–104, 135
  acting of, 6
  class inferiority of, 96
  compared to David Garrick, 90
  Cox vs Kean prosecution, 91, 101
  The Examiner's role in launching Kean's success, 94
  identified as feminised, 99
  and notoriety, 6–7, 95
  as Othello, 93
  physical appearance, 90
  position in late Georgian society, 90
  reappearance at Drury Lane after trial, 91
  revolutionising acting style, 90
  as Richard III, 93–4
  as symbol of Romantic inspiration, 90
  transgression of, 6–7, 91
  use of Shakespeare in his letters, 92
Kemble, John Philip, 6, 8, 90–1, 96, 135, 204–6
  brother of Sarah Siddons, 192, 204
  earnings, 156
  and O.P. riots of 1809, 91, 96
  resemblance to Charles I, 205
Kenrick, William, 127–30, 144
  Love in the Suds, 128, 144
Kenyon, Mel, 116, 120
Kerslake, John, 210n
King, Thomas, 165n
Kingston, Duchess of, 83–4
Kinservik, Matthew, 85n, 89n, 167n
Knipp, Elizabeth, 129
Kobialka, Michael, 145n
Kustow, Michael, 123n
Kynaston, Thomas, 149

Lafler, Joanne, 167n
Langhans, Edward, 166n

Langridge, Natasha, 122
Langtry, Lillie, 31, 170–6, 179–80, 182, 184
  affair with Prince of Wales, 172–3
  and association between actress and prostitution, 172
  as box-office draw, 173
  The Days I Knew, 173, 176
  friendship with Oscar Wilde, 172
  playing Shakespeare, 173, 175
  private life of, 8, 176
  production of *As You Like It*, 173–4
  rejects part in *Lady Windermere's Fan*, 176
  whitewashing of her image, 175
Laughton, Charles, 222
Lawrence, Thomas, 193–4, 197, 200
  Mrs Siddons, 197–8
  portrait of Queen Charlotte, 200, 203
Lee, Nathaniel, 162
  The Rival Queens, 162
Leigh, Vivien, 217–18, 220–3, 226–8
Leonard, Mark, 211n
Leverson, Ada, 32, 40–4
Levey, Michael, 212n
Licensing Act [1737], 67, 69
Lloyd, Robert, 70
Lorraine, Lorn, 56
Lumby, Catherine, 86n, 89n
Lynch, Deirdre, 81, 85n, 89n

Macaulay, Alistair, 117
Macaulay, Catherine, 67, 77
Macdonald, James, 111, 113–14, 118
Macklin, Charles, 74–5, 133, 136, 156, 195
Madigan, Danny, 214, 216, 218
Maland, Charles, 208n
Mallin, Eric, 229n
Marie Antoinette, 26
markets, 1, 7–8, 34, 70, 85, 112, 114, 125, 154–64, 171–2, 218
Marshall, P. D., 11n
Marshall, Rebecca, 23, 156
Maxim, 15
McBean, Angus, 217
McCreery, Cindy, 86n
McGowen, Randall, 89n
McKellen, Sir Ian, 217, 230n
McPherson, Heather, 211n

McTiernan, John, 214, 221, 229n
media, 1, 3, 9, 49, 58, 73, 81, 84, 91, 93, 110–12, 114, 117, 121, 148, 161, 163, 191
 media hype, 8, 133
memoirs, 150, 153, 159, 171, 210n
Melville, Alan, 228
Milhous, Judith, 166n, 167n, 168n
Miller, Jonathan, 230n
Miller, Ruby, 51
Milling, Jane, 10n, 11n, 105n
mimicry, 65, 67–8, 70–1, 77–8, 80
monarchy, 2, 9–10, 18, 21, 24, 153, 159, 162, 200–1, 204–6, 208–9, 222
Monroe, Marilyn, 15, 225
Moody, Jane, 105n
Morley, Sheridan, 109, 113, 120, 121n, 122n
More, Hannah, 83
Munns, Jessica, 166n

nation, 4, 9, 18–19, 28, 49–50, 75, 81, 91, 93, 97, 115, 134, 186, 189, 206, 225, 227
National Theatre, 108, 216, 217
Neilson, Anthony, 112
Nicholson, Colin, 165n
Norton, Victor, 147n
notoriety, 5–7, 32, 45, 50, 52, 56, 58, 63, 80–1, 95, 107, 110–16, 118, 130, 151, 171–3, 191
Novello, Ivor, 51–2

O'Connor, Garry, 227, 229n
O'Hara, Scarlett, 226
Old Vic Theatre, 226–7
Oldfield, Anne, 129, 153, 155–6, 159, 161
 biography of, 155
 in *The Careless Husband*, 153
 charitable acts of, 158
 earnings, 156
 memoirs of, 159
 as mistress, 153
Olivier, Laurence, 8, 125, 135, 139, 214–19
 and advertising, 216–18
 and ambigous sexuality, 9, 219–21
 autobiography, 216
 creating public self, 222

Englishness, 9, 217, 222–3, 225
 fascination with make-up, 220
 film roles, 226–7
 knighthood, 223–5
 and monarchical images, 9, 222
Orr, Clarissa, 213n
Osborne, John, 58, 110–11, 223
 The Entertainer, 220
 Look Back in Anger, 110
Ottaway, Susannah, 210n, 211n
outrage, 49, 93, 97, 107, 110

paragraph journalism, 69, 73
parody, 39, 76, 199, 218
 of Shakespeare, 214
 of Wilde, 40, 42
partisanship, 8, 93, 134
patronage, 6, 51, 91–2, 151–3, 158
Payne, Deborah, 165n
Pepys, Samuel, 20–3, 25, 28, 129
 visits Nell Gwyn and Rebecca Marshall backstage, 23, 156
performance, 1–8, 17, 21–3, 37, 44, 55, 67–9, 72, 75, 84, 91–2, 94, 96, 98, 110, 117, 135, 141, 149–51, 158, 163, 171, 173, 175–6, 178–9, 181–4, 186, 194, 196, 204, 215, 218–17
 of monarchy, 10
 of queenliness, 9
Perreau, Daniel and Robert, 82
Peter, John, 108, 113
photography, 171
Pickford, Mary, 22, 27
Pinero, Arthur Wing, 31, 176
 The Notorious Mrs Ebbsmith, 176
 The Second Mrs Tanqueray, 176
Pinter, Harold, 58, 117, 120
 The Collection, 218
Plath, Sylvia, 120–1
playwright, 3, 5–6, 8, 31, 36, 48–52, 54–5, 58, 65, 67–70, 72, 76, 83, 109–15, 117, 120, 127–8, 144, 148, 151, 154–5, 158, 173
Plowright, Joan, 221–2
Pope, Alexander, 129
portraiture, 9, 97, 191, 193
Postlewait, Thomas, 1, 104n, 188n
Powell, Kerry, 44, 47n

presence, 1–2, 17, 21, 25, 50, 53, 78, 91, 95, 98–9, 148, 192–3, 200, 219–20, 224
proximity, 4, 81, 84, 176
public intimacy, 4–5, 8, 14–16, 19, 21, 23–8, 150–2, 164
Public Leader, 127
publicity, 8, 54, 71–3, 76–7, 82, 111–15, 117, 139, 141, 169–70, 172–3, 175, 178
  thriving on partisanship, 134
Punch, 32, 34, 40–2, 45
  cartoons of Oscar Wilde, 32, 34, 40, 42
  Francis Burnand, editor of, 40

Queen Charlotte, 200–8
Queen Victoria, 18–19, 28
Quin, James, 5, 8, 70, 127, 130–44
  acting style of, 5, 70
  as Coriolanus, 141
  as Falstaff, 139
  as Horatio, 139
  Dublin engagement in 1741, 133
  established as England's leading actor, 130
  in *The Provok'd Wife*, 132
  political interests of, 134
Quinn, Michael L., 2, 10n
Quintilian, 17

Rabey, David Ian, 121, 124n
Ravenhill, Mark, 112, 115–17
  Shopping and Fucking, 112
Rawlings, Margaret, 52
Rebellato, Dan, 122n
Reform Act [1832], 92
reputation, 1, 6–8, 10, 41, 45, 49, 70–3, 75, 77–8, 81, 95, 107, 114, 130, 134, 141, 148, 151, 162–3, 169–72, 177–8, 180–2, 184, 192–3, 199, 208
Restoration, 20–1, 92, 98, 129, 149
  and actresses, 21, 149–50, 152
  theatre, 20, 129, 149
Reynolds, Joshua, 140–4, 194, 197, 200, 206
  portraiture theory of, 197
  Siddons as the Tragic Muse, 200, 202, 205
Ribeiro, Aileen, 168n
Rich, John, 70, 133, 134

Richards, Penny, 166n
Richards, Sandra, 166n, 168n, 188n
Richardson, Ralph, 225–6
rivalry, 7–8, 31, 74–5, 95, 127–44, 159–63
Roach, Joseph, 5, 11n, 165n
Roberts, Philip, 122n
Rojek, Chris, 2–3, 23, 25, 52, 171, 186n, 191, 208, 209n
Roscius, 74
Rose, Jacqueline, 85n, 105n
Rosenthal, Laura, 152, 165n
Rousseau, Jean-Jacques, 128
Royal Court Theatre, 107–18
royalty, 21–2, 24, 201, 205, 208, 222, 226–9
Rudd, Caroline, 81–3
Ruskin, John, 33, 180
Russell, Gillian, 105n
Ryan, Lacy, 70, 139

Saatchi, Charles, 114
Sackville-West, Vita, 50
satire, 33, 67–71, 73–5, 77–8, 80–1, 83–4, 85n, 128, 144, 179
Saturday Review, 31
Saunders, Graham, 110, 122n
scandal, 6, 20, 80–1, 127, 129, 136, 151, 173, 175, 193, 216
Schama, Simon, 213n
Schickel, Richard, 4, 11n
Schwarzenegger, Arnold, 214
Scott, Clement, 173, 181
  on Ellen Terry, 182
  on Lillie Langtry, 172
  A Wife's Peril, 173
Sellar, Tom, 121n
Seneca, 109, 112
Senelick, Laurence, 145n
sensation, 6–7, 49, 53, 91–2, 110, 112, 114, 116, 135
sexuality, 6, 80, 84, 96, 121, 128, 142, 150, 218–20
Shakespeare, William, 4, 9, 13, 51–2, 92, 95, 109, 129, 132, 134–5, 149, 173, 175, 179–80, 182, 199, 204–5, 214, 223–4
  As You Like It, 13, 173–4, 226
  Hamlet, 95, 214, 223, 226
  Henry VIII, 204

Shakespeare, William – *continued*
  King John, 135
  King Lear, 109
  Much Ado About Nothing, 4
  Richard III, 223
  Twelfth Night, 129
Shapiro, Michael, 164n
Shaw, George Bernard, 31, 36, 40
  attack on West End theatre, 31
  correspondence with Ellen Terry, 182–3
  as an English aristocrat, 36
  on Ellen Terry, 181, 184
  love letters to Mrs Patrick Campbell, 178
  on Mrs Patrick Campbell's performance, 176
Sheridan, Richard Brinsley, 73
  The Critic, 73, 221
Siddons, Sarah, 5, 9–10, 24, 26, 97, 156, 163, 191–208
  acting style, 26, 192–3
  ageing, 5, 26, 192, 196–7, 200
  as British icon, 9, 206
  discovered by David Garrick, 192
  disdain for breeches parts, 195
  earnings, 7
  evades scandals, 193
  image management, 192–4, 197
  last portrait of, 200
  negotiating benefits, 157, 159
  obesity, 24, 192, 196–7
  patriotism of, 206
  portraits of, 193–4, 197
  pregnancy of, 192, 196
  readings of Shakespeare and Milton, 199
  Reminiscences, 193–4
  rendering acting profession respectable, 193
  representation as queen, 200–1, 204–6, 208
Sierz, Aleks, 112, 122n
Simpson, Helen, 54
Simpson, O. J., 89n
Sketch, 42
Smith, Chris, 114
Solkin, David, 212n
Speedie, Julie, 46n
Spencer, Charles, 108

St James's Chronicle, 128
St James's Gazette, 40
stage, 1–3, 7–8, 18, 21–4, 26, 31, 34, 36, 41, 45, 48–9, 52, 72, 77, 81–2, 90–2, 95–9, 109, 114–15, 128–30, 133–6, 138–9, 144, 149–6, 158–9, 162, 164, 169, 171–2, 175–6, 177–8, 180–1, 183–4, 186, 192–5, 199, 204–5, 215, 218, 220–1, 226–8
star, 2–5, 7–8, 17, 23–4, 48, 53, 55, 92, 100, 148, 150, 152–5, 157, 176, 181, 191–2, 206, 214, 218, 220–1, 226–7
  definition of, 7
stardom, 3, 94, 163, 214, 221, 226–7
Steele, Richard, 25, 28
Stephenson, Heidi, 122n
Sterne, Laurence, 140
Stevens, George Alexander, 69
stigmata, 5, 24, 26
Stokes, John, 10n
Stowell, Sheila, 60n, 187n
Straub, Kristina, 106n, 145n, 167n

Tabert, Nils, 115, 117
tabloids, 81, 86n, 89n, 107–10
Tarlton, Richard, 4
Taylor, Paul, 108
Taylor, Valerie, 58
technology, 71
Terry, Ellen, 8, 13, 31, 54, 170–1, 175, 179–84, 185
  acting as Henry Irving's consort, 180
  Edward Gordon Craig's biography of, 183
  financial success of, 8, 180
  as icon of traditional femininity, 179
  in *A Pageant of Great Women*, 185–6
  playing Shakespearean heroines, 180, 182
  private life of, 180–1
  The Story of My Life, 181
Thane, Pat, 211n
theatre, 1–4, 7, 9–10, 18, 20–2, 24, 26, 31–2, 34, 36, 40–2, 44, 48, 51, 56–8, 65, 67, 70–3, 81, 83–5, 90–7, 99, 101, 108, 110–15, 118, 127–30, 134–6, 138, 142, 144, 148–9, 151–7, 159, 162–3, 173, 193–4, 196, 216, 218, 221–3, 225–9
  and censorship, 3

theatre – *continued*
  and class and gender disputes, 99
  history, 4–5, 48, 57, 80, 91, 133
  industry, 56, 114, 118
  and nineteenth-century morality, 98–9
  and nineteenth-century public, 32
  and prostitution, 98
  as public sphere, 91–2, 150
  and sexuality, 144
Thomas, David, 29n
Thompson, James, 165n
Thorndyke, Sybil, 52
Thurman, Uma, 15
Times, 91–4, 99, 101–4, 107, 180
Tinker, Jack, 108
Tinkler, Penny, 230n
transgression, 5–7, 67, 80, 91, 99, 107–10, 114, 169–70, 172–3
Travolta, John, 216
Trefussis, Violet, 50
Trump, Ivana, 226
Tscherny, Nadia, 197, 210n
Turner, Cheryl, 167n

Valentino, Rudolph, 27

Wachman, Gay, 60n
Wanko, Cheryl, 107, 165n, 166n, 209n
Ward, Geneviève, 171
Warlikowski, Kyzysztof, 115
Weber, Max, 17, 29n
Werkmeister, Lucyle, 87n
West, Shearer, 146n
Whistler, James, 33
Whitefield, George, 77–8, 83, 134
Wilde, Oscar, 5, 31–45, 49, 63, 172, 175–6
  De Profundis, 45
  An Ideal Husband, 31, 34, 40, 43, 45
  The Importance of Being Earnest, 31–2, 34, 37–8, 44, 45
  Lady Windermere's Fan, 32, 34, 176
  libel suit against the Marquess of Queensberry, 32
  name removed from playbills, 45
  notoriety of, 5, 32, 45
  'The Remarkable Rocket', 31–3, 36, 45
  Salome, 37
  weariness of fame, 43
  A Woman of No Importance, 31–2, 34
Wilkes, John, 73
Wilkinson, Tate, 69–70, 73, 75, 78
Williams, David, 72
Williams, Tennessee, 218
Williamson, Nicol, 125, 217
Wilson, Harold, 223
Winston, James, 92–3, 95, 98–100
Woffington, Peg, 70, 137, 141, 151–2, 155–6, 159–60, 186
  charitable acts of, 158
  competition with Anne Bellamy, 163
  family background of, 154
  memoirs of, 150
women, 8, 20–1, 27–8, 48–54, 56, 58, 67, 80–1, 84, 94, 96–9, 107, 109–11, 120, 128, 137, 144, 148–56, 158–9, 162–4, 175, 177–8, 180, 184, 186, 192–3, 195, 200, 204, 217, 228
  fallen women, 8, 99
wonder, 26, 129, 153
Woods, Leigh, 1–2, 10n, 104n
Woolf, Virginia, 58, 117
Worthing Gazette, 39
Wright, Nicholas, 110, 121, 122n

Young British Artists ('YBA'), 114

Zeami, 17